BAD BLOOD

CREDITS

BAD BLOOD
An Illustrated Guide To Psycho Cinema
Christian Fuchs
CREATION CINEMA COLLECTION VOLUME 18
ISBN 1 84068 025 3
First published 1996 as *Kino Killer*
Translated into English by Otmar Lichtenwoerther
Edited by Jack Hunter
Additional info: Jack Hunter, Mikita Brottman
English edition first published 2002 by Creation Books
www.creationbooks.com
Copyright © Christian Fuchs 1996, 2002
All world rights reserved
Design/Setting:
WhiteLight/The Tears Corporation
Illustrations:
British Film Institute, Christian Fuchs, Jack Hunter Collection, Museum Of Modern Art New York, by courtesy of the original production companies and distributors. All film photographs are official publicity shots and used as intended. Carl Panzram picture and Manson crime scene pictures courtesy of Amok Books. *Seul Contre Tous* shots courtesy Gaspar Noé.

Acknowledgements
The author would like to thank the following people: Peter Hiess, who initiated this book, James Williamson at Creation Books, Jörg Buttgereit (for his preface and his films crawling under your skin), and last but definitely not least Mr. Joe Coleman, who has inspired many of the book's texts as a border-crossing artist and personality.

Extra thanks go to:

Elisabeth Habitzl, who wrote many killer-biographies, corrected many (German) texts and made several contributions to the essay on "Murderous Women".
Otmar Lichtenwoerther, without whose translation this book simply would not be possible.
Herbert Pfoestl, for tracking down many rare quotes, and our murderous conversations once upon a time. Thanks also to Anne Gibbs-Pfoestl.
Harald und Irma Dolezal for their helpful background information, the collection of many filmographies and numerous pictures from the Dolezal archive.
Heimo Sver for tracking down many films, phoning me so often, and his help in general.

Without all their help and encouragement this book couldn't have been written.

This book is dedicated to Claudia.

CONTENTS

FOREWORD

Real killers are not filmed when killing. We only see them sit guiltily in the dock avoiding looking into our eyes on the other side of the news-camera. Their piercing psychopaths' eyes stare at us madly from the cover of *Life Magazine*. But we do not see the filthy deeds they are famous for. "Seeing is believing".

The killers have laid bare deeply rooted forces within ourselves and excited our imagination. What has really happened? To capture this on celluloid in all its necessary atrocity only seems too natural. "What you are about to see is true!"

Moreover, it is only human – or shall I say inhuman? – when the freedom of art tempts us to go slightly berserk. A dribbling senile farmer may quickly become a chainsaw-swinging butcher with a skin mask in ravening bloodlust. "And remember: it's only a movie!"

Killers may take photos for themselves. As a souvenir, as a fetish. But they will withhold them from us. Too cruel for inexperienced eyes. Isn't it our duty to record every juicy detail for future generations? "So that things as horrible as these never happen again".

Killers are losers. Poor creeps that have lost the battle within themselves. What partly reminds us romantic dreamers of an anarchic outbreak from a society based on constraint is nothing but a cry for help. A too late cry for love and harmony nobody wants to hear now. The killer has decided to use more effective means to engage our interest. Who does not want to listen, must suffer. Attention at any price.

But the killers also kill for us. In spite of all their horror, their deeds have a relieving effect. Like a valve in our souls damaged by civilization and full of pent-up aggression.

Killers suit us fine in the uneventfulness of our well-protected lives. We use and abuse them as we please, either as scapegoats, or as postmodern anti-heroes.

As creators and recipients of cinema killers we will still have to justify ourselves, even after this book. We are to be pitied.

With love, Jörg Buttgereit

Since his debut film NEKROMANTIK (1987) the German director Jörg Buttgereit from Berlin has stood for cinematic subversion "Made in Germany". In four full-length movies and several short films up to now he has been operating uncompromisingly in the twilight zone between the breaking of taboos, splatter shocks, and, especially, extreme emotions. Buttgereit shoots radical cinema of emotions. Murderous characters come up again and again in films like DER TODESKING and NEKROMANTIK 2. Finally, in SCHRAMM (1993), he puts a serial killer squarely into the centre of the story. Neglecting the commercial laws of the mainstream taste-police, Buttgereit provides us with deep insight into the psyche of the murderer.

INTRODUCTION
NO-ONE GETS OUT OF HERE ALIVE: KILLER MOVIES AND MOVIE KILLERS

"And this is what people don't want to look at, that life exists only through the suffering and death of other life. That's the only thing that keeps the world going. Science comes up with incredible ways to keep things alive and moralists are begging for ways to keep people from being cruel to animals or other people, but that's what nature is. Nature is cruel."
–Joe Coleman

"It ain't that in their hearts they're bad. They'd stick by you if they could. But that's just bullshit, People just ain't no good"
–Nick Cave

"When Father Flanagan said, 'There's no such thing as a bad boy' – well, Father Flanagan was wrong."
–Joseph Wambaugh

We are afraid of them because their deeds defy reason and threaten our society in an incalculable way. Psychoanalysis and sociology try to explain their irrational acts of violence and shed some light upon the dark of their actions with a vast number of diagnoses and theories: the mass murderers, serial killers, and rapist killers flooding the second half of the 20th century with "motiveless" violent crimes. The media has built monuments for them, has lionized them, analyzed and dissected them. It has either stylized them to monstrous human beasts or to forerunners of the outlaw-myth. Cinema plays an important role in the enormous influence of the serial killer and mass murderer-phenomenon on contemporary popular culture (numerous underground-bands, cartoonists, and writers refer to it). The romantic frenzy in BADLANDS (1973) inspired by the true case of the young killer couple Charlie Starkweather and Caril Fugate; the disturbing terror of HENRY – PORTRAIT OF A SERIAL KILLER (1986) on the track of the mass murderer Henry Lee Lucas; the raging massacre of TAXI DRIVER (1975) influenced by Arthur Bremer, an unsuccessful assassin. The journey into the dark side of human existence is also a journey into the most exciting zones of the cinematic medium.

Watching Suffering Does One Good
"To see others suffer does one good, to make others suffer even more: this is a hard saying but an ancient, mighty, human, all-too-human principle to which even the apes might subscribe; for it has been said that in devising bizarre cruelties they anticipate

man and are, as it were, his 'prelude'. Without cruelty there is no festival: thus the longest and most ancient part of human history teaches."
–Friedrich Nietzsche

Whether you want to admit it or not, it is the lust of watching other people being punished by fate that hides behind today's True Crime movie fashion. It is the same voyeuristic glance that already at the turn of the century contributed to the great success of newspapers, pamphlets, and detective magazines with horrid murder reports and detailed descriptions of the deeds. Since its pioneer days cinema, developed from the *laterna magica* and always closely related to side-shows, freak circuses and funhouses, has stood for sensationalism and gooseflesh. Like love stories, comedies and fantasy movies, gloomy melodramas and abysmal horror have always been part of the standard repertory of this new medium.

"It is as if cinema feels called upon to take stock of all the motives of horror", Siegfried Kracauer declared in 1940. "We thought we could dismiss this trait of cinema as mere speculation caused by the sensationalism of the masses. It may be true that quite often such speculations play a role. Nevertheless, their presence does not at all justify the aesthetic ban of the cinematic treatment of the themes mentioned here." In these words the film theorist Kracauer answered those critics who already in those early days were worried about the mental welfare of society because of violent content on the screen. Tacky moralism and a deeply rooted fear of the motion picture's power have always been significant for the portrayal of "evil" in cinema.

The modern dispute between the representatives of the imitation theory, who regard man as a will-less remote-controlled zombie, and the advocates of catharsis, who believe in the liberating power of fictitious filmic violence, has been raging since the beginnings of cinema. Many directors regarded the cinematic depiction of the shadow zones of human existence as a necessity (Luis Buñuel's UN CHIEN ANDALOU, 1928, is an early highly artistic example), others persisted in banning violence and crime from cinema. Moreover, one should not forget the modern alliance of "prohibitionists", which goes from right wing to left, from conservative censors and advocates of a "clean screen" to feminists and culture-pessimistic critics. Hopeless journalists believe in the most simplistic interaction of film and reality in their mentally ill gibberings, and regard the audience as a bunch of puppets as stupid as they before the media barrage.

It's Only A Movie

But progressive media theorists have already realized that one should by all means distinguish between cinematic violence and reality. "That those films may be fatal for anybody is only those people's wishful thinking whose primary concern is to build up constantly new enemy images in order to divert from their own activities of much higher range and accuracy of aim." (German film critic Maerz).

Nobody becomes a brutish man of violence or even a killer merely because he has seen too many True Crime or horror movies. Of course, there are cases like the one of John Hinckley, who attempted to assassinate Ronald Reagan in 1981 and declared that TAXI DRIVER had inspired him to do this. The assassin fantasised of the relationship between Travis Bickle (Robert De Niro), who runs amok in the film, and the infant hooker Iris (Jodie Foster) whereby Hinckley imagined the role of De Niro for himself and wanted to make a sacrifice to the actress Jodie Foster. But a time bomb like that definitely explodes some time or other. Practically everything can suffice as an ignition spark. A newspaper article, an offensive phrase of a fellow citizen, or, last but not least, a movie. Who once wheels towards the point of no return to kill other people because he is driven by his parents/environmental influences/social conditions/certain genes/the "evil" per se (tick off according to your world view), will translate his aim into action. Cinema will neither particularly encourage him nor prevent him from doing it [see also Postscript].

For the overwhelming majority of viewers the difference is clear. Murderous cinema, i.e. cinema about murderers, always means illusion, even if a flick claims to be highly realistic. Fiction, not reality. Not for nothing is the slogan "It's only a movie" emblazoned on the poster for Wes Craven's disturbing debut LAST HOUSE ON THE LEFT (1972). Attention! This *is* only a movie.

To find a killer in a movie interesting, romantic, or deplorable does not automatically mean to accept the real killer out there. The loud thrill that is mediated by films like BONNIE AND CLYDE (1967) quickly disappears when you study the real case of Bonny Parker and Clyde Barrow. Two cold-blooded killers shooting everyone who happened to come across their triggers, hiding behind the outlaw facade. The mass murderer Charlie Starkweather is another random example; a wrecked loser in every respect, a neurotic garbage disposal man suffering from language and motion disturbances who dreamed of being a proud rebel like his idol James Dean. BADLANDS' Kit Carruthers, Starkweather's movie version actually *is* a rebel, a killer displaying a scarcely penetrable, almost unnatural coolness. The fantasy world of cinema has its own laws.

Different people have different approaches. For the one True Crime cinema is a profound analysis of moral philosophy and the abysses of the human soul, for the vast majority it is merely horrible entertainment in the already mentioned primeval tradition of cinema. But you should definitely distinguish between screened violence and the real one. Whoever engages in the cinematic game of projected wishes, fears, and desires is interested in a way that has nothing in common with the nowadays fashionable appetite for obscene Reality TV shows. Moreover, it has nothing to do with a real confrontation with death like witnessing a car accident by chance. On the contrary: it is cinema that thematises, criticizes or works up the narcotic deluge of images in our Reality TV world in films like HENRY, NATURAL BORN KILLERS (1994) or C'EST ARRIVÉ PRÈS DE CHEZ VOUS (MAN BITES DOG, 1992). By means of abstraction and refraction such films can provide us with an insight into the inner mechanisms of murderers that by far exceeds the usual media depiction.

The observation of real death scenes via documentary material, all those exploitation videos *à la* FACES OF DEATH, or the frequently quoted and also doubted Snuff movies are a completely different topic that *Bad Blood* is going to touch upon only rather sporadically and vaguely. I recommend *Killing For Culture* by David Kerekes and David Slater, an extensive study of real death in cinema. The dark thrill that is caused by many of the films discussed in that seminal book has only partly to do with the things discussed here, and works according to its own rules.

Violent Culture – Cultural Violence

"To sing of love! To me, love is hate, wailing, crying, shame, mourning, tears, blood, cadavers, bones, remorse. I have not known other kinds."

–Petrus Borel (1833)

"To avoid creating simplifying analogies between imaginary and real violence you have to go one step beyond moral valuation or even interpretation and to confess: ***violence fascinates*** *– not only labile children and pathologic monsters."*

(Quote from a special edition about "Aesthetics And Violence" of the German cultural magazine *Heaven's End*.)

At a close look this confession runs like a blood-red thread through cultural history. The evil, the horror, and art, no matter if high art or low art, have always been partners in crime, old allies.

A smell of murder and manslaughter, quite often varnished with difficulty by vindication and moral constructs, from the first cave drawings to the paintings of Bosch and Gruenemann, from the extreme body art of the Viennese Aktionist group to the "Guts' n' Gore" obscenities of the Splatter movies, has been running all through the history of art. Writers as well as painters have been inspired to create masterpieces by the interconnection of crime, sex, and death, from the Greek tragedy with its mass carnage (Aristotle is the origin of the term catharsis), or the Elizabethan tragedy and the Gothic novel of the late 18th and 19th century. According to *Melmoth The Wanderer*, a key work of the genre: "it is quite possible to enjoy suffering... You will call this cruelty, I call it curiosity – that curiosity that brings thousands to witness a tragedy, and makes the most delicate female feast on groans and agonies", notes the book.

The dark side of Romanticism, that among others goes back to D.A.F. de Sade, the "Divine Marquis", glorified the murderer as a literary hero and waded knee-high in a sea of blood, tears and other body fluids. England and especially France (significantly enough the mother-country of the guillotine) distinguished themselves with a number of hand-picked specialists in manslaughter. Barbey d'Aurevilly concluded that "happiness lies in crime", Charles Baudelaire wrote murderous poems, Thomas De Quincey an aesthetic essay titled "On Murder Considered As One Of The Fine Arts". Writers like Octave Mirbeau, or the infamous Comte de Lautréamont constructed philosophies of crime in the best Sadean tradition. In the States Edgar Allan Poe enrolled in the annals of evil: "This spirit of perverseness, I say, came to my final overthrow. It was this unfathomable longing of the soul to vex itself – to offer violence to its own nature – to do wrong for the wrong's sake only – that urged me to continue and finally to consummate the injury I had inflicted upon the unoffending brute [...] because I knew that in so doing I was committing a sin – a deadly sin that would so jeopardize my immortal soul as to place it – if such a thing were possible – even beyond the reach of the infinite mercy of the Most merciful and Most Terrible God".

Happiness In Crime

In France there followed a seamless transition from the 19th to the 20th century, from Parisian Grand Guignol theatre squirting artificial blood to the Surrealists and, later, the Existentialists with their passion for all sorts of crime. The followers of André Breton rehabilitated murderers like Joseph Vacher or the Papin sisters. Georges Bataille, a masterly thinker who worked in the surrealistic atmosphere for a short time, regarded both the murder of passion and eroticism as man's means to transcend his limited existence. He wrote: "We can only reach a state of ecstasy when we are conscious of death or annihilation, even if remotely".

Simone de Beauvoir was convinced that "in every person there lurks [...] an indestructible kernel of darkness, something that cannot break up social conventions or the common currency of human speech, but does, now and then, burst out in a particularly scandalous fashion." As in Albert Camus' classic novel *L'Étranger*, where out of a whim motiveless murder happens in broad daylight, an opus that reminds of the American *série noire*, the pop-cultural pulp fiction equivalent to French existentialism.

The representatives of this gloomy kind of literature like James M. Cain, Dashiell Hammett and Cornell Woolrich triggered off the light-and-shadowplays of Film Noir, which from the Thirties to the Fifties depicted a world full of immoral cops, femmes fatales, and tragic murderers, and became cinema history through its lionization by French film critics. Putting the killer into the centre of his stories the pulp-writer Jim Thompson, a late follower of Hammett & Co., radicalised the mutually quite similar themes of the *série noire*. His hard-boiled novels like *Pop. 1280* (1964) or *The Killer Inside Me* (1952) were dark stories told from the perspective of men who massacre their wives and their best friends without batting an eyelash.

Influenced by the authentic violence of real world phenomena like the Vietnam War or brutal student riots, the American horror movie genre of the Sixties finally got rid of its outdated Gothic monsters. Realistically depicted violence began to dominate instead of Gothic horror. Hitchcock's Norman Bates appears behind the shower curtain, Bonnie and Clyde die in a slow motion blood-bath.

At the same time the Viennese Aktionist group blasted the art business with their taboo-breaking ideas. They were preoccupied with simulating social violence and repression in symbolic battles of material and transforming it into cathartic energy. "One just had to grasp at any form of liberation, at any means of liberation. I simply slashed and whipped the pictures more", protagonist Günter Brus said later. Author Veit Loers writes: "Masturbation, vomiting and bowel movements, not for nothing the traditional weapons of political caricature, lead on to castration, mutilation and murder." Finally the avant garde in Vienna celebrated orgies of bodies, guts, blood and sperms, like autopsy photos from hell. Oswald Wiener, an Austrian theorist of Aktionism, announced: "Kids and teenagers! Torpedo your families wherever you can. Laugh at your fathers, beat them, if you are strong enough! Take their wives! Kill! Do not reason, and never reveal your motives!"

With some detours a track of violence leads from the wild Sixties and Seventies to horror cinema of the Eighties with the serial killer as teenager idol (Freddy Krueger & co.), and the literary battle of material of the splatter punk of the Nineties – as well as the topical and growing fascination with crime in all areas of the media.

Cinema Killers

As already mentioned, the murderer has been part of the inventory of cinema since its beginnings. No matter whether action thriller, Western, whodunit or horror movie, in every third film somebody is violently annihilated. Not to count war movies and period pictures where the list of victims goes into thousands, or even millions.

Moreover, there have always been real cases that have been exploited by the film industry. What in the early days of cinema began with Fritz Lang's classic M – EINE STADT SUCHT EINEN MÖRDER (M, 1931), modelled on Peter Kuerten, a murderer from Weimar, boomed inexorably into the True Crime genre of the last few years. Some examples?

–Ted Bundy, who killed more than twenty women and is said to have received love letters even in Death Row, was impersonated by housewives' darling Mark Harmon in THE DELIBERATE STRANGER (1986).

–Ed Gein, the necrophiliac transvestite from Wisconsin, became the legendary model for horror classics like PSYCHO (1960), THE TEXAS CHAINSAW MASSACRE (1974), or the character of "Buffalo Bill" in THE SILENCE OF THE LAMBS (1990).

–Bonnie Parker and Clyde Barrow, two idols for more than one killer hot for publicity. Already in 1930 they wrote their own public relations articles, a poem ("The Ballad Of Bonnie And Clyde") and were fully concerned with the making of their myth. The life of this famous gangster couple was adapted for the screen several times.

–Perry Smith and Dick Hickock, who annihilated an entire farmer family, were immortalised by Truman Capote in his best-selling novel *In Cold Blood* (1965) and Richard Brooks' film of the same title.

–Charlie Starkweather, the greasy-haired teenage idol among the mass murderers became the darling of the media in the Fifties. Together with his girlfriend Caril he killed eleven people and smiled into the cameras until he died. BADLANDS is only the most famous picture about the young couple. It reconstructs their life and killing spree in romantic images.

These are just the tip of a huge, ever-melting cinematic iceberg.

As very dubious stars, many killers have already assisted industrially in the making of films about their gory deeds. For instance, the murderer Gary Gilmore closely co-operated with the director Lawrence Schiller in the captivating TV production THE EXECUTIONER'S SONG (1982). Moreover, some criminals delivered precise proposals about which actor should actually take their part.

Very often only a few elements of life and "work" of a murderer sufficed as inspiration for movie artists. Such was the case with Ed Gein, as well as with Charles Manson, the diabolic sect-guru whose so-called family put a bloody end to the hippie era. Jonathan Demme's world-wide success THE SILENCE OF THE LAMBS, at the latest, partly influenced by Ed Gein, established the serial killer as a cliché figure of the mainstream thriller. Since Demme's picture the serial killer has finally replaced the classic stock figures of horror. Since then he has been grimacing through the different genres as a nightmarish figure with evil instincts – from screwball comedies to erotic thrillers.

Films That Bite

"Some films were never meant to entertain an audience. Many were designed along the lines of a Drano enema... get inside you, deep into the soft parts, and rip your guts out. In many instances, the filmmaker is not looking for any new friends or fans: he wants fear, loathing, repulsion and reaction from his audience. He is not asking you to like him or his work. But he is issuing a challenge, perhaps even a warning, to any potential viewer: Watch this film at your own risk!"

–Chas Balun

The quality of True Crime movies differs considerably. Many productions employ the language of the Yellow Press and completely distort the facts. But on the other hand, strict seriousness and clinging to the facts often results in a boring, cinematically uninteresting TV-style production that rather plays down the horror and restricts itself exclusively to the perspective of the cops investigating the case. Speculative exploitation melodramas can often display a deeper insight into the topic. Moreover, it is not always necessary to orient oneself painstakingly along the line of strict realism. Cinema may exaggerate. Cinema *shall* exaggerate.

Some ambitious directors like Martin Scorsese or William Friedkin tried their hands in unfathomable psychological studies beyond hero-worship and law-and-order mentality. The screams of the victims in their films still reverberate a long time after watching them, their pain has been burnt into the viewer's retina. But at the same time you gain deep insight into the desert of the delinquent's soul. Richard Brooks is such a director. In IN COLD BLOOD (1967) he masterfully combined factual report and high art. Unfortunately, such serious films striving for authenticity are rare for financial reasons. Really controversial topics have always been unpopular in Hollywood – and today they are even a bigger nuisance.

Pictures on whose cinematic surface a viewer can lose his footing as if on a slippery floor have become especially rare. But art should always attempt to be subversive. At best it should bite, hurt, and leave deep traces. Therefore it must be allowed to cross all borders and to leave behind all areas of taboo in the filmic discussion of crime and death. John McNaughton's HENRY – PORTRAIT OF A SERIAL

KILLER; Koiji Wakamatsu's OKASARETA BYAKUI (VIOLATED ANGELS, 1966), Lodge Kerrigan's CLEAN, SHAVEN (1994) or Gaspar Noé's SEUL CONTRE TOUS (I STAND ALONE, 1998) belong to this rare species from the poison-cabinet of the history of film. They hardly deliver any clearly recognizable ideology and do not allow escape into the realm of the metaphysical (like so many horror films do). Their only aim is consternation. This is what makes them so hard to gulp down – and so important.

Criteria Of Selection: Murder Is Not Always Murder

"Yes, I believe in pain, I believe in corruption and anger and hate. I believe in murder."

–monologue from THE EXORCIST III

In the face of the vast amount of works relevant for this book I had to find some criteria according to which the selection of cases and their cinematic treatment could work. It was important for me to crystallise a subjective principle according to which I wanted to investigate the films, a point of view on the margin of the conventional ones. Beyond the academic discourse and the bloodless approaches of many film theorists, far away from the clinical eye of doctors and court psychologists, contrary to the flourishing True Crime industry, whose most relevant motto is "the more victims and atrocities, the better", but tries to conceal greedy sensationalism with cheap moralism. If you judged mass murderers according to the spectacular content of their deeds, films about dictators and blood-thirsty tyrants would have to be included in this book. But this was by no means the intention of this work.

Even a really interesting author like Colin Wilson, who is specialised in the discussion of murder, often misses the point because he randomly mingles political terrorists, dictators, serial killers and Mafiosi in his standard books such as *The Murderers' Who's Who*. For Wilson they all represent the principal increase of violence and brutalization in the 20th century. But isn't that a too random common denominator? In a society of psychotic lone wolves like the "amok" James Huberty, the "vampire" Richard Chase, and the "cannibal" Ed Gein, traditional gangsters like Bugsy Siegel who work in intricate hierarchies, or political terrorists like the members of the german RAF simply do not fit. In the fictional celluloid universe, too, Robert De Niro running amok in Martin Scorsese's TAXI DRIVER is far different from the mass of interchangeable angels of sanitised vengeance from the conveyor belts of action cinema.

"Useful" Versus "Senseless" Murder

It sounds macabre, but there *are* different categories of murderers. Some capital crimes will never be digested by society; others, though they affect us deeply, somehow fit into the picture we have from society.

The amok gunman who blindly runs into a diner and starts to shoot at random and without warning, the criminal lovers who annihilate themselves as well as others on the run in order to conserve their love before it becomes paralysed by everyday routine; the little employee in a small business who stages a massacre in his office because he cannot bear being nothing but a dust particle in the infinity of the universe. Not only do they drown the victims and their survivors in blood and tears, their acts simply do not have any place in common-sense experience, because they lack sense and orientation – whereas an opponent of the system who methodically blasts a train station or a crowded department store in order to fight a restrictive state of the society is a stock figure of revolutionary mythology. Political killers like those concisely depicted in NADA (THE NADA GANG, 1973) or PATTY HEARST (1988), two vaguely sarcastic movies about terrorism, are "the necessary opposite of order which would be deprived of legitimisation without its declared enemies" (Bernd Mattheus). They represent the counteracting force necessary for a government to justify its forms of surveillance and punishment. Whereas someone running amok seems to be an antithesis to this world, driven by incomprehensible forces, the terrorist actually appears to be a piece in a big game of chess acting according to instruction.

Borderlines between mass murderers on a manhunt (James Huberty announced his deeds with "I'll go hunting humans") and the clean vigilante groups and urban avengers who want to get rid of the big cities' scum are sometimes difficult to draw. Some serial killers, too, believe in their mission to free the world from "worthless life". But, in fact, there is an enormous difference. Manic figures like Richard Ramirez, Charles Whitman, or the fictional "Red Dragon" are only licensed to kill by their own psychotic subconscious. Bernhard Goetz, the celebrated subway avenger from New York, and his cinematic equivalent Charles Bronson in the notorious DEATH WISH series act in conformity with the logic of the system and rally a mass of fans round themselves in an environment progressively heading towards an almost fascist conservatism. For the Punisher and the Exterminator protect our society from the "vermin" (like Ramirez & Co.) even when our society's own protection mechanisms have become non-effective through corruption and cowardice.

Just as these vigilante acts are already highly accepted, murders committed in the heat of passion or in self-defence, like the one in the feminist road movie THELMA AND LOUISE (1991), quite understandably enjoy the highest degree of acceptability and are part of the standard repertory of "controversial" talk-shows.

Murderer and murderer are not the same. Political fanatics and avengers *à la* Dirty Harry kill to cause a change, whereas the movie cannibal Hannibal Lecter kills because he enjoys fingering the guts of his victims. Many more people become killers for materialistic and mercenary reasons, either to bully their enemies or to raise their bank account. The Mafia and other forms of organised crime annihilate people solely for profiteering, thus manifesting prototypically violent capitalist forms of expression. Mafiosi, murderers and robbers, vigilantes and terrorists, they all kill for a profit. After all, profit is the highest value in a world totally ruled by economical purposes. The Canadian anthropologist Elliot Leyton wrote: "Multiple murder for profit is merely one form of making a living, one in which the murder is incidental to the goal. Those who practise this 'profession' would undoubtedly follow another if they were offered more money."

Leyton, unlike Wilson, really endeavours to distinguish between the different types of murderers. He writes: "Neither are we studying the professional state-employed torturers and murderers who are essentially bureaucrats, wreaking havoc on their fellows on behalf of the rulers of modern governments [...] We are concerned only with those who appear to kill for its own sake, those for whom killing alone is the apparent goal."

"Motiveless" Murder As Revolt

Anthropologists like Elliot Leyton are interested in the unsolved mystery behind the motives of serial killers, runners amok, and mass murderers. Unlike materialistically orientated delinquents, they exist in a world outside common sense.

Whoever seemingly acts senselessly and purposelessly, whoever does not fit into the system, cannot be countenanced any more. Not even for the other "conventional" criminals. A key sequence dealing with this idea can be found in Fritz Lang's M. Here the child-slaughterer impersonated by Peter Lorre has to justify himself in front of a court of criminals because he has stained their "professional honour". Motiveless murder, the killer that kills for killing's sake, only evokes one thing beyond disgust, fear, and anger: total consternation.

But many directors and other artists, like John McNaughton, Terence Malick, or the American painter Joe Coleman, are in search of exactly this consternation effect, because they smell the aura of subversion in it. For them, as for Leyton, the mysterious shadow-zone of motives hidden in the dark represents the most fascinating aspect of the discussion of murder. According to the cynical American magazine *Answer Me*, a kind of bible for armchair misanthropes, "it is the seemingly senseless and aimless nature of their slaughtering that makes serial killers and mass murderers so captivating and stupefying". On the occasion of a printed list of the 100 "most creative" murderers, the editors justify their choice as follows: "We expect politicians and gangsters to kill, as it's been their stock in trade for thousands of years. We'd be very disappointed if they didn't kill. We might even cry. But you won't see Al Capone or Adolf Hitler on this list. Their motive was obvious: Power. For this article we operate by one maxim: The lesser the motive, the better the murder".

Of course, *Answer Me* especially wants to contrast the phoney moralism of commercial True Crime stuff with nasty humour. But the irreverent American underground magazine's credo "the lesser the motive, the better" has a long tradition. Stylizing the character of the "motiveless" murderer as a radical counterpart to society, some writers, especially those working on a post-structuralist and surrealist basis, have continued provoking us in the tradition of gothicism, romanticism, de Sade, and Nietzsche. Basically, the murderer executes as a last consequence what many anarchist, rebellious, and antisocial bohemians and philosophers have been raving about. The runner amok as a rebel against the *corps social* and the serial killer as *homme sauvage* who breaks out of the frame of civilisation rules – both manifest an exaggerated form of individual anarchism evading all commonsensical moral values. Luis Buñuel, too, the past master of subversive cinema, was attracted by the image of the murderer as anarchist against sense and order, as drastic prison-breaker from the status quo: "The symbolism of terrorism, which is a feature of our century has always attracted me. I mean total terrorism aiming at the destruction of any society, the entire human race. But I can only despise those who make terrorism a political weapon in their fight for a purpose."

It does not matter if someone is driven by circumstances, acts unpremeditatedly or fully consciously: megalomaniac born losers who burned in powder-smoke (James Huberty, Howard Unruh), vampiristic sado-masochists (Fritz Haarmann, Richard Chase), the lovers (Martha Beck & Raymond Fernandez, Charles Starkweather & Caril Fugate, Bonnie Parker & Clyde Barrow), who left behind a trace of blood in films like BLOODY WEDNESDAY (1984), THE SNIPER (1952), THE HONEYMOON KILLERS (1970), or BADLANDS; they are all, of course, disgusting psychotic characters without pity and morality. But in their unfathomable irrationality, consternation, and delusion, their obsession, madness, and lust of killing, their anti-morality and asocial behaviour between the most brutal outbursts of emotion and absolute emotional torpor, they stand for radical revolt serving neither a political, nor an ideological purpose. A revolt directed against "the superiority of nature" (de Sade), "the transitoriness and insignificance of the human condition" (Sartre), and "the rule of economy and reason" (Bataille), which, beside murder, can also be expressed through suicide, sacrifice, sexual ecstasy, and death itself. For such different minds as Jean Genet, André Breton, Norman Mailer, or Jean Baudrillard these phenomena are cracks and fissures blind with rage that can cause the collapse of our dominant moral/ethic world of ideas at any given second.

Murder As Art

"One is limiting art much too severely when one demands that only the composed

soul, suspended in moral balance, may express itself there. As in the plastic arts, there is in music and poetry an art of the ugly soul, as well as an art of the beautiful soul; and in achieving art's mightiest effects – breaking souls, moving stones, and humanizing animals – perhaps that very art has been most succesful."
–Friedrich Nietzsche

"Crime is beauty"
–Melvins

Stanislaw Ignazy Witkiewicz, himself an obsessive in his own way, wrote that "only madness or crime can break the wall of ordinariness, sometimes creative power, or not even it". This Polish writer, too, saw murder as a rebellious act. He put himself in the row of great poets who saw in the "anti-elite" of outcasts, from criminals and lepers to madmen, the last resistance in a hopelessly lost world.

I have already discussed how the world of art has always been fascinated by blind violence and "evil", but there is still much more to their interconnection and mutual influence. Writers and artists dealing intensely with murderers are only one side of the coin. On the other side there are real killers writing works of literature, which goes back to the 19th century Frenchman Pierre François Lacenaire and his contemporary Pierre Rivierre. Is it mere coincidence that notorious murderers like Jack Henry Abbott also wrote poetry and even whole novels? That killers as writers are nothing extraordinary can also be seen in the cases of Austrian Jack Unterweger and American Gary Gilmore. Others, like John Wayne Gacy, who killed 32 homosexual men and played Pogo the Clown on children's birthday parties, acquired a dubious reputation as painters. The paintings of the killer clown, who was put to death in 1994, sell well in the art business. As in the Sixties and early Seventies *art brut* and the art of madmen were highly demanded and soon had their place in renowned museums. Today the paintings and writings of serial killers are baiting people into the American galleries. A famous example for the multi-faced interplay between (popular) art and violent crime is Charles Manson. He would have become an underground folk-singer of the Seventies, if his followers had not disembowelled pregnant Sharon Tate and her friends. Reciprocally, radical artists working in the underground network like the American painter Joe Coleman claim that they would have been arrested for murder long time ago, if they had not been able to free their aggression and their murderous instincts in art. "I can sort of understand a person like James Huberty, who went into a McDonalds and started to shoot the people", says Coleman. "Huberty destroyed both himself and the people. That's obviously not the idea behind my art, but there are certain types of pain that need expression. The expression has to be equal to the pain, it has to be as extreme". The cleansing cathartic effect that many artists try to achieve, in Coleman's case as a self-therapy, is what certain serial killers, too, are looking for in their acts, if one can trust their biographies. Are art and crime two really comparable ways of purification, the reduction of one's instincts?

"The annihilation of mankind must be aimed at, as well as the annihilation of art. I hate the people and their institutions. I deeply hate whatever bears a human face. I love animals. I would have mankind wiped out to the number of people I necessarily need for entertainment". Phrases from the farewell letter of an amok gunman or the diary of a multiple serial killer? Not at all. Otto Muehl, a member of the Viennese Aktionist group wrote these lines in 1963.

"Visionary Killers"

"... the decision is to encourage the psychopath in oneself, to explore that domain of

experience where security is boredom and therefore sickness, and one exists in the present..."

–Norman Mailer

For Magnus Hirschfeld, a german psychiatrist of the Twenties, the poet Charles Baudelaire, and the killer Peter Kuerten were closely related cases. In a famous essay he called both dangerous psychopaths. But basically he agreed with Coleman. He concluded that Baudelaire would have become a potential Kuerten, if he, as intellectual, had not been able to divert his murderous forces. The artist as potential murderer/the murderer as artist ?

The fact is that the majority of "motiveless" crimes are committed by well-read, educated people with a high IQ. There are even cases in the history of crime like the one of the homosexual couple Nathan Leopold and Richard Loeb, who carried out the execution of a man as an "intellectual" act. One of the two killers in ROPE (1948), Hitchcock's cinematic realisation of the case, talks of "murder as art". Inspired by Leopold and Loeb, André Gide defined "motiveless" murder as "a culminating *acte gratuit* liberating man from the determination of the material universe, the point where man decides irreversibly for his freedom" (more about that in the chapter "Killers As Mythical Figures"). Of course, the bourgeois society must be shocked by the painters' and philosophers' glorification of murder, suicide, and running amok as downright existentialist revolt. This cries for being completely banned into the realm of madness. German author Bernd Mattheus says that "rational logic defends itself against acts without obvious motivation behind".

"This is why a tainted society has invented psychiatry to defend itself against the investigations of certain superior intellects whose faculties of divination would be troublesome". This was written by Antonin Artaud, a French poet labelled crazy and was, of course, interpreted as a sign for his madness by his psychiatrists. What if Artaud is right? What if there are really some visionaries locked away in padded rooms, isolation wings, and institutions for mentally ill criminals? "Indeed, most of psychology is childish. A census taker tried to quantify me once. I ate his liver with some fava beans and a big Amarone", retorts such a "visionary" as Hannibal Lecter.

The Bondage Of Psychology

"Most of us are aware how trivial, ephemeral, descriptive and meaningless psychiatric diagnoses are."

–William Gaylin, an American psychiatrist

"No psychology, this is always the worst."

–Jean Baudrillard

The fictional character of Hannibal Lecter has been deliberately chosen as a counterpart to all those psychologists who contribute their shallow comments to every TV-documentary about mass murderers, flood the book market with their theses, and hence profit considerably by the delinquents, and, especially in America, reduce the serial killer problem to charts and lists. The German magazine *Splatting Image* says: "In the USA psychology is likely to be treated as an exact field of science". It is that indexical simplicity, not Freud's early attempts to understand the wide land of the human soul, that Emil Gengenbach attacks when he rages: "It serves the psychiatrists right when they are called the inquisition of the bourgeoisie. Those who try to escape their utilitarian exploitation, suffer madly from their craziness". It is the institutionalised mechanisms, the psycho-tests and analyses which serve the dominating norms and accept the existing system of values as the only "normal" one. The FBI psychologists' computer programs, which should help them to cope with the serial killers' and mass murderers' onslaught, are apparently doomed to failure. Early childhood traumata and organic damage definitely are important factors, if one proceeds into the realm of bloodlust and amok. But do they alone drive a man to murder? Why do so many kids in the States grow up under identically bad conditions as Albert DeSalvo, The Strangler of Boston, but still do not commit such crimes? Why do so many people suffer from a brain tumour similar to the one of Charles Whitman, the sniper from Austin, and still never run amok? "All American Boy" Ted Bundy and his towering hate corrected once and for all the often employed image of the gentle guy disoriented and gone astray only because of his social circumstances. His childhood, his education, his relationships, everything was average. "Nothing happened to me, Officer Starling. I happened," Hannibal Lecter says; "you can't reduce me to a set of influences."

Sometimes the "evil" hits so massively that all "emotional model-kits" break down, and, essentially, the motiveless killer remains a mystery. It is the mystery hiding behind these delinquents that magnetically attracts so many of us. Some concerning themselves seriously with crime, like Coleman or the musician Jim Thirlwell, do not delight themselves with the gory details of a series of murders. For them, motiveless killers like Bundy are the last dark spots in a monotonous world that has been totally illuminated, deconstructed, and conditioned by the machinery of rationality. Whoever cannot be categorized in boxes, finally denies the image of the glass man, who as a blackbox functions according to predictable rules.

From the real killers to the killers in cinema: as forensic psychiatry can only attempt to explain true cases, the psychoanalytically determined film theory with its constructs of interpretation is locked up in a network of repetitive explanation patterns. Susan Sontag harshly protests against psychoanalytic as well as Marxist analysts in her famous essay "Against Interpretation", and sides with an entirely aesthetic view of art: "By reducing the work of art to its content and then interpreting that, one tames the work of art." And the American film theorist Stephen Shapiro states: "We are tired of endless discussions of the phallus, the castration complex and the problematics of the sexual representation. Psychoanalytic discourse, even at its ostensibly most critical, does nothing but reinscribe a universal history of lack and oppression" (from: "The Cinematic Body").

So I too have tried to omit explicit psychological explanations in this book in order to disengage myself from such dissatisfactory views.

Terms: "Schizophrenics", "Psychopaths", "Sado-Masochists"

Nevertheless one thing is clear: even if you are highly critical of the language of the police, psychiatry, and the courts, you cannot do without terms like psychopath or schizophrenic because they are already part of everyday language. Everybody uses popular psychological terms (cf. sadist and masochist, which have also lost every relation to their originators de Sade and Sacher-Masoch) without any deeper knowledge about the clinical picture behind, or even worse, without ever questioning their catalogues of symptoms.

Psychoanalysis in its trivial cartoon-form has become a common element of the horror and thriller genres. Alfred Hitchcock's films are an excellent example. Psychoanalytical terms are present everywhere, from the Yellow Press to boozy discussions in pubs: "This guy must have had an early childhood trauma!". Hence these terms are also employed in this book, not in their purely scientific sense, but as elements of popular culture and language. As I have already mentioned, this book shall not represent any particular psychoanalytical view nor any other specific scientific school. Oscillating between myth and truth and fully aware of all the stereotypes and clichés *Bad Blood* nevertheless cannot do without, I rather let the different approaches clash. An odyssey into the realm of burning madness, knives dripping with blood, and unbelievable phantasmagorias.

Perhaps, one gets to know a part of oneself that one never wanted to know. For "killing is a vital force inside us", wrote Octave Mirbeau. "All higher species are dominated by it, as well as the sex drive. [...] After all, we are all murderers to a greater or lesser extent."

The Killer Inside Me

"This rudderless world is not shaped by vague metaphysical forces. It is not God, who kills the children. Not fate that butchers them or destiny that feeds them to the dogs. It's us, only us."

–Alan Moore, Watchmen

"God help the beast in me."

–Johnny Cash

Only very few of us want to accept this part of us. We lock up the "evil", electrocute it, or hang it and leave it to the archives of criminal psychology.

The terms most frequently connected with extreme delinquents like "pathological", "perverted", or "abnormal" do not only serve to express justified emotions like fear or anger, but primarily to separate our own normal personality – which would never be capable of such acts – from the alien evil, that we stigmatise as sick. There is nothing that the Yellow Press and talk-show gurus love more than assigning a place outside humanity to runners amok and serial killers. This complete segregation of the criminal as the alien, the monstrous exception from the healthy rule, goes even much further than any punishment. Of course it is clear that every functioning social system must protect itself against the assaults of irrational killers via laws and moral values. Nevertheless, the exclusion I am talking about makes our world a phoney planet where every serious discussion of violence is repressed.

Yet the analysis of the alien could provoke results which, though not pleasant, lead to the core of the phenomenon of human violence: it lurks in every one of us. Violence is an essential part of our lives we cannot repress. "Gentle childbirth, bullshit!", says Emil Gengenbach. Artaud said that:"we have all been thrown violently into life, copulated and masturbated nine months through the membrane". No death can be more violent and painful.

Deep down in every one of us there is a ruthless, primal killer inside. Perhaps, this is the fundamental truth from which all censors, moralists and inveterate optimists flee in panic. Jim Thompson describes the killer inside so brutally and accurately in the characters of his books. Their message seem to be: It lies in all of us. Only most of us are too hypocritical and cowardly to actually do what they want.

To occupy oneself seriously with the unpleasant facets of one's own personality via literature, music, and film seems to be more productive and more fascinating than pushing it away into the schoolbooks of psychopathology. To follow the bizarre logic of the delinquents, to approach their thinking in books and films, to dive into their suffocating universe, all this makes it possible to trace one's own baser instincts. Doing it without glorification and damnation, this is what the book tries to accomplish. Of course, this is a bit risky. You can easily lose the ground under your feet, if you attempt to understand the motives of a "motiveless" killer. This happens in Michael Mann's film MANHUNTER (1986, based on a novel by Thomas Harris). The FBI agent Will Graham delves so deeply into the psyche of the mass-murdering "Red Dragon" that he almost cannot find the way back to the light (of reason).

But the risk pays well. According to all catharsis theorists of cinema, to face the abyss inside means to gain its familiarity a little bit. Siegfried Kracauer says that "every depiction plays with the depicted. Maybe the 'horror thing' aims at making the people get the knack of things in whose clutches they still are at the moment."

Cinema As Catharsis

All discussion of the horror that is evoked by mass murderers and serial killers is deeply rooted in the mastering of the fear of one's own death, the terror, and one's own murderous impulses. Behind the gloomy entertainment, the chilly kicks mediated by films like THE SILENCE OF THE LAMBS or HENRY there is the idea of film as a therapy to come to grips with the real horror. A mature audience learns to deal with the horror. Whoever can laugh about monstrosities and is not shocked, may be dangerous for a possible mass-outbursts of emotion, aimed at generating randomly definable expressions of will. "He who is not impressed by any form of violence [...] subverts the fundaments of a sound popular instinct. The more or less free living out of sado-masochist fantasies does not really threaten our society, but the repression of passion does". (Maerz)

The Japanese society with its deluge of extreme violence in the media, but at the same time a relatively low crime rate speaks for the thesis that murderous cinema can have a quasi-liberating function giving everybody the opportunity to compensate, hence satisfy his own latent violent obsessions. Oliver Stone, responsible for the fictional killer maelstrom NATURAL BORN KILLERS, is convinced of this theory: "I believe that all of us are born violent – we're natural born aggressors. We have a million-year-old reptilian brain with a neo-cortex of civilisation on top, but it's doing a bad job of concealing the aggression. Killing is a combination of genetics and environment. When I go to my son's school, I notice a lot of aggression in kids, a natural cruelty. How are we to deal with it? My way would be to show kids images of aggression – Kubrick's 2001 apemen, for instance – and say, this is you too. You are an animal. Next time you feel aggression in your schoolyard and want to slug your friend, recognise it as such – that's the beginning of getting a handle on it. If you know what it is that's making you blind with rage, you have taken the first step towards controlling the mood as opposed to having the mood control you".

Cinema as a drug, a cathartic pill. It is provocation and the raw material of nightmares. Face the horror. Get to know the killer inside. Plunge into your own dark abyss.

PART ONE
CASE HISTORIES

"Electric Chair" (1967), by Andy Warhol (© Warhol Museum)

JACK HENRY ABBOTT

Messages From The Belly Of The Beast

"...You sit in solitary confinement stewing in nothingness, not merely your own nothingness but the nothingness of society, others, the world. The lethargy of months that add up to years in a cell, alone, entwines itself about every 'physical' activity of the living body and strangles it slowly to death. You no longer do push-ups or other physical exercises in your small cell; you no longer masturbate; you can call forth no vision of eroticism in any form, and your genitals, like the limbs of your body, function only to keep your body alive. Time descends in your cell like the lid of a coffin in which you lie and watch it as it slowly closes over you. When you neither move nor think in your cell, you are awash in pure nothingness. Solitary confinement in prison can alter the ontological makeup of a stone."

–Jack Henry Abbott, *In The Belly Of The Beast*

The Case

Jack Henry Abbott is perhaps one of the most tragic symbols of an existence entirely spent "upstate". Born in Michigan in 1944 as the son of an Irish sailor and a Chinese hooker, he has only lived in freedom for a minute period of his life. From the age of 12 onwards he frequented several institutions for juvenile delinquents and was found guilty of forging a cheque at 18. A few years later he stabbed a fellow jailbird, but he managed to escape from the high security block. After a bank robbery he was arrested again.

In 1977 Jack H. Abbott wrote a letter to Norman Mailer, who was writing the non-fiction novel *The Executioner's Song* about the double murderer Gary Gilmore at that time. He had heard of Mailer's project and offered him authentic material about the life of murderers in prison. This was followed by an exchange of letters over a long period of time where Mailer and Abbott discussed politics, moral values, and, above all, Abbot's nightmarish twenty-year-long prison experience. The eternal jailbird that fought isolation madness in solitary confinement with reading

Norman Mailer

philosophical books turned out to have a lucid mind obsessively analysing the daily prison routine. Mailer called him a "romanticist and a mystic influenced by the contradictory worlds of Marx and Nietzsche, and formed by the brutality of his environment, finally, confinement was something like karma for him." In the end there remained almost one thousand narrowly written pages whose imagery captivated Norman Mailer. They were published as *In The Belly Of The Beast* in 1981. The book was highly successful. Norman Mailer even managed to bring the authorities to release his protégé earlier. On June 5, 1981, shortly after the book was published, Abbott was set free. But the man now being celebrated by the literary scene had been standing much too long with his back to the wall. Excluded and alienated from the world, he could not be rehabilitated anymore. On July 18, 1981 he stabbed the waiter Richard Adan in the course of a harmless row in a New York bar. Hence he was found guilty of "manslaughter in extreme arousal". Since then he has spent his time in the place he had desperately tried to escape from – the pit – and will remain there for the rest of his life. Abbott: "A man is taken away from his experience of society, taken away from the experience of a living planet of living things, when sent to prison."

GHOSTS OF THE CIVIL DEAD / Australia 1987

Directed by John Hillcoat. Written by Gene Konkie, Evan English, John Hillcoat, Nick Cave, Hugo Race. Camera: Paul Goldman & Graeme Wood. Music: Nick Cave, Blixa Bargeld, Mick Harvey. With Dave Field, Mike Bishop, Chris De Rose, Nick Cave, Dave Mason

Abbott's sad example of everyday hell behind bars became one of the main sources of inspiration for probably the coldest prison movie of all times. Two newcomers, the governor designate Officer Yale and the delinquent Wenzil, come into a "maximum security" prison in the middle of the Australian desert. In these two opposite characters GHOSTS OF THE CIVIL DEAD shows how prison dulls, erodes, and finally breaks people.

Far beyond the usual prison movie-romanticism, this film presents life in the high security hell as uneventful, vegetating. It is a pilot for the execution of sentence in the future. Muzak like in a supermarket fills the rooms and the convicts cower

Nick Cave, GHOSTS OF THE CIVIL DEAD

apathetically in their cells and stare into the void. Again and again the piercing boredom is interrupted by ultra-brutal outbursts of violence. A swearing inmate mutilating himself (impersonated by the rock singer Nick Cave) who brings the whole thing to an explosion with his hysteria, functions as a catalyst for pent-up aggression. Cave and all the others who participated in the writing of the script found detailed descriptions of dullness and emptiness in Abbott's book: "My body communicates with the cell. We exchange everything, temperature and breeze, smells and the remainders on the floor and on the walls." Forget the usual prison movie clichés in GHOSTS OF THE CIVIL DEAD, there is no deep friendship among men and no lonely guitarist singing the blues. Nick Cave says that before making the film he was "captivated by the image of prison in old Blues songs: 'Warden, warden, lock me up, it was a girl that brought me here' and rubbish like that. Doing time, now I know what this means, is a great deal gloomier, absolutely unromantic, the Evil as such".

The wardens too are portrayed neither as sympathetic nor extremely sadistic (like in Jules Dassin's paradigmatic prison-movie classic BRUTE FORCE, 1947), but rather reduced to mere observers (via video monitors). Austrian film critic Reinhard Jud states that "John Hillcoat shows the high-security prison as an allegorical place where, like rarely elsewhere, palpable processes of levelling and disintegration are highly condensed." At the end, when released again, the killer Wenzil is still shown as remote-controlled and monotonous as before; the film's message becomes apparent: the prison as a distillate of the world outside.

SADA ABE

The Case

On 16 May, 1936, an extraordinary murder case – in fact an astonishing crime of passion – came to light in Japan. 31-year-old Sada Abe, a low-class prostitute, strangled to death her lover Yoshizo (aka Kichizo) Ishida – believed to be a pimp – during an act of sadomasochistic love-making. This was the culmination of a sex session which apparently had lasted from 23 April to 7 May. Sada was picked up by the police as she wandered the streets in a state of strange elation. She was carrying a *furoshiki* (cloth for wrapping gifts) in which was discovered the severed penis of her dead lover. The case became notorious, and remains something of a feminist *cause célèbre* with its implications that the stereotype of submissive Japanese women is not as accurate as the patriarchal structure of their society seems to suggest.

The lovers had become so addicted to each other that they soon could not spend one minute without each other. Making love around the clock they finally forgot about the outer world. Even eating and drinking were performed as erotic rites, and the borderline between lust and pain soon disappeared.

AI NO CORRIDA (THE EMPIRE OF SENSES) / Japan 1976

Written and directed by Nagisa Oshima. Camera: Hideo Ito. Music: Minoru Miki. With Tatsuya Fuiji, Eiko Matsuda

Oshima told this extreme love story which could only result in death with very aesthetic, sensuous, and above all taboo-breaking images. Though avoiding banal voyeurism, the depiction of the two lovers' uncompromising devotion and pain contains explicit sexual imagery otherwise found only in hardcore pornography.

In his version of the true story of Sada and Kichi, the lovers abandoning themselves in an erotic frenzy, Nagisa Oshima achieves something remarkable. He works with the devices of pornographic film, showing genitals and ejaculations, yet transgresses subversively all conventions of the porno-genre. AI NO CORRIDA is about an empire of passions devouring everything, an empire far outside social reality. There is no safety for the lovers. It is an eroticism heading towards death. Aba Sada strangles Kichi and cuts off his penis, because she wants to carry it with her for all time. A filmic delirium unsurpassed in its intensity.

AI NO CORRIDA

JITSUROKU ABE SADA (ABE SADA STORY) / Japan 1975

Directed by Noburu Tanaka. Written by Ido Akio. Camera: Mori Masuru. Music: Sakata Koichi. With Myashita Junko, Ezumi Hideaki, Sakamoto Nagatoshi, Hnayagi Genshu, Koizumi Ikonusuke

The true story of the prostitute Sada, who killed her lover in 1936 and strayed through the streets with his cut-off penis, is an enduring one in Japan. Noburu Tanaka, who did a lot of surrealistically erotic "roman pornos" (Japanese soft-sex films), actually directed visions of Sada's excess one year before Oshima. Tanaka tells the story of tenderness and violence less explicitly, but highly poetically and passionately. A maelstrom of kisses, skin, sweat, and blood. At the end you can read "Following evidence was confiscated: a silk ribbon, a carving knife, a male genital". Tanaka's version of the story is full of flashbacks and refers to the authentic confessions of the real protagonist. Tanaka describes her as follows: "She is a typical Japanese woman who does not react logically but very physically. She does not only represent sacrifice and resignation, but rather the urge for life at any price, if only to be scorned for it. The vitality of Japanese women can be extreme."

What makes both film versions provocative is their reversal of sex roles taking place somewhere in the middle of the films. This can be interpreted as a subversive attack on the misogynist Japanese society: Kichi becomes more and more passive, and Sada begins to strangle him to increase her lust, whereby she finally kills him. She cuts off his penis and wanders entranced through the streets of Tokyo during a putsch until she is arrested. Before that the passionate murderess writes with blood "only Sada and Kichi" on a linen. Scenes of obsession, an erotic state of emergency.

SADA ABE STORY

JOE BALL

The Case

Joe Ball was a Texan ex-bootlegger, who had a tremendously prosperous "Sociable Inn" motel in Elmsdorf near San Antonio. The travellers were not only attracted by the road house because it was situated directly beside Highway 181, but primarily for hand-picked pretty waitresses and other attractions – like the pool behind the house with five alligators swimming in it. The proud owner used to entertain his guests with feedings. He started them with big bloody slices of meat. Sadistically, he then went on to living cats and dogs as 'gator dinner. After a particularly pretty waitress had disappeared without leaving a trace, Mr. Ball laconically commented on the frequent change of personnel as follows: "You know how they are. They come and they go." When Ball's third wife disappeared too, rumours came up and the police intervened. When the cops visited him in September 1938, he drew his gun without any visible sign of emotion and blew out his own brains. Investigations revealed that the motel owner had killed at least five girls who had worked for him and had fed them to the pets in the bone-filled pool. The girl-eating alligators came into the San Antonio zoo, and became curiosities many people marvelled at.

EATEN ALIVE aka DEATH-TRAP aka SLAUGHTER HOTEL aka STARLIGHT SLAUGHTER aka HORROR HOTEL MASSACRE / USA 1976

Written and directed by Tobe Hooper. Camera: Hardy Rustam. Music: Tobe Hooper and Wayne Bell. With Neville Brand, Robert Englund, Mel Ferrer, Stuart Whitman, Marilyn Burns

Judd, a mad soliloquising hotel owner in Louisiana, kills young, preferably female, tourists with a scythe and dumps them into the alligator pond behind the house where a huge hungry pet is already waiting. With this trashy movie vacillating between horror and only partly funny gags, Tobe Hooper followed his terror-classic THE TEXAS CHAINSAW MASSACRE. As in the case of the preceding film with its allusions to Ed Gein, a true case was the starting point. But Tobe Hooper was not only inspired by the Texan alligator breeder Joe Ball, but also by Hitchcock's immortal film character Norman Bates, who is in his turn also based on Ed Gein. Thanks to his total

EATEN ALIVE

overacting, Neville Brand starring as Judd is really entertaining. But you need a looking glass, if you want to find gory splatter-scenes. At least the sleaze factor is high due to the participation of the young Robert Englund (in pre-Freddy Krueger days) and some fucked-up Hollywood stars like Stuart Whitman and Mel Ferrer. Further credit points: a short performance by Hooper's chainsaw-stricken Scream Queen Marilyn Burns. Likewise, the artificiality of the cheap, hence totally unnatural studio decoration. Illuminating every scene in glaring red and blue, Tobe Hooper anticipates the ghost train atmosphere of later films like FUNHOUSE (1981) and especially THE TEXAS CHAINSAW MASSACRE II (1986).

The primal terror of being eaten alive by alligators also informs such sub-JAWS exploitation fare as KROCODILE (Hong Kong/Thailand 1976) and Lewis Teague's ALLIGATOR (1980), only to resurface with a vengeance 20 years later in LAKE PLACID (2000), Tobe Hooper's CROCODILE (2000), and James Hickox's BLOOD SURF (2000).

The Case
Arizona Donnie Clark alias Kate "Ma" Barker is probably America's most notorious mother. She was born in Missouri in 1872. Her childhood idol was the gunman Jesse James. In 1892 she married the farm-worker George Barker and soon gave birth to her beloved sons Herman, Lloyd, Arthur ("Doc"), and Freddie, her favourite son. Growing up in poverty and "educated" by Ma alone, the four boys incurred punishment in their very early youth. In 1914 the family moved to Oklahoma where the boys committed a few robberies and were sentenced to longer terms of imprisonment. Herman shot himself when facing a superior police force. After these events Kate walked out on her husband and set up a hideout for fugitive capital criminals that brought her thousands of dollars. She used the money to get her sons out of prison. When Freddie was released in March 1931, the Barker Gang began to take shape. Ma planned the robberies and kept in the background, Freddie and his friends carried them out. The boys killed and robbed at will, while Kate was listening to hillbilly songs and solving crossword puzzles at home. Contacts to other gangs and corrupt politicians saved them for a long time from police prosecution. But after they had kidnapped two entrepreneurs, the FBI was at their heels. On January 16, 1935 FBI agents hunted down the Barker Gang in their hideout in Florida. Whether Kate died in the hail of bullets that tore the house to pieces, or committed suicide, remains a mystery. Anyway, there are numerous legends about her. Moreover, we will never get to really know if she was the over-thoughtful mother, the brutal criminal mastermind that commanded her helpless sons, or, on the contrary, a helpless mother who was used as a front by her sons to escape harsher punishment. But legend has her down as a killer.

BIG BAD MAMA / USA 1974
Directed by Steve Carver. Written by William Northon & Frances Doel. Camera: Bruce Logan. Music: David Grisman. With Angie Dickinson, William Shatner, Tom Skerritt, Susan Sennett, Dick Miller
A funny, trashy film from Roger Corman's "New World" production company, obviously influenced by Ma Barker. But in this pseudo-feminist version the robbing

MEN, MONEY and MOONSHINE
WHEN IT COMES TO VICE, MAMA KNOWS BEST!
HOT LEAD
HOT CARS
HOT DAMN!
ANGIE DICKINSON
BIG BAD MAMA
WILLIAM SHATNER · TOM SKERRITT · SUSAN SENNETT · ROBBIE LEE
R
RESTRICTED
WILLIAM NORTON & FRANCES DOEL
STEVE CARVER
ROGER CORMAN
A NEW WORLD PICTURE · METROCOLOR

BLOODY MAMA

and killing mother gathers murderous daughters instead of sons around her. The gang robs men, abuses them sexually, and shoots them after consumption. The sex scene between Angie Dickinson (from the TV series *Police Woman*) and William Shatner (alias Capt. Kirk from *Star Trek*) caused no little scandal at the time.

BIG BAD MAMA 2 / USA 1987

Written and directed by Jim Wynorsky. Camera: Robert C. New. Music: Chuck Cirino. With Angie Dickinson, Robert Culp, Danielle Brisebois, Bruce Glover

After Mama Angie Dickinson has fallen victim to corrupt doings in the Thirties (her husband has been shot and she herself has been robbed of all her belongings), she robs banks together with her daughters and sets up a gang. In a story that rather reminds of a female Jesse James than of the Barker gang, she is made a folk hero by the press. After several dates with a cosmetic surgeon, ageing Angie Dickinson again plays the role of "Big Bad Mama". Roger Corman, who initiated this even sleazier version, completely neglects the fact that she dies a violent death in the end of Part One. He has his favourite director Jim Wynorsky do the remake including many of Corman's own preferences, i.e. sexism (many gratuitously naked girls), cheap action scenes, and the denunciation of the authorities.

BLOODY MAMA / USA 1970

Directed by Roger Corman. Written by Robert Thom based on a report by Don Peters and Robert Thom. Camera: John A. Alonzo. Music: Don Randi. With Shelley Winters, Pat Hingle, Don Stroud, Diane Varsi, Bruce Dern, Robert de Niro

CRAZY MAMA

Roger Corman, the Godfather of exploitation cinema, seems to be fascinated by the myth of Ma Barker. She was a main inspiration for many films he produced. This opus, which perhaps can be taken the most seriously, marks the beginning of all his "Bad Mama" films and was directed by the B-movie mogul himself. Corman's classical virtues can be found here, whereas his later "New World" movies often degenerated into pure trash. The man who represented the rare example of a leftist liberal capitalist in Hollywood, confronted attempts to detect auteurism and social criticism in his work with blasts of pure exploitation. This mélange stands true in films like Scorsese's BOXCAR BERTHA (1971), or Corman's BLOODY MAMA. In these films reality is presented roughly, obscenely, and brutally, but also humorously. Proletarian drive-in cinema at its best.

Thanks to a method acting-steeled cast (beside an ingeniously abysmal Shelley Winters, young Robert De Niro excels in a minor part) Corman succeeds in an adequate realisation of the Barker case. Only roughly realistic, but on the whole following the historical events, BLOODY MAMA takes up and exploits all the myths around Ma Barker – her psychotic brutality, her brood-hen-like neurotic behaviour binding her boys to herself. Moreover, only Corman would dare to bring up the incestuous relationship Ma Barker might have had with some of her sons. With a tragi-comic scalpel he lays bare the madness that must have boiled in this family. When you consider the scene where Shelley Winters drowns a girl that has had sex with her favourite son without any signs of emotion in the bathtub, the end title changes its meaning: "In Memory of the Mothers of America" on a 3-cent-stamp.

THE GRISSOM GANG

CRAZY MAMA / USA 1975

Directed by Jonathan Demme. Written by Robert Thom. Camera: Bruce Logan. With Cloris Leachman, Stuart Whitman, Ann Southern, Linda Purl

Another opus from the B-movie factory "New World" that hardly reminds one of the real Ma Barker case, but once again tells Roger Corman's favourite story of a ferocious gang of women. The same story of the widow of a murdered farmer who sets out to take revenge was already filmed as BIG BAD MAMA one year before and later in BIG BAD MAMA 2. Here Cloris Leachman has the Angie Dickinson part. What is most remarkable about this film, is Jonathan Demme's cartoon-like *mise-en-scène*, creating a colourful mélange of crime story, rock'n'roll farce, and social satire.

THE GRISSOM GANG / USA 1970

Directed by Robert Aldrich. Written by Leon Griffith, based on a novel by James Hadley Chase. Camera: Joseph F. Biroc. Music: Gerald Fried. With Kim Barby, Scott Wilson, Tony Musante, Robert Lansing, Irene Daily

Relying on the legends about Ma Barker, Robert Aldrich delivered a movie that is by all means comparable to Corman's adaptation and even beats it in viciousness and gloom. Together with Russ Meyer's MUDHONEY (1965) and John Huston's WISE BLOOD (1979), THE GRISSOM GANG ranks among the most venomous ever Hillbilly-dramas: Welcome to Hellville, USA! Aldrich, who is well-known for his dealing with neurotic woman characters (WHATEVER HAPPENED TO BABY JANE; HUSH HUSH, SWEET CHARLOTTE etc.) portrays Ma Grissom/alias Barker as a monster hardened by life in the Depression days. Always having an eye on her own interests and without

Shelley Winter's touch of an incestuous "super-mother", she kills, robs and blackmails like a pitiless character from a Jim Thompson novel. But her sons (touching: Scott Wilson; frightening: Tony Musante; full of moronic redneck charm: Ralph Waite, the "Daddy" in TVs *The Waltons*) are her equal.

When the young daughter of a millionaire is kidnapped by the gang, she gets a taste of hell during her captivity. Only Ma's cretinous son Floyd, whom she abhors when he molests her drooling and gasping in the beginning, saves her life. Floyd (Scott Wilson, who after IN COLD BLOOD enters his name once again in the gallery of ingenious sidemen) makes her his "wife", hence taboo for the rest of the gang. In a story-twist typical for Robert Aldrich, the tortured girl gradually loses her disgust of him and replaces repulsion by traces of sympathy. In the final shoot-out (the police storm the gang's hideout just as in the real Barker case), all are executed: Ma Grissom and the whole gang including Floyd, who surrenders unarmed. Finally getting back his daughter from the claws of the now-slaughtered gangsters, the old businessman turns away from her in disgust. Her pity for, and her (bodily) desecration by, white trash "scum" has thoroughly sullied the honour of the family. He would have preferred a dead daughter, hence an undefiled reputation. So the girl falls into sad apathy, as numb as the protagonist at the end of a gory horror film.

In the end of Robert Aldrich's film you finally experience that pity and mercy are words devoid of meaning. Always being appreciated as a brilliant craftsman, but never considered a really great artist due to his pulp predilections, Aldrich here created another highlight in a career already pulsing with gloomy jewels (such as KISS ME DEADLY/1955). In THE GRISSOM GANG envy, greed, and hatred are not an exclusive feature of the poor classes (films about the Depression days bear the danger of such a denunciation); in this opus there is hardly a character, no matter to which class he belongs, that is not rotten inside. THE GRISSOM GANG conjures a twilight world of amorality, hypocrisy and emotional sterility.

GUNS DON'T ARGUE / USA 1957

Directed by Bill Karn and Richard C. Kahn. Camera: William H. Clothier, Clark Ramsey & Guy Roe. Music: Paul Dunlap. With Jean Harvey, Myron Healy, Sam Edwards, Richard Cram

A kind of campaign for the agents of the Federal Bureau of Investigation, where in contrast to the vicious Barker gang, they are provided with some sort of glory. Decades later the public learned that in the FBI, abysses similar to that created by the Barker family yawn under the veil of crime-elimination. Then stories about FBI boss Edgar J. Hoover came up, a radical right-wing, decidedly "upright" American who wore sexy underwear in private, ordered the killing of innocent people, and would doubtless have roasted communists on the spit, if he had been allowed to.

MA BARKER'S KILLER BROOD / USA 1960

Directed by Bill Karn. Written by Paul Hall. Camera: Clark Ramsey. Music: Gene Kanauer. With Lurene Tuttle, Tris Coffin, Paul Dubov, Myrna Dell, Nelson Leigh

Keeping close to the historical background, this film begins with Ma Barker's criminal career in Oklahoma and follows her rise and fall until the bloody shoot-out in Florida. Unfortunately, the film never goes beyond the surface. The inner lives and the motivations of the characters remain entirely in the dark. Lurene Tuttle as the impressive killer mother is most outstanding in this average low-budget adaptation of the case. Some well-done action scenes (especially the showdown) compensate for long moments of boredom in a film that consists of several re-edited episodes of a TV mini-series.

GUNS DON'T ARGUE

QUEEN OF THE MOB / USA 1940

Directed by James Hogan. Written by Horace McCoy and William R. Lipman after the novel Persons in Hiding by J. Edgar Hoover. Camera: Theodor Sparkuhl. With Blanche Yurka, Ralph Bellamy, Jack Carson, Richard Denning

Although names and settings were changed, this short thriller (61 minutes) based on a chapter from the best-seller *Persons In Hiding* by J. Edgar Hoover definitely retells the case of Ma Barker and her gang. Here the FBI chases a woman called Webster with her three sons Denning, Seavy, and Kelly. The gang leaves behind a track of bank robbery and murder, and kills everyone who crosses their path. But the hero, a brave G-man, is right at Ma Webster's heels and in a series of gunfights one thug after the other dies by the bullets of FBI agents. In the end the FBI team hunts down "Bloody Mama" in her house, where she is just decorating the Christmas tree for the children of the village. After one shot has felled her last remaining son, the mother surrenders with her hands up: "All right, G-man, you've won."

Obviously, this film does not care much about the facts. Blanche Yurka, starring as Ma Webster portrays her as a murderess with humane traits who not only cares for her own sons, but also for the children of the neighbourhood. An ideal mother, so to speak, who, of course, cannot die in a hail of bullets. In 1940 Hollywood was not yet mature enough for an uncompromising depiction of the murderous Kate Barker.

CLYDE BARROW

Clyde BARROW & Bonnie PARKER
The Legend of Bonnie & Clyde

"Some day they will go down together/And they will bury them side by side/To a few it means grief/To the law it's relief/But it's death to Bonnie and Clyde"
from: *"The Ballad Of Bonnie & Clyde"* by Bonnie Parker

The Case

In 1909 Clyde Barrow was born as one of eight children on a farm in Telice, Texas. As he was never interested in school, larceny, a longer while in a reformatory school and a latent sadistic vein (he liked torturing animals) marked Clyde's childhood. At the age of 21 the juvenile delinquent met 19-year-old Bonnie Parker. The girl from a Baptist family was already married, but her husband had walked out on her. For both it was love at first sight, though with some obstacles. Clyde was threatened with 14 years behind bars for some thefts. But he was released on probation and the couple could fully concentrate on their criminal career. They gathered a gang around them (which among other things served Clyde's occasional homosexual predelictions) and became notorious as the Clyde Barrow Gang. They held up shops and banks. Most of the times the killed the owners or employees. Between the robberies they photographed each other in outlaw poses, slept in luxurious motels, and enjoyed life. Their motto was "Kiss. Drive. Kill." Cops who came too near to the gang paid for their recklessness with their lives. There was no exception. In July 1932 they suffered from the first throw-back: Clyde's brother Buck and his wife Blanche were shot by the police.

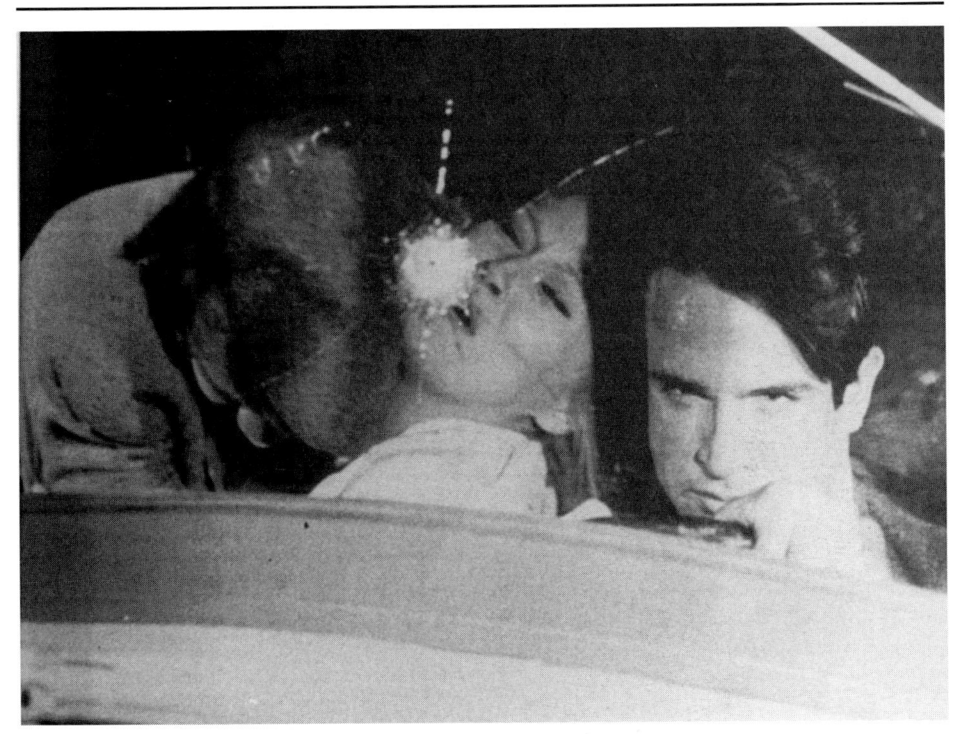

BONNIE AND CLYDE

On May 23, 1934 the "legend of Bonnie & Clyde" finally ended in a massacre of powder-smoke and lead. Cornered by six cops, the couple were torn to pieces by some 160 bullets. Souvenir-hunters snatched bundles of bloody hair before the coroner came. Leaving the myths aside, Bonnie and Clyde were no desperadoes of the depression era with Robin Hood proclivities, but simply two psychopaths running amok on the road.

BONNIE AND CLYDE / USA 1967

Directed by Arthur Penn. Written by David Newman & Robert Benton. Camera: Burnett Guffey. Music: Charles Strouse & Earl Scruggs. With Faye Dunaway, Warren Beatty, Gene Hackman, Michael J. Pollard, Estelle Parsons, Dub Taylor, Evans Evans, Gene Wilder, James Stiver

Though Arthur Penn's classic of Sixties cinema garbles the historical image of Bonnie and Clyde, it works perfectly as an outlaw-ballad influenced by the Nouvelle Vague and remaining independent from the facts. David Thompson notes that "David Newman and Robert Benton, the two journalists and scriptwriters adore the young men in France. They love AU BOUT DE SOUFFLE and JULES ET JIM and let themselves be inspired by these works."

The film begins with comedy-undertones. Good-looking Clyde wants to impress the attractive blonde Bonnie (both mutated from White Trash to Beautiful People *à la* Hollywood) with a hold-up. It works. And after Bonnie has begun to enjoy the thrill of danger they begin to rob banks. Their gang becomes bigger and bigger, their activities more and more spectacular. Suddenly the film topples over. An innocent clerk dies in a bank-robbery and the cat-and-mouse game with the police enters a different, more serious stage. Bonnie and Clyde are hunted down pitilessly all across the states of America. Their bloody end is only a question of time.

The film's shocking final scene, where Faye Dunaway and Warren Beatty are hit by a barrage of bullets in a bloody slow-motion-dance, altered the history of cinema with its explicitness. Arthur Penn anticipated the slow motion-violence of Sam Peckinpah (THE WILD BUNCH, two years later), Walter Hill, and many others. The breaking in of violence into the world of cinema is a symptom of the time. It is no coincidence that Penn depicts the "system's" reaction against two outsiders in such a brutal way. He only mirrors the real violence that was in the air then, the brutality of Vietnam and the police-attacks against the students' protests. Film critic Alexander Horvath analyses: "The two beautiful rebellious killers of the film describe a 'leftist myth', cool, anti-authoritarian, pop-heroic, but they follow the same crazy and 'senseless' tracks as their opponents. [...] BONNIE & CLYDE is the happiest (and perhaps the saddest too) in the American cinema of the Sixties. The elements flow together and for short magical moment they light a nosegay of sparklers."

BONNIE & CLYDE: THE TRUE STORY / USA 1992 (TV)

Written and directed by Gary Hoffmann. Camera: Ron Schmidt. Music: Scott Page-Pagter, John Valentino. With Tracey Needham, Dana Ashbrook, Doug Savant, Billy Morrisette, Michael Bowen

The sanitised, sympathetic faces of Warren Beatty and Faye Dunaway transformed the gangster couple Bonnie and Clyde to an immortal legend. They remained dangerous criminals, but also became synonyms for misunderstood juvenile rebellion. The truth is that they were rude, violent killers. They shot and robbed their way through five states, fired at everyone standing in their way, and left behind a trail of blood and tears. When they robbed a farmer, they did it painstakingly to his last penny. Then they fired a bullet into the helplessly trembling victim's head. Just for fun and to impress Clyde, Bonnie Parker once shot off a policeman's head in Oklahoma City. On another occasion they fired without warning at a highway patrolman on his motorbike and bulldozed his corpse again and again. Worried about their "code of honour" other gangsters distanced themselves from these dangerous, kill-crazy punks.

Instead of telling "the true story" as the title promises (which might have been a highly thrilling and provocative enterprise), Gary Hoffmann rather continues with the more peaceful moments of Arthur Penn's film. He does not excavate the ugly reality from under thick layers of gooey myths, but delivers a soft version for teenagers . He shows Bonnie and Clyde as two attractive young people (*Twin Peaks* beau Dana Ashbrook and cute Tracy Needham) slightly confusedly and naively escaping from the hopelessness of the depression era into crime. Scriptwriter Gary Hoffmann tries to put the blame for the decisive crimes leading to the couple's notoriety on some minor characters. Almost white-washed from all guilt, Bonnie and Clyde resurrect as typical juvenile soap-figures of the Nineties, almost unbroken heroes and victims of a desolate epoch. The true story? Hardly.

THE BONNIE PARKER STORY / USA 1958

Directed by William Witney. Written by Stanley Sheptner. Camera: Jack Marta. Music: Ronald Stein. With Dorothy Provine, Jack Hogan, Richard Bakalyan, Joseph Turkel, William Stevens, Douglas Kennedy

When her husband is sentenced to 175 years behind bars and she is all alone in the hard depression times, the waitress Bonnie transforms into a gangster-lady more than matching her male counterparts in roughness and brutality. She learns to handle machine-guns and to kill without batting an eyelash, together with her new

THE BONNIE PARKER STORY

boyfriend Clyde Barrow (called Guy Darrow here).

This black-and-white sleaze-version from the late Fifties deals very freely with the real story. Nevertheless, its brutal and pitiless characters are much closer to the real Bonnie and Clyde than the teenage-idols of the later movies. Here Bonnie Parker is no victim blindfolded by love as in the other cinematic versions. Dorothy Provine immortalises her as a cigar-puffing, big-bosomed killer-blonde representing the dominant part of the legendary duo. Whipped by a pulsating score in the midst of cheap filthy scenery, she guns herself through this beautifully immoral B-movie.

THE OTHER SIDE OF BONNIE & CLYDE / USA 1968

Written and directed by Larry Buchanan. With Jo Enterentree, Lucky Mosley, Floyd Hamilton, Mrs. Frank Hamer, Frank Hamer Jr., Burl Ives (narrator)

A pseudo-documentary compiling authentic material (there are interviews with the ex-gangster and contemporary Floyd Hamilton and Texas Ranger Frank Hamer & family) and cheap acted scenes. The then already sacked US-Country singer Burl Ives told the story from the off. Bizarre Z-film-specialist Larry Buchanan, notorious for his approaches to other historical figures like Lee Harvey Oswald (THE TRIAL OF LEE HARVEY OSWALD/1964) and trash-classics like NAUGHTY DALLAS (1964), THE NAKED WITCH (1965) and MARS NEEDS WOMEN (1966), is responsible for this attempt to exploit Arthur Penn's success. THE OTHER SIDE OF BONNIE & CLYDE is a dubious concoction. Yet it contains authentic pictures of Bonnie's and Clyde's bullet-riddled corpses torn to pieces and justifies its title, calling in question many of Arthur Penn's romantic outlaw-motives.

MARTHA BECK

Martha BECK & Raymond FERNANDEZ

"I wanna shout it out: I love Martha! What do the public know about love?"
–Ray Fernandez's official last words

"My story is a love story. But only those tortured by love can know what I mean [...] Imprisonment in the Death House has only strengthened my feeling for Raymond."
–Martha Beck's last words to the press

The Case

It was love at first sight. When Ray Fernandez and Martha Beck met in 1947 for the simple reason of a newspaper ad, they soon realised that they were soulmates. The Chicano Raymond Fernandez was born in 1914 and got through life as a marriage impostor who claimed to have an irresistible power over women. Martha was six years younger and worked as a children's nurse. She was overweight since her teenage days and had been raped by her brother. Apparently, Fernandez shared her preoccupation for bizarre sex as well as her contempt of other people. Together they answered contact ads and eased widows out of their savings.

During these fake marriages Martha moved in into the household as his sister. Because of her raging jealousy she tried to prevent Raymond from his "matrimonial duties" in every thinkable way. In August and December 1948 the couple killed two women. One was poisoned with barbiturates, the second Martha knocked down with a hammer and Fernandez strangled her to death. Delphine Downing, the third victim, was narcotised with barbiturates before she was shot. Then Martha, who worked in a home for deformed children, drowned her two-year-old daughter in the bathtub. "The Lonely Hearts Killers" walled in the corpses in the cellar. But soon watchful neighbours informed the police and the couple were arrested.

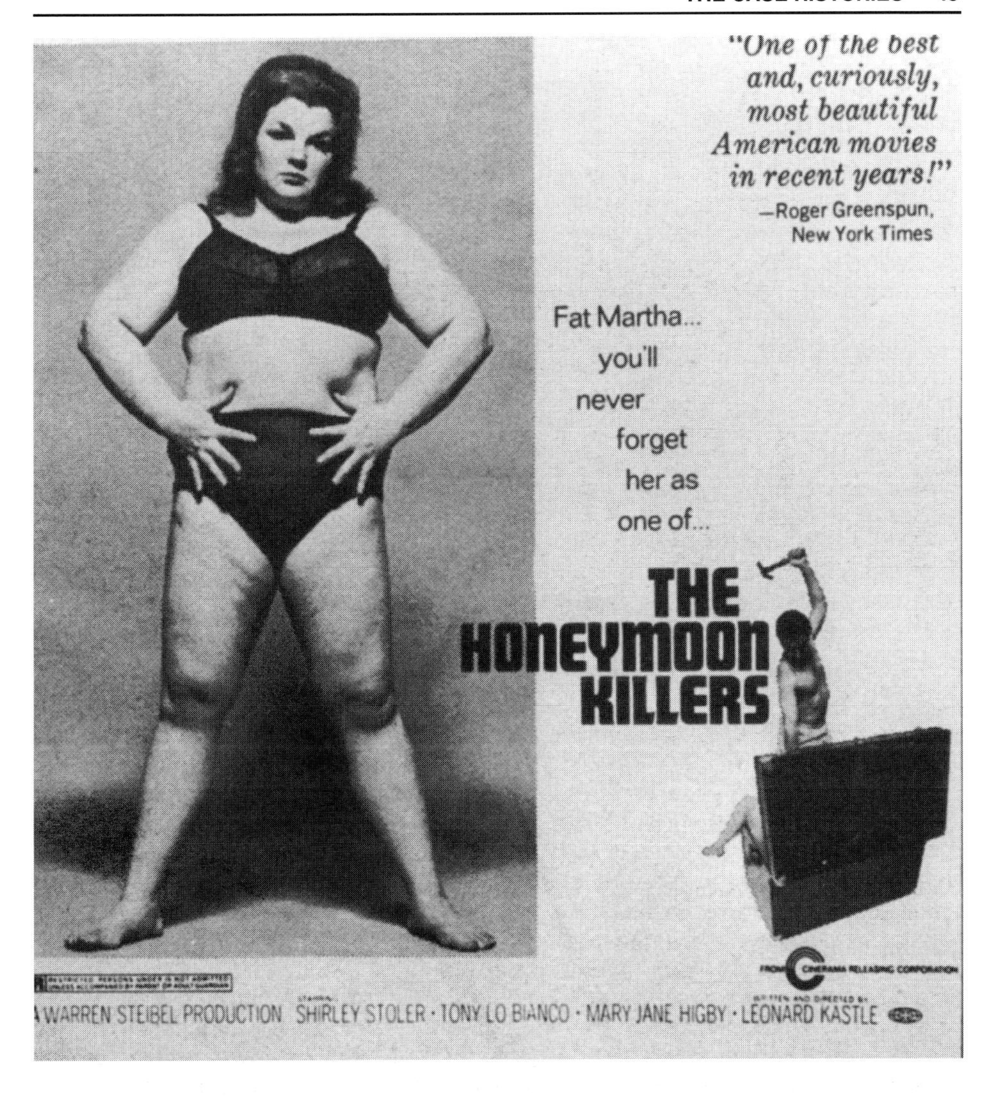

The trial began on June 9, 1949 and became a big media event predominantly due to the extreme sex life of the couple, which was made public. "The monster" and "the fat cannibal" were accused of 20 murders, but only three could be proved. Even from Death Row they sent themselves hot lover's oaths. On March 8, 1951 the "Honeymoon Killers" were electrocuted in Sing Sing prison.

THE HONEYMOON KILLERS / USA 1970

Written and directed by Leonard Kastle. Camera: Oliver Wood. Music: Gustav Mahler. Production: Roxanne. With Tony LoBianco, Shirley Toler, Doris Roberts, Mary Jane Highby

A classic of the sub-genre "Murderous Couples". Though THE HONEYMOON KILLERS keeps rather precisely to the facts of the original case, it transcends dry documentary. The French director Francois Truffaut once said that "in the last 20 years only very few American films have similarly impressed me".

Leonard Kastle's film, which was first scheduled to have been shot by Martin

Scorsese, has deservedly developed from a box-office flop to a fixed repertoire movie of midnight specials appreciated by cineasts as much as by trash connoisseurs. Kastle tells the story of Ray Fernandez and Martha Beck, the "Lonely Hearts Killers" as a sombre black and white melodrama that is broken time and again by moments of morbid comedy. Tony LoBianco and especially Shirley Stoler, who has already achieved cult status, excel themselves as marriage impostors travelling across the USA, whereby the slippery gigolo Ray always introduces Martha, weighing 200 pounds, as his sister. While he eases lonely middle class women out of their savings promising marriage, or actually marries them under a false name, Martha assists with pills, hammer, and revolver in difficult cases. Kastle leaves open whether the unequal partners are really in love as they affirm solemnly in their lovers' oaths, or, if it is (at least in the case of Ray) only a means to an end. THE HONEYMOON KILLERS ends where the real killers ended: in the electric chair.

A tasteful as well as tasteless conjuration of the dreams and nightmares of middle class America, a B-movie from a time when it seemed still possibe to film solid little independent-jewels with little financial backing.

THE HONEYMOON KILLERS

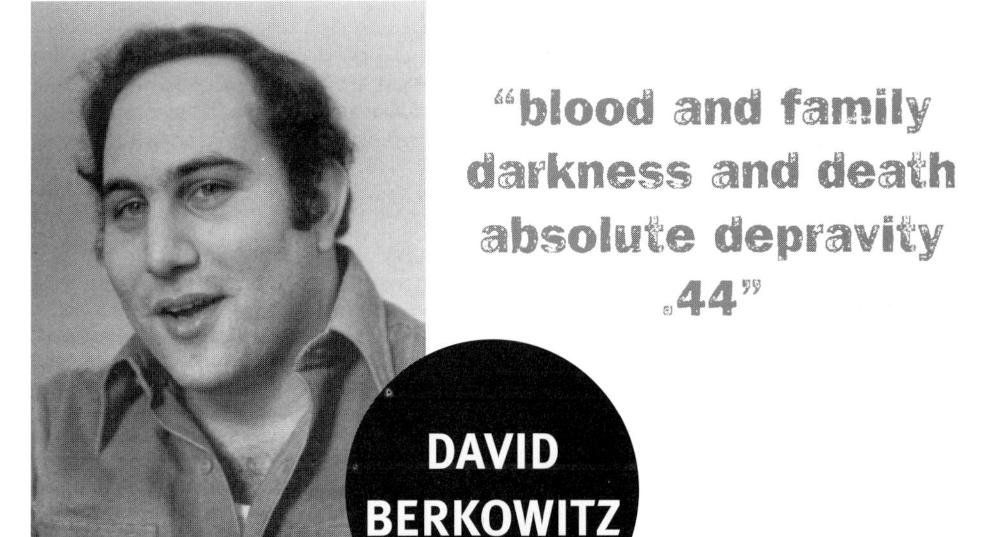

"blood and family
darkness and death
absolute depravity
.44"
DAVID
BERKOWITZ

The Son Of Sam

"WHEN FATHER SAM GETS DRUNK HE GETS MEAN. HE BEATS HIS FAMILY. SOMETIMES HE TIES ME UP TO THE BACK OF THE HOUSE. OTHER TIMES HE LOCKS ME IN THE GARAGE. SAM LOVES TO DRINK BLOOD. 'GO OUT AND KILL' COMMANDS FATHER SAM."

–Letter of April 17, 1977 from David Berkowitz addressed to Queens police detective Captain Joseph Borelli

"I have several children who I'm Turning Into Killers. WAIT TIL they grow up"

–Graffiti on David Berkowitz's walls.

"...While the defendant shows paranoid traits, they do not interfere with his fitness to stand trial."

–Dr. David Abrahamsen, psychiatrist for the prosecution during the Berkowitz trial

Within a year, from July 29, 1976 to July 31, 1977 the New York postman David Berkowitz killed five women and a man and injured seven other people seriously. The victims of the then 24-year-old killer who was first called "44 Caliber Killer" in the newspaper headlines and later, when his letters had been published by the police and the press, "Son of Sam", were almost always young couples, who Berkowitz begrudged their happiness.

Born on June 1, 1953 as Richard David Falco, the future nightmare of the Big Apple was the result of his mother's quick affair with an anonymous businessman. Released for adoption immediately, the baby ended up in the home of a Jewish couple that had a little shop in the Bronx. David Richard Berkowitz, as he was re-baptised by his new parents became a highly difficult and shy teenager. He was haunted by depression and outbursts of anger. When his beloved adoptive mother died of cancer in 1967, he freaked out completely."When this feeling came over me",

Berkowitz confessed later, "I would hide under my bed for hours. I would also lock myself in a closet and sit in total darkness from morning until afternoon. I had a craving for the darkness and I felt an urge to flee away from people." About the time he went into the Army the later Son Of Sam found out he'd been adopted. But he failed to establish contact with his real mother. Moreover, he was unable to establish any contacts with girls.

Some people might turn to alcohol and drugs in such situations, or simply find a way to move on with their lives. Well, first David Berkowitz turned into an arsonist and then – step 2 – he bought a .44 calibre gun. "Eventually I crossed that invisible line of no return. After years of mental torment, behavioural problems, deep inner struggles and my own rebellious ways, I became the criminal that, at the time, it seemed as if it was my destiny to become", Berkowitz said in 1999. First in Queens, then in other boroughs of NYC, he fired at young women and couples. Finally, thanks to the observations of a witness, he was arrested on August 10, 1977. First he claimed that his neighbour, the pensioner Sam Carr, had forced him to commit his deeds with the help of his dog. Allegedly, the dog had sent Papa Sam's Satanic messages to poor Son David (a.k.a. Chubby Behemoth) via hypnosis.

Only many years later, as a lifer, would Berkowitz give up his crazy Son of Sam idea. But the today born-again Christian with his own homepage on the internet still holds occult powers responsible for his frenzy: "I am utterly convinced that something Satanic had entered into my mind and that, looking back at all that happened, I realize that I had been slowly deceived".

OUT OF THE DARKNESS / USA 1985 (TV)

Directed by Jud Taylor. Written by T. S Cook. With Martin Sheen, Hector Elizondo, Matt Clark, Robert Trebor, Jennifer Salt, Charlie Sheen

No surprise: Like so many others, this mixture of documentary and feature film does not focus on the psyche of a serial killer, but places the story of a stubborn cop who puts all his life into his investigations in the centre. Martin Sheen, an old hand, plays the New York detective Ed Zigo, who has to suffer a lot until he finally tracks down the Son of Sam in his apartment. After about two thirds of the film Robert Trebor has the opportunity to do a short but impressive portrayal of David Berkowitz. "I am not playing Berkowitz as a foaming-at-the-mouth character," the actor says in an interview. "There are a lot of layers to the role (...) I tried to get the facts right on Berkowitz. It is important to know that he was adopted. And that he was born a Catholic and raised a Jew, although he got involved in cults and went away from Judaism." Trebor, who belongs to the comedian stock cast of TV-shows like *Hercules* and *Xena*, was working intensely on a role that fascinated him. "It is important to study the darker sides of man, just to know where the clouds are forming. There are murderers all around us. They are not from Mars. We should know why things happen. After all, Nazis don't just drop out of spaceships."

SUMMER OF SAM / USA 1999

Directed by Spike Lee. Written by Victor Colicchio & Michael Imperioli & Spike Lee. Camera: Ellen Kuras. Music: Terence Blanchard. With John Leguizamo, Adrien Brody, Mira Sorvino, Jennifer Esposito, Michael Badalucco

In this film, one of the best and at the same time most under-estimated Spike Lee efforts, David Berkowitz does not only stand in the centre, but also serves as a culmination point for several interwoven story lines. Lee beams us into the city of New York of 1977, where in the hot "Summer of Sam" the city is trembling with fear of the mysterious serial killer who shoots lovers in their cars in the night. Hysteria is in the air and it smells of cold sweat and lynching. Yet the fun junkies want to have their fun, the masses partying in the disco groove, a small minority raving to the music of the Sex Pistols and The Clash. It's the heyday of Studio 54 and CBGBs, dancing and slam-dancing. The time of pre-Aids decadence. But while orgiastic parties are being celebrated somewhere in the Big Apple and tons of white powder is being sniffed, the Son of Sam is squatting in his filthy apartment which – in Lee's version – might have come right out of the video-clip purgatory of SEVEN. "Kill for Sam Carr. Sam Carr My Master" is written somewhere on a wall full of crazy epigrams. Flies are buzzing around rotting meals. Berkowitz is tossing and turning in his bed tormented by visions in which the dead dog of his neighbour comes again and again giving lethal orders. Soon shots can be heard somewhere...

SUMMER OF SAM tries to put as many different approaches to the key year of 1977 as possible into one shining and blood-stained kaleidoscope. The film manages this with a flood of highly colourful and stimulating images that often remind us of Martin Scorsese's best moments. Various individual lives mirror the atmosphere of the Italian community where love and hate, sex, drugs and religious tradition clash until, finally, everything culminates in one big climax, the arrest of Mr. Berkowitz.

I AM THE "MONSTER" –
"BEELZEBUB" – THE
"CHUBBY BEHEMOUTH".

The Hillside Stranglers

"It wasn't fuckin' wrong! Why is it wrong to get rid of some fuckin' cunts?"
–Kenneth Bianchi (as Steve, his alter ego)

"He would not hurt a canary bird".
–A witness about Angelo Buono

The Case
Kenneth Bianchi and his adopted cousin Angelo Buono raped, tortured, and strangled at least ten women and got rid of the corpses in the hills of Los Angeles, events which made the newspapers write of a "Hillside Strangler". Between October 1977 and February 1978 the "Hillside Strangler" (the press assumed a single offender for a long time) was the most atrocious nightmare for all women living in the conurbation of L.A. The first victims were hookers who had been approached by Bianchi. Then the guys dragged girls picked at random into their torture basement in Angelo's house.

In January 1979 the police tracked down a man working for a surveillance company who had been seen with one of the victims shortly before her death. His name: Kenneth Bianchi. Hoping to get off with a milder sentence Bianchi testified against his cousin Angelo Buono. Concerning himself, he held his violent alter ego "Steve" exclusively responsible for the murders and tried to give the impression of an incompetent split personality in front of the criminal psychologists. But the experts found Bianchi, who had been studying psychology and hypnosis, guilty of fraud after many tests. It became the most expensive trial in the history of Los Angeles and lasted more than two years. Kenneth Bianchi received a life sentence with some chance to be released before he dies because he declared himself guilty and testified against his cousin. Buono received a life sentence without any possibility of pardon.

THE CASE OF THE HILLSIDE STRANGLERS / USA 1988 (TV)

Directed by Steven Gethers. Produced by Carole Coates Prod. Camera: Ronald M. Lautore. Music: Gil Melle. With Richard Crenna, Dennis Farina, Billy Zane, James Tolkans

A typical example of a true crime documentary drama made for television that reminds of a soap drama in suspense as well as *mise-en-scène*. The film follows the chronological sequence of events beginning with the first murders in October 1977 until the arrest of the delinquents and the trial, including the episode of Bianchi's "split personality" that has made the headlines. But Gethers meticulously follows the laws of the television play in his version of the Hillside murders, which ends up in sterility, reserve, and stereotyped character descriptions.

Billy Zane, a designated *Twin Peaks* beau and in the same year feverishly nervous in DEAD CALM, impersonates Kenneth Bianchi without leaving any considerable impression. Likewise, the TV actor Dennis Farina is colourless as Angelo Buono. Not a tinge of the suffocating horror that happened in their torture-garage can be felt in THE CASE OF THE HILLSIDE STRANGLERS. And one gains just as little insight into the psyche of the killers.

TED BUNDY

"Killers are very rational people. The more people they kill, the better they get at disposing of bodies...You only find the bodies that a serial killer wants you to find. There's plenty more you'll never find... I don't feel guilty for anything... I feel sorry for people who feel guilt... I'm the coldest motherfucker you'll ever put your eyes on."
–Ted Bundy

The Case
Ted Bundy is a special case among comparable serial killers. The man who killed between 30 and 40 women had a relatively ordered childhood without any conspicuous events, studied successfully and stood at the beginning of a political career in the Republican party. He was said to be handsome and sociable, an "All-American Guy" who had achieved his social rise with intelligence and charm. Bundy himself talked of an "increased sexual appetite", but the motive of his crimes remains mysterious.

Theodore Robert Cowell was born on November 24, 1946 as the illegitimate child of the 22-year-old Eleanor and grew up with his grandparents. For a long time he believed that his mother was his sister. Later she married John Bundy. After he had finished psychology with honours, Ted Bundy registered at the University of Salt Lake City in 1973 to study law. In January 1974 girls began to disappear in the region around Seattle. This was the beginning of a series of murders lasting for four years. All the victims were of the same age, were attractive and had long dark hair with a centre parting. The police hunted a certain "Ted" with phantom pictures. In the autumn of 1974 a murder series began in Salt Lake City. Three women disappeared, one managed to get away. Her evidence helped the police to track down Ted Bundy. After five additional murders in the skiing resorts of Colorado he was arrested in August 1975, but the killer managed to escape. Only after entering forcibly a residential home for girls and killing a twelve-year-old girl soon afterwards, was he finally seized in 1978.

The trial was broadcast live by some US TV networks. There, the serial killer defended himself eloquently. Although Ted Bundy denied the murders persistently, his guilt could be proved by bites that had been found on one of the corpses. He used to rape the women, hit them with iron bars, strangle them, and bite them before he killed them. Finally, Bundy was found guilty in three cases and sentenced to death. Already years in prison, Ted, the lady-killer married his girlfriend Carol Boone. He made her pregnant before he was put to death on the electric chair on January 24, 1989. Furious citizens celebrated a public festival in front of Raiford State Prison, Florida while he was electrocuted. "Die, Bundy, Die!", the crowd cheered.

THE DELIBERATE STRANGER / USA 1986 (TV)

Directed by Marvin Chomsky. Written by Hesper Anderson based on a novel by Richard W. Larsen. Camera: Michael D. Marguolis. Music: Gil Melle. With Mark Harmon, Frederic Forrest, George Grizzard, Ben Masters

Mark Harmon, sunny Mr. Nice-Guy in many American TV-serials (*Flamingo Road*) and films, is the serial killer Theodore "Ted" Bundy in this sticky adaptation by Marvin Chomsky, an industrious but rather mediocre tele-play director. A 177-minute video was released for the German market. In the original version it is an NBC production with two parts based on the novel *The Deliberate Stranger* by Richard Larsen.

The film follows chronologically the tracks of Ted Bundy, from the first murders to his seizure and his conviction in 1980. What happened afterwards, especially Bundy's execution and the festival-like atmosphere in front of the prison, had to be omitted. After all, the film was released in 1986. Perhaps, the conceited Mr. Bundy could even watch it himself behind prison bars.

Beside the meticulous police investigation, THE DELIBERATE STRANGER concentrates on his facade of the handsome friendly guy every mother would have welcomed as her son-in-law. Behind the facade there lurked an extraordinarily intelligent serial killer compared to "normal" sex killers, who are said to be ugly, shy, and rather stupid. Moreover, he killed an extraordinarily high number of people. Within two years Mr. Bundy killed more than 20 girls after he had most brutally beaten and raped them. Only to a very restricted extent can Mark Harmon mediate this dualism between the handsome campaign worker for the Republican Party and the sadist woman killer. The rest of the cast, including the gifted Frederic Forrest are surplus anyway.

The murders, as always in television plays, happen off-screen or are at best hinted at. The responsible networks explain that they want to avoid the glorification of violence and voyeurism for reasons of piety. Of course, this is a lie because people like Marvin Chomsky are far more interested in audience ratings than in the feelings of the survivors or the peace of the victims. Only the worthy laws of US television, that ban bare breasts as well as the realistic depiction of violence, define form and content of films like THE DELIBERATE STRANGER. Dealing with an extremely violent subject like the Bundy case without making the audience strongly aware of its inherent sexual atrocity and butchery, means playing down reality to a ludicrous degree. The serial killer degenerates to the equivalent of an arbitrary *Dallas* or *Dynasty* villain, the cop to his honest and brave opponent. True Crime entertainment as a little kick between the commercials and daily game-show imbecility.

The Case

"Gojo Cardinas was a man who killed 30 women. For this he was famous in Mexico. He was put into a mental institution and the doctors declared him healed some time later. Free again he became a lawyer and a journalist, married, and had two children. A perfectly normal person. [...] I was working for a newspaper then and met him in a bar. He did not remember his deeds, but he was feeling pretty good in his second life. He was a very nice man – but he had killed 30 women."

(Alejandro Jodorowsky in *Dark Stars: Interviews With 10 Directors*)

SANTA SANGRE / Italy-Mexico 1989

Directed by Alejandro Jodorowsky. Written by Alejandro Jodorowsky, Roberto Leoni, Claudio Argento. Camera: Daniele Nannuzzi. Music: Simon Boswell. With Axel Jodorowsky, Sabrina Dennison, Guy Stockwell, Blanca Guerra

If the murderer Gojo Cardinas really existed, or whether he was only a fantasy of long-bearded Alejandro Jodorowsky, an illusionist loving violence and esoteric psycho-drama, remains unclear. Nevertheless SANTA SANGRE is included in this book for its surrealist approach to the True Crime subject. In the mid-Seventies Jodorowsky's films were renegade trips in intellectual hippie-circles, and Jodorowsky himself was regarded as a taboo breaker and an orgiastic sensualist. The close friend of Fernando Arrabal and Roland Topor got his reputation as a notorious non-conformist with two movies: EL TOPO (1970) and MONTANA SACRA (THE HOLY MOUNTAIN, 1973); the former a Zen-Buddhist Italo-Western, a splatter movie in the spirit of surrealism, the latter telling the Christian history of salvation refined with Marx and Sartre as well as influences of Taoism and Hinduism. His films were shown together with NIGHT OF THE LIVING DEAD (1968) or ERASERHEAD in the midnight double features of many avant-garde cinemas and the audience realised that these films could be seen as pure pop entertainment without caring too much for sense and symbolism.

The writer/theatre director/activist/comic-strip author and film-maker made SANTA SANGRE; i.e. "holy blood", in 1989 after a long creative break. The film is Jodorowsky's homage to the horror genre, which he adores, and was produced by the

SANTA SANGRE

brother of the Italian "Godfather of Terror" Dario Argento. Inspired by the real (?) case of Gojo Cardinas, he tells the story of the young woman-murderer as a phantasmagoria broken by psychedelic visions, a chain of grotesque episodes. The killer strikes on behalf of his armless mother, acts as her hands.

In spite of many genre elements Jodorowsky still sticks to his main sources of influence. He still industriously quotes Buñuel, Godard, and Sergio Leone, beside comic strips and Sixties drug culture. Sometimes SANTA SANGRE looks like a collaboration of Dario Argento and Federico Fellini, in which the Fellinian element is the only weak point worth mentioning. If you don't like the exhibitions of freakish characters, you will be in despair watching Jodorowsky. SANTA SANGRE is a freak show of the deformed, clowns, fat women, and "ugly" types of all sorts, revelling in the violent underbelly of Mexico where savage murder is common and life is cheap. But amidst that Jodorowsky can follow again and again his old underground tropes, staging scenes of strangely bizarre beauty.

RICHARD CHASE

The Vampire Of Sacramento

"...and as the Eucharist touched his tongue he thrust his hand almost unnoticeably forward and the organ screamed in his head and his whole being screamed with his soul sickness and his head suddenly jerked back and his eyes snapped open as the beloved Cardinal stood erect with his arms outstretched, his shadow forming a large cross, and his eyes staring above him and his mouth open in a silent scream and the chords of the organ thundered through the cathedral and the choir sang the ALLELUIA as the sun shone in almost blinding brilliance on the long gold carved handle of the knife sticking out from between the ribs of the Cardinal, after penetrating his body almost to the spine, and the Cardinal's blood flowed forth splattering the fallen Hosts and the shimmering gold protruding from his body and Harry rose from his knees and leaned on the railing and looked into the face and mouth of the man of God, the light from the gold handle slashing his eyes, and shouted at him, SPEAK! FOR THE LOVE OF FUCKING CHRIST, SPEAK! SAY IT!"

–Hubert Selby, *The Demon*

"I will end the world by flooding if I get killed. Gott!"

–Richard Chase

The Case

Richard Chase killed for the blood. He was obsessed by the idea that his blood was poisoned. In order to purify himself, or better in order to survive he had to drink the red sap of life. The blood of animals first, then human blood.

Born in 1950, Chase grows up under a parental roof of quarrel and aggression. His mother often suspects that his father wants to poison her. Richard, the friendless young boy has drug problems and is arrested for illegal possession of arms in 1973. The doctors diagnose paranoid schizophrenia. He is put into a mental institution after he has injected himself with rabbit blood, but already in autumn he is released. Chase begins to complement his diet with birds, cats, and dogs. He kills them, drinks their blood, and eats their raw intestines. Besides this, he keeps a diary about the consistency and taste of the different kinds of blood. In August 1977 he is found naked and smeared with blood in a field. He has slaughtered two cows.

Then the chronology of horror begins. He starts shooting practice, he fires at occupied houses, and kills a man in front of his house in December 1977. In January 1978 he follows the pregnant Theresa Wallin into her house, shoots at her, and slashes the dying woman. He catches her blood in a glass, drinks it, and covers his face and his body with it. Within the same month he butchers a young woman, her six-year-old son, her 52-year-old boyfriend, and a 22-month-old baby. Chase cuts up the woman, decants her blood, as well as that of the baby. Finally he flees with the baby's corpse. On the next day the "Vampire of Sacramento" is arrested. When the police search his apartment, they find a horror chamber. All furniture, wallpaper, clothing is soaked with blood. There are bullet-holes everywhere and human and animal organs in the freezer. In spite of his diminished responsibility, Richard Chase is sentenced to death. But on Christmas Eve 1979, the "Vampire of Sacramento" evades punishment with an overdose of pills; perhaps to escape his execution, maybe only to cleanse his blood.

RAMPAGE / USA 1987

Directed by William Friedkin. Written by William Friedkin after a novel by William P. Wood. Camera: Robert Yeoman. Music: Ennio Morricone. With Alex McArthur, Michael Biehn, Nicholas Campbell, Deborah Van Valkenburgh, Grace Zabriskie

The first scene: an aerial shot – the camera hovers over vast acres and fields, comes deeper and deeper, until a lonesome stroller can be seen. Then a cut: typically American suburbia where neat one-family houses stand in a row. A place where well-to-do upright middle-class families dwell. A pre-Christmas atmosphere, a climate of peace and tranquillity.

But like every True Crime movie idyll, this one is deceptive. Ennio Morricone's portentous tunes tell of the ominous destruction of this self-satisfied middle-class world. The terror nears in the shape of a stroller in a blazingly red anorak. Smiling coolly the young man with shades heads toward a house, and when an elderly woman opens the door, the stranger disrupts the peaceful atmosphere with one single shot of his gun. Further bullets follow. The stupefied family has only a few seconds to realise that death has come to visit them in the shape of a seemingly icy cold boy without any emotion, who is nearing his wounded, but still living victims with a kitchen knife.

The murderous intruder is Charles Reece, a youngster who devastates American family idylls until he is caught and sentenced to death. In the last moments he evades punishment by suicide. Reece and the plot of RAMPAGE refer in many details to the Chase case. The names were only changed for legal reasons.

Visions and dream-walking sequences pervade the film. They break the realism of the central law court-drama in regular intervals. Where does responsibility end? Where does madness begin? Is the death penalty justified as an instrument of punishment? These are the questions Michael Biehn asks himself in the central role of a young D.A. In his example, William Friedkin elucidates all the questions that come up when a killer like Reece/Chase leads his one-man-war against society: the problems

RAMPAGE

of legislation, the helplessness of science, the infinite grief of the survivors. Moreover, the film shows strong sympathy for the victims. The scene where father and son find the disembowelled wife and mother is very subtly staged, but shakes you profoundly and remains unforgettably in your mind.

But at the same time Friedkin explores the motives of the delinquent and, unlike the superficial novel, takes him rather seriously, although it would have been easy enough to portray Reece as a gobbling monster that drinks the blood of people and animals. Like Chase, he fantasises of powers that draw his blood and vital energy and want to poison him. A transcendental element is inherent in his murderous deeds. Alex McArthur, who portrays the killer says that his character is on a "mission" in search of salvation and purifying catharsis. This leads him into a church in the end and provokes the "Communion scene"; Reece drinks the blood of a priest, a key sequence.

The religious aspect can be detected in many scenes. Icons of bourgeois happiness, like figures of saints in the garden, or an Advent wreath, come up repeatedly. McArthur's constantly red clothing evoking the associations of danger, threat, and, of course, blood fits well into this. "Red: Expression of the consuming power of hellfire or untameable desire and passion", says *The Lexicon Of Symbols*. If you add the blood of the martyrs, the Body of Christ, and the idea of sacrifice of the Old Testament, the circle closes to the associations to archaic religions, sacrifice, and heathen rituals ghosting through the film. Charles Reece/Richard Chase repeatedly talks about Satan, of a "Devil's Station" on the air, which influences him negatively with hidden messages. Many radical sects claim things like that, too. The oscillation between blasphemy, strict fundamentalism, and religious mania is a speciality of William Friedkin. Just think of THE EXORCIST (1973), a film appreciated by the high clergy (the Pope!) just because of its extreme style drowned in putrefaction, slime, and obscenity. The script and the novel the EXORCIST is based on were written by Peter Blatty, a religiously motivated best-selling author who intelligently dealt with the ritual aspects of serial murder in EXORCIST III, a film he directed himself.

Up to the present moment RAMPAGE is one of the most complex, most intelligent attempts of an approximation to the serial killer phenomenon. One of the suppressed masterpieces dusting on the shelves of the distributors. A film where the total assault of irrationality upon reason takes place in a most disturbing way. "The greatest impetus for me was the feeling that psychiatry had always been playing an unholy role in America" (William Friedkin). A perfect, though not easily digestible thriller. What remains are unsolved questions and icy silence.

Unfortunately, Friedkin's film was re-edited and released as a "Director's Cut" in 1993 (again with little success). This version lacks many strong moments of the original and offers unnecessary explanatory sequences instead.

ANDREI CHILATILO

"What I did was not for sexual pleasure. Rather it brought me some peace of mind."
–Andrei Chikatilo

"I wanted to see this man who could rip open my son's stomach and then stuff mud in his mouth so that he would not cry out. I wanted to know what he looked like, to know which mother could bear such an animal."
–Nina Beletskaya, mother of a victim

The Case

The prototypical example of horror rising from banal ordinariness, and perhaps the most atrocious killer in sheep's clothes: Andrei Romanovic Chikatilo, one of the most extreme killers spewed out by the 20th century. When he was caught in 1990 the 56-year-old former teacher from Russia confessed to have killed, raped, and dismembered 55 people, mainly young girls and boys, over a period of some ten years. There was evidence of 53 victims, though a higher estimated number of unknown cases is still highly probable.

Outwardly, Chikatilo was the perfect citizen of the USSR. A well educated and rather mousy husband and father of a grown-up son and a daughter who played chess excellently and always looked away timidly when there was violence in a film(!). But a brutality of unthinkable dimensions was boiling under the ordinary surface. Chikatilo, who had been fired as a teacher because he had molested some children, then worked for the Russian railroad company. There he was considered shy, odd, and colourless, but also a good worker. But a private circle of a sexual void, hate, and madness drove the "Red Ripper" to bizarre crime. In the night he attacked minors in the forests not far away from where he worked, and performed his "operations". First he cut the tongues out of his still-living victims to prevent them from crying for help, then he pierced the auditory canals and tore their eyeballs out of their sockets. Finally he sexually mutilated his victims. These explosions of violence satisfied him for a short moment (Chikatilo's semen was found on the torn sexual organs and in the eye sockets of the children) and briefly took the constant pressure from his psyche. The man his friends remembered as a "tender loving grandfather" asked himself, "Why do even drunkards and hobos have a functioning sex-life, whereas I don't?". Andrei Chikatilo was executed by a firing squad in 1994.

CITIZEN X / USA 1995

Written and directed by Chris Gerolmo. Camera: Robert Fraisse. Music: Randy Edelmann. With Stephen Rea, Donald Sutherland, Max Von Sydow, Jeffery De Munn, Joss Ackland, John Wood

As one might have expected it wasn't Russian television but an American cable-network that brought up the Chikatilo murders. As a matter of fact, the spectacular case of the "Ripper of Rostov" has stirred worldwide attention and was just what the serial killer-addicted US-audience was waiting for. Moreover, when he was finally caught, the Russian nation was so traumatized by Chikatilo's gory deeds that the shock waves still hadn't ebbed away when the first scriptwriters threw themselves at the topic. The case massively shook many taboos of the past, and it seemed that without some kind of corrupt entanglement within the communist security apparatus Chikatilo wouldn't have been able to kill without hindrance.

Against all odds the final product is really captivating and expands considerably the otherwise rather narrow limits of documentary drama on television. And this despite the fact that CITIZEN X at first follows all conventions of the genre, focusing on the killer's hunter and his investigations and not on the killer himself. Police detective Bukarov (Stephen Rea) believes in a serial killer behind the shocking corpses of children found not far away from Rostov. Yet, in 1982 the introverted cop is totally alone with this view and opposes the lines of the official propaganda, which denies the existence of "such decadent Western phenomena" in the glorious Soviet Union. Nevertheless, supported by the mighty Colonel Fetisov, Bukarov continues his investigations and in 1984 the trap closes with a snap. A certain Andrei Romanovic Chikatilo is caught by the detectives controlling all the train stations in the area of Rostov. But the suspect's blood does not fit to the semen found on the victims. As comrade Chikatilo reveals himself as faithful member of the Communist Party, some higher echelons automatically regard him as innocent. So he is released and a few months later the brutal series of murders recommences.

Bukarov, torn and already falling prey to depression, has to start out right from the beginning. Only after he has been provided with a greater team years too late and has also included a psychiatrist (a taboo!), does the noose around the delinquent's neck get tighter again. When he is arrested again in 1990, the evidence seems to suffocate petty bourgeois Chikatilo, but it isn't until his interview with the psychiatrist (Max von Sydow) that he breaks down. The excited crowd celebrates Bukarov as a hero and even the serial killer task-force of the FBI sends congratulatory telegrams.

Of course, you only get a vague idea of the horror happening in the woods of Rostov in CITIZEN X. The author and director Chris Gerolmo has to obey the rules of the medium. The film must be okay for prime time and an explicit approach to the dark sides of human nature is forbidden. Nevertheless, Gerolmo delivered a stifling opus different from the usual playing down TV-trash. It is not the conventional plot (and the acting, especially Joss Ackland as communist *par excellence*) that lifts CITIZEN X beyond the average, but its ambitious adaptation. Miles away from the tough US-cliché-cop, Stephen Rea tumbles through the barren, often apathetic atmosphere created by Chris Gerolmo. Jeffrey De Munn as Chikatilo moves as silent, invisible and remote-controlled. Only in some short and terrifying moments does "the monster" flare up. CITIZEN X was awarded several prizes at diverse festivals, and Donald Sutherland (as Colonel Fetisov) received an Emmy for the best minor part.

"Once again I experienced that quiet, peaceful thrill. I had no regrets."
–John Reginald Christie describing his state after murder

The Case

The murders committed by the then 55-year-old John Christie severely moved the people of London in 1953, because thereby an error of justice happened that cost the life of an innocent. On March 24, 1953 a tenant renovating the former house of John Christie at 10 Rillington Place finds three female corpses in a hiding place in the wall. Another two are found buried in the garden. The remains of his wife, missing for one year, lie under the living room floor. The discovery ends an almost 14-year-long series of murders.

The weak and frequently ill John has a hard childhood. He commits several little offences and is imprisoned for a while, but in the war he is accepted into the police as a volunteer. As he becomes seriously hypochondriac, he devotes himself extensively to auto-didactic medical studies. Probably he uses the resulting knowledge for illegal abortions. He marries in 1920. His entire matrimonial life suffers from his odd sexual behaviour oscillating between repression and perverse fantasies. Presumably, this is the key to the murders, almost all of which share the same pattern: the women, among them three prostitutes, are tempted into the house under the pretence of medical help. There they are narcotised with gas and raped. The victims must be unconscious for the rapist killer, before he is able to abuse them. Then Christie kills the women, mostly by strangulation. Sometimes sexual abuse occurs *post mortem* too.

In his trial beginning in June 1953 the honest man wearing glasses confesses to various murders, among them that of his former neighbour Beryl Evans from 1949. But Beryl's almost cretinous husband Tim had been accused of murdering his wife and his daughter. Tim Evans, who first confessed to the crimes, but then accused Christie, lost himself in a network of contradictions and was hanged for double murder in 1950. Until today it is not clear for some people who was the real delinquent, but after decades of investigation experts are convinced that Christie killed the woman,

TEN RILLINGTON PLACE

and the illiterate Evans killed the baby in despair. Officially, the corpse of the executed man has been exhumed much later and buried again with all honours.

Although he has been pleading for insanity, John Reginald Christie, the real murderer, has to feel the noose around his neck on July 15, 1953.

TEN RILLINGTON PLACE / GB 1971

Directed by Richard Fleischer. Written by Clive Exton after a novel by Ludovic Kennedy. Camera: Denys Coop. Music: John Dankworth. With Richard Attenborough, John Hurt, Judy Geeson, Isobel Black

For True Crime specialist Richard Fleischer (THE BOSTON STRANGLER, COMPULSION) the evidence in the Christie case was clear: the elderly care-taker of notorious 10 Rillington Place had committed all the crimes, the moronic illiterate Tim Evans was an innocent victim of justice.

TEN RILLINGTON PLACE introduces its protagonist with a murder: Christie makes a woman suffering from asthma take an allegedly healing gas. When she realises her mistake, the delinquent is already fingering a rubber hose in order to strangle his victim. (Later in the film you get to know that Christie fell prey to a gas assault in WW1, which paralysed him for a long time).Then the mousy killer buries the corpse in the garden behind the house. When the working class-couple Evans and their baby move into the shabby block of flats, Christie (the British director/actor Richard Attenborough) follows the blonde Beryl with his gazes. A second, unwanted pregnancy drives the young couple into despair and the unsuspecting woman directly into the claws of the murderer.

Christie offers her his medical knowledge and promises a quick and painless abortion. Beryl agrees to this and practically signs her death warrant: gas, attempted rape, strangulation. The ignorant husband (John Hurt, captivating), being let in into the secret abortion plans, finds his dead wife in the evening and even believes her murderer's lame excuse of an ill-starred operation. Christie drives Evans to escape and strangles the baby in his absence. When the nervous wreck of a husband finally gives himself up to the police, fate takes its run. The mass murderer goes on hiding behind the mask of the petty bourgeoisie, while an innocent iman s hanged instead of him. It takes time until the police find the real murderer by chance. In the meantime certain things begin to dawn on Christie's wife...

Richard Fleischer, who did not only intend to study the anatomy of a case of murder, but also wanted to condemn the deplorable death of Tim Evans, stages his film as a claustrophobic, intimate play. Narrowness, anxiety, dank walls behind which atrocious secrets lie. The events outside the house hardly matter. TEN RILLINGTON PLACE is shot almost exclusively inside the walls of this specific address in London. Fleischer went as far as shooting the film in the original setting. Just in time, as one year later 10 Rillington Place was a parking garage.

A limited setting demands a limited number of actors. After Fleischer had analysed the difficulties of legislation from many different points of view in COMPULSION (based on Nathan Leopold & Richard Loeb), and had discussed the mass hysteria around Albert DeSalvo in THE BOSTON STRANGLER, he totally concentrated on the character of the delinquent when working up the Christie case. The camera sticks at Christie/Attenborough and does not allow itself any experiment. Frosty realism replaces the manneristic techniques of the film's predecessors (split screen, etc.). A grim, suffocating realism that makes Richard Fleischer's opus a forerunner of John McNaughton's HENRY and some of the other chilling shockers created in more recent years.

JEFFREY DAHMER

"I won't hurt you if you let me handcuff you and take some pictures. You have to be nude."

–Jeffrey Dahmer to a victim

"I've always felt he was somewhat of a social misfit. I tried my damnedest to instil interests, in trying to become interested in something in life, education, trying to get to accept him Christ."

–Jeffrey Dahmer's father

The Case

Jeffrey Dahmer could smarten himself up with the sad fame of setting new standards in the rich catalogue of extreme cases in the US-serial killer history. When the police stormed his notorious apartment 213 in a house in Milwaukee, the cannibal had stored parts of corpses everywhere in his room. Two corpses lay in the bathtub. The frozen heads of his victims were found in the refrigerator.

Like many comparable cases, the chronology of this serial killer begins with a "pretty normal" childhood. On May 21, 1960 Jeffrey Dahmer was born in Milwaukee, Wisconsin as the son of a well-to-do family. Very early, well-protected little Jeffrey keeps out of the way of other children as well as adults. From the outside he is a shy but polite little boy who is teased by his classmates for his reserve and self-chosen isolation. As a response he retires even more into his shell. Like many other children Jeffrey develops fantasies of power and violence. Moreover, he likes playing with guts and dead dogs. His father watches him gather animals hit by cars from the street and bury them in his own little "pet cemetery" behind the house. Jeff secretly experiments with the cadavers and tries to dissolve them in acid. "What can I say, he was a typical lone wolf", a US criminologist answered in later years when asked about the Dahmer case.

Sex was taboo under the parental roof, his latent homosexual disposition no subject Jeffrey would have ever discussed. Later Dahmer reports that already his earliest sexual fantasies involved killing.

In 1978, 18 years old, he lures a hitchhiker into the house in the absence of

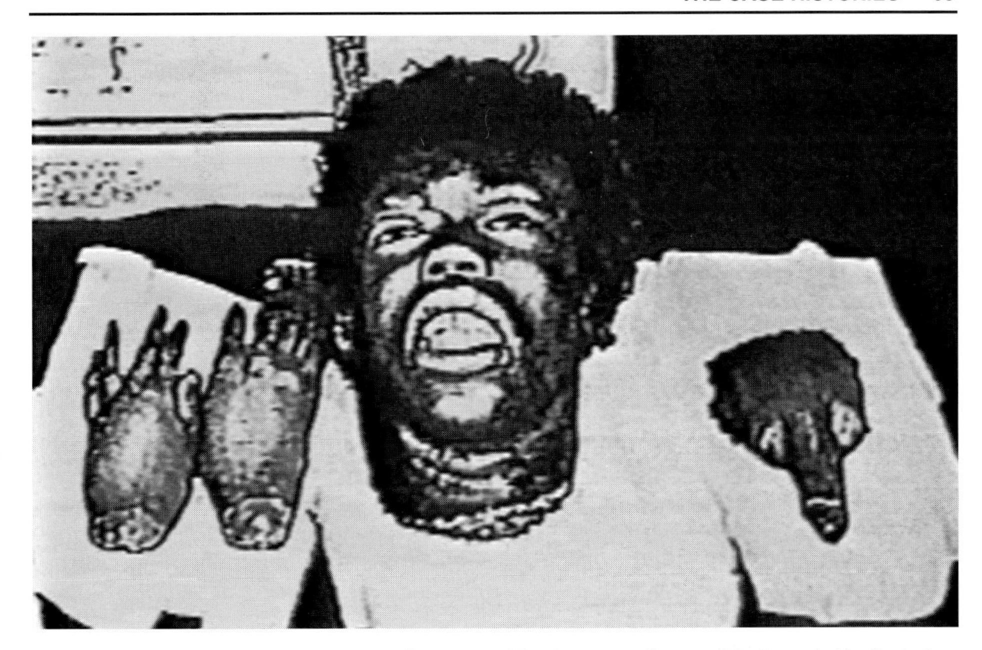

The severed body parts of one of Dahmer's black victims

his parents and hits him on the head. He chops the corpse into tiny pieces and buries them in the woods. In 1987, when labile Jeffrey is living with his grandmother, the series of murders causing the death of 17 victims commences. All are young man who the delinquent approaches in bars. Similarly to Dennis Nilsen, another homosexual serial killer, hate was not his motive. He longs for his victims as objects, wants to keep them forever, make them submissive. Sometimes he drills holes into their heads and fills them with battery-acid when they are still alive in order to make them "zombies". He pushes his power fantasies with his favourite films STAR WARS, HELLRAISER, and THE EXORCIST I and III. He identifies with Darth Vader and Pinhead, the ultimate black-leather heroes of his gloomy fetishist world. Finally, after losing his job and vegetating in his apartment in the middle of fresh corpses, the police put an end to his activities.

Homophobia and racism are central subjects of his trial, for the majority of Dahmer's victims were black. It hailed protests all over America, because police investigation was not exactly fast or meticulous when gay Afro-Americans from lousy neighbourhoods disappeared without a trace.

On February 17, 1991 Jeffrey Dahmer was sentenced to 15 times life. In the meantime he had become an exceptional case of media exploitation. Father and son Dahmer met on US television at the best broadcasting time to talk openly about his bloody deeds for the first time. Unlike the reporters that interviewed Charles Manson, his talk show-host treated him rather amiably. A calm and composed serial killer without screams and tears looked into the cameras. The "Cannibal of Milwaukee" seems to have been the exact opposite of a foaming maniac. In 1994 Jeffrey Dahmer was killed by a fellow jailbird, bludgeoned to death in the latrines.

THE SECRET LIFE aka JEFFREY DAHMER: THE SECRET LIFE / USA 1993
Directed by David R. Bowen. Written by Carl Crew. Music: David R. Bowen. With Carl Crew, Cassidy Phillips, J.R. Brown, Jeanne Rascom, G. J. Reed, Alex Scott

This cheap video-production somehow achieves what many much more expensive True Crime TV productions do not: the real names of all the victims and all the other people involved including Jeffrey Dahmer and his family are used. Though this might increase the pseudo-documentary shock-effect of the film, it cannot however make up for its formal insufficiency and bad acting. Produced immediately after the Dahmer trials, THE SECRET LIFE never left the rearmost corners of US video stores. But this would be no reason to disqualify the film. Sometimes you can find real jewels there in the recesses. Quite probably, Dahmer's family brought an action against the makers of the film.

Pseudo-director Bowen begins his home video showing episodes of a serial killer's life at the time when 22-year-old Jeffrey Dahmer moves into the house of his grandmother. Expressionless video sequences accompanied by gooey *National Geographic* or soap-keyboard muzak line up in a row. In addition to this the protagonist's monotonous off-screen voice murmurs about his emotional scars and traumata. Only the fact that the Dahmer in the film speaks in the same perversely gentle voice, gives THE SECRET LIFE some sort of atmosphere, at least periodically.

The first murder in front of the camera: Jeffrey kills a hitchhiker, while his grandmother is sitting in front of the sewing-machine in the adjoining room. Time-jumps into Jeffrey's childhood when he plays with dead animals. Some bad splatter scenes, fade-out. Dahmer kills and kills. First in his grandma's house, then in the notorious apartment 213.

The years from 1988 to the bitter end in 1991. Subtitles inform us about the events. Dahmer sneaks into bars in the night, talks to young men, offers them money for nude pictures. Always the same foul play. Then a little Irish Coffee spiced with sedatives in Jeffrey's apartment, a thrust with a knife, a stranglehold, or a blow to the neck. The camera fades out when the killer goes on to the body-dismembering, corpse-fucking afterplay. More and more victims, Dahmer caught in the vicious circle of his deeds, again and again giving way to his murderous forces after short phases of cold turkey. He cooks organs, tastes them. Cannibalism too is caused by an urge for power. The author Joel Norris writes: "Some serial killers try to preserve the intensity of the murder, to prolong the feeling of power and triumph over their pasts, by attempting to preserve the body through a ritualistic dismemberment of the dead victim. Either the victim's genitals are cut off and carried away, or the limbs are severed, or the head is removed. Serial killers have eaten parts of the victims' remains, carried off parts of the body with them for later preservation in jars or scrapbooks, buried parts of their victims' bodies in isolated 'sacred' spots, or shown them to their subsequent victims." Dahmer must get rid of 17 bodies in his serial killer "career", an enormous physical and mental effort. Bones have to be sawed to pieces, sinews cut, guts packed into plastic bags. On July 22, 1991 the police save him from the horror of his existence. Then the credits. After so much simplistic exploitation it only appears hypocritical that the film is dedicated to the victims, as it is emphasised in the credits.

THE SECRET LIFE is a typical product from the garbage dumps of American amateur film. Take a camera and portray your favourite serial killer. Some of the minor parts are okay, and the atmosphere of the killer-apartment is positively rotten and wrecked. But, as in many other "Z-movies", this is merely a by-product of an abortive *mise-en-scène* and by no means intentional. It is a pity that again a low-low budget film-maker lets slip the opportunity to approach a subject uncompromisingly. Bowen and his scriptwriter/protagonist Crew had no studios behind them that could have forced them into the one or other direction. Nevertheless, they involuntarily imitated the usual television plays. THE SECRET LIFE lacks the mental horror that Dahmer was living through, as well as the utmost terror his victims had to experience in the face of death. This has nothing to do with the budget.

ALBERT HENRY DeSALVO

The Boston Strangler

"Once I stabbed her once, I couldn't stop... I keep hitting her and hitting her with that knife... She keep bleeding from the throat... I hit her and hit her and hit her..."
–Albert DeSalvo confessing to the murder of a 23-year-old student

The Case
Albert Henry DeSalvo terrorised Boston between June 1962 and January 1964 creating a climate of hysteria and paralysing panic. "The Boston Strangler", in "real life" an average family father, abused, hit, and strangled 13 women between 19 and 85 years of age. Disguised as a gas man or a messenger, he was let into the apartments of his victims. In many cases he strangled the women immediately, in others he first tied them to the bed, raped them, and killed them afterwards. He undressed the corpses completely, spread their legs, and draped stockings or slips around their necks in cute little knots; some were left with broomsticks or bottles rammed into their vaginas, or covered in bite marks. DeSalvo was driven by his manic sexuality and wanted to have sexual intercourse five or six times per day. In 1955 he also began to molest children. During the 18 months of his terror campaign against the female sex the Boston strangler harassed almost 300 women. Nevertheless, for lack of evidence not a single murder could be proved. DeSalvo, diagnosed irresponsible and schizophrenic, got a life sentence for a number of minor sexual offences and was sent to the Bridgewater Institute for Mental Criminals. From there he was referred to the Walpole State Prison, Massachusetts where he ended up himself as a victim of murder.

THE BOSTON STRANGLER / USA 1968
Directed by Richard Fleischer. Written by Edward Anhalt after the novel "The Boston Strangler" by Gerold Frank. Camera: Richard H. Kline. Music: Lionel Newman. With Tony Curtis, Henry Fonda, George Kennedy, Jeff Corey, Sally Kellerman

THE BOSTON STRANGLER

Richard Fleischer's film is practically split into two parts. The first half is dedicated to the development of the hysterical atmosphere paralysing Boston for months. Then the film deals exclusively with the killer and his split personality. The movies of Richard Fleischer, a hyper-productive director with an enormous output, oscillate between rather awkward productions and examples of flawless craftsmanship. This film ranges among the latter, beside True Crime classics like COMPULSION, or TEN RILLINGTON PLACE. This cool analysis of a killer may be seen as one of the most impressing contributions to the history of serial killer movies.

THE BOSTON STRANGLER meticulously stages Gerold Frank's novel, a best-selling detailed report on the DeSalvo case. From the first murder he follows the events chronologically, observing the police investigation, as well as the coverage in the media and the victims' reactions. This all happens simultaneously most of the times due to the fashion in Sixties cinema to split the screen into several segments showing parallel events. Constant split screen-technique and a rather over-ambitious formalism reduces the horror of the story a little bit, but gives the film a distanced documentary touch over long stretches. The delinquent himself only comes up late in the film. Fleischer introduces him in a highly convincing scene: after the police have published a possible personality profile of the killer, the camera shows a typical well-behaved American family idyll. Father is watching the funeral of JFK on television, talking soothingly to his children. Mother is working in the kitchen. The audience knows immediately that this pretty normal husband (Tony Curtis!) must be the Boston Strangler. The dream of the intact family as a refuge from a merciless world (a world symbolised by the Kennedy assassination) is smashed into a thousand smithereens in the following scenes showing DeSalvo gag and kill.

The two chapters "A City In Fear", and "The Capture Of The Strangler" are followed by a long final sequence in the lunatic asylum entirely devoted to Tony Curtis's dead and empty stare. Curtis, who definitely delivers one of his most demanding performances in an otherwise predominantly comedic or costume-drama career, rises above himself in the role of the killer. By the way, he even resembles him physically. Totally apathetic, haunted by inner demons, he is gradually losing contact with reality. In the clinically white atmosphere of the bare interrogation room he finally gives in to madness. His body resembles a lifeless envelope, with the strangler's mind hidden somewhere way inside.

"I did not know why I shot him. I was just very upset."
–Ruth Ellis

The Case

Ruth Ellis entered criminal history as the last woman who was hanged in England. Her crime: she shot dead her lover David Blakely in broad daylight.

The 28-year-old peroxide-blonde had a stormy life. Working in a night-club she gave birth to an illegitimate child at the age of 18. She married George Ellis, with whom she had a daughter. After divorce Ruth was call girl, nude model, and finally manager of the bar where she got to know David Blakely, a well-to-do heir and unsuccessful car-racer. Their turbulent affair was accompanied by David's alcoholic excesses and violent quarrels. Then David spent Easter 1955 with a befriended couple without informing Ruth. In a jealous frenzy she observed his house for nights, and finally decided to shoot him. She shot at her lover six times in front of a pub in Hampstead. Then she asked a passer-by to call the police.

During the trial Ruth Ellis hardly ever tried to claim extenuating circumstances or elicit understanding for her deed. From Death Row she wrote to a friend about her imminent execution, "Don't worry. It's like pulling teeth, and they will give me a glass of brandy before".

DANCE WITH A STRANGER / GB 1985

Directed by Mike Newell. Written by Shelag Delaney. Camera: Peter Hannan. Music: Richard Harley. With Miranda Richardson, Rupert Everett, Ian Holm, Matthew Carrol
In the middle of the Eighties England faces a film boom, directors like Neil Jordan, Chris Bernard, and Alex Cox created a media craze about New British Cinema, a longed-for artistic and commercial counter-force to US cinema superiority. As in the Free Cinema Movement of the Sixties, typically British stories were told again. Directors like Cox or Julian Temple thoroughly worked up the roots of British pop culture. The producer Roger Randall Cuttler sees the murderess Ruth Ellis from this perspective. For him she represents something like the first rebel, the "pioneer of a

YIELD TO THE NIGHT

dawning youth culture", a representative of the lower classes reacting violently against the humiliation received from her high society lover. Cuttler participates in the script and the casting, chooses the protagonist Miranda Richardson, and enthuses to Mike Newell about the project.

Visually a cool melodrama, DANCE WITH A STRANGER does not tell Ruth Ellis's story from an objective distance, but from the perspective of the delinquent. Nevertheless her bourgeois lover David Blakely is more than a hypocrite antagonist. Like Ruth, he is a prisoner of the still very restrictive British society of the Fifties.

Admittedly, Blakely has a weak character and is a plaything for his friends and prompters. With this deficiency he ruins Ruth's life, and hence he has to die. Nevertheless, he is a victim, too. The flux of the story is not always convincing. Sometimes the film seems to stop at an invisible margin, unable to get through to the feelings of the characters; but as Ruth is slowly heading for a lethal solution, DANCE WITH A STRANGER becomes denser and more emotional. Miranda Richardson's face freezes to a painted mask mirroring the full extent of the tragedy.

"The luxury she has been working for, her effort to break down social barriers for her obsession resulting in her drift into madness, all this is not depicted superficially psychologically, but physically in this film", notes film critic Reinhard Jud.

YIELD TO THE NIGHT / GB 1956

Directed by J Lee Thompson. Written by John Cresswell, from the novel by Joan Henry. Camera: Gilbert Taylor. Music: Ray Martin. With Diana Dors, Michael Craig

Made just a year after Ruth Ellis was hanged, YIELD TO THE NIGHT never refers directly to her case but is an obvious response to the horror and revulsion felt by many at the execution of the blonde killer. Diana Dors, whose peroxide aura perfectly evokes Ellis, gives her best ever performance as the murderess condemned to death, living out her last days in prison confinement. A powerful, claustrophobic and moving plea for humanitarianism.

JOHN WAYNE GACY

The Blood Crimes Of Pogo The Clown

"The only thing they can get me for is running a funeral parlor without a license."
–John Wayne Gacy after his arrest

The Case

John Wayne Gacy, one of the most sadistic killers of the USA, entered the annals of criminal history as the "Killer Clown".

Born in Iowa in 1942, John is a fat sickly boy suffering from the beatings and insults of his father, a boozer. Nevertheless he starts a quite successful career, engages in the political and social matters of his community, marries and has two children. In 1968 the owner of a fast-food restaurant is sentenced to 10 years in prison for sexually molesting two teenagers. But 18 months later he is released for good conduct. After his divorce Gacy moves to a suburb of Chicago where he opens a prospering construction business. In 1971 he is again accused of sexual harassment of a teenage boy, but the charge is dropped. Early in 1972 he marries a second time and re-starts his political activities, especially for the Democratic Party. John's second wife suffers from his lack of sexual interest and his violent character.

In 1978 a 27-year-old man accuses Gacy of chloroforming him, raping him several times, and finally dumping him in a park. But the police lack sufficient evidence for an arrest. When in December 1978 a 15-year-old boy disappears after an interview with Gacy, the police visit him after a long phase of observation. There the police detectives encounter the pungent smell of putrefaction. During the search the policemen find 28 corpses in various stages of putrefaction buried in the basement, in the garden, or in cement pits. The remaining five victims mentioned by Gacy have been thrown into the river nearby. The community is shocked. Only Mr. Gacy's respectable facade has been known to them prior to this hideous revelation.

Disguised as "Pogo the Clown", John had been a popular entertainer at kiddie birthday parties. Moreover, Gacy was a promising amateur artist. The great number of paintings done by the killer in prison very quickly became wanted collector's items among movie stars and rock musicians.

Gacy began to kill in 1972, ostensibly in self-defence. Yet the series of murders broke out after his second divorce in 1976. His method was to lure young men into his house under a pretence to show them the so-called "handcuff trick". When they were hand-cuffed, he raped them most brutally and strangled them with a rope. In the interrogations the then 36-year-old J.W. Gacy denied being homosexual and repeated vehemently that he hated homosexual people. "The Killer Clown" dished up a completely different story: It was his evil alter ego Jack that committed the murders while John was mentally absent. So the defence pleaded for irresponsibility, but in March 1980 Gacy was found guilty in all cases and sentenced to death. In 1994 "Pogo, the Mass Murderer" was put to death in the electric chair.

TO CATCH A KILLER / USA 1992 (TV)

Directed by Eric Till. Written by Judd Kinberg. Camera: René Oloshi. Music: Paul Zaza. With Brian Dennehy, Michael Riley, Martin Julien, Michael Copeman, Meg Foster, Margot Kidder, Maria Ricossa

Like Ed Gein and Charles Manson, John Wayne Gacy, the killer of at least 33 boys and young men, has managed to become a part of the death-addicted US popular culture. Probably the spectacular details of the case are the reason of the enormous media popularity of the heavy-weight killer: the well-to-do citizen owning a flourishing business, once photographed together with First Lady Rosalyn Carter as a local politician, the nice clown Pogo always ready for a sleight of hand, and finally the amateur artist whose naive paintings made it to galleries and private collections. But in his secret life Gacy frequented gay bars, where he approached young homosexuals and took them home. He chloroformed the victims, raped them anally and killed them. The remains of 28 corpses were found under the basement of his house in Summerdale, Illinois.

This perverse double life provided Gacy with a fixed place among the Top Ten killers of mass murder history.

Of course, mankind could not do without a TV adaptation of Gacy's case in the general media feding-frenzy. Rather belatedly, Eric Till carried out the film in 1992. TO CATCH A KILLER is a three-hour, two part-production. Pseudonyms are employed for some victims and other persons involved, but the delinquent himself is explicitly named. The film enters the case at Christmas 1978 when the Illinois police become strongly alert to him for the first time, after 15-year-old Robert Piest has disappeared. A war of nerves lasting for months breaks out where the killer constantly threatens with charges, and the cops try to break him with wearing-down tactics. All means are justified to convict Pogo, who wriggles like an eel. But finally a fortune-teller (metaphysically and typically for TV) provides the police with the decisive hint.

Compared to the bunch of TV serial killer soaps seemingly even more hollow and arbitrary than the cheap paperbacks on the True Crime shelves of the bookstores, TO CATCH A KILLER makes a solid impression. Yet the unbelievable horror is compressed to TV dimensions and processed according to the laws of advertising. Judd Kinberg has constructed his script along a typical mainstream pattern. The identification figure for the audience is put in the foreground. As almost always in such TV epics it is the heroic police detective and his criminal investigation that is focused. Joe Kozenczak is a stubborn young detective convinced of respectable Mr. Gacy's guilt, who does not give up until he has brought the fat clown to Death Row.

Right from the off, we only learn about the atrocious murders from files and interviews. Eric Till shows Gacy's basement only in half-darkness. The audience is not (cannot be) provided with a deeper insight into the horrors of anal rape and dismemberment. The brilliant Brian Dennehy, who impersonates John Wayne Gacy convincingly, caters for certain moments of suspense. Nevertheless, the actor often famous for complex character roles does not really rise above himself here. The soap opera corset forces him to restrict himself to rather one-sided acting. Gacy as a demonic, grinning and sweating TV bad guy. The most atrocious aspect, that the chubby boy-butcher was basically a "normal" respected fellow, is only slightly hinted at, for all that the Gacy case would have been an opportunity to poke in some fundamental wounds of the US psyche.

Many serial killers believe that they do society some good if they kill certain kinds of people, hence also erasing taboo sides of themselves. "The victims symbolize something in their murderer's pasts", says Joel Norris, "Gacy killed male prostitutes because he was extremely homophobic, and he was killing the hated homosexual part of himself." So he directed the self-hatred he was overcome by when following his desires and having sexual contact with men, against the victims. In truth, he only wanted to erase the homosexual component of his own self.

The Wisconsin Necrophile

"Good old Ed. Kind of a loner and maybe a little bit odd with that sense of humour of his, but just the guy to call in to sit with the kiddies when me and the old lady want to go to the show."

–One of Ed Gein's neighbours

The Case

Ed Gein is one of the most absolutely macabre cult figures of mass murder history, and an established part of American popular myth. The farmer from Wisconsin with morbid hobbies like necrophilia, cannibalism, and thrdesecration of graves inspired epoch-making masterpieces of movie horror, besides numerous songs and books.

Ed Gein was born in Plainfield, Wisconsin, the rural backwater of the American Midwest, in 1906. His father died early and Ed grew up dominated by his mother in a climate of hard labour and rare entertainment. Contacts to women were taboo for him and his brother Henry, who later died in a fire. Ed's mother was struck by a heart attack in 1945. After that Ed Gein sealed off the rooms used by his mother and restricted himself to the kitchen and a small bedroom. Step by step the ticks and sick fantasies fed by his mother's misogyny and stored up inside him came to the surface. He had always been a weirdo with odd preferences, but the presence of his family had held his tendencies under control.

Alone with his deranged mind Ed was brooding on the remote farm. From the outside he was a classical lone wolf, a harmless queer fish working for his neighbours over the day doing little household chores or baby-sitting. In the night he did "his own little jobs": studying anatomy books, digging out corpses from the local cemetery in order to study their build, and to fabricate trophies from their parts, such as sewn belts of nipples (part Ed's famous human-skin suit). Soon Ed was not satisfied with his night business any more. In 1954 he killed the 54-year-old Mary Hogan, ambushing her after frequenting a bar. Three years later Bernice Worden, an elderly woman working in a Plainfield ironware-store, vanished without a trace. Witnesses reported seeing Ed Gein in town parking his pick-up truck in front of the store.

Victim Bernice Worden

Gein skinned two women in the way hunters do it with shot deer, and added certain private parts to his collection. The officers of Plainfield Sheriff Office would never forget November 16, 1957: when the police finally visited the old-timer on his farm, they found Ed's macabre collection: items like a carton full of vaginas, and numerous human organs in the refrigerator. Moreover, the killer had hung the headless corpse of Mrs Worden on a cross-bar and pulley in the stable like a dressed animal. Her head – with nails driven through the ears – was found in a muslin sack.

Ed Gein was put into a mental institution for the rest of his life and died there in the Eighties. His house was burnt down by his neighbours and his car toured fairs as "Ed Gein's Car!". Lux Interior, singer of garage-rockabilly band The Cramps, once wrote: "There are many good man, but only a few big men. Ed was one of the big men, but no good one. Eddie the digger, he's much bigger than you."

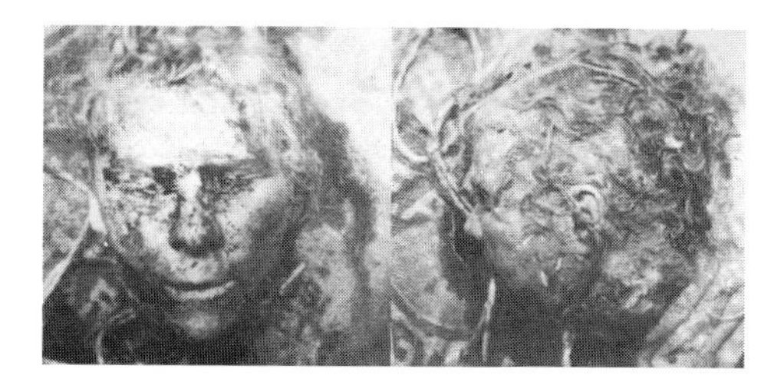

Victim's head

DERANGED

DERANGED / USA 1974

Written and directed by Jeff Gillen & Alan Ormsby. Camera: Jack McGowan. Music: Carl Zittrer. With Roberts Blossom, Cosette Lee, Robert Warner, Marcia Diamond, Brian Sneage, Robert McHeady, Micky Moore, Pat Orr, Marion Waldman

An unfortunately little-known trashy pearl which, nevertheless, can be counted among the best productions of the True Crime genre. Only the names have been changed for legal and protective reasons (Ed Gein is called Ezra Cobb). Otherwise it is undoubtedly a character analysis of Mister Gein, the ghoul dancing lonely in moonlit nights wearing a costume of human skin.

The setting: a remote farm in Wisconsin inhabited by a lonesome old queer who has never learnt to deal with the world. After his mother's death which has left him behind deeply depressed, he takes back her corpse from the cemetery. Old Ezra mummifies Mum's body and soon excavates other corpses for her company. It does not take long until the first murder happens. Mrs. Cobb has never taught her son how to deal with women.

Tom Savini, well known for his later special effects-wizardry in various George Romero zombie films, created the stark, but atmospheric gore and make-up effects. The pseudo-documentary design of the film is another major achievement. A reporter standing in the middle of Ezra's living room factually/dryly/naively comments on the macabre events, "Perhaps, we can learn from it". Roberts Blossom is a rather unknown minor actor, who in his only lead approaches the real Ed Gein (as we know him from True Crime literature) in a fascinating way. He does not portray him as a bloodthirsty madman, but as a whimsical old farmer, a naive childlike guy who simply has a murderous spleen. Jeff Gillen and Alan Ormsby, two B-movie professionals in the field of cheap but amusing horror films, provide us with insight into a deranged mind. Sometimes they do this in a very bizarre, very funny way. But it is an undertaker-humour similar to the one cultivated by US-Noise bands like Killdozer or Big Black.

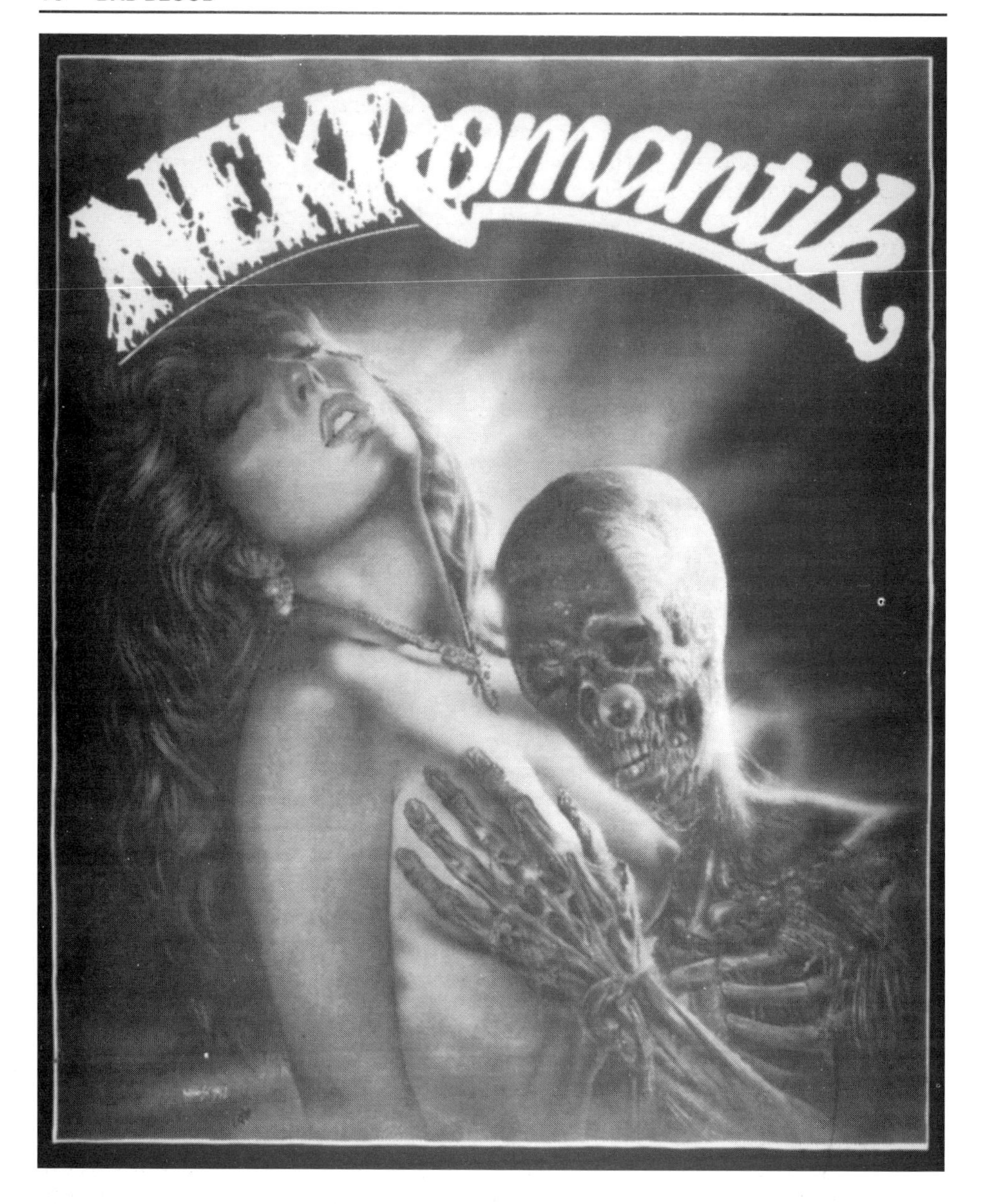

ED GEIN aka IN THE LIGHT OF THE MOON aka /USA 2000

Directed by Chuck Parello. Written by Stephen Jonston. Camera: Vanja Cernjul. Music: Robert McNaughton. With Steve Railsback, Carrie Snodgress, Ryan Thomas Brockington, Bill Cross, Colette Marshall

Finally, a film which deals with the actual facts of the Ed Gein case. Steve Railsback (who portrayed Charlie Manson in HELTER SKELTER/1976) essays the deranged farmer. His background in hard, rural Wisconsin is covered adequately – the only problem is, the true story now seems a bit tame when compared to the many extravagant films which have been based on Gein's nocturnal exploits. Most of the protagonists' and victims' real names are used.

NEKROMANTIK / Germany 1987

Directed by Jörg Buttgereit. Written by Jörg Buttgereit & Franz Rodenkirchen. Camera: Uwe Bohrer. Music: J. B. Walton, Hermann Kopp, Daktari Lenz. With Daktari Lenz, Beatrice M., Harald Lundt, Susa Kohlstedt, Heike S.

"Love for man and what remains from him" is what the protagonist of this provocative underground movie and the "bad old necrophile" from Wisconsin share. Injecting a strong dose of subversion and taboo-breaking into the already dead-beat splatter-genre Buttgereit, an outspoken "Geinophile", and his co-scriptwriter Rodenkirchen try to save what can be saved. Robert "Rob" S. works for a "cleansing firm" removing corpses of all sorts from scenes of accidents by official order. The job supplies him with "material" for his abysmal private life. He shares a dark obsession with his girl-friend Betty. They only get satisfaction in carnal-necrophile lust. The film is radical in its mélange of the unbelievable (sex with mouldy rotten corpses) and the romantic (music and camera transfigure the disgusting sequences to moments of bizarre beauty). NEKROMANTIK is not really a film about killers, since the couple's lovers are already dead when they find them; but in the context of Ed Gein and his bizarre predelictions, it deserves inclusion here. Finally, Buttgereit's movie takes its title really seriously; hence, at least in its ambitions, it is perhaps to be seen in the framework of Wakamatsu or Pasolini than only within the limits of the horror genre.

This and its sequel, NEKROMANTIK 2, were only rivalled by the full-on necro-psycho assault of LUCKER, which spewed out of Belgium in 1986.

PSYCHO / USA 1960

Directed by Alfred Hitchcock. Written by Joseph Stefano after the novel by Robert Bloch. Camera: John L. Russel. Music: Bernhard Hermann. With Anthony Perkins, Janet Leigh, Vera Miles, Martin Balsam, John Gavin

Ed Gein can hardly be recognised in the figure of the most famous of all psycho killers, hyper-sensitive and schizophrenic Norman Bates in Alfred Hitchcock's epoch-making shocker. But at a closer look you find the same mother fixation, the dissection and stuffing of dead items, as well as a tendency towards transvestism. Moreover, Robert Bloch's novel *Psycho* is strongly influenced by Edward, the man in the skin suit. Living in Wisconsin at the time of the Gein case, Robert Bloch wrote the book within a very short time, after he had heard of the atrocious farmer in Plainfield.

Hitchcock's phenomenal command of filmic techniques, his innovative camera-work, his subversive dealing with expectations (the film's heroine dies within the first third of the film, which at the time of the film's release really shook the audience), Anthony Perkins' unsurpassed rendering of Norman the crazy mother's boy, and, of course, the famous, a thousand times analysed shower-scene, all this makes PSYCHO the classic deserving its place in the history of cinema.

Three more or less superfluous sequels have been made, none of them elaborating on the Gein-related nature of the Bates character. Then, in 1998, Gus Van Sant made his shot-for-shot colour remake, also called PSYCHO. This apparently redundant action was deliberate cinematic provocation. And a pre-programmed failure. The makers of this film have probably kept cool as Christopher Doyle, director of photography, confessed in an interview with the author of this book: "I don't think Gus or myself even give a shit about what people think about the movie [...] 'Psycho' is a conceptual artwork. It asks 'What is a masterpiece?' 'What is structure?' 'What is fame?' Nobody under 25 knows about 'Psycho', and most of them haven't heard about Hitchcock. All this stuff about the purity of a masterpiece going down the drain, that's what Gus is addressing. Don't think about it as a movie, you don't even have to see it. He took 20 million dollars from these Hollywood assholes and made his PhD in Fine Arts."

"Buffalo Bill", SILENCE OF THE LAMBS

THE SILENCE OF THE LAMBS / USA 1990

Directed by Jonathan Demme. Written by Ted Tally after a novel by Thomas Harris. Camera: Tak Fujimoto. Musik: Howard Shore. With Jodie Foster, Anthony Hopkins, Scott Glenn, Ted Lavine, Charles Napier, Tracey Walter, Roger Corman, Chris Isaak

He hits under cover of the night. Young, tall and lonesome women are his victims. After a martyrdom of several days he finally skins them. That is why he is called Buffalo Bill. This name hovers over the American continent like a foul, pungent stench. In order to stop the sex killer the FBI dares an experiment. They are going to work together with already arrested serial killers to draw up a psychological profile.

Enter Clarice Starling, a young FBI agent still in training, and Dr. Hannibal Lecter, the ingenious cannibal in solitary confinement. A subtle cat and mouse game, a mixture of psychoanalysis and methodical madness, develops between the two. Clarice must tell Lecter intimate details about her life in order to get precious coded information as a reward. Finally Lecter effects a bloody escape, establishing his "übermensch" credentials.

"Pretty much anytime you see anything in a movie about human skin suits, you're seeing Ed Gein's legacy", notes Maitland McDonagh. THE SILENCE OF THE LAMBS is definitely such a case. Buffalo Bill has by all means been inspired by Ed Gein. In 1990 Jonathan Demme, before only known for exploitation works, surprises with an aura of constant threat. Numerous hyper-texts lie under the entertaining frame. THE SILENCE OF THE LAMBS is a film about motivations and circles around the origins and the stimuli of human behaviour as well as the impenetrability of the mind. Which impulses drive people to massacres like that, or, vice versa, why does someone want to play the hero and becomes an FBI agent? Meanwhile Bill, though only briefly glimpsed in his skin drag, remains one of the most terrifying creations to spew from the Gein heritage.

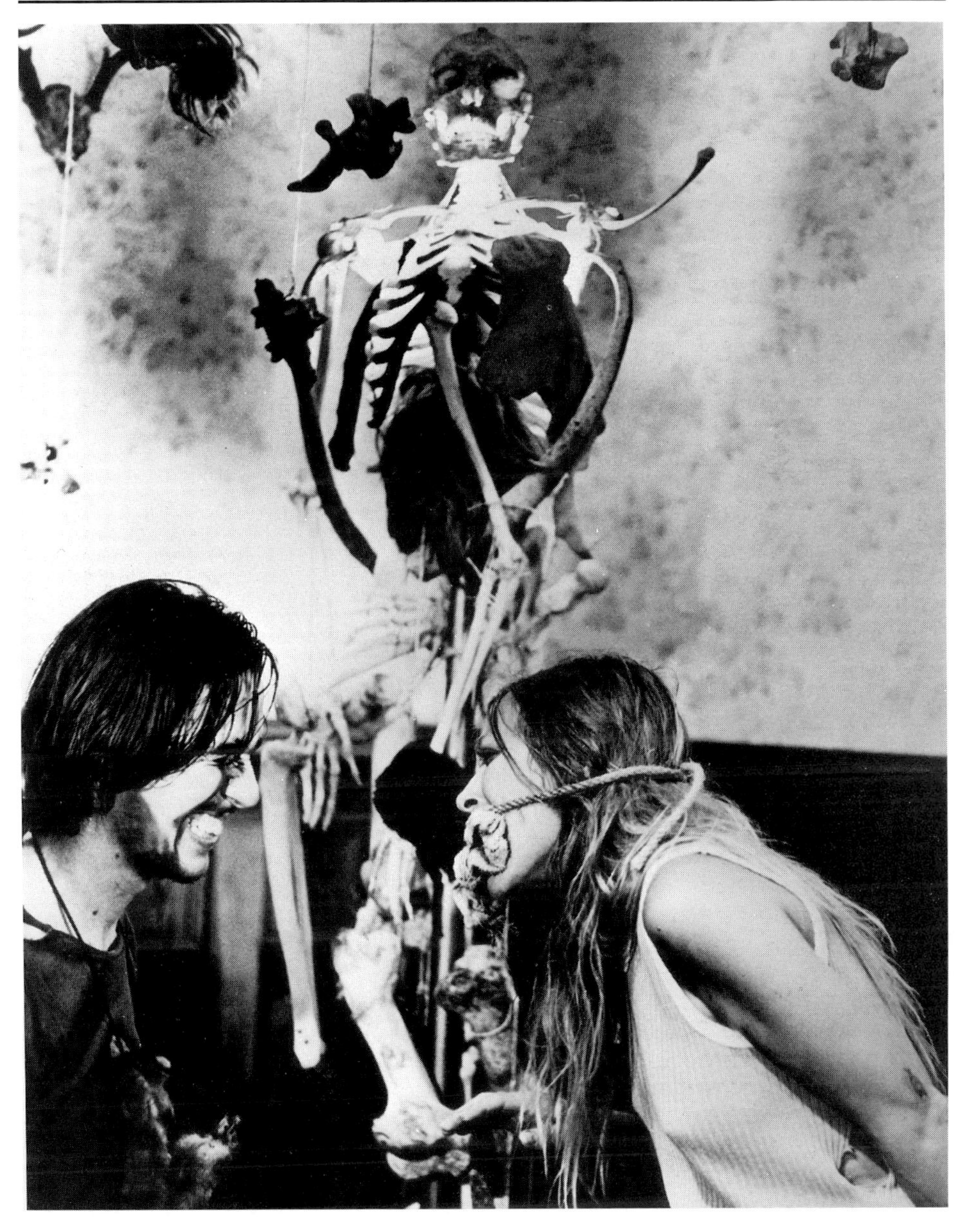

TEXAS CHAINSAW MASSACRE

THE TEXAS CHAINSAW MASSACRE / USA 1974

Directed by Tobe Hooper. Written by Kim Henkel & Tobe Hooper. Camera: Daniel Pearl. Music: Tobe Hooper & Wayne Bell. With Marilyn Burns, Allen Danziger, Gunnar Hansen, Jim Siedow, Edwin Neal, Paul A. Partain

A bunch of youngsters are travelling through Texas in a microbus. After meeting a weird hitchhiker, having a rest in a lonesome deserted farmhouse becomes their doom. A nightmarish family led by "Leatherface", a monstrous slaughterer wearing a mask of human skin and swinging a chainsaw as weapon, hides inside the ghastly building. Sally is the only survivor of their confrontation with the infernal "family", and the horror is written in her face forever.

When the two young Independent film makers Tobe Hooper and Kim Henkel are looking for a publicity-stirring subject for a low budget 16mm-film in the early Seventies, the legendary Ed Gein case is more than okay for them. They write the script within six weeks, not caring much about the facts: the killer dressing in human skin becomes a whole bunch of brothers living and killing in a remote farmhouse in Texas (instead of Wisconsin). Though Hooper and Henkel do not care at all about the facts, the spirit of Ed Gein becomes much more apparent in THE TEXAS CHAINSAW MASSACRE than in most of the other films. There are mouldy farm rooms full of bone sculptures, the smell of dried blood and guts, the perverted redneck mentality of the killers regarding women as animals, cannibalism and desecration of graves. And there is a further dark spot on the US psyche which is taken up by Hooper and Henkel: the idea of the psychotic "family", the latently violent climate of the post-Sixties (after the breakdown of all Hippie-ideals). All this has its roots in the thematic complex around Charles Manson.

The critics have stigmatised Hooper's debut as a "splatter-orgy" for years, overlooking the film's real motivation. On the contrary, real gore-freaks won't enjoy the film. THE TEXAS CHAINSAW MASSACRE is subtly staged and very little blood is spilled. Like PSYCHO, the film works with the imagination of the audience and creates an atmosphere of terror where you believe in seeing things that are not there.

MOTEL HELL (1980) and SLAUGHTERHOUSE (1987) are among the more interesting of the many films inspired by Hooper's masterpiece.

TEXAS CHAINSAW MASSACRE 2 / USA 1986

Directed by Tobe Hooper. Written by L.M. Kit Carson. Camera: Richard Kooris. Music: Tobe Hooper & Jerry Lambert. With Dennis Hopper, Caroline Williams, Jim Siedow, Bill Moseley, Bill Johnson

As THE TEXAS CHAINSAW MASSACRE was a distorted snapshot of the early Seventies (peaceful kids are disembowelled by brutal rednecks), the highly underestimated sequel is about the consumerist Eighties. This time two show-offish yuppies are the first to be converted into "yuppie meat" by Leatherface. A radio moderator hearing the murder over CB-radio gets into a blood-soaked maelstrom of violence and, like Sally in part one, she experiences what it means to get caught by Leatherface, the cook, and the rest of the Texas Chainsaw family. Only a fanatical Texas Ranger (Dennis Hopper at his maniacal best) can free the DJ-lady from this horror nightmare.

Knowing full well that he won't be able to repeat the concentrated terror of his debut, Tobe Hooper is much more explicit concerning splatter and sarcasm now. In spite of financial problems, badly worked distribution, and censorship, TEXAS CHAINSAW MASSACRE 2 like only few other films oscillates brilliantly between pitch-dark humour and rigid, uncompromising brutality. Absurdly enough, but unsurprisingly given its unstinting gore, the ironic comic-book style sequel has more problems with censorship than the truly disturbing original in many countries (e.g. Germany, England).

TEXAS CHAINSAW MASSACRE 3: LEATHERFACE / USA 1989

Directed by Jeff Burr. Written by David Schow. Camera: James L. Carter. Music: Jim Manzie. With Kate Hodge, Ken Foree, R.A. Mihailoff, Viggo Mortensen

After the undeserved flop of the sequel, Hooper & Co. sold the rights of the Leatherface myth to another company. Hence this absolutely superfluous continuation of the story neither follows up part 2, nor has anything to do with the

THREE ON A MEATHOOK

original vision of Hooper. It is rather an uninspired remake of part 1, and still not the end to the series: in 1994, Kim Henkel the co-author of the original, tried to recreate the Chainsaw spirit. The only thing worth mentioning about his effort, RETURN OF THE TEXAS CHAINSAW MASSACRE (1994) is that his young main actors Matthew McConaughey and Renee Zellweger are now hot stars in Hollywood – though obviously not because of Henkel's picture.

THREE ON A MEATHOOK / USA 1973

Directed by William Girdler. Produced by John Asman, Lee Jones. Camera: William L. Asman. Music: Edward Dempley & William Girdler. With Charles Kissinger, James Pickett

The deserted countryside; meathooks, girls disappear. An old farmer kills young girls in bloodlust and makes his son responsible for these deeds. The immediate "Geinsploitation" forerunner of TEXAS CHAINSAW MASSACRE and DERANGED hardly achieves in any scene the intensity and atmosphere of its successors. Typical trash-filth of the early Seventies, creeping along viscously until it tears the viewer out of his lethargy with a few splatter scenes. Girdler has since remained faithful to the horror genre, but in his later films like GRIZZLY (1976) and THE MANITOU (1978) he devoted himself to man-eating bears and mutated demons.

GARY GILMORE

"Let's do it."

–Gary Gilmore's last words to the firing-squad

The Case

Gary Gilmore's doom stirred much publicity in the United states – especially because the murderer stood up for being sentenced to death, and some famous writers were interested in him.

Born in Oregon on December 4, 1940 Gary grew up full of hate against his alcoholic father. But he loved his mother and his younger brother. At the age of twelve his criminal "career" began with car theft and burglary. At fourteen he stole guns and soon he found himself in an institution for juvenile delinquents. Despite his intelligence and his talent for painting he soon went to the bad again after his release. At the age of 22 he was booked for robbery. The psychiatrists there called him "a classical sociopath". At the age of 35 Gary had already spent 18 years behind bars, many of them in solitary confinement. In 1976 he was released on probation and moved to his relatives'. He also got a job there.

Gary tried to narcotise himself with alcohol and painkillers. Nevertheless, his anger against society broke out. On July 19, 1976 he drove to a petrol station armed with a gun and robbed the attendant Max Jensen. Then he dragged the 24-year-old law student to the toilet, made him kneel down, and shot two bullets into his head. Looking for his girlfriend Nicole Barker on the following day he attacked 25-year-old Bernie Bushnell in a motel. Bushnell had to lie down on the ground with his face down. Then Gilmore shot him into the back of his head.

When the killer wanted to throw away his gun, he accidentally shot into his hand. A filling station attendant noticed that and phoned the police. Gary was soon seized. In his trial he did not defend himself, but insisted on being sentenced to death

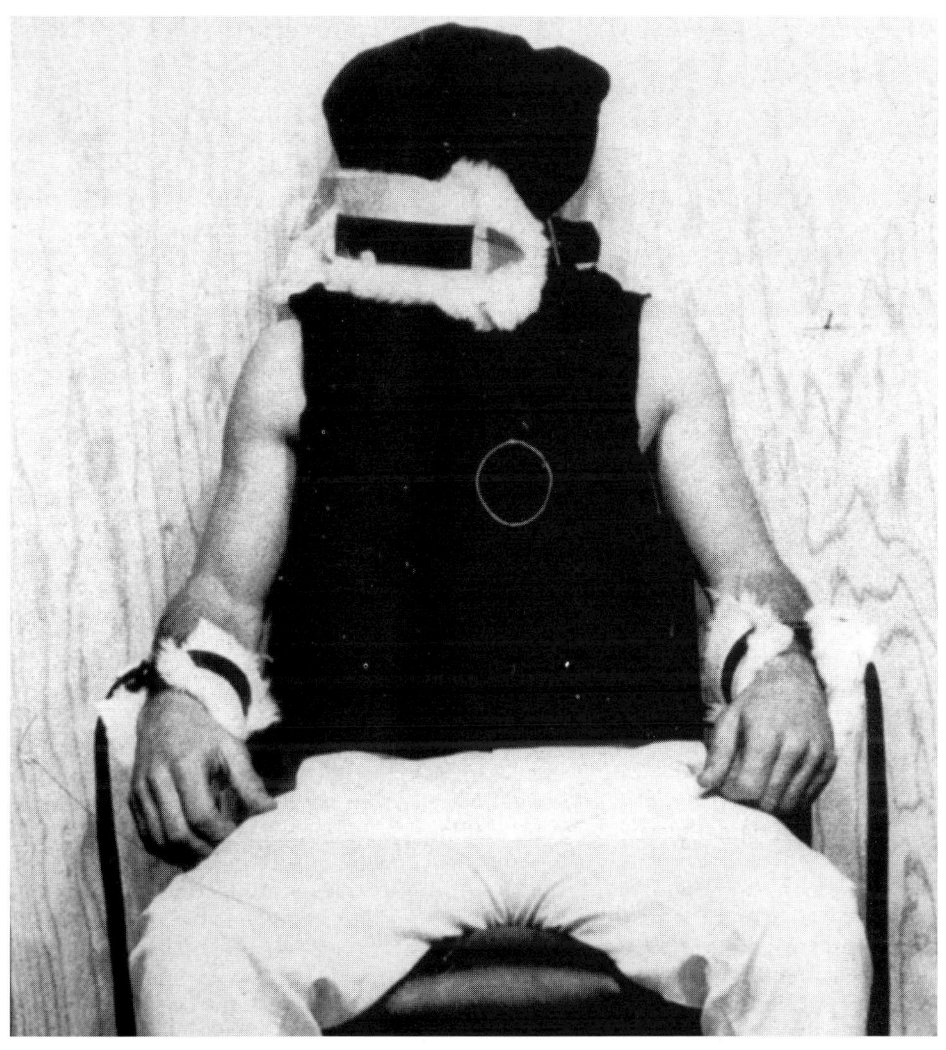

THE EXECUTIONER'S SONG

and executed as soon as possible. He was allowed to choose between the noose and the firing squad. Gilmore chose the latter. His execution took place on January 17, 1977. Bound to a chair he was shot by four policemen. This was the first execution in the USA after a more than ten years' break.

THE EXECUTIONER'S SONG / USA 1982 (TV)
Written and directed by Lawrence Schiller after a novel by Norman Mailer. Camera: Freddie Francis. Music: John Cacawas & Waylon Jennings. With Tommy Lee Jones, Rosanna Arquette, Christine Lahti, Eli Wallach, Jordan Clark
Right from the beginning the media were highly interested in Gary Gilmore. Norman Mailer was fascinated by the strange killer and wrote the novel *The Executioner's Song* about Gilmore and with Gilmore's help. He was awarded the Pulitzer Prize for the book. Then, shortly before his execution, Gary Gilmore sold the film rights to the

journalist Lawrence Schiller. The film that Gilmore was not able to see turns out to be one of the very rare really masterly examples of that rather dubious genre, TV documentary. This melancholic and bitter country-ballad tells about life, love, and the death of a killer driven by hate and frustration.

The film begun with Gilmore's personal participation, fades into his life in April 1976. Gary is released on probation and tries to start a new life with his cousin Brenda in Orem, Utah. He plunges into a love affair with Nicole Barker, an attractive blonde, but their initial romance is soon shaded by outbursts of aggression and slaps into the face of the fragile girl. Seemingly Gary cannot get rid of his burning hate and the traces of his past. He cannot forget that he has spent half of his life in reformatory schools and prisons, partly in high-security solitary confinement. Nicole sacrifices herself and there really are some flashes of hope, but then Gary commits the robbery and the two cold-blooded, motiveless murders in 1976.

In the ensuing trial the killer insists on being sentenced to death, although the death penalty has not been carried out in the States for ten years. Already on Death Row, the man who fights for his right to die attempts suicide twice with an overdose of pills after making a suicide pact with Nicole.

On a snowy winter's day in January 1977 Gary Gilmore celebrates his imminent extinction in prison together with his relatives, as the country singer Waylon Jennings is grievously crooning on the soundtrack. The following day he is executed by a firing-squad.

Beside the subtle camera work and the moving soundtrack (Gilmore himself suggested Jennings and his ballads) Lawrence Schiller owes everything to his superb actors, especially the then highly underrated, but since deservedly Oscar-decorated Tommy Lee Jones, who melts entirely into his character. His furrowed face mirrors the killer's pain, anger, and dark tragedy: Jones *is* Gilmore. He portrays the delinquent as a victim, but without excusing for a second his atrocious murders. Beside his sympathetic acting Rosanna Arquette impresses in one of her best roles, bringing Nicole to vivid life.

Postscript: During the writing of this book directress Agnieszka Holland prepared SHOT IN THE HEART, a cinematic version of the book by the same title of Mikal Gilmore, Gary's brother. The usually intense Elias Koteas (CRASH, 1996) will play the convicted murderer, also starring Giovanni Ribisi as Mikal, Sam Shepard as Frank Gilmore Sr., and Erik Bogosian as Lawrence Schiller.

The Werewolf Of Hanover

"Warte, warte nur ein Weilchen/dann kommt Haarmann auch zu dir/ mit dem kleinen Hackebeilchen/und er macht Hackefleisch aus dir." (Wait, wait a little moment, then Haarmann comes to you/With his little cleaver/he makes mincemeat of you.)

–German folksong

The Case

Haarmann's murder series deeply shook Hanover in the unstable and famine-stricken years after WW1 , a time when black-marketeers, refugees, and crooks tried to scrape a desperate living.

Friedrich Haarmann was born in Hanover as the last child of six. His father was a brutish ill-tempered boozer and seducer who often beat his son. His seven-year-older wife was slightly moronic and early bed-ridden, but she had brought a little fortune into the marriage. Spoilt by her, Fritz idolised his mother, but hated his father from an early age. He wished him in prison for the rest of his life. The pampered imbecile boy playing with dolls was to be drilled in military school, but was soon dismissed because of epilepsy. He molested little children and was committed to a mental institution. But soon he broke out. From then on he lived on minor thefts and frauds and repeatedly served his time. Moreover, he came into conflict with the police because of homosexual contacts; but when he began to work as an informer, they did not disturb his "business" anymore.

It remains a mystery when Haarmann began to kill, but his bloodlust increased from 1919 onwards. In 1919 he met Hans Grans, 20 years younger than him and from then on his partner in sex and crime. Hans Grans was a cynical fellow dominating his mentally inferior partner. Fritz Haarmann was in bondage to him and lived like a servant in their flat.

Haarmann preferably selected his victims at the train station. There he accosted mainly impoverished young men between 13 and 20. As in most of the cases they were looking for a job, he offered help and food and took them home. There he killed them – according to his own words – biting through their throats. Then he expertly cleaved the corpses, sold the flesh on the black market, and threw the skulls and the bones into the River Leine. He either sold his victims' clothes and belongings, or gave them Hans Grans.

When playing, some children found skulls in the river in May 1924. In an organised search 500 human bones were found. The public was shocked and terribly afraid of the child-slaughtering "werewolf". Becoming more and more suspicious the police began to observe Haarmann. On June 22 he was arrested for sexually molesting a boy. The police searched Haarmann's flat and discovered the clothes of some missing youths as well as some blood on the walls. The 45-year-old killer finally confessed, but also accused his lover Grans. He was charged with 27 murders. But he himself suggested it could have been 40.

Haarmann wanted to be sentenced to death rather than return to a mental institution. On the last day of his trial he said, "Do you believe I enjoyed killing people? I was sick for eight days after the first time. Sentence me to death. I am only asking for justice. I am not crazy. It is true that I often get into a state of mind where I don't know what I' m doing. But I am not crazy. Cut it short. Save me from this life which is only pain for me. I don't want to beg for mercy, nor will I appeal against my sentence. I only want to spend one last nice evening in my cell – with coffee, cheese, and cigars. Then I will curse my father and go to my execution as if it were my wedding."

On the following morning, December 20, 1924, Haarmann was beheaded. His accomplice Grans was sentenced to 12 years behind bars for aiding and abetting murder. The background of the case became known through the analysis *Haarmann – The Story Of A Werewolf* by Theodor Lessing, who followed the trial attentively.

FRITZ HAARMANN UND THEODOR LESSING — ZWEI DEUTSCHE SCHICKSALE / Germany 1990 (TV)

Directed by Gisela Marx & Andreas Thiel. Written by Gisela Marx. Camera: Thomas Erhard. With Michael Prelle, Walter Spiske, Frank Herzog

An instructive TV-documentary taking up and staging the detailed courtroom report of the contemporary writer Theodor Lessing. Not only Haarmann's way to the executioner is shown here, but also the atmosphere of his time, full of fear, social hardship and the growing influence of the Nazis. Lessing, a Jewish liberal and socialist condemned the society's merciless erasing of the "alien element" Haarmann, tried to put himself in the killer's mind, and criticised the circumstances of the time. This brought him serious conflicts with right-wing circles.

DER TOTMACHER (DEATHMAKER) / Germany 1995

Directed by Romuald Karmakar. Written by Romuald Karmakar & Michael Farin after the protocols of the conversations between Fritz Haarmann and Prof. Ernst Schulte. Camera: Fred Schuler. With Goetz George, Juergen Hentsch, Pierre Franckh, Hans Michael Rehberg

A film rigorously opting for cinematic anti-aesthetics and strictly opposing the usual approach to the topic of serial killing in the Nineties: no cop vs. killer plot crammed with action, no visual shocks, no spectacular make-up effects or morbid scenarios. DER TOTMACHER is a filmed intimate play based on the original interrogation files of the Haarmann case. Romuald Karmakar stages the protocols of a serial killer as a chilling psychological analysis very close to the borderline between film and drama. He only needs an interrogation room as the central setting, a doctor, a stenographer, and a killer. "To stage the film in only this room – this was the first important decision," Karmakar said in an interview. "I always let people tell stories in my films. But you are never shown what they are describing. As a viewer you have to try yourself to see the images behind the words".

DER TOTMACHER avoids obvious interpretations of the topic (e.g. Haarmann as a murderous herald of Hitler and the Nazi era) and depicts the case soberly and impartially. Karmakar totally refuses the moral position of comparable films. He wants to bewilder without delivering messages. An approach the young film-maker had already exemplified in a number of provocative and formally rigorous documentaries; e.g. in his last film WARHEADS (1993) mercenaries talk about their bloody and misanthropic profession over a length of three hours. In that film too the director does completely without comments, does not give any answers to many open questions, and hence sees himself confronted with a barrage of disapproval. "I refer to the motto of Immanuel Kant's enlightenment: 'Have the courage to make use of your own mind!' This is still valid today in the Nineties. Films where you have to think yourself are what I make."

DER TOTMACHER continues this uncompromising gesture into the feature film format. Again any reflection on the subject is left entirely to the viewer. That a scanty dialogue film like that has nevertheless become a box office-hit seems to be the merit of Germany's only superstar Goetz George, who lends Fritz Haarmann his voice and his face. Goetz George, who has probably seen the role of his life, breaks with his image from TV series and works himself into a histrionic t*our de force*. He gives the monster Haarmann human, tragic, sometimes even humorous traits. Yet behind these traits you can see his own virtuosity flicker more than once. Goetz George plays himself as Haarmann and changes the film into a personality show from time to time. Nevertheless, Romuald Karmakar's concept has succeeded and it can be regarded as genuinely sensational that DER TOTMACHER has already lured more than 500,000 people into the cinemas of Germany, the country of moronic, dull love & lifestyle comedies.

DIE ZAERTLICHKEIT DER WOELFE (TENDERNESS OF WOLVES) / Germany 1973

Directed by Ulli Lommel. Written by Kurt Raab. Camera: Juergen Juerges. Music: Johann Sebastian Bach, various hit-tunes, etc. With Kurt Raab, Jeff Roden, Margit Carstensen, Wolfgang Schreck, Rainer Werner Faßbinder, Ingrid Caven

This almost forgotten debut film of the Faßbinder-protégé Ulli Lommel shows scenes of the mass murderer's life in stylised images. Lommel transforms the real case into a homo-erotic vampire-fantasy. He reunites almost Faßbinder's entire crew. The mentor himself shortly appears as a slippery crook. But shaven-headed Kurt Raab, who portrays "The Werewolf of Hanover" and also wrote the script, ranges above all. As befits the film's title he plays Haarmann as a tender wolf, a sensitive, tenderly speaking paedophile strongly reminiscent of other examples in the history of cinema. When he bites into a boy's neck, Max Schreck's NOSFERATU – EINE SYMPHONIE DES GRAUENS (NOSFERATU, 1920) comes to one's mind. When Haarmann walks through foggy streets in the night, this evokes memories of Peter Lorre's child-slaughterer in Fritz Lang's M – EINE STADT SUCHT EINEN MOERDER.

Lommel sticks closely to the events depicted in Theodor Lessing's book, but although the Haarmann case is closely related to the time of the Weimar republic, he situates the story after WW2. Of course, post-war Hanover with all its black-marketeers, hookers, and fences is a good setting for Haarmann's bloody business, too, but the costumes are rather 1973. According to Paul Anthony Woods, Haarmann's lover appears "as a coiffured 70's smoothie, modelling the type of white suit/black skirt combination that Bryan Ferry would be found in that same year.

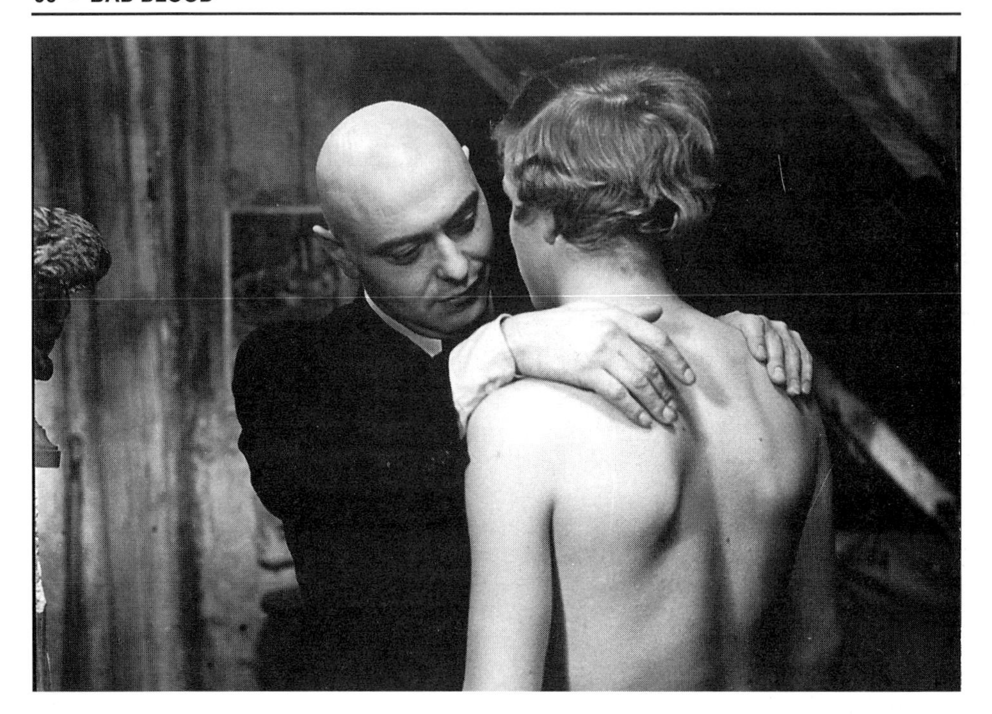

TENDERNESS OF WOLVES

Whether these touches are deliberate anachronisms or due to budget restrictions is anyone's guess." Abstraction, the breaking of conventions, or simply no money for historical costumes?

It is hard to say where Lommel's own directing begins and Faßbinder's influence ceases. Too many scenes in ZAERTLICHKEIT DER WOELFE are coined by this legend of German *film d'auteur*. There are the sentimental songs on the soundtrack, the conscious colour dramaturgy, and the filthy hangouts and bars visited by the murderer. The film wallows in a picturesque low-life milieu, but cannot convincingly mediate the horror taking place in Haarmann's claustrophobic attic room, the biting of Adam's apples and the dismembering of the corpses.

Soon Lommel left the circle around Faßbinder and headed to Hollywood. But he only became a negligible B-movie director there.

The McDonalds Killer

"Jimmy was a loner – not a bad boy, but someone who spent of his time by himself... He just did not want to mix, he didn't want to talk to people."
–A neighbour about James Huberty

The Case
In 1983, at the age of 41, James Huberty is fired from his place of work of many years' standing in Masillou, Ohio and falls into a crisis. In December 1983 he moves to San Ysidro with his family, because he hopes for better job-opportunities in California. Though he finds a job as a security-guard, he is soon fired again. This leads to frustration and depression. On July 1, 1984 Huberty leaves his apartment with a shotgun, a gun, a rifle, and plenty of ammo "to go hunting for humans", as he tells his wife. But she does not take her bewildered husband seriously. Yet he executes his intention in a most atrocious way in a nearby McDonalds restaurant, haphazardly spraying the junk-food temple with bullets. Within a few minutes 21 people die in the muzzle flash of the runner amok, 19 others are seriously injured. This mass shooting, one of the biggest in the US history of crime, only ends when Huberty himself dies in the hail of bullets from a rapidly-formed SWAT team.

BLOODY WEDNESDAY aka THE GREAT AMERICAN MASSACRE / USA 1985
Directed by Mark G. Gilhuis. Written by Philip Yordan. Camera: Robert Ryan. Music: Al Sendry. Produced by Gilmark-Visto. With Raymond Elemdorf, Pamela Baker, Navarre Perry, Teresa Mae Ellen, Jeff O'Haco
A man with a bag full of guns entering a McDonalds restaurant. The film begins to slacken, congeals to slow motion. Screams are hollering through the room, the click of the trigger sounds unnaturally loud and transforms into hysterical sustained fire. Panic breaking out, everywhere broken glass, jets of blood squirting onto the walls of the hamburger restaurant.

BLOODY WEDNESDAY

The suffocating final scene, reminiscent of Sam Peckinpah's films where the repressed madness of the amok killer breaks out at last, is everything you really remember of this B-movie. Within the 90 minutes leading up to this scene Gilhuis tries in vain to let the audience participate in the inner, mental war of the killer, a project doomed to failure by an over-taxed protagonist. This raw pseudo-psychological exploitation movie was produced immediately after Huberty's gruesome deed to profit from the US wide headlines. Gilhuis completely changes the character of the killer and the prehistory of the massacre. Borrowing from TAXI DRIVER and diverse horror movies he makes Huberty a typical hallucinating loser of amok-cinema, instead of the bewildered family father he really was.

The German Catholic Film Service hints at the film's unexpected cast: "a violent action film only interesting because the scriptwriter Philip Yordan has formerly excelled in JOHNNY GUITAR/1954, 55 DAYS AT PEKING/1963 or EL CID/1961, and the cutter Gene Ruggiero has worked for the Lubitsch-films NINOTCHKA, 1939 and THE SHOP AROUND THE CORNER, 1940". Names you would not have expected in the jungle of exploitation cinema.

JIM JONES

"Those who do not remember the past are condemned to repeat it."
–A slogan in the camp of Jim Jones

The Case

In the end of 1978 the pictures of a sect's collective suicide shocked the world-wide public. Almost 1000 corpses covered the ground deep in the jungle of Guyana. They had followed the last order of their psychopathic leader Jim Jones.

The later sect leader Jim Jones was born into a poor working-class family in Indiana in 1931. His father was a member of the local Ku Klux Klan and his mother allegedly an Indian. Already in his childhood the extraordinarily intelligent lone wolf was interested in the church, and began early to stand up against race hatred. He married in 1949, adopted seven children, and moved to Indianapolis as a preacher. In 1956 he founded "The Temple of the People" and was constantly attacked for his indefatigable dedication to the equal treatment of all races. In 1963 the sect moved to California with 150 members. Beside his preaching Jones engaged himself politically and founded two firms and several rehabilitation centres.

More and more people, predominantly African Americans, gathered around the charismatic man who was also celebrated as a faith-healer and a raiser from the dead from the early Seventies. Nevertheless, the Temple of the People and above all its leader slowly drifted into a turmoil of blackmail, abuse, sexual harassment, and – in the beginning only – verbal terror. Under pressure of numerous rumours and a negative image in the media, Reverend Jones transferred his temple to Guyana. There he founded Jonestown, praised by the sect as paradise on earth, in 1975. But armed guards stood at the doors of paradise. Iron discipline, hard compulsory work, and almost torture-like punishment ruled.

When in June 1978 some escaped members were spreading horror-news about Jonestown, congressman Ryan decided to check them out. On November 17, 1978 he arrived in Guyana accompanied by a TV team and the relatives of some Temple members. On the following day armed Jones disciples shot at the group at the

Jonestown, aftermath of "The White Night"

airport killing Ryan and three other people. Twenty people were seriously injured. That evening "The White Night", a weekly performed exercise in mass suicide, became horrible reality. Jones had a mixture of potassium cyanide and Kool-Aid, causing death within five minutes, distributed among his disciples. Little children died first. After a few minutes 912 people were dead – many after a little "assistance". Reverend Jones shot a bullet through his own head.

AMAZONIA aka INFERNO IN DIRETTA (CUT & RUN) / Italy 1985

Directed by Ruggero Deodato. Written by Cesare Frugani & Dardano Sacchetti. Camera: Emilio Loffredo. Music: Claudio Simonetti. With Lisa Blount, Leonard Mann, Willie Ames, Richard Bright, Richard Lynch, Michael Berryman, Eric Lasalle, Gabriele Tinti, John Steiner, Karen Black

Deodato, a veteran in the controversial, uniquely Italian genre of cannibal-film, made a name for himself with exceptionally shocking, realistic depictions of violence. Blood-operas like ULTIMO MONDO CANNIBALE (THE LAST SURVIVOR aka LAST CANNIBAL WORLD, 1976), or CANNIBAL HOLOCAUST (1979) lead to the justified suspicion that he had tortured and killed real animals without batting an eyelash. There were even rumours of sacrificed human lives. But Deodato merely had a very good special effects expert perfectly staging the brutal gore-scenes. You can argue about the cynical ideology of Deodato's oeuvre (if you want to apply such standards to "Z-movies" like that at all), but it is still a radical quality that CANNIBAL HOLOCAUST can really provoke and shock.

In AMAZONIA Deodato tries to repeat the success of his "classics" long after the ebbing away of the cannibal wave, but is thwarted by the strict censorship of the

AMAZONIA

Eighties. Again he sends a headline-horny team of reporters into the jungle, though instead of cannibals rivalling drug-gangs now reign there with brutal violence. You might ask what all this has to do with Jim Jones. Well, Deodato loves mixing reality with fiction. The head of one of the rivalling drug syndicates is a Vietnam veteran who had once been a faithful bloodhound of Jim Jones in Guyana.

BAD DREAMS / USA 1988

Directed by Andrew Fleming. Written by Andrew Fleming & Steven E. de Souza. Camera: Alexander Gruszynski. Music: Jay Ferguson. With Jennifer Rubin, Richard Lynch, Bruce Abbott, Harris Yulin, Sly Richardson

A "Jim Jones meets Charles Manson" conflation. After more than ten years of deep sleep the only survivor of a mass suicide finally wakes up. Then, in 1974, Cynthia had been a member of a cult called "Unity Fields" lead by a dangerous, charismatic preacher named Harris. Now, in 1988, she returns from her coma-like sleep. She is taken to a neuropsychiatric clinic where she is introduced to a Dr. Berrisford. He wants to help her to remember the events leading to the self-annihilation of the sect.

So the sensitive patient takes part in a group therapy for people with personality disturbances. In the course of the treatment traumatic fragmentary pieces of memory come up. It seems as if "Unity Fields" is not extinguished yet. More and more often Cynthia finds her way back to the origin of the disaster, a ritual self-burning whereby all the other members of the cult died in the flames. Dead Mr. Harris appears to her like a zombie who wants to have back his "child of love". Seemingly motiveless suicides happen around the tortured girl. It seems as if the dreadful guru

GUYANA TRAGEDY: THE STORY OF JIM JONES

had not died, but is going to re-incorporate his "servant" into the community.

While the idea of mass suicide and the icy character of Harris are obviously based on Jim Jones and his "Kool-Aid-festival" in Guyana, there are also inspirations derived from the Manson-murders woven into the film. BAD DREAMS, Fleming's debut, derives its charm from the clash of past and present as well as a subliminally psychedelic atmosphere. There are moments of forceful intensity (e.g. when musical quotes from the Sixties are contrasted to shocking dream-sequences). When a juvenile suicidal of Cynthia's therapy group slashes himself to the chords of Sid Vicious' version of "My Way", this is modern punk-nihilism.

Fleming's heroine must understand that nothing has changed while she has been sleeping. People are still on their quest for values and meanings – and failing. The therapy group where one after the other commits suicide is like her Hippie-commune of the Sixties. A void reigns where all ideals have been smashed to pieces. Finally it becomes evident that friendly Dr. Berrisford is the true madman. He drives his patients into suicide with overdoses of LSD.

GUYANA: CULT OF THE DAMNED / Mexico-Spain-Panama 1979

Written, directed, and produced by René Cardona jr. Camera: Leopoldo Villasenor. Music: George S. Price, Nelson Riddle & Bob Summers. With Stuart Whitman, Bradford Dillman, Gene Barry, Joseph Cotten, Yvonne De Carlo, Jennifer Ashley

This sensationalist quickshot from the Mexican exploitation king René Cardona Jr, whose father had already been notorious for his ultra-cheap wrestling movies (Santo), was scorned by critics as one of the most nauseous documentary drama of all times. Specialised in making films out of Yellow Press headlines he had also exploited the Bermuda Triangle (IL TRIANGOLO DELLE BERMUDE, 1978), tornadoes (CYCLONE, 1977) and the famous cannibal jet-crash in the Andes (SURVIVE!, 1976). For inexplicable reasons (or perhaps legal ones) the real names of the historical figures involved in the Jones case have been changed, though not to unintelligibility: Hollywood-B-relegated Stuart Whitman does not really deliver a Oscar-performance as Reverend Jim Johnson(!). "Extremely sleazy", writes *Psychotronic* specialist Michael Weldon. Not surprisingly, CULT OF THE DAMNED was to be seen in the States in a double-feature with AMIN: THE RISE AND FALL (1980), the Idi Amin saga.

GUYANA TRAGEDY: THE STORY OF JIM JONES / USA 1980 (TV)

Directed by William A. Graham. Camera: Gil Hubbs. Music: Elmer Bernstein. With Powers Boothe, Ned Beatty, Veronica Cartwright, Brad Dourif, James Earl Jones, Dianne Ladd, Randy Quaid, Meg Foster

As a 4-hour-long US TV production in two instalments, the story of the rise and fall of Reverend Jones, who took 912 people with him when he died, won several Emmys. Later on a 90-minute version was produced for the video market.

As you might have expected the film deals with the dubious inner life of the sect and focuses on the dark sides of Jim Jones, which became dominant in the course of the Seventies. Here is shown what disappointed ex-disciples told the media: instead of peace and equality, there was a strict hierarchy. Spying, hour-long interrogations, and physical punishment were the order of the day. Jones preached austerity, but lived in luxury, while his disciples lacked the most elementary things after they had given him all their property. Powers Boothe, who was awarded an Emmy, characterises the Reverend as a hypochondriac and conceited almost rock star-like figure addicted to pills. His disciples have to call him "father" and he claims the right to choose women and men for sexual service. He separates or brings together couples at pleasure, or takes children away from their parents. The everyday life in the jungle is depicted as rather frightening. The paranoid Reverend holds his more and more extreme sermons via loudspeakers, and threatens with mass suicide via CB-radio. Mass suicide is rehearsed once in a week in the so-called "White Night" and is a test of faith for his disciples. Unfortunately the film does not manage to transcend the framework of an average TV production when the "White Night" becomes reality. It remains in the censored mode of the medium and hints only vaguely at the horror. Finally THE GUYANA TRAGEDY remains a superficial collection of facts.

MANGIATI VIVI DAI CANNIBALI (EATEN ALIVE) / Italy 1980

Directed by Humbert Humbert alias Umberto Lenzi. Camera: Federico Zanni. Music: Carlo Maria Cordio & Maria Fiamma Maglione. With Mel Ferrer, Robert Kerman, Ivan Rassimov, Janet Agren, Paola Senatore, Me Me Lai, Meg Fleming

In the middle of New York fanatical sect-members shoot at people with poisoned blow-pipe arrows. Evidently, they are members of a group which, led by a certain Jonathan(!), had renounced civilisation in order to celebrate mystical rituals of purification in the jungle of Papua-New Guinea. The protagonist of the film has lost her sister to the dubious guru and is now on the way into the jungle to free her.

Arriving there she finds a sexist violent slave-hell you cannot escape from. For outside Jonathan's empire the cannibalistic natives of the island are hiding in ambush. While Jonathan and his disciples are committing collective suicide, people are dismembered and eaten alive outside the camp....

It's cannibal time! In the early Eighties this splatter sub-genre from Italy was in full bloom. Blood-spurting entertainment through pain, between involuntarily funny dialogue, racist intermezzos, and extreme sexism. If you can gulp all this down, it remains a gory trash classic from Lenzi, director of the superlative CANNIBAL FEROX.

WERNER KNIESEK

"I love it, when women tremble in fear of death in front of me. It is like an addiction. You cannot stop it."

–Werner Kniesek to the investigating judge

The Case

"Murder on a prison vacation, out of mere lust of killing!" This headline shocked the Austrian public in 1980 and lead to serious attacks against the Austrian practice of the execution of sentence. Probably the then 34-year-old Werner Kniesek from Salzburg, who had been diagnosed "seriously abnormal but not mentally ill" by a court psychiatrist, should have been locked away from mankind for the rest of his life.

Werner Kniesek was born in 1946 as the illegitimate son of a widow and an African-American GI. Werner, the cute "nigger-baby" and everybody's darling became a well-behaved polite boy. Only as an apprentice did he stray to the bad. He began to steal and ran away from home.

On June 5, 1962 Werner Kniesek decided to realise his long-planned escape abroad. He stole a greater amount of money from his mother, who had threatened to turn him over to welfare, and stabbed her with a bread-knife screaming "Yes, Mummy, you must die! You can't help it!". Then he left his seriously injured, bleeding mother behind and went to Hamburg by train. Two days later he was arrested.

He was sentenced, but two years later released from prison, though only for a little while. Soon the young man, who meanwhile had married a prostitute, found himself behind bars again for several burglaries and the attempted murder of a 73-year-old woman.

In January 1980 he was given a three days' holiday from prison in order to be able to look for a job. He was due to be released a few weeks later. From Upper Austria he travelled to St. Poelten where he sneaked into the villa of the 55-year-old widow Gertrude Altreiter. Walking through the house he met Gertrude Altreiter's 27-year-old handicapped son sitting in his wheelchair. "I'll kill you", Kniesek said, "but we have time."

When the mother came home from shopping with her daughter Ingrid, he threatened the women with a gas pistol, tied them, and dragged each of them in a separate room. The girl tore her clothes off and begged, "I'll do everything you want, but don't kill us." Kniesek only had a cruel smile for her fear. "I only want to see you all die", he replied. First he strangled the paralysed son, showed the seriously ill mother the corpse, then killed her, too. After sadistically abusing her for hours he finally strangled the 25-year-old girl. Even the Altreiters' cat had to die. "Her meowing annoyed me", he said later.

He spent the night sleeping beside the dead, stuffed the corpses into the trunk of their Mercedes, and drove to Salzburg. There he stirred suspicion, because he nervously fumbled in a briefcase full of money. When Kniesek returned to the stolen car, the cops were already waiting. After an unsuccessful suicide attempt in his cell he confessed his deeds. "I killed out of sheer lust [...] I gave the mother cardiac drops to make her experience her agony better."

Again diagnosed responsible for his deeds, the murderer himself asked for being committed to an institution for mentally abnormal delinquents. He confessed to have had a strong urge to kill from his childhood on, and added that he could not exclude further murders. Werner Kniesek got a life sentence. His attempt to escape in 1983 caused again a scandal.

ANGST aka FEAR / AUSTRIA 1983

Directed by Gerald Kargl. Written by Gerald Kargl & Zbigniew Rybczynski. Camera: Zbigniew Rybczynski. Music: Klaus Schulze, With Erwin Leder, Silvia Rabenreither, Edith Rosset, Rudolf Goetz

An exceptionally haunting contribution to the unfortunately rather boring post-war history of Austrian cinema. Whereas the majority of Austrian directors avoid controversial topics as well as straight genre-cinema, ANGST enters territories where True Crime film and horror melt into each other, twilight zones in which you can find most of the films discussed in this book. In his only film Gerald Kargl does not shrink back from staging taboo subjects like violence, repulsion, and sadism to full effect.

Kargl and his co-author and cameraman Zbigniew Rybczynski were inspired by the drastic case of Werner Kniesek, which excited the Austrian media as well as the Austrian public in 1980. But after studying the police files and some own investigation, they decided to change the names and the details.

Almost narrating in real time the film begins with the release of a criminal remaining nameless after ten years behind bars. This is paralleled with his immediate murder fantasies. Just having left the prison he tries to strangle a female cabdriver, but fails. Whipped by his feverish thoughts (spoken from off-screen they represent the lion's share of verbal communication on a soundtrack almost void of dialogue) and the pulsating synthesiser track by Klaus Schulze, the delinquent flees through a little forest and comes into a high-class suburban district. He breaks into an abandoned house and only meets a mentally handicapped young man in a wheelchair there. But a few minutes later the two other residents of the weekend villa, an elderly woman and her daughter, appear.

And while the killer is raving in off-screen about his destroyed childhood, sexual fantasies, rape and abuse (a monologue distilled from Kniesek's statements, but also from the confessions of the German mass murderer Peter Kuerten), he throws himself madly at the villa's residents and starts his acts of killing. He drowns the handicapped man in the bathtub, strangles the mother, and slaughters the daughter with a kitchen knife. Then he abuses her *post mortem*. This all is depicted in endlessly long scenes striving for realism, the camera rushing through the house like a runner amok. But an equal time-span is dedicated to the "afterplay" of the murders. The film shows the killer wash himself, drag the corpses into the trunk and finally, driven by madness, rush directly into the arms of the police.

It is a brave attempt to show three murders from beginning to end in all their

ANGST

gruesome and long-drawn-out details, without shortening them to effective shock moments. After all, Kargl wants to portray violence in all its bluntness and minuteness of detail. He is not at all interested in aestheticism. Yet reducing the plot exclusively to the murders themselves is not only radical, but also bears a flaw. Where no traditionally constructed story is told, where there are neither turns and twists in the plot, nor suspense in the dialogues, the viewer's tension and mental participation drop considerably in the course of the film. The intentional tormenting stretch of the plot might sometimes cause a viewer to slide nervously to and fro on his seat.

Nevertheless, ANGST deserves praise for its cinematic delivery of the evidence that the disorientated Austrian soul does not at all differ from the American, or the German, or whatever. Henry Lee Lucas could have told about his life in just the same way the impressive Erwin Leder describes his childhood in fragmented off-phrases. Fortunately, ANGST also reacts against the simplistic cataloguing of characters like Kniesek, in spite of some psychoanalytical reference in the spoken text. Nobody really manages to penetrate their surface. Concerning the species of court psychiatrists and their diagnoses as well as the whole difficult complex of "rehabilitation/illness and cure" the film simply says "Fuck you!" The film deals neither with the reactionary point of view – the legal three days off from prison caused the villa-murders – nor with a possible humanist counter-argument. ANGST only shows, depicts, but abstains from an own opinion.

Like MAN BITES DOG or HENRY, PORTRAIT OF A SERIAL KILLER, ANGST says the following: there are people among us who enjoy torturing and killing others, despite a century-long process of civilisation. Now deal with it.

The Bitch Of Buchenwald

Even within the rigid fascist hierarchies of the SS Death Camps – whose sole purpose was the facilitation of mass murder – one woman's activities mark her above the rest, and single her out as a rare example of a female psychopath in the tradition of "Countess Dracula" Elizabeth Bathory. While her colleagues merely carried out the prosaic extermination ordered by their superiors, Ilse Koch took advantage of the system to refine her own very special brand of maverick butchery and perversion.

Koch (born 1906) was married to the Kommandant of Buchenwald, one of the most notorious of the Nazi internment camps. She would ride around the camp on a white horse, savagely whipping prisoners at will, and also press-ganged many male inmates into sexual service, to satisfy her nymphomaniac urges. She was, by all accounts, singularly plain and unattractive. But Ilse Koch's real perversions were even more sinister, and place her in a category of necro-sadism rivalled only by Ed Gein and a few select others. She was regularly engaged in killing, and would order the death by lethal injection of any prisoner who bore an "interesting" tattoo. She would then remove the corpse's skin and fashion it into household artefacts such as lampshades or book bindings, or even articles of clothing such as gloves.

Koch was tried for mass murder after the liberation of Buchenwald, but escaped death by managing to get pregnant. She was later sentenced to life imprisonment, and at the time her psychiatric report described her as "a perverted, nymphomaniacal, hysterical, power-mad demon". She finally hanged herself in Aibach prison in 1967.

ILSA, SHE-WOLF OF THE SS / Canada 1974
Directed by Don Edmonds. Written by Jonah Royston. Camera: Glenn Roland. With Dyanne Thorne, Sandi Richman, Jo Jo Deville, Uschi Digard
In the Seventies, when liberal laws allowed daring films in many countries, exploitation genres like kung fu, cannibal, women in prison, and torture camp films flooded the market. Today these films, without regarding their "message" often

appear like sledgehammers into the face of mainstream common-sense. Despite a few unwittingly ridiculous moments, ILSA, SHE-WOLF OF THE SS ranks among the darkest oeuvres of that decade. The film "wants to show things to avoid them ever happening again", but does this in all possible explicitness and gloating detail. Ilsa, alias Dyanne Thorne, represents an almost Pasolinian combination of sadism and fascism, a

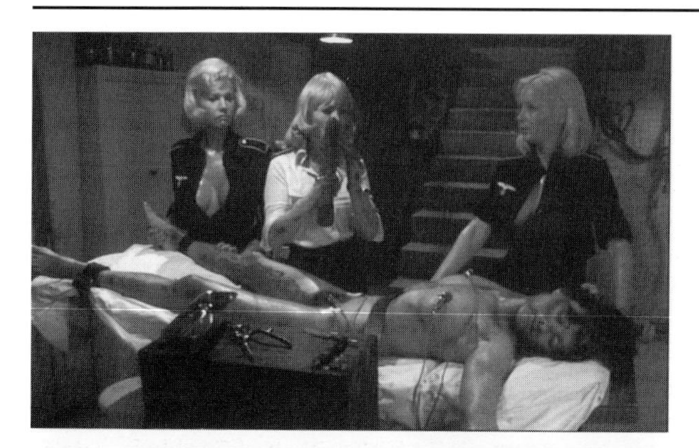

ILSA, SHE WOLF OF THE SS

dominatrix of death: the perfidious Nazi killer and pervert Ilse Koch in the body of a Russ Meyer ultra-vixen. Produced by exploitation mogul David Friedman, ILSA was the ultimate entry in a series of Nazi sleaze movies inaugurated by Lee Frost's LOVE CAMP 7 (1969) and John Hayes' SHE DEVILS OF THE SS (1970).

The atrocities committed in ILSA include: naked slave girls infected with disfiguring diseases and maggots; girls tortured by nail-pulling or being fucked with an electrified dildo; mass floggings and lynchings; and girls exploded in compression chambers or boiled alive. All this is served up with lashings of softcore sex focusing on Thorne's overdeveloped mammaries. Last but not least is Ilsa's preferred punishment for those male inmates who fail to satiate her ravenous sexual needs: the very next morning she has them viciously castrated without anaesthetic – often preferring to make the bloody cut herself.

A blonde "Hitlerjunge" shoots Ilsa at the end of the film, but this could not prevent its producers from doing two sequels: ILSA, HAREM KEEPER OF THE OIL-SHEIKS (1975) and ILSA, THE TIGRESS OF SIBERIA (1977). In these, Dyanne Thorne provides her sadistic talent for an Islamic and a Stalinist regime respectively, although neither is as graphic or disturbing as the original. In 1977 Thorne appeared in Jess Franco's WIP sleaze-trip GRETA, HOUSE WITHOUT MEN, which soon became known by the alternative title ILSA, THE WICKED WARDEN – much to the dismay of ILSA's creators.

MEIN KAMPF II aka SECRETS OF THE NAZI WAR CRIMINALS / Sweden 1956

Directed by Tore Sjoberg. Written by Erik Holm. With Ilse Koch, Josef Goebbels, Adolf Hitler, Heinrich Himmler et al

This harrowing documentary, which includes footage of mass extermination from the Nazi Death Camps, was the first film to expose the horrors of Ilse Koch and her collection of human skin ornaments, revealing her to be no "mere" war criminal, but a genuine female psychopath torturing, killing and skinning her victims under cover of night and fog.

The Case
The twins Ronald and Reginald Kray were born on October 24, 1933 and grew up in poverty in the notorious London East End. They allegedly had a very close, almost telepathic relation and a strong mother fixation.

Already as teenagers they performed as practised boxers and together with their older brother Charles they acted with extraordinary brutality in various street gangs. In 1954 they opened their first bar, which among other things became a meeting place for London criminals. The Kray twins called themselves "The Firm", an enterprise with Reg as the manager. Ron, called "Colonel" organised the bloody hold-ups and the battles with hostile gangs. In the end of 1956 Ron was sentenced to three years for grievous bodily harm. In 1959 he fell ill with schizophrenia. The illness, alcohol, and medication reinforced his outbursts of violence and made him more and more unpredictable. In 1966 he killed a rival gangster in rage. Reg, who had married in the meantime and had successfully expanded their criminal empire, was hardly able to stop his brother's escalation of violence. After Reg too had committed a murder in 1967, the Krays were betrayed to the police by their underlings, suffering from Ron's brutality.

Around New Year's Day 1969 their trial began. It was a big media event and became the longest and most expensive trial England had seen. On March, 8 the Krays both got a life sentence to be completed in separate prisons. Ronald Kray died in spring 1995, Reggie in 2001.

KRAYS, THE / GB 1990
Directed by Peter Medak. Written by Philip Ridley. Camera: Alex Thompson. Music: Michael Kamen. With Gary Kemp, Martin Kemp, Billie Whitelaw, Kate Hardie, Susan Fleetwood.
Oscillating between realism and stylisation, flashbacks of their childhood and their activities in the Sixties, Peter Medak's film shows snapshots from the life of the Kray

THE KRAYS

brothers. It tells of two violent criminals stylising themselves as the Robin Hoods of London, from their youth as boxers to the time of the "Firm". They live in luxury with blackmailed money and the profits of their bars, but also support poor families and donate plenty of money for charity performances. They are well known and feared throughout the city. Yet many VIPs, even from far away Hollywood are among their friends. Finally Ron drifts into schizophrenia. He beats up gang members or friends, attacks them with a knife, or shoots at them for banal reasons.

Medak's diagnosis is everything but romanticising. Together with his scriptwriter Philip Ridley (who directed the fantastic film THE REFLECTING SKIN, 1990) he works out stringently the psychotic, depressing aspects of the dangerous brothers. THE KRAYS avoids every typical attitude of a gangster ballad. Perhaps it was a bit daring to cast the ex-Spandau Ballet-poppers Gary and Martin Kemp as the Kray twins; though neither are at all embarrassing in their acting, they are not really captivating on the screen either.

It took another film to get to know Peter Medak's real talent. ROMEO IS BLEEDING (1993, featuring Gary Oldman) is a violent, paranoid noir-meditation on a corrupt cop in Los Angeles. A wicked masterpiece compared to which THE KRAYS seems like a preparatory exercise, though already showing some promise.

The Vampire Of Düsseldorf

"I used to stroll at night through the Hofgarten very often, and in the spring of 1930 I noticed a swan sleeping at the edge of the lake. I cut its throat. The blood spurted up, and I drank from the stump and ejaculated."

–Peter Kuerten

The Case

Peter Kuerten's series of murders triggered of mass hysteria in Germany in the late Twenties. His preoccupation with blood brought him the nickname "The Vampire of Düsseldorf".

In the beginning there was a youth whose early life was a virtual blueprint for mass murderers. In 1883 he was born in Cologne as one of 13 children and grew up in a poor family with a brutal father, a heavy drinker who raped his wife in front of the children and was imprisoned for attempted incest. According to his own confessions Peter Kuerten committed his first murders at the age of nine, when he drowned two playmates in the Rhine. He tortured animals, vagabonded, and stole as a youth. From the age of 13 onwards he satisfied his sex-drive with incestuous acts, excessive masturbation, and sodomy with sheep, pigs, and goats. He stabbed the animals during intercourse to get deeper satisfaction.

At the age of fourteen he was seized for theft. With short breaks he spent twenty years of his life in prison, especially for robbery and fraud, but also for the attempted strangulation of a girl. After a flunked attempt he committed his first sexual murder on March 25, 1913. He strangled a 13-year-old girl when she was asleep, slashed her throat, and pierced her private parts. Blood had always been an important sexual stimulant for him. He knocked down women in broad daylight, because their open wounds aroused him.

In 1921, after his release, he got to know a former prostitute who had been serving time for killing her fiancé, and married her. Until he died his wife was the only person for whom he was able to develop normal feelings of infatuation. In 1925 he

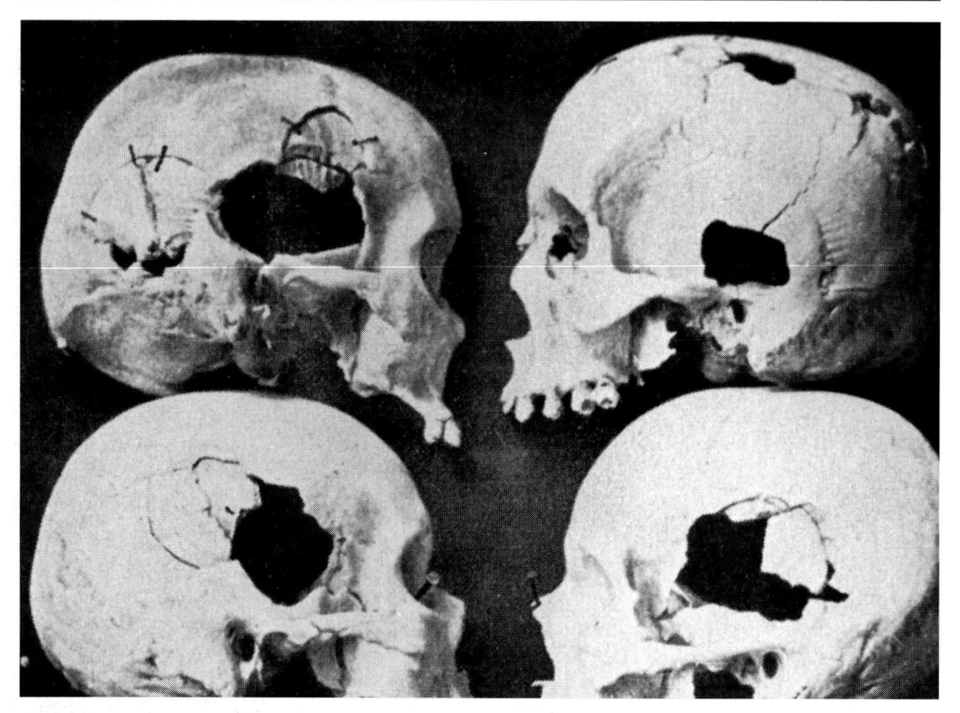

The smashed skulls of some of Kuerten's young victims

moved to Düsseldorf with her, got as job and seemingly lived a conventional life. But at the same time he started his most gruesome series of crimes. Between 1925 and 1928 he attempted to strangle four women and men and committed seventeen acts of arson. In February 1929 he stabbed a woman 27 times. A man whose blood he drank died of 24 stabs with a pair of scissors. In August he stabbed men and women in their backs in the streets. On August 24, 1929 "The Monster of Düsseldorf" garrotted a 5-year-old and a 14-year-old girl. In September and October he killed or injured several women with a hammer and raped them in some cases.

After annihilating a 5-year-old girl he wrote a letter to a newspaper telling where the corpse of an earlier victim could be found. Probably, this was an allusion to Jack the Ripper, who he strongly admired. Panic was reigning in Düsseldorf, but after ten months of terror the murders suddenly stopped. Only the attacks on women went on. On May 14, 1930 he tried to strangle a handmaid in a forest. This finally brought the police on his track. But Kuerten noticed the policemen when they were looking for him in his block of flats, and confessed to his wife that he was the monster. She should betray him to get the reward. On May 24, 1930 she gave in to his wish, reported him to the police, and ended one of the greatest searches in the history of Germany. 900,000 people had been denounced and interrogated as possible delinquents.

Neighbours and friends could not believe that Kuerten was the "vampire". He had always been regarded as quiet, intelligent, and industrious. He had refined manners and displayed a slight touch of a dandy. Because he was interested himself in the motives for his murders, he worked together with the psychiatrist Berg after his seizure. Finally he believed himself that they had been sexually motivated. Even the reconstruction of his murders and his confessions brought him orgasms. The trial

M (1951)

began on April 13, 1931. Peter Kuerten had to sit in a cage. "The King of Perverts" was sentenced to death for murder in nine cases, and on July 2 he was guillotined. He hoped to be able to hear his blood flow and called his execution "the pleasure that ends all pleasures".

M / USA 1951

Directed by Joseph Losey. Written by Norman Reilly Raine, Leo Katcher, and Waldo Salt (after a script by Thea von Harbou, Fritz Lang, Paul Falkenberg, Adolf Jansen, Karl Vash; based on an article by Egon Jacobson). Camera: Ernest Laszlo. Music: Michel Michelet. With David Wayne, Howard da Silva, Luther Adler, Raymond Burr

M (1931)

Seymour Nebenzahl, the second producer of Fritz Lang's original M was responsible for this Hollywood remake of the German classic. First Nebenzahl tried to recruit the director of the original version, but Fritz Lang declined with thanks as well as his protagonist Peter Lorre who, 20 years later, found himself too old for the role. So the difficult project was handed over to the Englishman Joseph Losey, who transplanted the story of the German child-murderer into Los Angeles in the Fifties – and hence did not refer much to Peter Kuerten any more.

Losey, an alert observant of neurotic bruises and human abysses – see his masterpiece THE SERVANT (1963) – basically copied Lang's original version, but foregrounded the sexual motives of the obsessed killer which had been concealed in 1931.

M – EINE STADT SUCHT EINEN MOERDER (M) / Germany 1931

Directed by Fritz Lang. Written by Thea von Harbou, Fritz Lang, Paul Falkenberg, Adolf Jansen, Karl Vash; based on an article by Egon Jacobson. Camera: Fritz Arno Wagner & Gustav Rathje. Music: Edvard Grieg (after motifs from "Peer Gynt"). With Peter Lorre, Ellen Widmann, Inge Landgut, Gustav Gruendgens

A classic of early German cinema shot in sharp black-and-white images. With the story of the child-murderer Franz Becker, who is not only chased by the police but also by gangsters (with his gruesome deeds Becker offends gangland's code of honour) the masterly filmmaker Fritz Lang managed to accomplish an important forerunner of modern psycho-killer films. Peter Lorre melts into the character of the friendly whistling wolf in sheep's clothes and delivers one of the most fascinating performances of his career.

"The Killer Is Among Us" was the first draft-title of the crime story elaborated by the productive couple Fritz Lang and Thea von Harbou. The Nazis, then rapidly gaining political influence smelled an allusion to Hitler in that title and demanded a change. But Lang did not have decidedly political intentions. He was rather inspired by Peter Kuerten's disturbing deeds and the panic and hysteria the "vampire" had caused in 1930. As the NS-bosses considered the mass murderer topic much more harmless than political criticism, Lang got the okay and could do the film.

The film censors fought the finished opus long before they allowed it to be screened and to captivate a world-wide audience with its dazzling description of a mass murderer.

LE VAMPIRE DE DÜSSELDORF / France-Italy-Spain 1964

Directed by Robert Hossein. Written by Robert Hossein & Claude Dessily, G. Tabet, A. Tabet. Camera: Emanuel Machuel. Music: André Hossein. With Robert Hossein, Marie-France Pisier, Roger Dutoit, Paloma Valdes, Annie Anderson

If you wanted to set up a macabre ranking of the most bestial sex-killers of the 20th century, Peter Kuerten would definitely be (at least) near the top. Studying the biography of "The Vampire of Düsseldorf", the details of his murders, and his filed confessions, you are hit by the pungent stench of death, a stench that is still overpowering in the modern age of more and more extreme serial killers and amok killers. So it should be regarded as a courageous act that someone like the director, initiator, and protagonist Robert Hossein dared to work up that case authentically and ambitiously in 1964. After all, at that time the story was still too shocking and disgusting for a wide audience.

But when you watch the film, you become aware of a fundamental misunderstanding. Hossein, a second-rate star of the French cinema of the Sixties (in mainstream films like the ANGELIQUE series) was more interested in an atmospheric picture of Germany on the eve of fascism than in a psychological analysis of a mass murderer. The "Evangelischer Filmdienst" (a Protestant film service) says correctly; "Hossein's symbolically overloaded Kuerten is a childish picture of the philistine German and a mysteriously gloomy pathological event. Yet the Nazis were no members of a secret society, but rather threatened Mabuse's craving for power at any price, if you want to use a film metaphor. Hossein has understood nothing of that."

Even worse than the blurred ideological significance of its Kuerten character is the film's vehement intention to correct the image of the sex monster in a human shape. Hossein portrays Kuerten as a silent, sensitive man whose facade does not give away anything of the inner nightmares tormenting him. Rather reminiscent of a painter or poet, the killer moves like an apathetic daydreamer through a scenery of backyards and night-clubs. What is the result of Hossein's interpretation? You do not even get an idea of the terror paralysing the city, Kuerten's sexual brutality, or his deeply rooted misanthropy.

Monsieur Bluebeard

"Is every smoking chimney and every bad smell proof that a body is being burned?"
–Henri-Désiré Landru

The Case

The hubbub of WW1 was in favour of the murderous activities of the French Bluebeard, Landru, who was put to death for murder in 11 cases.

Born in Paris in 1869, Landru initially wanted to become a clergyman. Then he went to the army, but ended up as a shop attendant. In 1893 he married a remotely related cousin and had all in all four children with her. After he had been duped by his boss, he started a criminal career full of thefts and frauds, only interrupted by several terms of imprisonment. Perhaps revenge had been his initial motif. From 1914 the bearded Landru scraped through as a marriage impostor. Through relevant adds he got to know wealthy middle-aged widows and exploited them financially and sexually.

Although he was rather small and not at all attractive, many women succumbed to his charm and moved into his out-of-the-way cottage near Paris. There the women, as well as the son of a widow and a destitute chambermaid, disappeared without a trace. One day the relatives of two missing women got to know each other in their investigation. Moreover, it came out that the mutual marriage impostor was Henri Landru, who was also wanted for other offences.

When he was arrested in April 1919, he unsuccessfully tried to hide a black notebook. It became the main incriminating evidence in his trial. The names of his victims, correspondence, profits, and expenses are painstakingly noted there. Yet when searching the cottage the police found neither corpses nor murder instruments, only numerous unidentifiable bone splinters beside a stove.

In the two years of detention pending trial Landru remained stubbornly silent. Then the trial began, observed by a large audience. "Bluebeard" bragged of having had 283 women, constantly protested his innocence eloquently, but refused to talk about the whereabouts of the missing women and the accusations of murder. His defence was entirely based on the missing corpses. His then 29-year-old mistress Segret, who left France later on, witnessed for him. But in spite of the jury's sympathy and his constant protests of innocence, Henri-Désiré Landru was sentenced to death and guillotined on February 25, 1922.

BARBE BLEU (BLUEBEARD) / Italy-France 1972

Directed by Luciano Sacripanti. Written by Edward Dmytryk, Ennio de Concini, and Maria Pia Fusco. Camera: Gabor Pogany. Music: Ennio Morricone. With Richard Burton, Raquel Welch, Virna Lisi, Natalie Delon, Marilu Tolo

The myth of mass-murderer Bluebeard is old. It goes back to Marshall Gilles de Rais, who in the 15th century kidnapped hundreds of boys and brutally slaughtered them in his castle. The term went through several permutations until the time of WW1, when the 50-year-old antique dealer Henri Landru was awarded this nickname (for the many women he killed in his out-of-the-way cottage and his eye-catching beard). Word of "Bluebeard" wandered through the international press and it even became a *mot*, a familiar quotation in France. The former killer of adolescent boys had become a charming gentleman promising marriage to women but tempting them into their doom.

In this version from 1972 Richard Burton plays an Austrian aristocrat, millionaire, and leader of a radical right-wing movement, who kills his wives to conceal his impotency. Scrapisanti clumsily tries to point out too simplistic relations between disturbed sexuality and fascism. BLUEBEARD culminates a row of films dealing with murderous marriage impostors and nice-guys becoming their mistresses' doom: BLUEBEARD (1944) by the exile-Austrian Edgar G. Ulmer (with John Carradine), and LOVE FROM A STRANGER (1937) with Basil Rathbone, only to name two examples.

BLUEBEARD'S TEN HONEYMOONS / GB 1960

Directed by W. Lee Wilder. Written by Myles Wilder. Produced by Roy Parkinson. Camera: Stephen Dade. Music: Albert Elms. With George Sanders, Corinne Calvet, Jean Kent, Patricia Roc, Greta Gynt

The story of the marriage impostor and woman-killer Landru as a British crime film with comical undertones. Instead of only employing the myth of Bluebeard (like many other films), this low budget-movie sticks to the real case, though taking facts and names not too literally. George Sanders, an English actor and dandy *par excellence* who committed suicide in 1972, is Landru. Sanders left a farewell letter saying that life bored him because he had already tried and experienced everything. He let this decadence and dark sarcasm flow into all his roles. This alone makes the otherwise rather negligible adaptation of Monsieur Landru's deeds worth seeing.

LANDRU / France 1962

Directed by Claude Chabrol. Written by Francoise Sagan. Music: Pierre Jansen. Camera: Jean Rabier. With Charles Denner, Stephane Audran, Danielle Darrieux, Michèle Morgan, Hildegard Knef

Although the story is based on Monsieur Landru's real deeds, Charles Denner almost looks like Landru, and some historical material from WW1 gives the film a documentary touch, the film basically alludes more to Charles Chaplin's MONSIEUR VERDOUX than to the real events. Claude Chabrol too is rather more concerned with a sarcastic, provoking portrait of an epoch, than an approach to the individual doom of the modern Bluebeard. Both films try to compare serial genocide in war (Chaplin's

LANDRU

film is about WWII) with an individual's serial killing. It is the time when human life does not count any more, when millions bleed to dead in their trenches, providing an immoral foundation for cynical Monsieur Landru and his wicked activities.

Chabrol, who made an art form of laying bare bourgeois idylls in the Sixties, should have been the ideal man for the study of a philistine killer, but he is thwarted by his indecision. Too many satirical moments weaken the horror of the murders, the camera and music seem too detached to involve the viewer.

By the way, Landru's mistress Segret, essayed in the film by Chabrol's wife and well-tried actress Stephane Audran, saw the film and sued its producers. She was awarded 10,000 francs damages. But even this did not make her happy. In 1968 she drowned herself at the age of 72.

MONSIEUR VERDOUX / USA 1947

Written and directed by Charles Chaplin. Camera: Roland Totheroh. Music: Charles Chaplin. With Charles Chaplin, Mady Corell, Allison Roddan, Robert Lewis, Audrey Betz

Monsieur Verdoux has the charming face of Charlie Chaplin, the famous comedian and alleged lady-killer. Yet a killer lurks behind this facade. The unemployed bank clerk Verdoux feeds his paralysed wife and his children by marrying rich ladies, killing them, and inheriting their money. But in a collapse of the stock market he loses all the money earned with serial murder and delivers himself up to justice.

The Landru case was the impulse for a black comedy appreciated by many film freaks today. Yet when it was released it bewildered Charlie Chaplin's fans. The admirers of "the little tramp" did not appreciate that murder could be funny.

LEOPOLD & LOEB

Nathan LEOPOLD & Richard LOEB
"The Perfect Murder"

The Case
One of the most spectacular cases in the US history of crime happened in Chicago in the Twenties. Nathan Leopold (19) and Richard Loeb (18) were young men coming froma good house, both living in the high-class suburban district of Hyde Park. The sons of millionaires were 14 respectively 13 when they met. Leopold, called "Babe" by his friends, suffered from various diseases of the glands and, allegedly, had already as a child been seduced into sex-games by his governess. He was said to have an IQ of 200, spoke nine languages, and was an expert in ornithology and botany. Nietzsche and his often misinterpreted philosophy of the "superman" were his ideals. Yet "Babe" felt too weak to become "superman" without the help of a partner. He found his partner in Richard Loeb. Dickie was an attractive, athletic, and similarly intelligent boy with a keen interest for detective stories and true crime.

Perfection was their key-word. To be perfect meant to stand above the others. They regarded themselves as beings beyond justice, law, and judgement. Leopold and Loeb entered a homosexual love affair and agreed to commit the perfect crime together. In the following years they committed minor larceny, arson, and similar malpractices. In 1924 they decided to kidnap someone, kill him, and go to Europe with the ransom (they did not need money, but would demand it only for the sake of credibility). Then they made all necessary preparations and set up a list of potential victims. Nevertheless, they randomly chose 14-year-old Bobby Franks when they saw him. They took the boy with them in a rented car. Leopold drove, and Loeb stabbed the boy four times with a chisel. It lasted fifteen minutes until Bobby had finally bled to death. Afterwards the killers drove to an out-of-the-way swamp area, undressed the corpse, and hid it in a sewer-pipe. Then they posted the blackmailing letter. But Bobby was quickly found on the following day. Moreover, the police found Leopold's glasses on the scene of the crime.

Only eight days after this "perfect crime" the boys were suspected of the deed and interrogated. The "strong" Loeb broke down first and confessed. The trial shook Chicago, and some people even called for lynching them. The "Thrill Killers", as they were called by the press, were defended by the famous lawyer Clarence Darrow, who argued with Freud's then rather new theories about sexuality and childhood. For their youth and the confession of their guilt they were not sentenced to death, but to imprisonment for life plus 99 years. Against the judge's order they came into the same prison, where they lived in relative luxury, were allowed to visit each other, and had a lot of other privileges. As Dickie Loeb time and again molested fellow jailbirds with homosexual attempts, one of them finally stabbed him in self-defence in 1936. Nathan Leopold, who wrote an autobiographical book behind bars, was released on March 13, 1958 and moved to Puerto Rico. There he worked in a parish and married in 1961. According to his own statements he had not spent a day in his life without thinking of the murder. He died of a heart attack in 1971.

COMPULSION / USA 1959

Directed by Richard Fleischer. Written by Richard Murphy after the novel "Compulsion" by Meyer Levin. Camera: William C. Mellor. Music: Lionel Newman. With Dean Stockwell, Bradford Dillman, Orson Welles, Dianne Vorsi, E. C. Marshall

"What's a man's life?", Artie Straus (Richard Loeb) and Judd Steiner (Nathan Leopold), two lads coming from a good house ask themselves. In COMPULSION this question drives them first to theft, then to murder. The camera observes their heated discussions, the misanthropic braggadocio, and the elitist student milieu where all this takes place. The inhuman deeds happen off-screen.

After the more labile Judd (fantastic: Dean Stockwell, who much later appeared in BLUE VELVET) has lost his glasses on the scene of the crime, the noose tightens around their necks. When the two killers are arrested the outrage is rabid, and the death penalty only a question of time. Two rich Jewish guys (homosexual too) killing a child for the fun of it. What a projection for class warfare and anti-Semite tendencies! But the expensive star – defending counsel Jonathan Wilk (Orson Welles) tries to oversee the case without prejudices and to save the two young misanthropes from the executioner.

Meyer Levin, a former colleague of the deadly duo Leopold & Loeb wrote the novel this film by True Crime expert Richard Fleischer (THE BOSTON STRANGLER, TEN RILLINGTON PLACE) is based on. Though weakened in its seriousness by some shrill exploitation effects, Fleischer's film has probably the most stringent approach to Leopold and Loeb. The loud intro (rushing in a sports car to hectic music Artie and Judd almost hit a hobo) fits into the tradition of other juvenile rascals of the US cinema of the Fifties, all the High School-rebels, Hellcats, and anti-social teenagers. Later on Fleischer's character description becomes subtler and more accurate, leaves the usual bad-boy patterns. Psychology, the milieu, and the parental home are important for Richard Fleischer, but he avoids simplistic general explanations.

The film is strictly divided into two parts. Whereas the first half tells about the killers and their motives, feverishly rushing along tand alking of bewildered sexuality and violence fetishism ("Do you know how much beauty lies in Evil?", Judd asks a girl in an ill-fated approach), the second part comes to a standstill. It shows the trial, the difficult decision of the jury, and, especially, the counsel's speech against the death penalty delivered by Orson Welles, who dominates the film. But when the killers only crack jokes about his speech, the lawyer doubts his own motivations for a moment.

ROPE

ROPE / USA 1948

Directed by Alfred Hitchcock. Written by Arthur Laurents after a play by Patrick Hamilton. Camera: Josef Valentine. Music: Leo F. Forbstein. With James Stewart, John Dall, Farley Granger, Joan Chandler, Cedric Hardwicks

An apartment in an American city. Just when the college-students Brandon and Philip are strangling a fellow student, the camera plunges into the event. They commit the murder to corroborate their thesis of "perfect crime", or "murder as art", a theory allowing the more intelligent individuals to place themselves above the "mediocre" rest of mankind. The liaison of eros and thanatos is always present in many of Hitchcock's films. After their deed the two killers are empty and exhausted, as if after a long orgasm. Under the surface murder becomes a metaphor for the sexual act.

To enhance the thrill of the crime, the two delinquents give a party at the crime scene and invite, among other people, the father of their victim. He does not know that the corpse of his missing son lies in the box on which dinner is served. The boys' favourite professor, Rupert Cadell, who has been feeding their icy-cold world-view with daring Nietzsche interpretations, has also been invited. The party suffers from Brandon's scornful malice and Philip's hyper-nervous behaviour. Moreover, the atmosphere remains rather chilly because a certain guest, the victim of murder, does not show up.

Shrewd Professor Cadell comes back into the apartment after the ill-starred dinner party has already been over for a while and realises to his horror what damage the cynical mind-games in his lectures have done. Instead of being solidly behind the "perfect" duo, he reports his "disciples" to the police.

Hitchcock was concerned with two things in the first screen adaptation of the Leopold/Loeb-case. One the one hand he wanted to criticise the intellectual arrogance and hubris of the unequal duo, but on the other hand, on the perhaps more important formal level, he intended to deliver the first genuine chamber-play in the history of cinema. He brilliantly succeeded in letting a story take place in almost real time in only one setting, but still generating suspense. Concerning the film's story Hitchcock provides his audience with emotional hot-cold treatment. The film's focus of suspense lies in the fact that the corpse in the box is not found, that the audience trembles with Brandon and Philip. While from the beginning Hitchcock provides us with two immoral protagonists as identification figures (admittedly, a rather remorseful Philip), ROPE is at the same time a warning against their ideology.

SWOON / USA 1991

Written and directed by Tom Kalin. Camera: Ellen Kuras. Music: James Bennett. With Daniel Schlachet, Craig Chester, Ron Vawter, Michael Kirby, Michael Stumm, Valda Z. Drabla, Natalie Stanford

An ambitious new adaptation of the "Thrill Killer" case, constructed of facts, myths, past adaptations, and biographies, and attempting to challenge the official history of the Leopold/Loeb-case for the first time. It was the main issue of the young independent director Tom Kalin, to emphasise the homosexual aspect of Leopold & Loeb that had been passed over in silence in all the other adaptations. Kalin, himself involved in the Gay Movement, thinks that it was more Babe's and Dickie's mutual emotional and sexual dependence than their "superman" philosophy that triggered off the murder of Bobby Franks. Suppressing and concealing their emotions in a repressive time and environment, they were victimised themselves. Armond White writes: "Leopold-Loeb becomes a test case for the director Tom Kalin, because in their time their sexual orientation was regarded as a reason for 'pathological' behaviour (a sentence also used by their ingenious defendant Clarence Darrow in his Counsel's speech). Moreover, imitating several scenes Kalin hints at the cultural misinterpretation of homosexuality in Hollywood's own Leopold-Loeb legends like Hitchcock's ROPE and Fleischer's COMPULSION. It is Kalin's intention to present a more sensitive, morally responsible view of things and he tries to exclude the typical cinematic gay erotic and a culturally anchored homophobia."

As praiseworthy Kalin's effort to get rid of sexual taboos and myths is, it becomes dry and fleshless in its actual staging. What could have become the most controversial adaptation of an extreme case, merely amounts to be a collection of boring, pseudo-artistic black-and-white images in the final analysis.

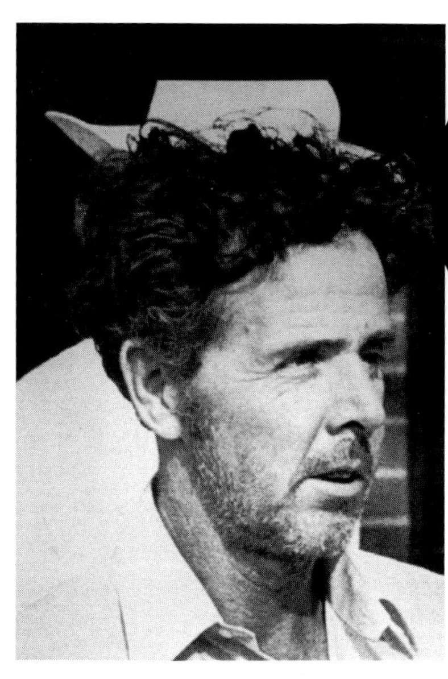

HENRY LEE LUCAS

"I was death on women. I didn't feel they need to exist. I hated them and I wanted to destroy every one I could find. I was doing a good job of it. I've got [killed] 360 people. I've got thirty-six states in three different countries. My victims never knew what was happening to them. I had shootings, knifings, strangulations, beatings and I've participated in actual crucifixions of humans. All across the country, there's people just like me , who set out to destroy human life."

–Henry Lee Lucas

The Case

Up to the present day nobody knows exactly how many people Henry Lee Lucas has killed. The police suspect him of 167 victims, Lucas himself claims more than 300(!), two dozen are without doubt. Together with the Russian Chikatilo he is regarded as one of the most atrocious serial killers of all times. Henry, the man with the glass eye who never took a bath and always ran around in filthy clothes spreading an intense stench, got his vital kicks and thrills from killing women.

Henry Lee Lucas had a childhood like something out of a third-rate horror movie. Growing up in a whorehouse, little Henry had to watch his mother, a prostitute, sleeping with her customers. She forced him to wear girls' clothes in school. Moreover, he was often beaten and sexually abused. Later the killer claimed to have attacked a teacher sexually and killed her at the age of 13. At the age of 24 he stabbed his then 74-year-old mother. From 1960 to 1965 he was kept in a psychiatric institution for capital criminals, the following five years in the State Penitentiary. Shortly after his release he kidnapped two teenage girls, and hence spent four additional years behind bars. Released again, Henry Lee Lucas finally became a murder-machine, the personified "American Psycho". Alone or together with his homosexual partner Ottis Toole he tramped from state to state, always on the road, always killing in a different way, leaving behind himself an atrocious track of blood across the USA. Toole, a vicious killer in his own right, was also a pyromaniac and confessed cannibal.

In November 1983 Henry was sentenced for murder of his minor wife Becky

Henry Lee Lucas arrested, age 23

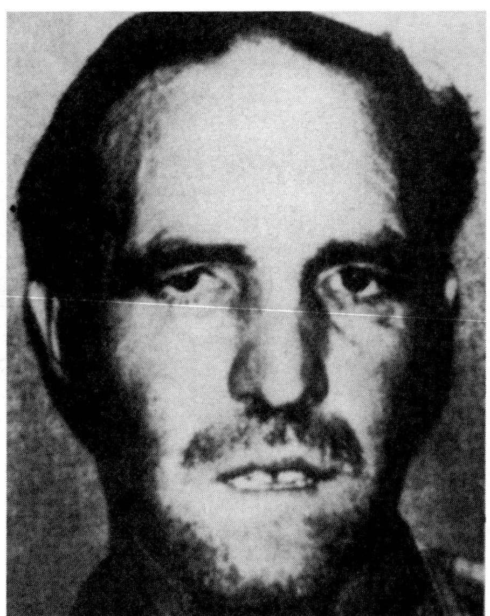

Ottis Toole

(Toole's sister). But the police could never prove the numerous murders they suspected were attributable to Lucas and Toole, although Lucas, who is still sitting in jail today – though his death sentence has now been commuted to life without remission – has allegedly confessed details only known to the medical experts.

CONFESSIONS OF A SERIAL KILLER / USA 1987

Written and directed by Mark Blair. Camera: Layton Blaylock. Music: William Penn. With Robert A. Burnes, Dennis Hill, Berkely Garrett, Sidney Bremer

"The following motion picture is based on a true story", is to be read in the credits. What is meant here is the true story of Henry Lee Lucas and Otis Toole, here called Daniel Ray Hawkins and Moon Lewton. Despite changing names and settings the film is closer to the biography of the travelling murder-machine Henry Lee Lucas than John McNaughton's rather free adaptation HENRY. Though never reaching the stifling atmosphere and shock effect of the latter, the film's depiction of the case deserves to be seen as a gritty, fact-oriented, and well-cast comment on a subject often otherwise only dealt with by third-rate TV directors.

Blair begins with the delinquent's capture and lets his serial killer Hawkins deliver the confessions alluded to in the film's title to an old cop. Hereby the most important events in the killer's life are shown in flashbacks. There is his childhood, the over-dominant elderly mother selling her body for some lousy dollars, the weak father, the first murder in early days, the trips from state to state. Finally he meets his murderous companion Lewton and his sister. Hitting the road, killing, hitting the road again. Like the real killer Daniel brags about his deeds, his fantasies of unbelievably high killing-counts taking his patient listener's breath away. It remains unclear where the border lies between absurd fiction and vomitous truth. Anyway, the number of victims is, unquestionably, horribly high.

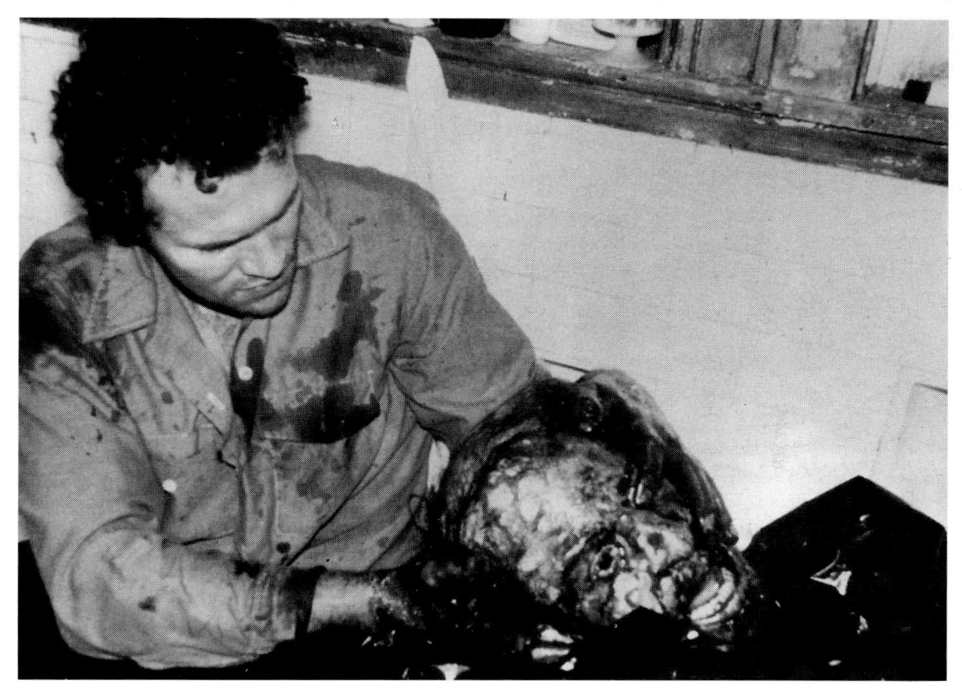

HENRY, PORTRAIT OF A SERIAL KILLER

HENRY, PORTRAIT OF A SERIAL KILLER / USA 1986-89

Directed by John McNaughton. Written by Richard Fire and John McNaughton. Camera: Charlie Liebermann. Music: Robert McNaughton, Ken Hale, and Steven A. Jones. With Michael Rooker, Tracy Arnold, Tom Towles, Ray Atherton

There are many ways to approach the subject of serial murder in film. Beside factual documentaries, artistic flourishes, and exploitation shockers, films like this one, without any recoverable moral intention, cut deepest into the viewer's emotional surface. John McNaughton's cheap independent movie had been threatened for years by the financially disastrous X-rating. It took years until it found a US distributor and became a "sleeper" hit of repertory cinema.

John McNaughton has distilled some archetypal episodes from the case of Henry Lee Lucas, who was sweeping like a death-tornado over America in the Eighties, for his low budget opus. Lee Lucas' life seems to be just what psychoanalysts have been waiting for, a childhood only consisting of torture and sexual abuse, many years of doing time, then finally the murder of his dominant mother. All these aspects might have been the physical and mental beatings favouring his development to a cold-blooded slaughter-machine. Yet the film does not insist on such theories, only restricts itself to fragmentary dialogues and allusions, and does without traumatic flashbacks into his childhood, Freudian symbolism, and other stock devices of the genre. John McNaughton said: "There will always be people like him. We've been critized for not 'explaining' why he kills. That's ridiculous. We're a long way from being able to explain such things. Of course, you could say it was his mother's fault, or society's, or he was abused, he was in jail, but then he could have had a twin brother who became a heart surgeon. I grew up with two brothers, one became a criminal, the other the lawyer of a big company. One drives a fancy car and wears a suit and a tie, the other forges cheques, cheats with credit cards and steals. Both come from the same parental home." (quoted from the book *Dark Stars*).

HENRY (with changed names and settings) does not stage catharsis, nor death ecstasy like RAMPAGE, nor ambiguity in its dealing with violence like A CLOCKWORK ORANGE, nor aestheticism like BLUE STEEL: you can neither love nor duplicate this film. It totally lacks the spirit of human rebellion that makes the hopelessness of other films (DRILLER KILLER, COMBAT SHOCK etc.) at least bearable. The characters act like the living dead. Henry, the protagonist, is no spectacular film-weirdo, no exciting psycho-killer. He is not driven by lucid madness, but drastically represents perverted normality/banality, hence personifies a serial killer much more appropriately than many characters in other films dealing with that topic. It seems quite obvious why there are so few films like HENRY presenting a murderous protagonist without traceable motives. "The audience cannot deal with them. So there must always be delivered a form of the Satanic Evil or mental deformation." (film critic Maerz).

HENRY perfectly mirrors the bluntness and void of its characters with its glum, cynical images similar to snuff-porno aesthetics. McNaughton's stone classic of independent cinema painfully weighs upon your memory, as hot and heavy as molten lead. And this is its great achievement. The violent film mirrors a violent reality.

PS: In 1997, a dull sequel (HENRY, PORTRAIT OF A SERIAL KILLER 2 – MASK OF SANITY) produced by a completely different team, appeared.

BRUNO LUEDKE

The Berlin Strangler

The Case

In 1909 Bruno Luedke was born, feeble-minded, in Germany. The casual thief and sadist who liked torturing animals once knocked down a woman with a carriage. At the age of 18 he began to kill.

During WW2, a chaotic time facilitating his murderous activities, he was arrested for a sexual offence and sterilised by order of the SS. But this did not weaken his killer instinct. He went on killing unnoticed. When in January 1943 an elderly woman was found strangled in a Berlin forest, the police interrogated all registered criminals. Luedke was among them and confessed after brutally attacking the policemen. But he pleaded mental irresponsibility. He confessed to killing 85 women since 1928, after raping them. He also robbed them in many cases.

After investigating the relevant cases for one year it seemed highly probable to the experts that Luedke had been the murderer in almost all of them. Yet the police avoided all publicity around Bruno Luedke, because several innocents had been arrested and sentenced instead of him. The NS-bosses decided to cover up the case. Luedke was taken to a Viennese hospital where he was abused as a guinea pig for some Nazi experiments, and died of the after-effect of an injection in April 1944.

NACHTS, WENN DER TEUFEL KAM (THE DEVIL CAME AT NIGHT) / Germany 1957
Directed by Robert Siodmak. Written by Werner Joerg Lueddecke after an article with the same title in a Bavarian magazine. Camera: Georg Krause. Music: Siegfried Franz. With Mario Adorf, Annemarie Dueringer, Werner Peters, Claus Holm, Hannes Messemer, Monika John

The Devil is Bruno Luedke, the mass murderer who killed dozens of women and girls in Berlin and Hamburg and their surroundings protected by the chaos of WW2.

Bombs hit the city. People flee into bunkers, and searchlights flood the night streets. Some women disappear without a trace in this turmoil. Later their corpses are found buried in a forest or in gravel pits.

Mario Adorf in one of his first and most intense roles, plays Bruno Luedke. He has the face of a blunt, hulking man on one hand appearing as a naive child, then as a madman driven by violent forces. He is not at all intelligent, but instinctively realises that he has little trouble in a time when dying has become a main element in everyday life anyway. Lacking motivation, the police do not really investigate intensely. "It is dull and hopeless, every day thousands of people are killed at the front, and we supervise a huge apparatus for a few single cases here", a detective complains.

Inspector Kersten, a war-disabled person, slowly tracks down the killer after years of homicides without anybody establishing a relation between Luedke and his deeds. "The Homicide Commission seems to be the quietest department," Kersten says, happy to have escaped the trenches when starting his new job. But this hope retreats the closer he gets to Luedke. The highest NSDAP-circles do not like the idea that the (unfailing) German police have not been able to detect a mass murderer for such a long time. When the killer reveals himself as a German (and not as a Jew, gypsy or other non-Aryan) one thing is clear: the Luedke case has to be covered up as a "Geheime Reichssache", Luedke himself erased, and his last murder saddled on another man. Kersten tries to intervene, but to no avail. He is sent back to the front as cannon-fodder. Moreover, the Gestapo is waiting for his girlfriend and confidante.

In Robert Siodmak's film someone tells the story of a German soldier whose speciality it is to sneak into the enemy's camp and strangle numerous men with his bare hands. He has been awarded the Iron Cross for that skill. Bruno Luedke strangles too, but more motivated by bloodlust than by decoration. A high SS officer can only shrug his shoulders about Luedke's more than 80 victims. Participating in organised mass murder day by day, he is used to completely different numbers as thousands perish in the concentration camp ovens. Siodmak does not juxtapose corpses, yet manages to mediate the absurdity of the murderer in a murderous era highly convincingly.

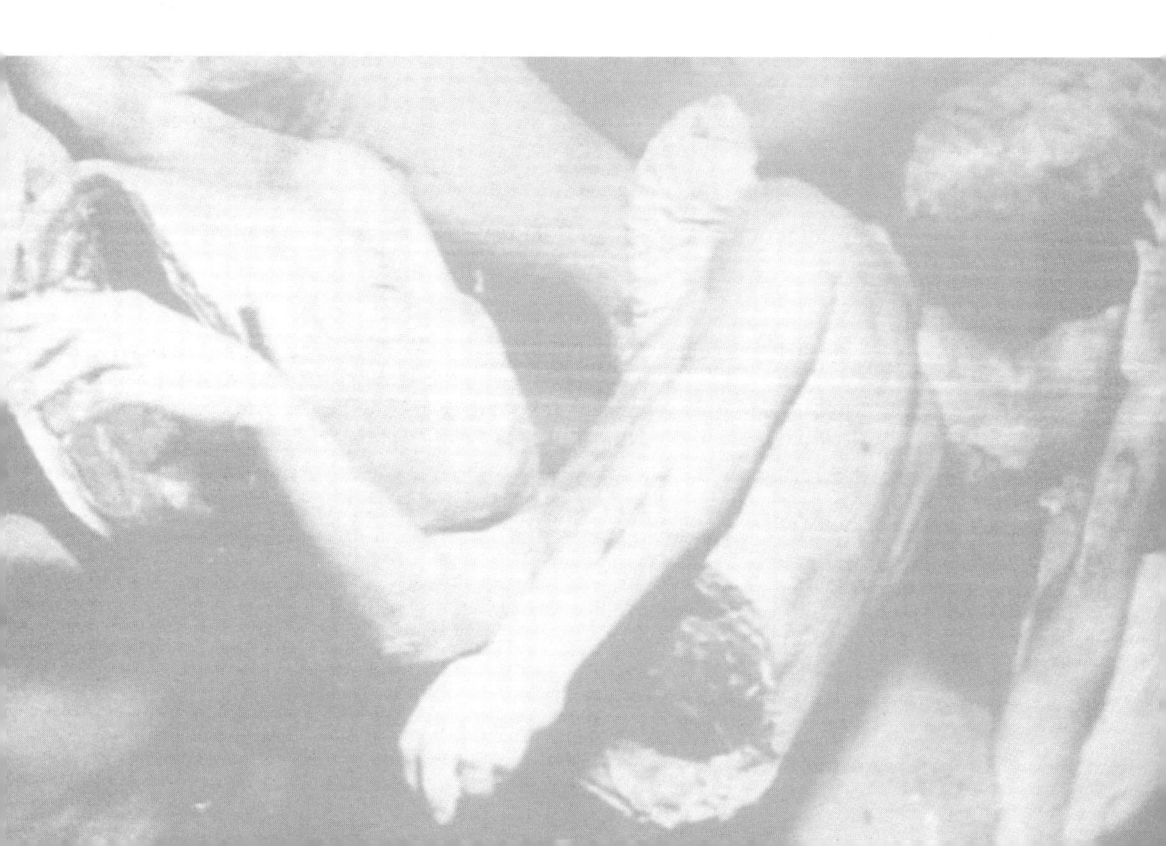

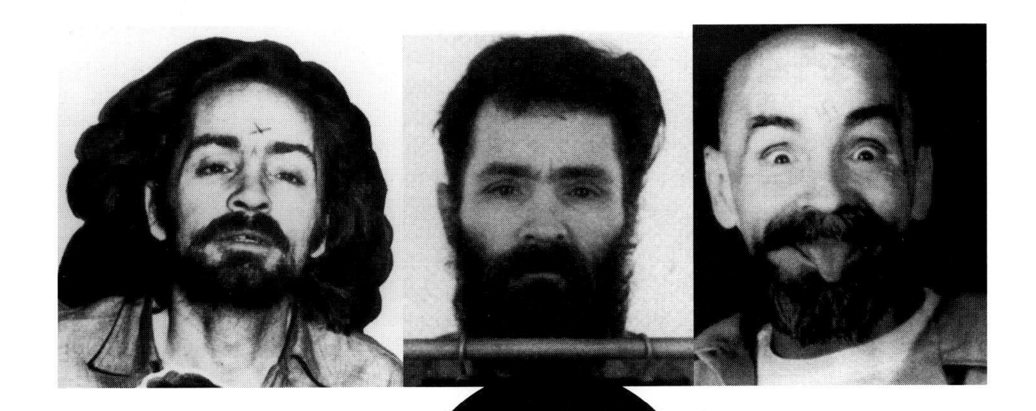

CHARLES MANSON

"I Am Jesus Christ And The Devil!"

"These children that come at you with knives, they are your children. You taught them. I didn't teach them. I just tried to help them stand up."
–Charles Manson

"I love love-ins. They're fascinating. They're fun. I think the hippies are great: they just want to be left alone and they want everything to be nice and peaceful."
–Sharon Tate

"I'm the Devil. I'm here to do the Devil's business."
–Tex Watson

The Case
On the night of August 8 to August 9, 1969 a case of murder shook the American Dream to its core. Sharon Tate, Roman Polanski's wife, was killed together with a group of friends in her villa in Los Angeles. The house on Cielo Drive, over the hills of Hollywood resembled a battlefield. Sharon Tate, Voytek Frykowski, Abigail Folger, Jay Sebring and her neighbour Steve Parent died in a thirty minutes' massacre. A macabre calculation based on the wounds of the victims brought up that every twenty seconds a knife was forced into a victim's body. Sharon Tate had been far advanced in pregnancy.

A gang of juvenile scavenger hippies was responsible for the massacre: Tex Watson, Susan Atkins, Leslie Van Houten, and Patricia Krenwinkel, all between 20 and 21. In their trial they stated that they had followed blindly and devoid of free will a murderous command. The alleged mandator: a charismatic ex-prisoner the disoriented kids regarded as a guru-like father figure: Charles Manson.

On August 10, one day after the Tate murders, another killer-gang struck in the night. The victims: Leno La Bianca and his wife, the owners of a supermarket-chain. A knife stuck in Leno La Bianca's mouth, a fork in his abdomen. Moreover, the killers had carved "War" into his abdominal wall. The doors and walls had been covered with one-liners "Kill the pigs!" written with blood. Months later a chain of hints lead to the delinquents.

Manson lived with his followers, juvenile runaways, on the desolate Spahn Movie Ranch in the hills of L.A. and in the scorched Death Valley. What appeared to be a typical hippie community from the outside, was a group-dynamic pandemonium inside. The legend tells of power-and-submission games and a lot of "liberated" sex and violent escapades. Naive Sixties ideals were mixed with racism and conspiracy-theories, exaggerated drug consumption and esoteric idiocy were the order of the day. According to half-serious sources Manson's and his followers' mood fell into a paranoid abyss at a certain time. Beside the Tate/La Bianca-murders the surroundings of the Family are ascribed some further crimes: the murder of the music teacher Gary Hinman by Bobby Beausoleil, and the mysterious death of the stuntman Shorty Shea.

These incidents abruptly ended the peaceful dreams of the Sixties. The children of Flower Power had become flowers of Evil. What had really happened, the motives and the background of the murders, all this disappeared in a media jungle of horror stories and hysteria. Manson himself, who paradoxically is regarded as one of the most notorious mass murderers of all times though he has never been proven to be on a scene of crime, had always denied any responsibility in the Tate/La Bianca-murders. Nevertheless, it remains a fact that Sharon Tate's death in that hot summer night of August 8, 1969 was more than "only" one more murder among many in L.A., a metropolis of violence. It was the funeral chant of a utopia: "Kill the pigs" instead of "Love & Peace".

Manson, "Satan in a human shape", as the Yellow Press called him, has become the ultimate personification of "Evil" in the pop-myths of the late 20th century, and has probably inspired cinema to produce more films than all the other killers portrayed in this book altogether.

FILMS AND DOCUMENTARIES BASED DIRECTLY ON CHARLES MANSON AND THE "FAMILY":

THE BOOK OF MANSON / USA 1989

Directed and written by Raymond Pettibon. With Robert Hecker, Joe Cole, Shannon Smith, Dave Markey, Dez Cadena

Charles Manson, claiming to be the Second Coming, leads his young followers down the path of sex and murder in this bizarre homage by renowned artist Raymond Pettibon.

CHARLES MANSON SUPERSTAR / USA 1989 (DOCUMENTARY)

Directed by Nikolas Schreck.

Charles Manson, the sect founder imprisoned for the rest of his life has long been incorporated in our big entertainment machinery. B-movie directors have stylised him as a surrogate Satan in a hippie's shape and commercialised him as a spooky pop-icon. Manson's face was used for selling washing-powder, numerous T-shirts, and popular little mass murderer-pictures for school children. This documentary shows the "other" side of the "Messiah" Manson, the "blunt country boy" as philosopher and social revolutionary. The video contains a long exhaustive interview with a lot of essential information about the case, though from the rather subjective point of view of the

CHARLIE'S FAMILY

Manson expert Nikolas Schreck, who also positions himself as his subject's talk-partner.

CHARLIE'S FAMILY / USA 1992

Directed and written by Jim Van Bebber. With Marcelo Games, Marc Pitman, Leslie Orr, Maureen Alisse, Amy Yates, Michelle Briggs, Sherri Rickman

"The time is going to come when all men will judge themselves before God. It'll be the worst Hell on Earth. It'll make Nazi Germany look like a picnic!" So speaks Patty, Manson Family member, in Jim Van Bebber's awesome work-in-progress. CHARLIE'S FAMILY is already the best Manson movie ever, portraying the events of '69 with deadly accuracy whilst juxtaposing them against the actions of a modern-day group of punkish terrorists. Psychedelic sex orgies, drug burns, and the blood-drenched Tate murders themselves are recreated in ultra-vivid relief, soundtracked by intense death metal crescendos. Unfinished at time of writing, CHARLIE'S FAMILY is a film which demands to be completed and distributed with the utmost expediency.

DEATH VALLEY 69 / USA 1986

Directed by Richard Kern and Judith Barry. With Sonic Youth, Lydia Lunch

Splatterpunk Richard Kern does his take on Manson in the form of a short rock video featuring Sonic Youth. Elements of the Manson story merge with modern post-pun k imagery showing the continuum between Manson's anti-hippies and latterday rebels.

HELTER SKELTER / USA 1976 (TV)

Directed and produced by Tom Gries. Written by J. P. Miller after a novel by Vincent Bugliosi. Camera: Jules Brenner. Music: Billy Goldenberg. With Steve Railsback, Nancy Wolfe, George Di Cenzo, Marilyn Burns

This TV-documentary drama is completely contrary to CHARLES MANSON SUPERSTAR.

DEATH VALLEY 69

MANSON

Perhaps, the truth lies somewhere in between. HELTER SKELTER is based on the famous and disputed novel by D.A. Vincent Bugliosi and mixes the facts of thousands of pages of trial files with the author's personal opinions. Although this film is similar to exploitation movies in its treatment of the events, it is far less rough and cynical than the latter, not to mention its lack of sex & crime. But the actors compensate for many of its drawbacks. Above all Steve Railsback as Charles Manson, who almost plays the real guru into the ground, so fascinatingly manic is his acting. Nancy Wolfe is a threatening Susan Atkins, and George Di Cenzo is so cold and disagreeable as Bugliosi that the real hero of the book and the film, the district attorney is rather discredited.

MANSON / USA 1974 (DOCUMENTARY)

Directed by Robert Hendrickson & Lawrence Merrick

"The news gives you 5% of what's going on and even that's distorted" (Manson). This rare documentary tried to throw light upon the case and is still banned in California despite its Oscar-nomination. Though the title promises a little bit too much (Manson himself can only be seen in short interview passages) it has become a cult-object for collectors. MANSON contains interviews with almost all members of the "Family", especially "Squeaky" Fromme. Rare Super-8 sequences complete the picture. Two bizarre events around the film deserve our attention: firstly, co-director Lawrence Merrick fell prey to a highly mysterious murder. Secondly, MANSON's success in New York in a double-feature with Polanski's MACBETH, which caused the latter's reputation as a bloody working-up of Sharon Tate's doom.

MANSON FAMILY MOVIES / USA 1984

Directed by John Aes-Nihil

Anyone hoping for the lost home-movies that were allegedly shot in the surroundings of the Spahn Ranch, or even the mysterious snuff films mentioned by Ed Sanders in

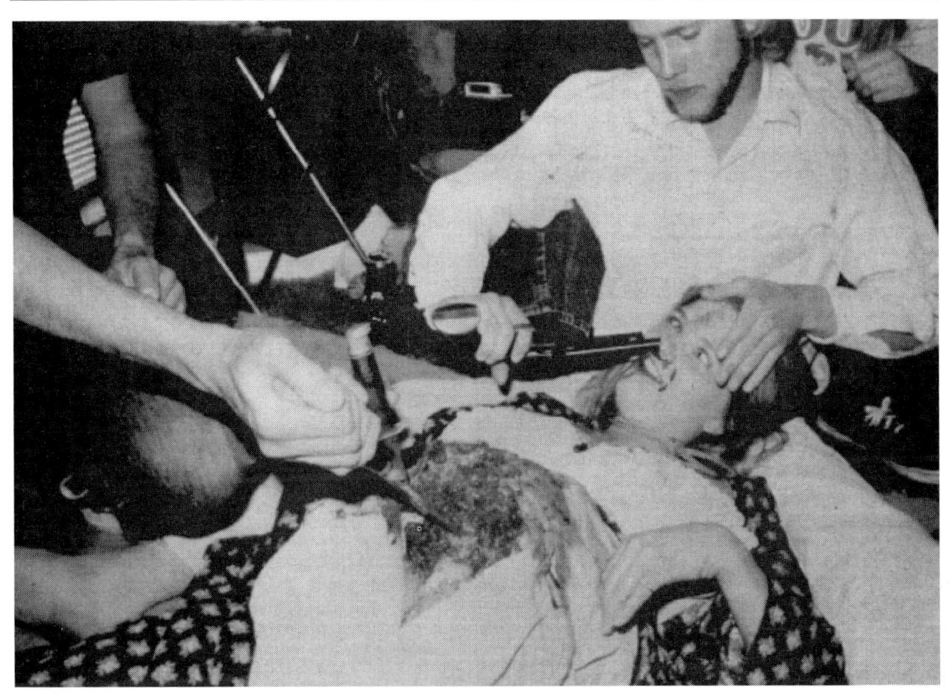

MANSON FAMILY MOVIES

his book *The Family*, will have to realise that this film has only been produced by a group of inveterate Manson fans delivering a tribute to their idol. On the video's cover you can read: "There are rumours that the Manson Family have filmed their activities. Here you see how these films might have looked like." The magazine *Film Threat* called this homage by John Aes-Nihil, who owns a Manson souvenir mail order service and is co-author of *The Manson Files*, a "poorly done Super-8 that is almost unwatchable". Yet John Waters praised it with the following words: "A primitive, obsessional, fetishistic tribute to mayhem, murder, and madness."

MURDERERS, MOBSTERS & MADMEN: CHARLES MANSON / GB 1992 (DOCUMENTARY)

Directed by Nick Bougas

A very informative documentary covering all aspects of the subject. In 1967 Charles Manson, who spent most of his life in prison for theft and pimping, burst onto the hippie-scene at the age of 33. His hatred, gathered during many years behind bars, mixed with the kids' non-conformist messages to become an explosive cocktail. Basically, Manson was a prototypical redneck: a shrewd macho conservative suspicious of "niggers". But he preached romantic outlaw-ideals, and the Flower Power children hung upon his words. Bougas, a notorious Manson fan, remains fairly objective.

THE OTHER SIDE OF MADNESS aka THE HELTER SKELTER MURDERERS / USA 1972

Directed & photographed by Wade Williams. Written by J. J. Wilkie. Soundtrack: Sean Bonniwell and Music Machine. With Gary Donovan, Richard Kaplan, Erica Bigelow, Kelly Cap, Debbie Duff, Paula Shannon

A psychedelic trash cult-film and a good example of what exploitation cinema can deliver in its best moments. Besides gorgeously tasteless entertainment this film flashes some sparks of obsession which lift it to the level of masterpieces like IN COLD BLOOD in his best moments. The longest scene in THE OTHER SIDE OF MADNESS is "in cold blood" too, the murders in the Tate villa depicted in every minute detail. Frank Howard does not follow a fixed plot, he only flashlights single images. Scenes from the trial, open-air concerts, life on the Spahn Ranch are seemingly randomly shown. In the middle of all this Sharon Tate appears as actress on the set, the film becomes coloured, and Johann Strauss's "Blue Danube" is to be heard. Later she says to her henchmen "Please, let me keep my baby" when they are going to kill her.

No actors in the film look like the real figures. Yet, though it sticks much less to the facts, this pseudo-documentary is by far superior to the fact-oriented HELTER SKELTER. You can almost smell and feel the perfectly conserved atmosphere of 1969. Moments of chill and stupid ridiculous scenes clash against each other. Perhaps, that's why the film corresponds much more than all the others to Manson's personality: the Family leader himself stands for dangerous threat as well as wishy-washy hippie-babble. Last but not least there is Sean Bonniwell's electrifying soundtrack. Manson himself appears on the song "Mechanical Man".

A SELECTION OF FILMS INFLUENCED BY MANSON AND THE "FAMILY":

BEYOND THE VALLEY OF THE DOLLS / USA 1970

Directed by Russ Meyer. Written by Roger Ebert & Russ Meyer. Camera: Fred J. Koenekamp. Music: William Loose & Stu Phillips. With Dolly Read, Cynthia Myers, Marcia McBroom, Charles Napier, Erica Gavin, Michael Blodgett, Haji

Though the title suggests a sequel to VALLEY OF THE DOLLS (1967, starring Sharon Tate), this is not the case. It is in fact the rare case of a big budget exploitation movie, done by a B-movie specialist recruited by 20th Century Fox: the tit-fetishist Russ Meyer. Together with the later well-known film critic Roger Ebert he wrote the story of Kelly, Casey, and Petronella, three girls who want to conquer Hollywood as a psychedelic girlie-band,"The Kelly Affair". The band come into the wonderland of stars and starlets, drug parties, sex, Sodom and Gomorrah. The decadent "Hollywood Babylon" of the fashion-hippies, starlets, and bohemians as Meyer depicts it must have been quite close to the reality where Charles Manson was a welcome party-guest, and many stars from Nancy Sinatra to Peter Sellers considered it chic to surround themselves with stoners and freaks. According to relevant sources Roman Polanski and Sharon Tate were especially known for their LSD-and-occult happenings.

At the end Russ Meyer lets violence break into this atmosphere of camp-humour and sex in the shape of a mad transvestite beheading, stabbing, and shooting the Beautiful People. As Ebert has explained: "We knew we would have the murder orgy... we were working before the Tate case was solved, and it was one of the exploitable elements we wanted to use".

BLUE SUNSHINE / USA 1977

Written and directed by Jeff Lieberman. Camera: Don Knight. Music: Charles Gross. With Zalman King, Deborah Winters, Mark Goddard

When Woodstock ended, Sharon Tate was already dead for a week. In 1969 the psychedelic soap bubble burst and the people woke up from the dream of a peaceful solution for all problems with a terrible hangover. This is the atmosphere of Jeff Lieberman's bizarre Horror/Trash-movie about a clique of Flower-Children. Ten years later these Sixties veterans have already become bourgeois, but they have not

reckoned with the after-effects of an LSD-type drug they had used back in the old days. "Blue Sunshine" leads to alopecia and murderous psychopathic tendencies. The ex-Hippies mutate to brutal, bald killer-machines. "The Flower-Children have become the living dead", writes the critic Kim Newman, and *Film Threat* calls the B-movie a homage to the Manson Family's "Yul Brynner-phase", i. e. the time during the trials when the girl members of the clan shaved their heads to show that they stuck together in support of their captured leader.

CANNIBAL GIRLS / Canada 1972

Directed by Ivan Reitman. Written by Robert Sandler. Camera: Robert Soad. Music: Doug Riley. With Eugene Levy, Andrea Martin, Ronald Ulrich, Randall Carpenter

Ivan Reitman, today widely known for his mainstream comedies, started his career with this involuntarily funny shocker. A young couple gets lost and falls prey to the girls mentioned in the title, who live in an out-of-the-way house together with the "Reverend", their leader. They live on human flesh – as the couple finds out in the course of time. Beside the bearded, long-haired "Reverend" with obvious traits of Charles Manson, it is particularly the dingy girls that remind of the Family. Cheap fun giving way to boredom.

THE COMMUNE / USA 1970

Director unknown. With Robert Harry, Joan Stormer, Sheri Nixon, Nancy Gold

This highly obscure hippie-shocker was promoted with the slogan "Worship him! Kill for him! Make love for him! Die for him!" One of those cheap productions released shortly after the Tate/La Bianca-murders to profit from their medial sell-out. Its ingredients were soft-sex and violence, and a certain Robert Harry impersonated the leader of the gang.

THE CULT / USA 1971

Written and directed by Kentucky Jones. Camera: Robert Maxwell. Music: Clark de Will. With Blaisdell Makee, Debbie Osbourne, Sean Kennedy, Candice Roman, John Vincent, Cindy Barrett

From a review by the German Catholic Film Service: "On the whole the film is anti-social and legitimates crime as the social outsider's right to work off his frustrations". Yet anyone expecting a consciously subversive film, perhaps even a message, after this review, will be seriously disappointed. Kentucky Jones' extremely cheap production is nothing but a soft-sex shocker with an equal share of violence and nudie-scenes. But there definitely *is* an anti-social tendency in the film. Its protagonists are a megalomaniac guru and a bunch of wild girls enslaved to him. In endless flashbacks we are told about their lives. A bourgeois mother catches her daughter making lesbian love. Another woman rapes her son, and a father his daughter. Rape, SM-spanking, incest, drug abuse, and group-sex permanently alternate with each other, and the chain of excessive crime culminates in a murder-orgy where (surprise, surprise!) a blonde starlet and her friends are slaughtered. The cult-leader and his beauties escape unharmed and satisfied. Kentucky Jones, who leaves off nothing that could shock a "bourgeois" viewer, provides his protagonists with an immoral happy ending without punishment.

CULT OF THE DAMNED aka ANGEL, ANGEL, DOWN WE GO / USA 1969

Written and directed by Robert Thom. Music: Barry Mann & Cynthia Weil. With Jennifer Jones, Jordan Christopher, Roddy McDowell, Holly Near

This film exemplifies how fast the film industry reacted to the Manson Family. ANGEL, ANGEL, DOWN WE GO was produced in 1969, even before the spectacular murders, but the story of drugs, ritual murders, and psychedelic rock bands in rotten decadent Hollywood provided a wonderful parable for the even more sensational reality. After Charlie and his "kids" had dominated the headlines of the Yellow Press for weeks, the promotion department of AIP decided to rename Robert Thom's film CULT OF THE DAMNED and alluded to the bloody events with suggestive slogans.

THE DEATHMASTER

THE DEATHMASTER / USA 1972

Directed by Ray Danton. Written by R. L. Grove. Camera: Wilmer C. Butler. Music: Bill Marx. With Robert Quarry, Bill Ewing, Betty Anne Rees, John Fiedler

Strictly speaking a vampire film starring Robert Quarry, an actor experienced in the genre, this production is also mentioned by Manson-chroniclers. For Korda, the film's bloodsucker, is a bearded, long-haired descendant of Transylvanian ancestors stranded on a Californian beach(!) at the beginning of the film. He stays there and gathers a crowd of hippie-followers around himself.

THE FEMALE BUNCH / USA 1971

Directed by Al Adamson. Written by Jale Lockwood & Brent Nimrod. Camera: Paul Glickman. Music: Jaime Mendoza-Nava. With Russ Tamblyn, Regina Carrol, Lon Chaney Jr. Jennifer Bishop

An ultra-trashy variation of the myth of the blood-thirsty Manson girls staged by Z-movie-director Al Adamson. A group of sadistic girls live on a farm together with an old factotum torturing their male prisoner. In their torture games the girls appeal to their idol Charles Manson. Adamson used the Spahn Movie Ranch, the Family's well-known hideout around 1969, as location. Tagline: "They dare to do what other women only dream about".

(Adamson had previously exploited the Manson case when promoting his ultra-violent biker flick, SATAN'S SADISTS/1969, with the tagline: "NOW: see on the screen the SHOCKING STORIES you are reading about in the newspapers TODAY!".)

GABRIELLE / USA 1970

Directed by Arlo Shiffen

Definite Manson elements in this sexploitationer. Our heroine, after a brutal rape, comes under the care of a certain Dr Matson. Matson is the head of a group known as the Family. He's a psycho, and encourages sexual excess and murder. Coincidence?

HITCHHIKERS / USA 1972

Produced, written, photographed and directed by Ferd & Beverly Sebastian. Music: Danny Cohen. With Misty Rowe, Norman Klar, Linda Avery, Tommy Gibbs

Maggie, a pregnant girl, leaves home to go to the ranch of Benson (!), a charismatic hippie-leader. She becomes a member of a harem together with four other girls. As hitchhikers garbed only in their underwear, these girls ambush lonesome motorists. The dusty highways and desert roads are not safe any more. Benson and his girls rob and rape throughout this "road-movie meets nudie", and similarities to real events are definitely not coincidental.

I DRINK YOUR BLOOD / USA 1971

Directed by David Durston. Camera: Jacques Demarceaux. Music: Clay Pitts. With Bhaskar, Jadine Wong, Ronda Fultz

A ferocious hippie-gang in a wild post-Manson style threatens honourable American citizens. Brutal conflicts develop in the course of which a little boy poisons the gang with infected meat-pies. Diagnosis: rabies. The madness caused by the disease and nesting in the brains of the youths makes them, as always in such films, unpredictable and murderous. "Eye for eye, and tooth for tooth" is the motto of the following massacre. Durston's weird story transforms from a Satanic ritual-shocker to an almost-zombie film openly alluding to Romero's NIGHT OF THE LIVING DEAD. A splatter-classic with a trebly synthesiser-soundtrack and perversely illuminated scenes, highly rated by trash aficionados. The perverse way the generation conflict is fought is well worth seeing too.

IGOR AND THE LUNATICS / USA 1986

Directed by Billy Parolini. Written by Jocelyn Beard & Billy Parolini. Camera: John Raugalis. With Joseph Eero, Joe Niola, Mary Ann Schacht. T. J. Michaels

How low can you go? Unavoidably, the producers Michael Herz and Lloyd Kaufmann flirted with the subject of sect mania and the Manson-myth. Production companies like Troma ruined the image of "good" exploitation cinema (*à la* Corman) with films like this one, and discredited rehabilitated terms like trash or B-movie again.

INVOCATION OF MY DEMON BROTHER / USA 1969

Directed by Kenneth Anger. Music: Mick Jagger. With Robert "Bobby" Beausoleil

Not really influenced by the Family, but inextricably linked, this fantastic 11-minute film by Kenneth Anger has a very special protagonist. Besides Anton LaVey, the high priest of the Satanic Church of San Francisco, Robert "Bobby" Beausoleil, Family-member and cconvicted murderer of Gary Hinman acts in it. He and Kenneth Anger also worked together on the underground classic LUCIFER RISING. The legend tells that Beausoleil had stolen the illuminated material and handed it over to Charles Manson, who buried it in Death Valley. INVOCATION OF MY DEMON BROTHER, one of Anger's masterpieces, is a hypnotic, colourful journey into the symbolist world of psychedelic rites of Satan, conjuration dances, etc. without becoming ridiculous despite all its mysticism. It is a great achievement of Kenneth Anger to shoot collage-like experimental films as thrilling and full of ideas as "real" motion pictures (e.g. SCORPIO RISING, 1964). Perhaps, this can be attributed to his dandified way of life and his camp thinking. Anger preferred to film the mythical universe of rock and pop culture rather than ban political manifestos on celluloid like the rest of the experimental cinema of the Sixties.

MULTIPLE MANIACS / USA 1970

Written and directed by John Waters. Camera: John Waters. With Divine, David Lochary, Mink Stole, Edith Massey

John Waters about his film: "In 1969, right before I started to shoot MULTIPLE MANIACS, Sharon Tate was murdered. This crime would have a profound influence over the entire making of the film. Since the real killer hadn't been apprehended yet, I decided that Divine would take credit for the murders in the film. I figured that if the murderers were never caught, there would always be the possibility that maybe Divine really *did* do it. We wanted "to scare the world", just like the unheard-of Manson Family, but we used a movie camera instead of deadly weapons. The murder became an obsession, and I talked about it so much that one of our new actors flipped out in the middle of the scene and ran from the set, screaming: "I know that's a police camera. You've tricked me into confessing to the Tate murders, and now I'll be arrested!" As I was completing the film, the Manson Family was caught, so I quickly changed the ending, explaining that Divine really hadn't done it. Nobody, not even Divine, could upstage Charles Manson."

Today Waters' first talkie seems like a stoned college prank. Waters himself collects Manson material and has contact to some Family members. His connection to them was underlined by a scene in PINK FLAMINGOS (1972) where the slogan "FREE TEX WATSON" is clearly visible spray-painted on a wall.

THE NIGHT GOD SCREAMED / USA 1971

Directed by Lee Madden. Written by Gil Lasky & David Spelling. With Jeanne Crain, Alex Nicol

A preacher is crucified by psychotic Jesus freaks, who then turn on his wife. Another Manson-style, crazy homicidal cult.

THE NIGHT OF THE WITCHES / USA 1970

Written and directed by Keith Erik Burt. Camera: Herbert V. Theis. Music: Sean Bonniwell. With Keith Erik Burt, Ronald Taft, Anakorida

A certain Keith Larsen, who had already performed in films like WOMEN OF THE PREHISTORIC PLANET, stands behind this pseudonym. Here he portrays a raping preacher with Mansonesque traits. An almost unknown little sex & horror film.

THE OMEGA MAN / USA 1971

Directed by Boris Sagal. Written by John William Corrington, from the novel "I Am Legend" by Richard Matheson. Music by Ron Grainer. Camera: Russell Metty. With Charlton Heston, Anthony Zerbe, Rosalind Cash

Heston plays the last uninfected man on an Earth ravaged by a man-made virus which has reduced its victims to nocturnal albinos. These freaks have banded together in a cult known as the "Family", led by the sinister Zerbe. At the centre of the film lies a primal struggle between the forces of light and dark – perhaps a metaphor for the death of Sixties optimism at the hands of Manson's death squad and other "Satanic"

SNUFF

forces. Certainly, these elements are absent from the original novel and the first film version (THE LAST MAN ON EARTH/1964).

SNUFF aka THE SLAUGHTER aka AMERICAN CANNIBALE / USA-Argentina 1974
Directed by Roberta and Michael Findlay. Cast: unknown
The origin of a myth created by a couple who produced films according to the formula "minimal shooting time, minimal budget & sex'n'gore". What Mr. and Mrs. Findlay were shooting in Argentina within a few days was an awful botch titled SLAUGHTER, a sect-prostitution-murder-story influenced by Charles Manson. Finally, the product was considered so fouled up that it was not released. Then Allan Shackleton, the promoter, had a clever idea. He cut off the last third of the film (in the middle of a scene) and inserted a new scene, rather awkwardly staged, showing a film crew dismembering a pretty starlet. Believe it, or not, shrewd Mr. Shackleton managed to sell these four minutes on celluloid as a genuine snuff movie "made in Argentina, where life is cheap" (an original promotion text). So with a new title (SNUFF) SLAUGHTER became a big success and lured many voyeurs into cinemas all over the world.

SWEET SAVIOR / USA 1971
Directed by Robert L. Roberts. Written by Matt Cavanaugh. Camera: Victor Petrashevic. Music: Jeff Berry & Gilbert Slavin. With Troy Donahoe, Renay Granville, Francine Middleton
A typical mass product from the trashy abysses of US cinema, with the ex-kiddie-star Troy Donahoe as a Manson-style guru called Moon. Some describe this as being the first fictionalized account of the Manson case. The action is switched to the East Coast (New York), but the same sex-and-violence situations unfurl. When the cult members

SWEET SAVIOR

inevitably turn to mass murder, one of their victims is a pregnant actress. Some years later the notorious low-budget company Troma bought this film and re-titled it THE LOVE-THRILL MURDERS.

THOU SHALT NOT KILL, EXCEPT aka STRYKER'S WAR / USA 1987
Written, directed and photographed by Josh Becker. Music: Joseph Lo Duca. With Brian Schultz, John Manfredi, Robert Rickman, Tim Quill, Sam Raimi
An entertaining splatter-film, set in 1969, from the ensemble of the US director Sam Raimi, who delivers a guest performance as a Manson-like sect leader. A malicious hippie-clan terrorizes, rapes, and kills the poor citizens of a small town. So some good men (Vietnam veterans *à la* Rambo) set out to end the gloomy goings-on. The makers of this cheap and crazy epic obviously also wanted to maintain a certain trash-film tradition, as well as the tradition of the post-Manson films.

The Case

In the Seventies Jacques Mesrine was one of the most dangerous and most wanted criminals of French origin. In Canada and France he was actually regarded as Public Enemy Number One.

Born in Paris in 1936 as the son of a teacher and a fashion designer, he grew up in an orderly environment. But the youngster was expelled from various schools and was rather interested in cinema and weapons. In the night he roamed about through bars and whorehouses, and committed several thefts and burglaries. At the age of 18 he married a coloured student to legalize her pregnancy. Two years later, in the course of the Algerian War, he was drafted and divorced his wife. In April 1959 Mesrine returned to Paris decorated with a medal. Disappointed by the absurd war and society, he decided to take vengeance and become a "real" criminal. He committed numerous burglaries on apartments with two friends and frequented the hooker and gambling underworld. There he stabbed the pimp of a sweetheart of his youth in rage. In 1960 he met his second wife in Spain. She hated his way of life but gave birth to a daughter . Soon he committed his first contract murder in Italy. In 1961 he was arrested in a bank robbery and was imprisoned until July 1963. Then he took a job and lived a normal bourgeois life for two years.

Then Jacques Mesrine had a criminal relapse. He stole again, killed an accomplice in 1966, worked as a contract-killer in gangland feuds, and dealt with counterfeit money. Besides France, he also operated in Italy, Spain, and Switzerland. In that time he left his family. In 1968 he brutally butchered two pimps of his new mistress Janou and fled to Canada with her. There he became Public Enemy Number One. And this was his "career": the kidnapping of a billionaire, 11 years confinement for armed robbery, break-out, and a second capture, jailbreak from the safest prison of Canada, two bank robberies, shoot-outs with the police, the killing of two frontier guards. He broke into the State Prison to free some friends, and managed to get out of the country in spite of a dragnet operation. First he went to New York City, then he lived in Venezuela for a while. In 1972 he returned to France. In March 1973 Mesrine was arrested again, but he managed to escape during his trial. Only a special "anti-gangster commando" was able to hunt down the Public Enemy.

MESRINE

In 1974 he participated in hunger-strikes in prison to push through better conditions of detention, which brought him solitary confinement. Finally he was taken to a high-security unit built exclusively for him. There he wrote his autobiography, which was published in 1977. The trial began in May 1977, and he was finally sentenced to 20 years. One year later he broke out again with an accomplice, committed several robberies, and kidnapped high-ranking persons. On October 24, 1979 Jacques Mesrine was shot dead in his car by a special commando of the police.

MESRINE / France 1983

Directed by André Génovès. Written by André Génovès after Mesrine's autobiography. Camera: Jean-Claude Coutry. Music: Jean-Pierre Rusconi. With Nicolas Siberg, Caroline Aguilar, Gérard Sergues, Michel Poujade

The film refers to Mesrine's autobiography published in 1977, and significantly titled *The Death Instinct*. In this book the Public Enemy depicts his criminal career uncompromisingly and in glowing terms. He states that he became a criminal out of his own free will and was not driven by the forces of circumstance. About his cruel and brutal crimes he says that he "loved action and liked living dangerously". On the one hand Mesrine is a killer who does not fear anything, murders, and follows gangland's code of honour, on the other he is a loving father and son who repeatedly tries to get in touch with his parents and his daughter, even if it may cost his head. He describes himself as follows: "In the course of the years I have become brutal and dangerous. I was feared and felt in a way satisfied about that. I was only gentle and mild with children and old people. My milieu is like a jungle where the strong ones make the law. Everybody knew that I did not hesitate to kill."

Nevertheless, Mesrine time and again attacks a society which leaves the individual no choice, because it does not care for him. For him society is phonier and more immoral than gangland. His hate of society and the bourgeoisie is a central feature of Mesrine and an important motive for his deeds: "Personally I live from crime. From a certain kind of crime which does not consist of attacking aged people but banks and certain factories. I am a straight guy [...] Normally I do what I say. I don't do it for the publicity and risk my life every time. I am no angel of vengeance, but a revolutionary who lives his fury [...]."

In prison Mesrine fights for better conditions, and he complains about the inhuman system of the high-security units in interviews and letters to the editor. With his eloquent and profound commitment he uncovers some scandalous defects of the French administration of justice. Unfortunately, these facets and contradictions in Mesrine's personality are hardly dealt with in the film. MESRINE rather emphasizes the spectacular events of his careers, like daring jailbreaks and shootings. The film is highly factitious but lacks background information, so the director of this not really exciting, and often clumsily staged film misses out the opportunity of a serious analysis of a complex murderer and gangster.

DENNIS NILSEN

"Loneliness is a long, unbearable pain... There was never a place for me in the scheme of things... I had become a living fantasy on a theme in dark, endless dirges... I made another world, and real men would enter it and they would never really get hurt at all in the vivid, unreal laws of the dream. I caused dreams which caused death. This is my crime."

–Dennis Nilsen

The Case

He is Great Britain's serial killer with the most victims (with the probable exception of Dr Harold Shipman, whose kill-count of moribund old ladies has yet to be verified). Like Jeffrey Dahmer, the Scotsman Dennis Nilsen killed to have company according to a biographer. He did not kill for sex or money. The murders were the products of his loneliness.

Born in 1945 Nilsen grew up in disordered circumstances. His parents were divorced, and little Dennis was sent off to his grandfather. When his beloved grandfather died, the six-year-old boy saw his corpse completely unprepared and was deeply shocked. From 1961 to 1972 he worked as a cook in the army. Then he went into the police. Later he also held a job in a labour exchange. He developed an inclination for homosexuality and death fantasies. He often watched himself in the mirror lying motionless with his body painted white and his lips painted blue. On New Year's Eve 1978 the shy intelligent man committed his first murder. He took a drunk teenager to his place, then strangled and drowned him. Then he painstakingly washed him and even changed the victim's underpants. Nilsen lived with the corpse for a week, then he hid it under the floor. He maintained this ritual in his following murders. After washing them he watched TV with the dead. They kept him company for a fortnight, then he chopped them and burnt them in the garden piece by piece or stored them under the floor. Within one year the lonely killer committed nine murders. Though some potential victims were able to escape, he was not suspected. Late in 1981 Nilsen moved into a different neighbourhood and tried to change his

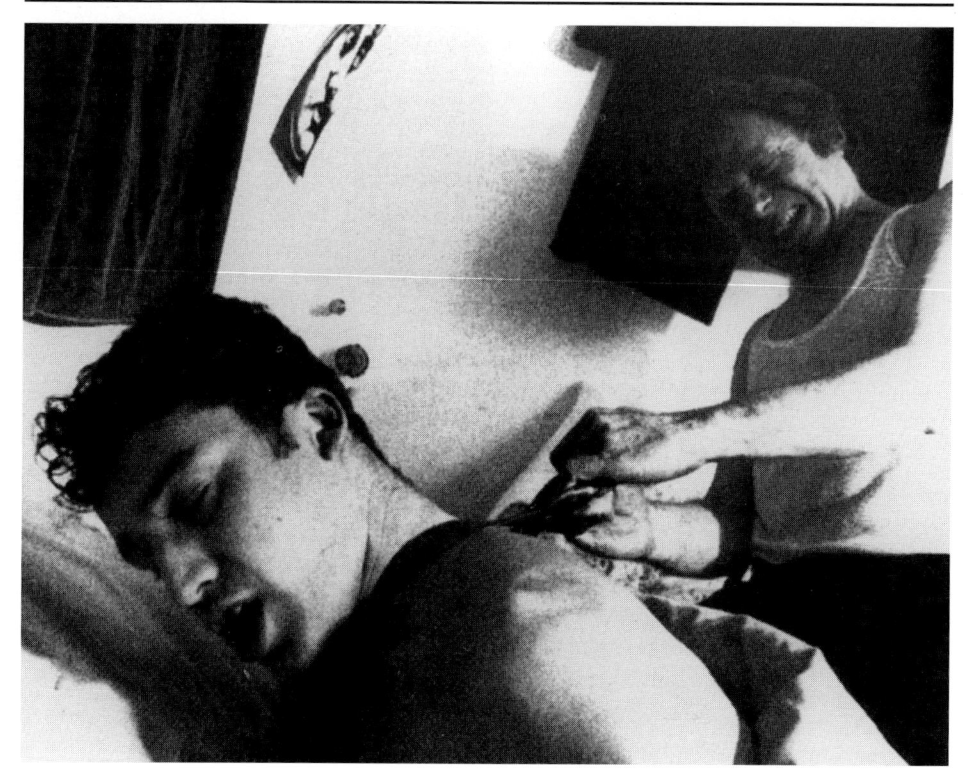

COLD LIGHT OF DAY

life, but by March 1982 he had killed again. He cooked the victims' remains in large pots or flushed them down the toilet. This became his doom. After some neighbours had complained about stopped-up waste pipes, the plumber made a gruesome discovery. 40 chunks of human remains had caused the defect. Though he removed most of the body parts in the night, he voluntarily opened the door for the police and confessed 15 murders. But only six could be proved against him. On November 4, 1983 Nilsen was sentenced to imprisonment for life. Later he wrote an open and uncompromising description of a murderer's feelings.

THE COLD LIGHT OF DAY / GB 1989-90

Written and directed by Fiona Lewis. Camera: Nigel Axworthy. Music: Paul Stewart Davies. With Bob Flag, Martin Bryne-Quinn, Geoffrey Greenhill, Andrew Edmans

In 1983 the British public is shaken. The ex-policeman and social worker Dennis Nilsen is arrested in his flat in North-London, after a plumber has noticed that parts of corpses had caused a blocked waste pipe. Within a few hours Nilsen confesses the murder of fifteen young men and so becomes one of the most atrocious serial killers in the UK 's criminal history.

What would have been a story for various exploitation films in America, or, at least, would have been adapted for a tele-play, is no topic for the censorship-ridden English film business. It has been left to the newcomer Fiona Lewis to adapt the story, with almost no money but still high artistic ambitions. Says Lewis in an interview: "I did a lot of research before I started this film [...] From the very first idea to the script I decided to do the film in a way that the audience remains 'outside'. This is why there are only very few close-ups. There is only one piece of music at the end of the film, after March's (Nilsen's) arrest, some sort of spooky requiem. Considering the topic it was extremely important for me not to use music. I felt that music was going to the audience too much in the events, was going to captivate it emotionally. This is what I wanted to avoid, because mass murder should not be glorified."

The cold light of day: depressive snapshots from the life of a serial killer. Of course, it is the homosexual killer Dennis Nilsen, though the name has been changed for legal reasons. Deliberate chill, isolation, an atmosphere like an icebox.

Fiona Lewis' approach can be best compared to John McNaughton's HENRY, PORTRAIT OF A SERIAL KILLER; though the Englishwoman had considerably less money at her disposal than the already cheap US production. This must be clearly stated, because the ambitious débutante is thwarted by the too slip-shod nature of her film. In every minute of COLD LIGHT OF DAY you see that it lacks the financial means for its intended rendering: coarse-grained, badly illuminated 16mm images, clumsy montage, and at times overtaxed actors undermine every profound artistic intention. What remains is a trashy, filthy film corresponding stylistically to Dennis Nilsen's revolting deeds (instead of playing down the murders via aestheticism), obviously caused by financial problems as well as a lack of craftsmanship. The German director Jörg Buttgereit showed how you can stage more subversive images with even less money in his killer-study SCHRAMM.

VIOLETTE NOZIÈRE

"I'm glad I killed him – he was a satyr!"
–Violette Nozière

The Case

The case of Violette Nozière stirred a lot of interest in Paris in the Thirties. The trial against the only 18-year-old-poisoner became a political issue.

Violette grew up in a poor and narrow environment. Her father, who worked for the French railroad company, was very strict and authoritarian. Yet her parents idolized their only child and made her believe that nothing was good enough for her. So pretty young Violette dreamt of a life in luxury and freedom. She tried to escape the petty-bourgeois narrowness and roved about in the bars of the Quartier Latin in the night, pretended to be a posh student, and earnt the necessary money as a casual prostitute. Her parents did not know anything of her double-life and even did not sense anything when they were told about her syphilis.

In January 1933 Violette leaves school. On March 23 she gave her parents poison for the first time, telling them it was medicine. Then she set fire to the flat. But the neighbours were able to save the narcotised victims just in time. Only a fortnight later she committed the second onslaught, this time with barbiturates, but it failed too. Finally Violette met the young student Jean Dabin and became his slave. He was the great love of her life, and she wanted to marry him under any circumstances. To win his love she gave him the money she earned as a prostitute and pretended that she was going to inherit 200,000 francs. She assumed that her parents had saved this sum. To get to the money she again added barbiturates to their drinks and turned on the gas in their apartment on August 21. Her father died, but her mother survived and reported her daughter to the police.

After her arrest Violette Nozière said that her father had sexually abused her when she was 13. She killed him because she hated him. But this accusation could never be proved. During her trial ultra-conservative circles demanded rigorous punishment for her onslaught on the fundamental values of family. Yet young people sided with the parricide because she symbolised an escape from petty-bourgeois bigotry for them. The Surrealists declared her to be their idol, for she had abolished conventional morals and lived as her true nature dictated. Violette was sentenced to death by the guillotine, but after vehement protests the sentence was altered to lifelong hard labour. In 1945 she was prematurely amnestied by Charles de Gaulle. Then she married and gave birth to five children. She owned a restaurant and also became reconciled with her mother. Almost 30 years after her deed Violette was even rehabilitated, and died in Paris in 1966.

VIOLETTE NOZIÈRE / France-Canada 1977

Directed by Claude Chabrol. Written by Odile Barski, Hervé Bromberger & Frederic Grendel after a novel by Jean-Marie Fittère. Camera: Jean Rabier. Music: Pierre Jansen. With Isabelle Huppert, Stéphane Audran, Jean Carmet, Jean Francois Garraud, Bernard Alane

Claude Chabrol tells the case of the 18-year-old poisoner from Violette's perspective. A bus ride after the deed is the starting point. The protagonist, Isabelle Huppert, who was awarded the Silver Palm for her performance in Cannes 1978, in her dark clothes. The press text is more poetical: "A silhouette black as mourning, lips red as blood, this is Violette when she walks through the city in the night. Mousy and gloomy as an autumn rain, this is Violette when she is at home again, under the roof of 'respectable people'."

One after the other fragments of her story come up in many flashbacks, complicating the viewer's effort to follow the chain of events. Memories from her early childhood, her authoritarian upbringing, the family's life in narrowest circumstances. Chabrol moves the solving of the case to the time after Violette's seizure. In this time she is also confronted with her surviving mother. The beautiful murderess' many ploys and lies are shown too. To be able to duplicate the circumstances of the crime as well as the psychological state of its protagonist, the film emphasizes detailed historical costumes and settings. Chabrol, who even went as far as using camera lenses from the Thirties, explained: "I did not try to deliver a historical depiction of the epoch of the Thirties, but I attempted to roll the film as I would have done it in 1933. [...] What interested me most was not the 'how' of the crime, this was no problem at all, but the 'why' of this parricide seemed to be relevant for me. So in the first place I had to try to understand Violette."

The real Violette Nozière was an idol of the Surrealists. Max Ernst painted an "homage" for her, a collection of poems by Breton, Eluard, and René Char illustrated by Salvador Dali was dedicated to her. Chabrol brings in the phenomenon of great admiration, because he sees himself in the same line of admirers: "Violette has fascinated me, like Eluard, Aragon, Margritte, Simone de Beauvoir and Pierre Brasseur before, especially the contradictions: murderess or saint, liar or faithful mistress, child or genius. I have tried to stage her dreams and her everyday life. First I was interested in her, because I am interested in poisoners and their motives. I have dealt with her profoundly and I love her for the things I found out about her. She was a young girl without any special education who as early as 1933 found out things which the women of today are trying to grasp with a great effort. I agree that women should liberate themselves to be able to live as women in freedom. I am only against it when they do it and behave like men afterwards. I love women too much for this. And I believe that Violette Nozière wanted to emancipate in this sense, namely to look for the optimal space within her femininity and finally to find this freedom. Probably, in her case this was only possible via murder, which Isabelle Huppert achieves to make astonishingly plausible."

Despite this admiration for its protagonist the film remains unbiased and sober. Emotions hardly reach the surface. The objectivity towards the central character makes it difficult for the viewer to identify and feel with her, a problem Chabrol wrestles with in his film about Landru too. That's why VIOLETTE NOZIERE succeeds in its beautiful photography and décor; whereas it otherwise lacks the suspense and urgency of plot we expect from "True Crime" cinema.

CARL PANZRAM

"While you were trying me here, I was trying all of you, too. I've found you guilty. Some of you, I've executed. If I live , I'll execute some more of you. I hate the whole human race [...] You think I'm playing crazy, don't you? I'm not. I know right from wrong. No delusions. I don't hear anything you don't hear. My conscience doesn't bother me. I have no conscience. I believe the whole human race should be exterminated. I'll do my best to do it every chance I get."

–Carl Panzram during his trial, 1928

"If you see me comin', better step aside, a lot of men didn't, a lot of men died. One fist of iron, the other of steel, if the left one don't get'cha, then the right one will."

–"16 Tons", an old blues ballad

"Today I am dirty, tomorrow I'll be just DIRT"

–Carl Panzram, from a letter written the day before his execution

The Case

With legendary human monsters of history like Marshall Gilles De Rais, Countess Erszebeth Bathory or Vlad Tepesz, the thin line between fiction and reality remains in the dark. We will never get to know the true extent and, above all, the real motives of their bloody deeds. In the case of Carl Panzram, who raged in the first decades of the 20th century, we don't need the reports of others. The serial killer documented his extreme crimes himself. Panzram's autobiography, first hand-written in Death Row then published as *Killer: A Journal of Murder*, shares the philosophical basis of De Rais & co: "This is not only about murder, it's a warcry against humanity. In my lifetime I have murdered 21 human beings", Panzram noted. "I have committed thousands of burglaries, robberies, larcenies, arsons and last but not least I have committed sodomy on more than 1,000 male human beings. For all of these things I am not the least bit sorry."

Yet his origin is a central point that separates Carl Panzram from the immoral libertines of the past. Whereas De Rais or Bathory acted out of their aristocratic or bourgeois positions and regarded the ordinary people merely as "material" for their lethal desires, the US killer comes from the other side of the system. Panzram suffered from aclassic underdog childhood that had alreadyby the age of eight brought him into conflict with the law. Born on a small farm in Minnesota, he was an alcoholic at the age of nine, from then on he spent a lot of time in corrective institutions, where he was brutalised more and more. Locked up early in a vicious circle of crime and punishment, Panzram spent 20 of his 38 years in prison.

Repentance remained a foreign word for the serial killer until the end. When liberal protests tried to prevent his dream of execution, he threatened, "I have no desire to reform myself, my only desire is to reform people who try to reform me and I believe that the only way to reform people is to kill em. My motto is, Rob em all, Rape em all and Kill em all."

Carl Panzram was hanged on September 5, 1930 at 6:01 a.m. His last words to the hangman are legendary. "Hurry it up, you Hoosier bastard! I could hang a dozen men while you're fooling around!"

KILLER: A JOURNAL OF MURDER / USA 1996

Directed by Tim Metcalfe. Written by Thomas E. Gaddis, James O. Long, Tim Metcalfe. Camera: Ken Kelsch. Music: Graeme Revell. With James Woods, Harold Gould, Robert Sean Leonard, Jeffrey DeMunn, Richard Council, Cara Buono, Ellen Greene, Robert John Burke, Steve Forrest

The first thing wrong with this movie is the title. Tim Metcalfe does not in the least try to screen Panzram's notorious autobiography, but rather the circumstances that led to these memoirs. Carl Panzram, one of the most cold-blooded killers of all times, placed confidence in a prison guard when he was in jail.

The historical facts: when rookie guard Henry Lesser doed his rounds in the Washington District Jail in August 1928, he hears of a failed jailbreak attempt by a new prisoner. Moreover, he gets to know that on the warden's orders this man has been abused sadistically by his colleagues – so much so that one of his testicles is ruptured and has to be removed. He is shocked by the extent of the torture and when he hears that the prisoner, a certain Carl Panzram, is completely broke, he gives him a dollar. This symbolic gift breaks the delinquent's emotional armour for a moment and Henry Lesser has a new confidant. "We became very friendly, and a spirit of *entente cordiale* prevailed between us", he notes later. The things Panzram tells him cut the ground from under the young liberal's feet. It is the story of survival of a tormented guy who, full of white-hot hatred, paid back every blow he suffered doubly and more. With the stationery Lesser has smuggled into his cell, Panzram immortalizes his life in aggressive torrents of words. When he is transferred to Leavenworth, Kansas after a sensational trial in the course of which he confesses his 21 murders, the guard and the killer remain in mail contact until the latter's execution. Of course, Lesser isn't able to convince the mean machine Panzram of his Christian Democrat ethics. Yet until the bitter end the two guys struggle with words and ideas. A conflict that leaves us cold in KILLER: A JOURNAL OF MURDER.

Metcalfe, who wrote the screenplay for the Yuppie-shocker KALIFORNIA, strings together long dialogue scenes and would-be authentic sepia prison images, but fails to evoke any intense atmosphere or any deeper emotions. Vacillating between an indictment of the US legal system and a conventional character study, the film runs on meaninglessly. Here it is bad enough that the discussions of the educated benefactor Lesser (dull: Leonard) and Mr. Panzram (highly ambitious but a casting mistake: James Woods) remind us more than once of dedicated yet at the same time deadly boring TV discussions. Moreover, it is really a crime that Metcalfe smooths over the memoirs of a killer, containing scenes of mayhem which cannot at all be transformed into a film, to an R-rated TV level in black-and-white flashbacks. Therefore the case of Carl Panzram, a man whose utter malignancy made him a natural phenomenon, leaves one completely cold.

"I looked for a boy. I found one. He was our table waiter. I educated him in the art of sodomy as practised by civilized people. But he was only a savage and didn't appreciate the benefits of civilization. He told my boss and the Boss man fired me quick but before he did I licked the hell out of him [...] While I was sitting there, a little nigger boy about 11 or 12 years old came bumming around. He was looking for something. He found it too. I took him out to a gravel pit about a quarter mile from the main camp of the Sinclair oil Co. at Loanda. I left him there, but first I committed sodomy on him and killed him. His brains were coming out of his ears when I left him and he will never be any deader. He is still there. Then I went to town bought a ticket on the Belgian steamer to Lobito Bay down the coast. There I hired a canoe and 6 niggers and went out hunting in the bay and back waters. I was looking for crocodiles I found them. Plenty. They were all hungry. I fed them. I shot all 6 of those niggers and dumped em in. The crocks done the rest."

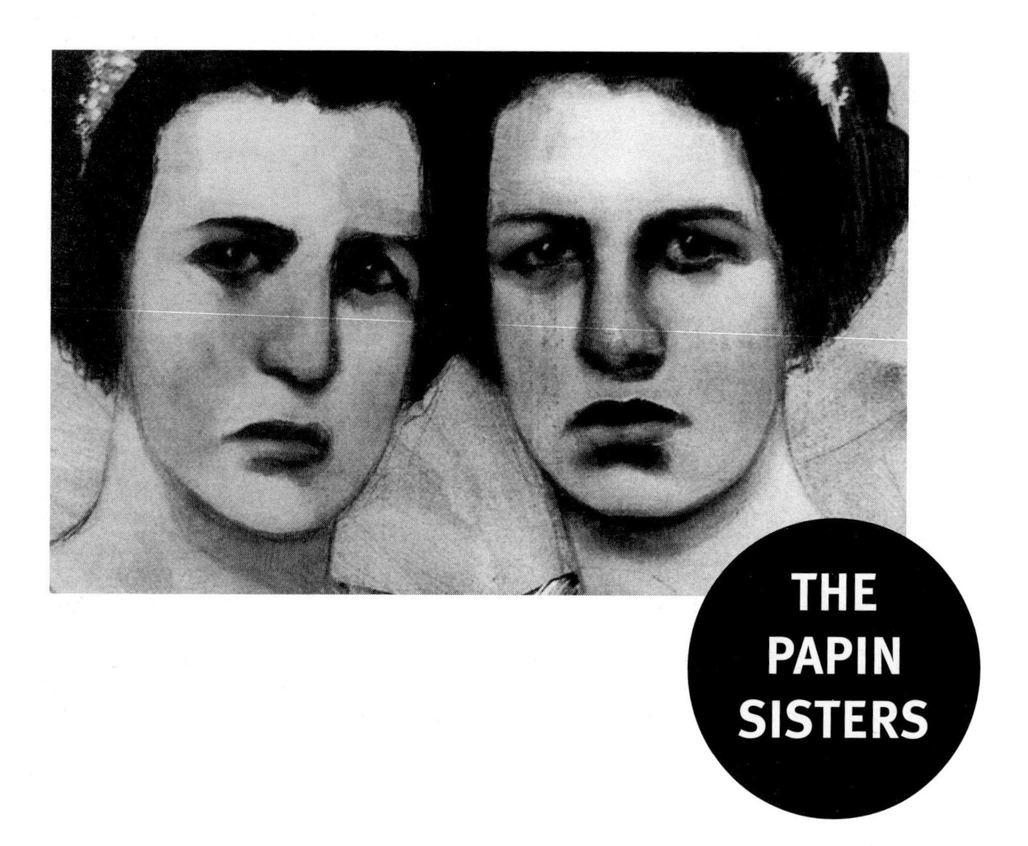

THE PAPIN SISTERS

"I explained to Madame that I was not able to iron because electricity had fallen out and then I saw that she was going to jump at me. So I anticipated her and scratched out her eyes with my fingers."
–Léa Papin at her trial

The Case

They were called "the Satanic sisters" or "the devils of Le Mans", but Christine and Léa Papin looked anything but diabolical. The two sisters in fact appeared to be full of shy restraint when they had to justify themselves before the jury for a gruesome double-murder in their hometown on September 20, 1933. Gazing shyly down to the floor they listened to the accusations.

The deed that had excited France had happened in a respectable bourgeois home on February 2 of the same year. Appreciated by Monsieur Lancelin, his wife, and his daughter, 28-year-old Christine and her 21-year-old sister Léa had already been working there as maids for years. But it remained open how the girls' relationship to their employers really was. Still, the world of the Lancelins' house could not have been as intact as it would be depicted later on. As a matter of fact, there must have been some serious conflicts between the women in the house. Léa damaged a flat-iron one month before the fatal deed, wherefore she was rebuked by her mistress and her salary was reduced.

But such a trifle cannot have triggered off what had happened on that Winter's evening. A clumsy mistake of the sisters caused an electric fallout when the family was out. A petty error, but Léa and Christine feared reprisals from their

LES ABYSSES

masters. When Madame Lancelin and her daughter returned and discovered the damage, a verbal conflict developed. Everything went extremely quickly – the sisters threw themselves at their mistresses and tore their eyes out of their sockets alive. "Then they attack the bodies of their victims with all within reach, hammer, tin jar, kitchen knife, smash their faces, strip their private parts and deeply slash the thighs and buttocks of the one to stain the other with her blood. Then they wash the tools of these atrocious rites, wash themselves and go to bed together." (Jacques Lacan in *Motives Of Paranoid Crime*).

Having a foreboding Monsieur Lancelin entered the pitch-dark building together with a policeman and found the corpses of his wife and his daughter mutilated past recognition. Then he found the two maids cowering together naked in bed. Dr. Logre, a well-known psychiatrist of the time pleaded for insanity, but the jury found Léa and Christine responsible and guilty. Regarded as the dominant one Christine was sentenced to death. Later her verdict was altered to imprisonment for life. She died in a lunatic asylum as early as 1937. Léa was sentenced to ten years. The motives of "the Devils of Le Mans" remain in dark despite the analyses of specialists like Jacques Lacan. "I do not regret anything", Christine said in front of the jury, "Neither I have planned my crime, nor have I felt hatred".

LES ABYSSES / France 1962

Directed by Nico Papatakis. Written by Jean Vauthier. Camera: Jean-Michel Boussaguet. Music: Pierre Barbaud. With Francine Bergé, Colette Bergé, Pascale de Boyson, Paul Bonias

Compared to other murderous women whose motives seemed evident (vengeance, jealousy, etc.), Léa and Christine Papin rank among the most irrational killers. Their enigmatic lack of motives fascinated artists like Jean Paul Sartre, Simone de Beauvoir, or André Gide. The Surrealists adored the Papin sisters as representatives – like Violette Nozière before them – of an individual revolt against the bourgeoisie.

"The Papin sisters were brought up in the monastery of Le Mans. Then their mother placed them with a 'bourgeois' family of the town. For six years they were totally enduring reprimands, unreasonable demands, and insults. Fear, fatigue and humiliation slowly nourished their hatred inside, this alcohol so mild which comforts you secretly, because it promises the passion to supported it sooner or later with physical violence. When the day had come, Léa and Christine paid their mistresses back for the injustice, as a matter of fact, salty. They literally massacred their mistresses, scratched out their eyes and smashed their heads. Then they washed themselves carefully and went to bed relieved and indifferent. The flash had struck, the wood was burnt, the sun had gone out forever." (Paul Eluard & Benjamin Péret).

This cinematic adaptation of the tragic events of Le Mans seems to have disappeared. Yet it was celebrated by the critics when it was released. Jean-Paul Sartre was so enthused that he called it "the first tragedy" of cinema. Jean Genet called it a "tornado from beginning to end". The two lead actresses (both ballet dancers) were driven to the verge of nervous collapse by director Papatakis, who refused to let them wash and goaded them into fights. It seems to have done the trick.

LES BLESSURES ASSASSINES (MURDEROUS MAIDS) / France 2001

Directed by Jean-Pierre Denis. Written by Jean-Pierre Denis & Michèle Halberstadt, after the book "L'affaire Papin" by Paulette Houdyer. Camera: Jean-Marc Fabre. With Sylvie Testud, Julie Marie Parmentier, Isabelle Renauld, Dominique Labourier, Jean-Gabriel Nordmann, François Levantal, Marie Donnio

This most recent film about Christine and Léa Papin was made during the writing of this book, demonstrating the enduring fascination of the case in France.

EN QUÊTE DES SOEURS PAPIN (THE SEARCH FOR THE PAPIN SISTERS) / France 2000 (Documentary)

Directed & photographed by Claude Ventura. Text by Philippe Paringaux. Music: Miklos Rozsa. Narrator: Pascale Thirode

What was life like for housemaids in a bourgeois household in Le Mans in the thirties? The Papin sisters worked for the Lancelin family for seven years; they even called Madame Lancelin 'maman' (mummy). Who were these people that the two young women were working for? How did the court cope with the fact that, although the murder weapons were found and a confession was made, no motive for the murder could be established? And what about Léa Papin, the younger of the two sisters? Léa finished serving her prison sentence, but her official date of death is not known. How did she live – and how did she die?

The idea for this documentary came from Laurent and Michèle Pétin, the producers of LES BLESSURES ASSASSINES, who wanted to try and tackle some of the questions raised by their film. Director Ventura previously made TV documentaries on rock music, classical music as well as portraits of artists such as Arthur Rubinstein, Andres Segovia and Yehudi Menuhin. His strictly sociolocical approach brings a lot of interesting facts about the Papin sisters on the surface, but fails to express the irrational truth about Christine and Léa – like all other movies about the case.

MAIDS, THE / GB 1974

Directed by Christopher Miles. Written by Robert Enders & Christopher Miles after the play by Jean Genet. Camera: Douglas Slocombe. Music: Laurie Johnson. With Glenda Jackson, Susannah York, Vivien Merchant, Mark Burns

THE MAIDS

Jean Genet was one of the poets deeply shocked but at the same time fascinated by the Papin sisters' terrible double-murder. His one-act play *The Maids,* performed for the first time in 1947 is based on the murderous servants, but transforms their blind motiveless act of violence to a more general social parable of class-circumstances and mechanisms of dependence. The maids Claire and Solange staging scenes with sado-masochist undertones while their mistress is away are the focus of this dialogue-staccato. They enact scenes where Claire plays the hated mistress and Solange her executioner. It is the sisters' greatest desire to poison their unloved employer. "We shall be that eternal couple, Solange, the two of us, the eternal couple of the criminal and the saint. We'll be saved, Solange, saved, I swear to you!"

The British star-actresses Glenda Jackson and Susannah York try hard to slip into the maids' roles, and to start a hysterical tragedy of emotions. They spit all their self-hatred and anger against their snobbish mistress into each other's face. Unlike the Papin sisters' cruelly delirious amok, the film (like Genet) sees them as women remaining servants forever. "When slaves love each other, it is no love." At the end Solange poisons her sister instead of the real Madame. Genet's revolt is only a fake slave-rebellion.

Christopher Miles should have anticipated that it is not enough to film a play like a stage performance. He completely trusts his actresses, puts them into a situation, and lets the camera run. What can grow into a captivating evening in the theatre, becomes a 90-minute display of verbosity and boredom in its cinematic version.

SISTER MY SISTER / GB 1994

Directed by Nancy Meckler. Written by Wendy Kesselmann after her book "My Sister In This House". Camera: Ashley Rowe. Music: Stephen Warbeck. With Joely Richardson, Jodhi May, Julie Walters, Sophie Thursfield

"That there is more going on than meets the eye is a huge thrill," David Lynch said once in an interview with Chris Rodley about his fascination with mystery in cinema. "So I think fragments of things are pretty interesting. You can dream the rest. Then you are a participant."

David Lynch in his best, i.e. most *enigmatic* moments would probably be the perfect candidate to make a film of the Papin case. This is what comes to your mind when you watch the adaptation of the tragedy of Le Mans in question. In spite of some good atmospheric attempts, the American director Nancy Meckler has given away too many chances trying to get a grip on the irrational with the tools of psychology and social analysis. Following Jean Genet's footsteps, it is again the suffocating bourgeois milieu that leads to the amok of the two sisters who are called Christina (Joely Richardson) and Rea (Jodhi May) here. Moreover, Nancy Meckler and her scriptwriter Wendy Kesselmann seem to put tons of feminist theory upon their work, for it is the symbolic figure of the mother that represents repression, clitorectomizes everything vividly female and directs it into dead-end channels in SISTER MY SISTER. That's why the film does without male protagonists and focuses on Madame and Mademoiselle Danzard (the latter is prevented from living and being a woman by her repressive *Maman*) versus the two maids in the attic. At first the innocent camera-eye watching the incestuous lesbian games of the sisters in the attic is juxtaposed with the suffocating atmosphere on the ground floor. Only after humiliation becomes more frequent in the house, does the relationship between Christina and Rea turn abysmal. Flashbacks telling, on the one hand, of convent school traumata and on the other about the mother's central status for the labile Rea. The claustrophobic attic chamber becomes a psycho-sexual isolation-cell, until a trifling incident triggers off all the sisters' stored-up hatred against their suppressers.

Does SISTER MY SISTER want to suggest that in a rigid era like the Thirties two women who could not communicate their inner and outer conflicts had no choice but murder? Hopefully not. For the Papin sisters' deed cannot be so banally deciphered. Furthermore, one really can't imagine any less adequate pioneers of the feminist issue than the "Devils of Le Mans".

Pauline PARKER & Juliet HULME

"I'm writing of this up in the morning before the death. I felt very excited and the night before Christmassy last night. I did not have pleasant dreams though. [...] Why could not mother die? Dozens of people, thousands of people are dying every day. So why not mother, and father too? Life is hard."

–From Pauline Parker's diary

The Case

In the late Forties Juliet Hulme, the 15-year-old daughter of an English scientist, came to New Zealand with her family to cure her tuberculosis. There she met Pauline Parker (16) in school. Pauline's parents had been pretending to be married for more than twenty years. Soon deep friendship developed between the two girls. They created their own imaginary world where they could let their fantasies flow. But their close contact was regarded "unhealthy" by their parents. So Juliet had to go to South Africa with her father, and Pauline was forbidden to accompany them by her mother. On June 22, 1954 the two girls slew Honora Parker with a brick wrapped in a stocking. 45 injuries were listed in the autopsy. Right from the beginning the police did not believe in the girls' version of an accident. So Pauline confessed the murder on the following day. In the meantime her diary had been found. It revealed the killing-plans made in despair about their imminent separation. The diary became the main evidence in a trial, laying bare the girls' exceptional relationship, and thus arousing the whole of New Zealand. "I am beyond the law", Juliet wrote in a passage and called Pauline and herself persons of genius. The highly intelligent girls created a world where they could take over different identities in their daydreams. So Juliet once became Charles II, emperor of Borôvia, then his mistress Deborah. Pauline imagined herself as Lancelot.

As the girls bathed together, slept in one bed quite often, and discussed sex, some doctors suspected a lesbian relationship. But this remained unproved. According to the diary there had been some erotic experiments where they had been "acting like saints making love in bed".

Pauline and Juliet were declared responsible for their deed and taken to separate prisons. They could not be sentenced to death because of their youth. In November 1959 Juliet Hulme was released and left New Zealand soon afterwards. Two weeks later Pauline Parker was dismissed and stayed in the country on probation until 1965. They were released on condition that they would never see each other again.

Today Juliet Hulme lives in England under the pseudonym Anne Perry, working as a successful writer of whodunits – as her agent announced at the première of HEAVENLY CREATURES. A final spicy detail: all her novels are situated in Victorian times and predominantly deal with the moral double standards and the repression of (female) emotions in that time.

HEAVENLY CREATURES / New Zealand 1994

Directed by Peter Jackson. Written by Peter Jackson & Frances Walsh. Camera: Alan Bollinger. Music: Peter Dasent. With Melanie Lynskey, Kate Winslet, Diana Kent, Sarah Peirse, Clive Morrison

"Innocence. Imagination. Obsession. Three words expressing everything which has made this film such a fascinating story: a murder mystery about love, a murder mystery without villains." (Peter Jackson)

No other director than Peter Jackson, the guru of the world-wide splatter-community since the weird slapstick-horror of BAD TASTE (1989) and BRAINDEAD (1992), suddenly reveals himself as a sensitive cinematic poet in his fourth film. Just as the New Zealander waded in blood and guts up to his ankles brilliantly in his earlier films, here he focuses with similar perfection on the mindscapes and adolescent disturbances of his young female protagonists. Yet there are similarities in Jackson's oeuvre as a whole. On the formal level there is the constantly moving, often rushing camera, and on the thematic level Jackson's disgust of suffocating bourgeois values, which he often attacks with crude humour (as in the super-mother tormenting the protagonist of BRAINDEAD).

After an electrifying pre-titles sequence HEAVENLY CREATURES tells the story of an exceptional friendship with exceptional consequences chronologically, like most True Crime films. Pauline, a shy chubby girl (Lynskey) growing up in the small town of Canterbury in well-ordered circumstances, meets Juliet (pneumatic future TITANIC-star Winslet), a pretty English girl, in school. They become close friends very quickly, because they perfectly complement each other. Juliet is extroverted, eloquent, and austerely charming. Pauline is the silent introverted author of the diary blessed with an abundant imagination. When she discovers one day that Juliet shares her interest in writing, the two girls become inseparable and escape into an imaginary realm of daydreams they call the "4th World", a metaphysical paradise with Borôvia, a medieval kingdom with court, princes, and princesses, as its epicentre. In HEAVENLY CREATURES this land is made visible by computer-animation, and forms a contrast to the lamentable reality.

The more Pauline and Juliet flee into their dream-world, the more school and parental home become insufferable for them. Borôvia is their kingdom of joy, sexual desires, and Mario Lanza (an idol of the girls singing his arias in their daydreams). There is even a Borôvian religion. But there are only enemies in everyday life: Juliet's father, who regards their close friendship as the beginning of a lesbian relationship, Pauline's mother, who suspects similarly "unhealthy" things, evil teachers, clumsy and blunted young suitors, etc. The personalities of the girls begin to change too. Pauline, once shy and hesitant, becomes more and more dominant, vice versa formerly eloquent Juliet becomes the passive half. The day of the murder, the day that will

HEAVENLY CREATURES

change everything, comes nearer and nearer.

HEAVENLY CREATURES by no means excuses or plays down the brutal murder, but shows it as a shockingly realistic rupture in the fabric of the girls' hallucinatory world. Yet the film still advocates a child's or teenager's right for dreams, visions, and escape from reality. Peter Jackson says: "This is an important point of reference for me. When I was 15 myself, I was living in my own world far away from the adults. Of course, I wasn't such an extreme example as the girls in the film, but in a way you can compare it. I fabricated models myself, did Super 8-films and had this whole imaginary world around me."

The film crew did not contact the real protagonists to protect their private sphere, but painstakingly scrutinized Pauline's diaries and other contemporary material. Together with co-author Frances Walsh, Peter Jackson above all wanted to correct the cliché of the evil-through-and-through "lesbian schoolgirl-killers" predominating in New Zealand. He emphasised: "I wanted to portray the girls as human beings, as real persons and not as cold-blooded monstrous creatures."

Among the films portraying obsessive friendships with lethal consequences HEAVENLY CREATURES is a special case, it manages to unite the levels of form and content highly convincingly. Whereas comparable films like SWOON and FUN (1994) restrict themselves to a shallow surface, Peter Jackson manages to submerge his audience deep into the minds of his (anti-)heroines.

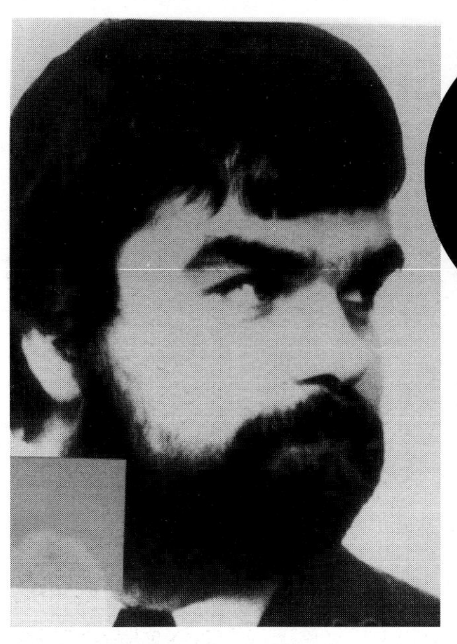

NORBERT POEHLKE

The Hammer-Killer

"'This is my life, mine and the life of the children. You don't fit into that, you bitch. Clean up here and look after the children during the day', Poehlke whispered into his wife's ear, 'you don't love them, I am the only one they love.' Inge gasped with tears running down her cheeks. 'Never do that again, never ask for Wagner again! Anyway, don't say I am the hammer-man!'

In a defiant movement he flung his wife away from him. Both hands around her neck she hit the corridor wall with her head. [...] Above you heard the dribbling of little feet and worried children's voices. Inge said, 'I'm only afraid that something happens again.' Poehlke did not hear it. He ran the back of his hand over his mouth to wipe off the spittle. Then he began to sing aloud like a priest, 'Kein schoener Land in dieser Zeit als hier das uns're weit und breit...'

'Who has screamed here?', one of the two boys shouted from above. Poehlke did not answer and went on singing, dragging his sons into their room."

–Fred Breinersdorfer, *The Hammer Killer*

The Case

Stealing cars and using them in a bank-robbery is criminal routine. People very rarely get hurt that way.

On May 3, 1984 a series of crimes ranking among the most terrible of post-war Germany begins in a German backwater, in the area of Heilbronn-Ludwigsburg. An unknown, obviously irrational delinquent cold-bloodedly shoots motorists in their cars just to get a getaway vehicle for bank robberies. The bank robberies all have the same pattern. A man with a Zorro mask enters the counter hall, smashes the teller's window with a heavy sledgehammer, and threatens everyone present with a gun. The media designates him "The Hammer-Killer"; after a long break he strikes again in December of the same year. Another car owner has to die, but shortly before the robbery the delinquent changes his mind. Within the same month he starts a second

THE HAMMER-KILLER

attempt. Swinging his hammer he seizees an enormous amount of money in a 'Volksbank' branch in Cleebronn. The owner of the getaway car is found with a bullet in his head in a nearby forest.

In the course of time it becomes more and more probable that "The Hammer-Killer" is a cop. On August 8, 1985 a special commission formed for this case addresses the public because the police believe they have found the delinquent from among their ranks. But the cops err, they have seized the wrong one.

On Monday, August 26 "The Hammer-Killer" commits his last robbery in Rosenberg. Two months later, on October 18, the corpses of a woman and a child are found in a little one-family house in the village Backnang-Strümpfelbach. The police assumes a typical man-shoots-wife-and-child-case, a family tragedy born of despair. But then the corpses of a wanted murderer and another shot child are found on a beach in Calabria, Italy, one thousand kilometres away from Germany. In the meantime, banknotes galore stuffed in hiding-places are found in the half-completed one-family house. Later the background of the case is reconstructed: Norbert Poehlke, a policeman in his early thirties turns out to be "The Hammer-Killer", who killed his family and himself after his wife had found him out. Poehlke was more than an ordinary murderer and robber. He represented the madness of normality. We will never get to know what forced him to shoot the people in their cars.

DER HAMMERMOERDER (THE HAMMER-KILLER) / Germany 1990 (TV)

Directed by Bernd Schadewald. Written by Fred Breinersdorfer after his own documentary novel. Camera: Ingo Hamer. Music: Ingfried Hoffmann. With Christian Redl, Ulrike Kriener, Silvan Oesterle, Timmy Vetter, Ulrich Pleitgen

A subtle, creeping film out of an emotional icebox. The way Bernd Schadewald slowly dissects the petty-bourgeois philistine world of his protagonist has something of John McNaughton's or Richard Brooks' grandeur, and shall be regarded as one of the best contributions to the True Crime genre.

The cop Norbert Poehlke, the father of two children, is dissatisfied with his underpaid job. After winning a few thousand deutschmarks in the lottery he dreams of a one-family house with a dream car in front of the door, an existence with "a little bit of luxury" for himself and his family. He begins to raise several loans whose repayment instalments far exceed his financial limits. Soon the family is in an absurd situation: they live in a half-completed house of their own, a Mercedes stands in front of the door, but they lack the money for everyday life. The Poehlkes starve and freeze at home, the bank threatens with imminent seizure of their belongings. So while despair is growing, "The Hammer-Killer" begins to strike.

Schadewald keeps precisely to Fred Breinersdorfer's book (this is rare too, especially if you consider numerous botched US TV productions), yet THE HAMMER-KILLER is more than a string of facts and names. Like Jörg Buttgereit's SCHRAMM the film delivers a merciless psychograph of the German petty bourgeois and his short circuits. The film depicts a man deluded by his capitalistic desires heading inexorably towards disaster and dragging his family with him.

His dreams of an expensive Mercedes and an idyllic house end on an Italian beach at dawn: "Still sitting Gabriel had fallen asleep, his head turned to the side. Poehlke stared at the little body, studied the face, and perceived the minute movements of breathing. Like a man turning coolly to the side to take a lighter out of his pocket, he turned a little bit, took out the gun and aimed it at the child's body. His face revealed something like worry. Then he shot. The detonation almost blasted his eardrums, blue powder-smoke filled the car. Poehlke drew back the weapon, lay down, and put the hot barrel into his mouth. Then he bit into it and pulled the trigger." (Fred Breinersdorfer, *The Hammer Killer*).

The Night Stalker

"You don't understand. You are not expected to. You are not capable of it. I am beyond your experience. I am beyond good and evil. Legions of the night, night breed. Repeat not the errors of the Night Prowler and show no mercy. I will be avenged [...] Lucifer dwells within us all."

–Richard Ramirez in front of the jury

The Case

Richard Ramirez, convicted for 14 murders and numerous rapes, terrorized Los Angeles between 1984 and1985. The ghost-like emaciated Satanist and Heavy Rock fan with long black hair and yellow teeth committed his gory deeds exclusively under cover of the night. Hence known as "The Night Stalker", Richard prowled the suburbs looking for open windows, or doors easy to open. When he found one, he broke into the house and raped and killed its petrified residents like a black angel of death.

At home in his mouldy apartment he listened again and again to his favourite song "Nightprowler" by the metal band AC/DC, dreaming of his victims' blood. In August 1985, when the police investigations and the hysteria of the people of Los Angeles had reached a climax, the killer's identity was revealed. Ramirez,

MANHUNT

whose face had already been on the title page of every newspaper for a few hours, was recognized by some residents when he tried to steal a car in East L.A. The people knocked the killer down and beat him until the police came. Richard Ramirez was sentenced to death thirteen times, which only cost him a scornful grin. There are rumours that the Night Stalker was visited in prison five times per day on average, only by women who had fallen in love with him.

MANHUNT: SEARCH FOR THE NIGHT STALKER / USA 1989 (TV)
Directed by Bruce Seth Green. Written by Joseph Gunn. Music: Silvester Levay. With A. Martinez, Richard Jordan, Lisa Eilbacher, Gerry Bamman, Jenny Sullivan
Again the same old story. Restricting itself to the naked facts MANHUNT is a mediocre TV adaptation of an highly interesting, shocking case. The film's highlights are the original settings and its rarely glimpsed killer's strong similarity to the real Richard Ramirez. MANHUNT never asks why the young man has become a blood-drinking Satanist, or what has driven him into his thoroughly sociopathic hallucinations. As in many television plays of the genre, the two cops investigating the case are the focus of interest, not the mental abysses of the killer, or the sheer terror in the eyes of the victims. The film circles around the cops' investigation problems, as well as their marriage troubles and other emotional trivia. Like Ramirez, one of the two detectives is of Mexican origin (A. Martinez, also to be seen in COLORS, 1988), which the film exploits as an opportunity to pretend to be politically correct and impartial.

"But I didn't realize what I'd done till I heard that sound. Like somebody drowning. Screaming under water. I handed the knife to Dick. I said, 'Finish him. You'll feel better.' Dick tried – or pretended to. But the man had the strength of ten men [...] Then I aimed the gun. The room just exploded. Went blue. Just blazed up. Jesus, I'll never understand why they didn't hear the noise twenty miles around."

–Truman Capote, *In Cold Blood*

The Case

On a Sunday morning in November 1959 a complete average family, father, mother, son, and daughter, are brutally murdered without any obvious motive in Holcomb, Kansas. Icy terror falls upon the inhabitants of the small town, who assume that the killer lives among them. Police investigation runs at full blast and the two delinquents, Perry Smith and Dick Hickock, two ex-prisoners and tramps, are soon arrested.

The murderous duo have been informed by a fellow jailbird that a huge sum of money is said to be stored in the house of the Clutter family. Yet when breaking into the farm house in the midst of wheat fields, they can't find any savings except 50

IN COLD BLOOD (1967)

dollars. What happens then, can only partly be explained by frustration and momentary anger. "The crime was a psychological accident, virtually an impersonal act; the victim might as well have been killed by lightning", Truman Capote writes in his famous new journalism-novel *In Cold Blood*. "A True Account Of A Multiple Murder And Its Consequences" is the subtitle of a novel painstakingly staging the Clutter case and thereby not only presenting the anatomy of a crime, but also drawing a critical picture of the American society torn between Puritanism and crime.

Perry Smith and Dick Hickock are sentenced to death. Yet it takes two long tormenting years until they are executed.

IN COLD BLOOD / USA 1967

Directed by Richard Brooks. Written by Richard Brooks after the novel by Truman Capote. Camera: Conrad Hall. Music: Quincy Jones. With Robert Blake, Scott Wilson, John Forsythe, Paul Stewart, John McLiam

IN COLD BLOOD, a film that, like Truman Capote's novel, can be read on several levels: as a committed plea against the death penalty, or a reflection on the paradox of a senseless massacre, and as a hallucinatory thriller investigating the deadly trance of the killers (despite its social realism).

In 1968 Richard Brooks adapted Truman Capote's best-selling novel with an obsession for facts and details unique in the history of film, but appropriate for the book. So most of the scenes were done on the original settings, like the real house of the Clutter family. Even some members of the actual jury took part in the court scenes. The two protagonists Robert Blake and Scott Wilson slipped perfectly into the roles of the killers. Scott Wilson, one of Hollywood's most underestimated actors, was almost exclusively given the roles of desperate frantic criminals.

Regarding Richard Brooks' icy kind of realism, Krisztoph Kieslowski's sombre murder-study KROTKI FILM O ZABIJANIU (A SHORT FILM ABOUT KILLING, Poland 1987) seems to be quite close. Both directors appear to be predominantly interested in thematizing the sense of capital punishment. Moreover, they both mercilessly dissect the killers' motives. Both Brooks and Kieslowski shock deeply, because they show murder as a "psychological accident" happening almost out of the blue. The delinquents act like remote-controlled and paralysed creatures without an obvious motive or pre-meditated killing intentions. Yet there are strong differences in the films' endings. Though Truman Capote's novel as well as its cinematic adaptation are definitely against capital punishment, the creation of bewilderment instead of too-simple social messages ensures the quality of Richard Brooks' opus.

Kieslowski finally weakens the mercilessness of his film with an ending oozing with perplexity. When the lawyer starts to cry after the execution of the murderer, it is as if Kieslowski wanted to say that there are still "morally unbroken" people in an ugly and hostile world (filmed through dark filters), and hence a slight glimmer of hope. IN COLD BLOOD, like William Friedkin's later related film RAMPAGE, spares you such an overly humanist epilogue. The cop Dewey, who arrests the killers "had imagined that with the deaths of Smith and Hickock, he would experience a sense of climax, release, of a design justly completed" (Capote). But after their execution there is nothing but a grey void and a queasy feeling. Whereas Kieslowski shows us a distorted grey civilisation and adds a considerable portion of humanist moralism, IN COLD BLOOD can be seen as a fatalist existentialist Film Noir where Hickock and Smith, the two outcasts, are creatures driven by the cosmic forces of fate. If you want to see the film entirely in such an emotional light, this is facilitated by Richard Brooks' atmospheric high-contrast black-and-white photography, which creates a gloomy suffocating aura from the beginning, Quincy Jones' pulsating jazz-soundtrack, and the protagonists' torn and bewildered gazes.

"It was midday deep in the Mojave Desert. Perry, sitting on a straw suitcase, was playing a harmonica. Dick was standing at the side of a black-surfaced highway, Route 66, his eyes fixed upon the immaculate emptiness as though the fervor of his gaze could force motorists to materialize. Few did, and none of those stopped for the hitchhikers [...] They were waiting for some solitary traveler in a decent car and with money in his billfold – a stranger to rob, strangle, discard on the desert." (*In Cold Blood*). Smith's and Hickock's trip to Mexico full of booze and cheap sex ends as a road movie, on empty desert roads under a scorching sun. From there it leads straight into disaster.

IN COLD BLOOD (TV) / USA 1996

Directed by Jonathan Kaplan. Written by Benedict Fitzgerald after the book by Truman Capote. Camera: Peter F. Woeste. Music: Hummie Mann. With Anthony Edwards, Eric Roberts, Sam Neill, Kevin Tighe, Gilian Barber

Thou shalt not remake an absolute movie classic. That's what an unwritten law of film-making says. Yet it is broken on a regular basis. Here, unlike Gus Van Sant's much-criticised remake of Hitchcock's PSYCHO , the makers of this four-hour TV epic have a good excuse at hand: "We're reinterpreting the book, not remaking the movie", Anthony "*ER*" Edwards, the actor playing Dick Hickock, says in an interview. "And the book is a classic of American literature – like *Catcher In The Rye*." Executive producer Robert Halmi Sr. adds: "Every great literary work needs a new interpretation for a different generation, who speak a different language and have a different morality." That's true, and an in-your-face Nineties version of Truman Capote's novel might have even been granted its place beside Richard Brooks' masterpiece. But, as is proven by many examples, American prime-time TV with all its restrictions isn't the right format for a film like this. Moreover, a producer like Robert Halmi Sr. , whose reputation is based on a series of dry and worthy TV adaptations of literary classics, is the most inadequate man in the background one can imagine.

Together with the anti-talent Eric Roberts as Perry Smith on his side, Anthony Edwards tries in vain to add new shades to the portrayal of the murderous male duo. His own style – he calls his slick, charming movie language "Dickspeak" – ricochets from Eric Roberts' stony facade. So even a director like Jonathan Kaplan (OVER THE EDGE, 1979), once a ray of hope in Roger Corman's B-movie dynasty, is of little help. The only lucid interval in thoroughly conventional spectacle: the matter-of-factly staged interrogation scenes in the second part. There you get a little bit of insight into the minds of the cold-blooded duo. And you forget the boring part one with its gooey portrait of the Clutter-family. But let us give Eric Roberts a second chance to defend the film: "No-one will find this cool. We demystify taking a life, we don't romanticize it [...] No-one's gonna watch this and buy the 'In Cold Blood' CD and go on and on like they did about 'Thelma And Louise' and 'Natural Born Killers'."

That's true, indeed. As a matter of fact nobody would have bought a possible soundtrack on CD. Because Mr. Roberts strumming the guitar and getting the blues is much more unbearable than the killing scene.

RICHARD SPECK

"Don't be afraid, I'm not going to kill you!"

–Richard Speck to Corazon Amurao, the only survivor of the Chicago nurse massacre

The Case

Chicago, July 13, 1966. Around midnight Corazon Amurao, a young nurse hears someone knocking on the door of the nurses' rooming house. She opens up sleepily, and a young pockmarked man strongly smelling of alcohol violently enters the house. It is 25-year-old Richard Speck, a man whose life has been determined by misogyny and sexual offences. Speck threatens the house's residents with a gun, ties them, and finally drags one after the other into an adjoining room. You can hear muffled screams from there. Richard Speck brutally strangles or stabs his helpless victims. One of the girls seems to remind him of his hated ex-wife (she was 15 when they married), he rapes her vaginally and anally before he mutilates her. All in all the crime cost eight girls' lives. Corazon Amurao survives the massacre hidden under a sofa and identifies Speck later, above all because of a tattoo on his arm – "Born to raise hell". In the course of investigation the police suspects that the nurse killer of Chicago is also responsible for a series of unsolved sex murders in the area of the Great Lakes. After all, he has been there at the time of the crimes.

The rockabilly-killer Richard Speck (with Elvis quiff and leather jacket) was duly sentenced to imprisonment for life ("600 years").

DIE HINRICHTUNG (BORN FOR HELL) / Germany-France-Italy-Canada 1975

Directed by Denis Heroux. Written by Denis Heroux & F.G. Ranger. Camera: Heinz Hoelscher. With Matthieu Carrière, Eva Mattes, Debbie Berger, Christine Boisson

This strange film oscillating between high artistic aims and horror cliché and obviously inspired by Richard Speck, moves the scene of the crime from Chicago to Belfast, Northern Ireland. A Vietnam veteran on his way through Ireland murders eight young nurses there. As he cast Matthieu Carrière, the ethereally boring favourite actor of all

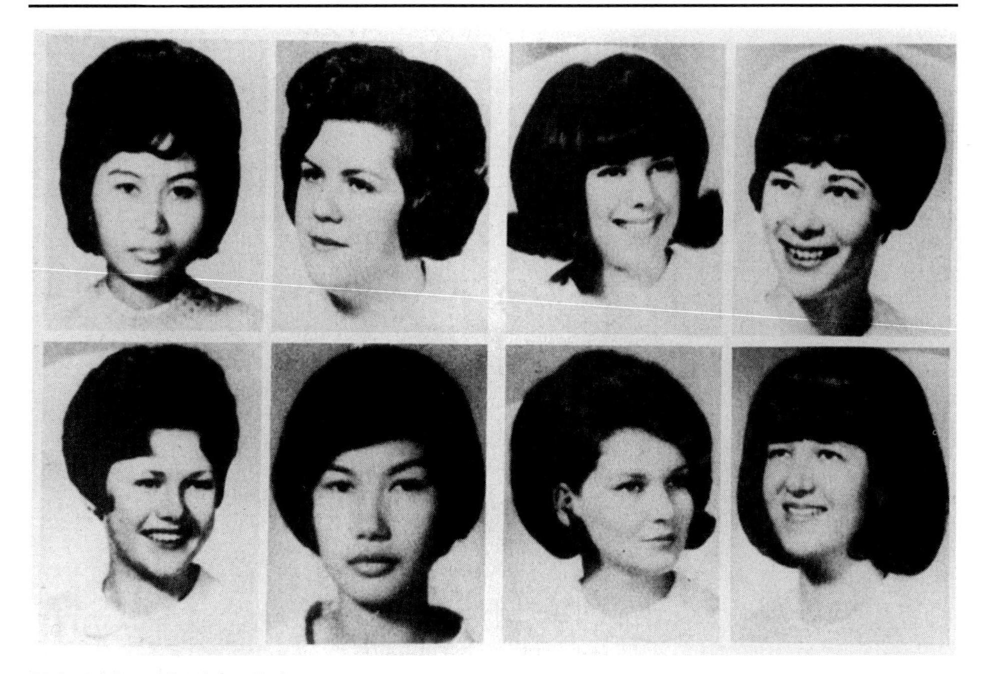

Richard Speck's eight victims

European authorial directors as killer, Denis Heroux probably wanted to get away as far as possible from the real story. The German Catholic Film Service writes, "A thriller about a mad killer based on a real case and flavoured with the topics of Vietnam and the Northern Irish civil war that loses much of its credibility through an abundance of motives and effects." After Heroux's and Koji Wakamatsu's completely abstract approaches, a realistic depiction of Richard Speck is still to be done. Though Robert De Niro in CAPE FEAR is physically already very close to him, one of the greasiest and meanest killers of criminal history definitely cries for a more profound cinematic analysis.

OKASARETA BYAKUI (VIOLATED ANGELS) / Japan 1967

Produced and directed by Koiji Wakamatsu. Written by Masao Adachi, Juro Kara & Koiji Wakamatsu. Camera: Hideo Ito. With Juro Kara, Michiko Sakamoto, Heiko Koyanagi

Richard Speck and the "Chicago Nurse Murders" as the main influence on a Japanese underground classic employing stunning, savage and bewildering form and content as a weapon against the viewer.

The film begins with a collage of commercial pornographic images. Then you see a young man throwing a weapon into the sea (the ocean is female and a mother symbol in the Japanese culture.). The guy breaks into a nurses' rooming house and watches some girls make lesbian love. This aspect drives him mad and triggers off an orgy of violence. He slaughters the passive girls one after the other. At the end he lies in the lap of the only surviving girl like a child. The black-and-white film because coloured for a blood-red moment. Cut. Collages of violent students' riots and terrorism.

While the deeds of real amok killers shock just because of their lack of motives, films about them almost always try to make sense of them. But nothing

VIOLATED ANGELS

weakens the shock of a criminal act more than making it explicable and plausible. Hence films circling around subjects like amok and serial killing without delivering justified explanations of the deeds are always the most gloomy and dangerous (e.g. John McNaughton's HENRY), but very rare. Koji Wakamatsu's OKASARETA BYAKUI – a film in the tradition of Genet and de Sade – is one of the most important works of this group, but at the same seldom screened in the West.

Although the bloody events almost entirely happen off-screen, the film has shocked even some open-minded critics. Amos Vogel, the author of *Film As A Subversive Art*, a standard publication on underground cinema, notes that Wakamatsu's artistic talent cannot be doubted, but criticizes heavily his "anti-feminist sadism which is not based on any ideological explanation and finally contributes a misanthropic flavour to his work".

Yet Vogel clearly does not understand that Wakamatsu (a *cinéaste maudit* being in touch with ultra-leftist radicals, but also with the Yakuza, the Japanese Mafia in the Sixties) deliberately omits every background explanation. What his protagonist does to a group of nurses in the course of this highly aesthetic black-and-white film is purposely devoid of ideology or logic. When, in the case of Richard Speck, the prison psychiatrist talks of a kind of trance in which the murders happened, then Koiji Wakamatsu comes very close to evoking this state of mind. After all, he has not intended a True Crime film rationally investigating the killer's motives. The film's protagonist has no "Born to raise hell" and no juvenile revolt tattooed on his flesh. Seemingly shy mediocrity, instead of Richard Speck's grimace distorted by hatred. Contrary to Richard Speck, this hyper-sensitive bewildered "hero" is not driven by an overwhelming sex drive, but by its exact opposite. A kind of hostile and violently asexual disposition forces him to break into the nurses' rooming house and torment, shoot, and slash its residents one after the other. It seems as if he executes the girls for their womanliness, their female sexuality (a lesbian couple is killed first) whereas he spares the youngest (as a manifestation of innocence). He confesses to the object of his adoration that he has killed the other girls in her honour.

Koiji Wakamatsu (alias Takashi Ito), a friend and protégé of Nagisa Oshima, whose masterpiece AI NO CORRIDA he co-produced, made the film one week after he had heard about the Richard Speck case. "The fact that only one girl hadn't been killed interested me", said the director 1998 in an interview with Romain Slocombe. "It seems that this girl was the only one to understand the boy's feelings, and that he just couldn't kill her. As for me, I am the youngest of seven brothers. We were all boys and we only had one mother. Spectators of my films often notice my Oedipus complex. I wonder if this personal tendency comes from my family situation during childhood. But apart from that, I feel admiration towards womanhood in general."

Wakamatsu only depicts the young man's bloodlust, and shows without judging the terrible events. Though the film's imagery is laden with metaphors and symbols (incest, sacrifice, phallic items, the Oedipal beginning with the murderer delivering a monologue to sea, a female symbol in Japan, the terrorist acts of violence at the end), OKASARETA BYAKUI can only partially be decoded. It remains a deeply disquieting film which, like the rest of Wakamatsu's seminal oeuvre, could only be regarded as S/M porn by utter udiots.

CHARLES STARKWEATHER

Charles STARKWEATHER & Caril FUGATE
James Dean, Rock'n'Roll, Mass Murder

"From the town of Lincoln in Nebraska with a sawed off .410 in my lap through the badlands of Wyoming, I killed everything in my path."
–Bruce Springsteen, "Nebraska"

"I had hated and been hated. I had my little world to keep alive as long as possible, and my gun. That was my answer. [...] It is not fair...it is not right...why was the world against me?"
–Charlie Starkweather

The Case

Charlie Starkweather seemed to be the prototype of the eternally misunderstood born loser. A Fifties psycho turned on by misanthropy, cheap booze, and rock'n'roll songs who identified with James Dean in REBEL WITHOUT A CAUSE (1955). Starkweather was born in Lincoln, Nebraska in 1940. He grew up in poor circumstances and soon the other children teased him for his stutter, his limp, his red hair and his modest height. Like many other social outcasts the garbageman Starkweather appeared silent and introvert, but towering rage and hatred were boiling inside him. Only when he met 14-year-old Caril Fugate, who was disappointed by the world too, did Starkweather find a true friend. A white trash romance developed between shooting practice in the desert and timid kisses in deserted trailer-parks. Caril's parents offered vehement resistance to the garbageman as their daughter's boyfriend.

On December 1, 1957 "angry young man" Charlie began his amok campaign against the world with a filling station hold-up. Boom! The attendant was his first victim. A little time passed by while the police were unsuccessfully searching for the killer, and Starkweather was brooding over plans of vengeance against the world. On January 28, the hateful 17-year-old would-be James Dean visited Caril's parental

The corpse of victim Robert Jensen

home. An argument developed, and after a scuffle Starkweather slaughtered her entire family. Later Caril denied any participation in these murders as well as in all those that ensued, but Starkweather strongly incriminated her in front of the jury. Charlie hid the corpses in the barn, and the the young lovers spent a few days filled with sex in the house. Charlie Starkweather: "The best time of my life!" When the neighbours became suspicious, they hit the road.

Boom, Boom, Boom! A murderous week on the run began. Again and again Charlie had to defend himself against various "enemies", most of the times shooting without warning into the backs of his often unarmed victims. The result: ten people dead, among them an old friend of the Starkweathers', a rich elderly couple and their maid, and a young High School couple (Robert Jensen and Carol King). Jensen's body was left in a storm cellar, his girlfriend King's partly denuded corpse on top. She had been viciously stabbed through the genitals and rectum. When Starkweather was finally cornered by the police, (Caril disassociated herself from the killer as soon as he was seized) he represented a perfect cliché-figure: cowboy boots, rolled-up jeans, and

a biker's leather jacket. The juvenile delinquent *par excellence*, born bad, born to murder. "Of course Starkweather was a product of the 50s", notes Jack Sargeant in his seminal study *Born Bad*, "for whom these now supposedly 'kitsch' icons were once actual symbols of rebellion".

After a spectacular trial where Starkweather did not show a sign of remorse, he ended up in the electric chair on June 24, 1959. A crowd of teenagers in jeans and leather jackets gathered in front of the jail to mourn their "rebel without a cause". The jury also refused to buy Caril Fugate's affirmations of innocence, so she was sentenced to life imprisonment.

BADLANDS / USA 1973

Written, directed, and produced by Terence Malick. Co-produced by Edward Pressman. Camera: Brian Probyn, Tak Fujimoto, and Steven Larmer. Music: George Tipton. With Martin Sheen, Sissy Spacek, Warren Oates, Ramon Bieri

Irritation instead of clarity, bewilderment instead of a politically correct message, the surrealistically romantic adaptation of the Starkweather & Fugate case. Neglecting the real facts the killer-tour of two gun-crazy kids all across Nebraska was transformed into a fascinatingly beautiful, lyrical story.

Terence Malick replaces social realism by a surreal, estranged atmosphere. The real Charlie Starkweather, a prototype of white trash America between Elvis and delinquency, would have been a completely different and much sadder story. Like many years later David Lynch in BLUE VELVET, Malick lays a dreamlike veil over

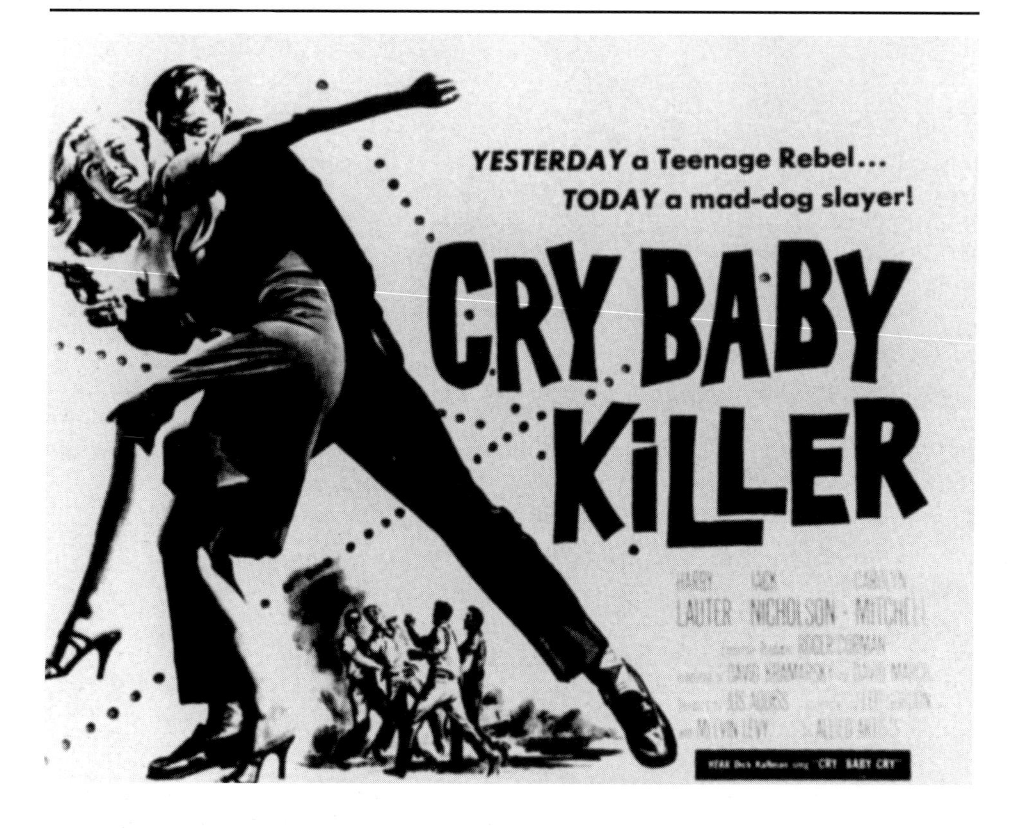

everyday life, and weaves American trivial myths, fairy-tales, and brutal outbursts of violence into his story of the outlaw couple Kit and Holly. The minor criminal couple starring the headlines all over America in the Fifties, inspired Malick to a narcotic, hypnotic work of art.

Kit Carruthers, laconically portrayed by Martin Sheen, breaks out of his petty-bourgeois circumstances together with his virginal girlfriend Holly (fantastic: Sissy Spacek), shoots her father, and burns down the house equally casually and coolly. Then he shoots several cops, an innocent couple, and even his best friend. The strangely apathetic, detached Holly naïvely asks the latter how dying feels like! Then Kit transforms from a teenage rebel to a tender lover and talented trapper (on the run the couple live in a tree house in the badlands of Montana). Then he is a cold killer, and finally a normal teenager again when he gives the cops autographs when they arrest him and lets himself celebrate like as hero. "Love is strange" can be heard on the soundtrack. So is Kit, who seems to be so much at the same time, James Dean plus his revolt and his asexual tendencies, a multiple killer, a naïve hero, a gun-crazy madman. Only one thing he is definitely not: predictable. His separation from once-loved Holly does not bother him, she in her turn has alienated herself from him.

Besides fascinating with hallucinatory images and a haunting score, the film always evades its viewers whenever they are convinced of having grasped the youngsters' motives. So BADLANDS is in this way comparable to VIOLATED ANGELS, Koiji Wakamatsu's rather free approach to the case of Richard Speck (Starkweather and Speck were both notorious as rockabilly-style juvenile delinquents in the teenage wasteland of the Fifties and Sixties). BADLANDS is an enigma, vehemently denies any palpable sense and oscillates between innocence and cold crime. Thus, together with its outstanding formal and technical qualities, it becomes a film "like a religious experience" (Quentin Tarantino), a stroke of genius constantly challenging one's imagination.

CRY BABY KILLER / USA 1958

Directed by Justus Addiss. Written by Leo Gordon and Melvin Levy. Camera: Floyd Crosby. Music: Gerald Fried & Dick Kallmann. With Jack Nicholson, Harry Lauter, Carolyn Mitchell, Brett Halsey; Ed Nelson, Mitzi McCall

At a time when the American public was still deeply shocked by the Starkweather case, and news of rock'n'roll and a new deluge of juvenile delinquency shook the country, Roger Corman, King of Exploitation, reacted as quickly as usual. He produced a short, rapidly done JD-film about a gun-crazy teenager (played by 21-year-old Jack Nicholson in his first film) who takes hostages and barricades himself in a drive-in cinema until the police attack with tear-gas. The film, running as double feature with HOT CAR GIRL (1958) was promoted with lurid taglines: "Yesterday a teenage rebel, today a mad dog slayer! A sizzling teenage shocker!". Clear evidence that a certain Charlie S. from Lincoln, Nebraska had completely changed the perception of the teenage "hooligan" in the USA. Teenagers wore tight jeans and leather jackets and quiffs. They were all potential runners amok and mass murderers.

MURDER IN THE HEARTLAND / USA 1993 (TV)

Directed by Robert Markowitz. Written by Michael O'Hara. Camera: Ron Garcia. Musik: Patrick Williams. With Tim Roth, Fairuza Balk, Kate Reid, Milo O 'Shea, Randy Quaid, Brian Dennehy, Roberts Blossom

Despite the clear biographical links of George F Hood's STARK RAVING MAD (1982), it took quite a long time until someone attempted to depict the Starkweather/Fugate rampage according to the facts, and naming names. Initially the film tells the story of Charlie and Caril chronologically, beginning with the filling station hold-up in December 1957 until their seizure and the electrocution of Starkweather. "Is there anything you want to say?" the executioner asks the young man. "Yes, tighten the straps, they are too loose."

This long (two and a half hours) and, for a TV production, rather captivating narration of the events seems to be preoccupied with destroying the myth of the romantic killer-couple. No road movie-like gun-crazy passion, no outlaw-existence on the run; Robert Markowitz sees Caril Fugate neither as the naïve partner of her incalculable boyfriend (BADLANDS), nor as a violent rock´n'roll slut (as in THE SADIST), but rather as a victim herself. MURDER IN THE HEARTLAND tries to restore Caril's reputation (she was released on probation in 1976) and to make plausible that the girl was threatened by her dangerous boyfriend and only followed him because she was scared to death. Later, in front of the jury, Starkweather was deeply disappointed by his "eternal love" and tried to take her with him to Hell by incriminating statements. The film shows the controversial murders from two perspectives, contrasting Caril's testimony with Charlie's. It is still unclear today if and to what extent Caril participated in the murders.

Compared to the rest of the boring TV genre, MURDER IN THE HEARTLAND definitely ranks above the average as a plausible rendering of facts. It is remarkable that all settings are authentic. Moreover, the characters' faces are well-chosen. Even many details concerning clothes and similar minutiae are painstakingly authentic. Tim Roth is a captivating Charlie Starkweather, while Fairuza Balk (though she does not look 14) portrays Caril as the perfect victim, despite many contrary reports on the case. But the film lacks the depth of narration and formal elements which might have transcended homely TV aesthetics. Compared to the weird hallucinatory world of

THE SADIST

BADLANDS, or THE SADIST's rebellious teenage nihilism, Markowitz's mere listing of events shrinks to the filmed version of a magazine article.

A postscript for True Crime film specialists: Brian Dennehy (John Wayne Gacy in TO CATCH A KILLER) and Roberts Blossom (Ed Gein in DERANGED) both appear briefly in the film.

THE SADIST / USA 1963

Written and directed by James Landis. Camera: Vilmos Zsigmond. With Arch Hall Jr., Marilyn Manning, Helen Hovey, Richard Alden, Don Russel

The exploitation version of Charlie Starkweather and Caril Fugate. A minor, unfortunately almost unknown opus from the poison-cupboard of B-movies, ideal for the drive-in cinema audience of the early Sixties.

At once, the pre-titles sequence is masterly: two eyes radiating madly in the dark accompanied by the off-screen voice of a doctor explaining typically sadistic behaviour. Then a zoom as quick as lightning to the psychotic pair of eyes, and above "THE SADIST" appears in big spooky letters. While the "official" Hollywood was working on the restoration of the image of a beautiful pure world, this black-and-white film, relegated to drive-ins, shows the opposite: brutal and evil people in a filthy reality.

THE SADIST begins (like the much later THE TEXAS CHAINSAW MASSACRE and every second splatter-movie) with a group of average citizens losing their way in an out-of-the-way place, and getting into an extreme situation. Here an abandoned petrol station and a junkyard in the desert are the location. Two teachers (classical Fifties philistines) and a young lady try to repair their car and to take in petrol. They are looking in vain for any helpful resident, waiting for hours in the scorching heat. The atmosphere is sweaty and the occasional small talk between the men and the woman is friendly only on the surface. Sexism and suggestiveness can hardly be hidden.

Enter the heavily armed young mass murderer, a James Dean-travesty, and his silent sexy girlfriend chewing bubble-gum (modelled on Starkweather and Fugate), the violent proletarian antithesis to the teachers. A psychodrama at close quarters begins (the junkyard is the only setting) where brutality, sex, and social differences become a dangerous mélange. Violence breaks out again and again in short, brutal, but also satirical detonations. The cartoon-like villain (brilliant: Arch Hall Jr.) lets one teacher have a bullet in the head with the cool valediction: "School's out, teacher!".

James Landis not only delivers solid B-movie entertainment, but also depicts a war of values and views of the world ("the teenager vs. "the teacher") that began in the Fifties and was continued by subsequent generations of desperate and rebellious youths. Allowing for its occasional, involuntary trash ridiculousness, THE SADIST probably comes nearest to evoking the spirit of white trash killer Charlie Starkweather.

STARK RAVING MAD / 1982/ USA

Directed by George F Hood. With Russ Fast, Marcie Severson

The least-known version of the Starkweather rampage is actually the nearest fictional approximation to the reality of the case. The film's young anti-hero, Richard Stark, is shown in prison, prior to execution; he reflects on the murderous spree perpetrated by himself and his 14-year-old girlfriend which led him to this fate, and we see the familiar tale unfold in flashback.

"we walk up to the cave and told her to come on out, she come out slow so caril pull her up alnost off her feet, i gave the 22 to caril f and said to keep a eye on her, i went on back to the car, i was jacking the car body up to get broads under the wheel, i heard a shot and ran back to the cave, the King girl was right where i left her befor when caril was there. Caril said that the King girl was running and shot her [...] i wish now i told this in my first statement. caril fugate was the [most] trigger-happy person i every seen."

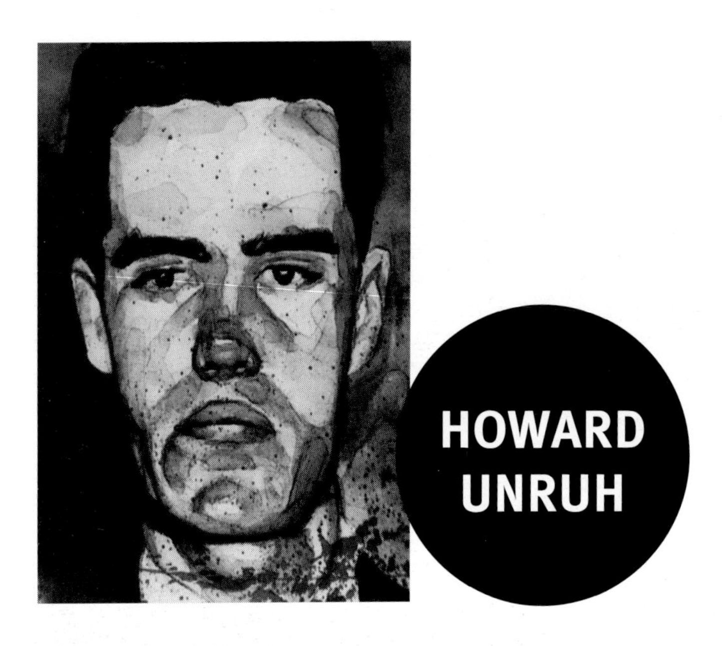

"I'm no psycho. I have a good mind."
–Howard Unruh

The Case
Born in 1921, Howard Unruh was a quiet and reserved student of theology and pharmacy who lived inconspicuously for many years. In 1941 he voluntarily joined the US Army and became an excellent sniper. His diary entries, where he noted details about every German he had killed during the war, the exact date, the circumstances, and the facial expression of the enemy when he was dying, are puzzling to say the least.

After the war Howard Unruh devoted himself to his studies, and guns. He built a shooting-stand in his basement and began to compose meticulous "hate-lists" of his neighbours containing data concerning the day he was going to "erase" them. Then Unruh raised a high fence around his house to protect his "mystery". When its door was stolen, his hour of vengeance had finally come. On September 6, 1949 he started his private campaign with a German Luger and a second gun. He shot almost all the people present in the houses and shops of his neighbourhood. In the street he shot a couple of friends who came to meet him. After only twelve minutes, thirteen people had been killed. Unruh walked home calmly as ever and reloaded his guns. In the meantime the police encircled his house and used tear gas. Soon, the murderous gun aficionado gave up without resistance. There was no trial. Howard Unruh was immediately put into a mental institution for the rest of his life. The taciturn killer has never explained his deed. He only said, "I would have killed a thousand people, if I'd had bullets enough."

SNIPER, THE / USA 1952
Directed by Edward Dmytryk. Written by Harry Brown after a story by Edna & Edward Anhalt. Camera: Burnett Guffy. Music: George Antheil. With Arthur Franz, Adolphe Menjou, Gerald Mohr, Marie Windsor, Frank Failen, Richard Kiley a. o.
Vaguely inspired by trigger-happy Howard Unruh, past master Dmytryk directed a classic of amok cinema, wrongfully lost and now lying in some archive.

THE SNIPER

No detail has specifically to do with Howard Unruh, neither the protagonist's age or his motives, but it rather seems as if in 1949 the extreme outburst of the killer had burnt itself as a collective shock into the subconscious of some directors. In Dmytryk's version of the mass-murderer theme Arthur Franz plays a passive, ordinary young man called Eddie Miller, who becomes a misogynist beast in his darkest moments. The quiet boy takes his precision rifle with telescopic sight and shoots unprotected women from a safe distance.

THE SNIPER depicts chronologically the killer's descent into a maelstrom of fear and aggression. The police investigations are staged simultaneously. What is remarkable about the film is its perspective: more than 20 years before Martin Scorsese's TAXI DRIVER, Miller had already been shown as a tragic manifestation of psychotic loneliness. He asks people for help, his friends, doctors. He deliberately burns his hand in a gas flame just to get into psychiatric hospital. But there the people cannot deal with his crisis, and let him go. So he completely falls prey to his obsession. He climbs up rooftops and starts firing at innocent women from there. Only an ambitious cop can stop him....

The gloomy atmosphere, obtuse camera angles and the obsessiveness of the actor place THE SNIPER somewhere into a zone between classical Film Noir and German Expressionism. Questions are raised but not answered, psychological explanations are reduced to a minimum, and the runner amok's paranoia is transferred to the audience; all this anticipates successful, later excursions into the realm of mass murder: RAMPAGE, THE BOSTON STRANGLER, HENRY, or COMBAT SHOCK.

JACK UNTERWEGER

"A new packet of razor blades is lying at hand. A long strong leather cord too. I am ready for the minute of my final decision. I see my body get limp, I see it escape this vegetable life in a last spasm [...]"

–From the book *Fegefeuer* by Jack Unterweger

The Case

Jack Unterweger was something like the tragic Austrian variant of the American-born loser, an existence with traces of Charlie Starkweather (the alienated and deformed childhood), Jack Henry Abbott (the criminal as an author), and Gary Gilmore (once in the vicious circle of juvenile prisons and solitary confinement there seemed to be no hope for rehabilitation).

Born in Judenburg, Styria on August 16, 1950 Unterweger had never met his father, a GI. As a little boy he came to his grandfather in Carinthia in February 1952, where he, as in the childhoods of Charles Manson and Henry Lee Lucas, spent his time among prostitutes, in an atmosphere of booze and beatings. In 1958 Jack was sent to foster parents, then, in 1962, he landed in a youth centre. What followed was an adolescence full of violence, misogyny, pimping, and a first sentence for theft in 1966 leading to his commission to a reformatory. After being released one year later, he held jobs of various kinds.

In December 1974 Jack Unterweger killed an 18-year-old girl and got a life sentence for doing so. Like Abbott, he wrote soulfully of the following years of isolation and loneliness in his cell. He got into contact with the outside, with writers around "Forum Stadtpark" and his autobiographical novel *Fegefeuer* (Translation: Purgatory) became a great success after it was published.

Unterweger, the writer, did not give up emphasizing his credentilas for reahbilitation into society and was released on probation in 1990. As a perfect example for rehabilitation he wrote and directed plays, worked as a journalist for the radio and the press. But on February 15, 1992 the curtain closed again: a warrant of arrest for suspicion of murder stopped the media-darling's new career of freedom.

Unterweger escaped to the United States, where he was finally tracked down. Back in Austria he was held responsible for a whole series of murders among prostitutes. The circumstantial evidence was not without gaps, and the author time and again protested his innocence. Questions after questions remain open.

Yet, in June 1994 Jack Unterweger was found guilty of murder in nine cases. Only six hours after the judgement Austria's "most famous" alleged serial killer hanged himself in his cell. He took with him the mystery of his deeds.

FEGEFEUER ODER DIE REISE INS ZUCHTHAUS / Austria 1988

Directed by Wilhelm Hengstler. Written by Wilhelm Hengstler, Bernhard Seiter & Jack Unterweger. Camera: Jiri Stibr. Music: Karlheinz Miklin. With Bobby Prem, Juergen Goslar, Jeanette Muehlmann, Ingrid Ettelmayer, Katharina Wressnig

Trying to avoid social realism with its inherent tendency toward exaggerated emotions, the Austrian director Willi Hengstler deliberately opted for stylisation in his adaptation of Jack Unterweger's autobiographical novel. Probably he was mindful not to adopt the loud approach of the Yellow Press. But this fear is based on the fundamental error that Yellow Press and True Crime magazine reports must always be a potpourri of dangerous lies, whereas sober fact-finding can only do justice to a case. Yet, whoever knows how to read between the lines of the tabloids, can sometimes get to know much more about the character of a murderer than in the sober articles of quality papers. The same goes for cinema: exploitation/trash greedy for sex and violence often comes nearer to the spirit of the one or other killer than many (pseudo) serious documentaries.

As he added time and again highly showy sex & crime scenes in his clinically monotonous novel, Unterweger seems to have been aware of the problem. Such scenes cry for an adaptation sticking very close to the protagonist and sucking in his sexual greed and cold sweat. But in FEGEFEUER the camera deliberately remains in the distance, as if it wanted to reverse and freeze the programmatic title of the film. Via artificiality the film is supposed to generate sober chill, and some theatrical alienation effects (the cops wear symbolic uniforms) represent a universality going far beyond the Unterweger case.

The flaw: W. Hengstler cannot stick to a clear-cut, unambiguous formal approach. FEGEFEUER is neither as full of passion as THE EXECUTIONER' S SONG, the elegiac US film about Gary Gilmore, nor as alienated and unreal as Terence Malick's BADLANDS, another social drama transformed into artificiality. All in all, the lives of the characters shown do not really touch the audience.

CHARLES WHITMAN

"I have just killed my mother. If there's a heaven, she is going there. If there is not a heaven, she is out of her pain and misery. I love my mother with all my heart."
–Charles Whitman in his farewell letter

The Case
Born on June 24, 1941 Charles Whitman seemed to be the prototypical all-American boy, a well-behaved bourgeois model youth and student at the University of Austin, Texas, who always did what his parents wanted. Moreover, he was a Marine, and was decorated as an excellent marksman.

In March 1966 some scratches on this harmonious facade appeared out of the blue. The gun aficionado repeatedly complained about a terrible headache, for which he held stress and overworking responsible. In addition to this, his mother threatened to leave his dominant father, which made Charles consult the college-psychologist in order to discuss his manic outbursts of anger. The previously sane world of Charles Whitman was slowly breaking apart.

But no mental grievance explains or justifies the amok kill-spree Charles performed on July 31 and August 1, 1966. In his farewell letter he wrote, "To whom it may concern, I don't understand what is compelling me to type this note. I've been having fears and violent impulses. I've had some tremendous headaches." Then he visited his mother and knifed her. After that he filled his Marines-bag with an arsenal of guns. Kathleen, a young woman whose belly he also slit open with a knife, was his second victim. The following morning he drove to the campus and took the elevator up the look-out tower. At 11.48 Whitman began to shoot blindly into the crowd below with a rifle with telescopic sight. A few minutes later 14 people were dying, 30 others were seriously injured. Only when some cops forcibly entered the tower and killed the sniper, was the massacre over.

In Whitman's autopsy a tumour affecting the aggression centre of the brain and causing his horrible headache was found. Yet it remains highly questionable if this tumour alone had made a killer out of the model boy. Charles Whitman has taken his motives for mass murder into the grave.

THE DEADLY TOWER

THE DEADLY TOWER / USA 1975 (TV)

Directed by Jerry Jameson. Written by William Douglas Lansford. Camera: Matthew F. Leonetti. Music: Don Ellis. With Kurt Russell, Ned Beatty, Pernell Roberts, John Forsythe

Here the detailed chronology of one of the most extreme instances of amok in US crime history – not lacking comparable explosion-like acts of violence – is condensed into a quite convincing TV drama. Of course, the usual TV practice of a nice-guy cop attracting the sympathy of the audience is a highly predictable cliché. Almost all comparable films about delinquents like Richard Ramirez or John Wayne Gacy are patterned in this way. In DEADLY TOWER it is the young cop Ramiro Martinez who fires the decisive bullet at Whitman, and hence he becomes Jameson's central hero. Ned Beatty as a nervous, but helpful civilian may also take the laurels for his courage. Beside the quasi-documentary handy-cam, the young Kurt Russell in one of his first roles blasts the frame of routine screen boredom. As Charles Whitman he has almost zero dialogue, silently carrying out his murderous (and suicidal) one-man-campaign, but his sweaty baby-face, his stiff movements, the twitching of his face when he shoots down into the crowd, all this is expressive enough. Not the stuff of repeated watchings, but nevertheless a concise True Crime study.

TARGETS aka BEFORE I DIE / USA 1968

Written and directed by Peter Bogdanovich. Camera: László Kovács. Music: Charles Greene & Brian Stone. With Boris Karloff, Tim O'Kelly, Nancy Hsueh, James Brown, Randy Quaid

The Whitman case is only a vague reference in Peter Bogdanovich's debut. Bogdanovich totally omits its weird motives and the medical explanations (the allegedly fully responsible tumour), he rather fits the singular case into a much larger social context, so his film can be understood as an appeal against US gun-fetishism and the increasing brutalization and emotional vacuum of post-Vietnam society.

Bobby, the young sniper in TARGETS is completely different from the conflict-stricken, ambiguous protagonists of Martin Scorsese (TAXI DRIVER) or Abel Ferrara (DRILLER KILLER). He is neither a noir-character, nor a charismatic anti-hero. Yet Bogdanovich's film is one of the best contributions to the category of "bourgeois amok". There is no cathartic effect in his acts of violence; one morning the outwardly nice guy and gun aficionado slays his family almost casually, and later on the same day he fires haphazardly into the crowd from a safe vantage-point. The campus of Austin University is replaced by a drive-in cinema in Bogdanovich's film (produced by B-movie guru Roger Corman). The audience is never seduced to sympathize with the killer, who is too emotionless and Vietnam-steeled. His dastardly ambushes, his deplorable capitulation in the end, all this reminds us of a spoilt and blunt child who has lost his proper sense of reality in his war games.

Initially TARGETS was planned as a straight horror movie for the Corman Factory, spliced together with some remaining material from the old horror film THE TERROR (1963) as a starting point. Moreover, Boris Karloff, an old and at the time already declining and battle-weary Hollywood star, still had to work out his contract. But after Charles Whitman's terrible deeds, Peter Bogdanovich realized that a new era of terror had dawned. Together with his first wife and co-author Polly Platt Bogdanovich he delivered a completely new storyboard. He introduced Boris Karloff as Byron Orlok, who played himself, an ageing Hollywood star, in one of his last roles, as a counterpart to the real horror represented by Bobby. In two parallel plot-lines we follow Bobby's and Orlok's lives until they finally intersect in the drive-in cinema. Romantic horror versus the naked truth. The era of cinematic Grand Guignol had long gone, the old monsters of cinema looked rather harmless compared to reality of Vietnam and the increasing violence among young people.

TARGETS

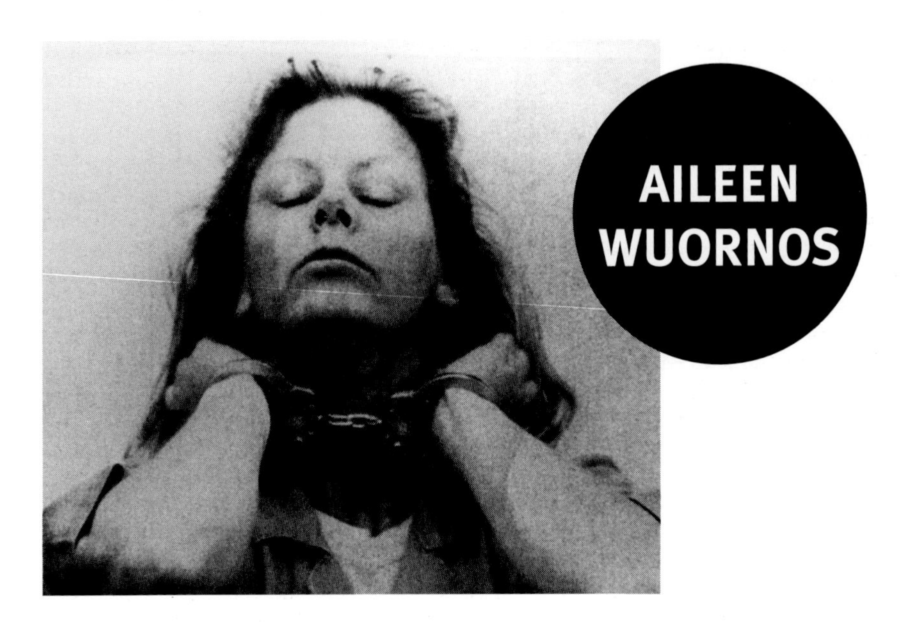

"They're gonna electrocute me, give me life in prison, and I don't deserve it... It was just self-defence."

–Aileen Lee Wuornos

The Case

As a female serial killer Aileen Wuornos is the great exception. The FBI, whose mass murderer profiles have been shaken by her, assumes that less than 5% of all serial killers are women, and those that are mainly kill direct relatives. Aileen's trial was broadcast live on television, film-makers and writers fought for the copyrights for her case, and the media alternately portrayed her as man-killing angel of vengeance, or as the victim of a brutal macho-society.

Between December 1989 and January 1991 six similar murders took place along a highway in Florida. The corpses of whites males between 40 and 60 were found in the woods, robbed and naked, in or near their cars. In November 1990 someone witnessed two women running away from the car of one of the victims. Their phantom pictures were published all over the country, and soon Aileen Wuornos and Tyria Moore, her lesbian lover, were identified. In the interrogations 28 year-old Tyria admitted to have known about the killings, but vehemently denied her participation.

In January 1991 34-year-old Lee, as she is called, was arrested and confessed to her crimes, which she claimed to have committed in self-defence, one after the other. She had been living a life on the road together with Tyria and had been working as a hooker to earn their living. So she'd got to know her later victims. According to her version she shot them because they did not want to pay, or wanted to rape her. The trial began in the Spring of 1991 and revealed the tragic story of her life.

Aileen was born in Michigan on February 29, 1956, and for eleven years she believed that her grandparents were her real parents. But then she was told that she and her slightly older brother Keith were the children of Diane, the Wuornos' eldest daughter, and that the people she had thought were her brother and sister were her uncle and aunt. Diane had been forced to give away her two children. Her grandfather, an alcoholic, was extremely strict and authoritarian. He regularly spanked Aileen with a leather belt and did not show any signs of love.

When she was eleven she began to offer her body for booze and cigarettes and tended to have extreme outbursts of anger. All through her adolescence she prostituted herself for drugs. In 1969, at the age of thirteen she became pregnant and released her baby for adoption. Again and again she escaped from home. Her brother was her only friend. She is also said to have been the victim of rape and incest, before her choleric grandfather threw her out of the house.

In 1971 her grandmother died, also an alcoholic, and a few years later her brother Keith. Her grandfather committed suicide. Aileen never got to know her real daddy, Leo Pittman, but heard about his death in prison. A nice daddy after all. By the age of 17 he had married her only 14-year-old mother. He had beaten her almost daily and had tormented her with his hyper-sexual urges. After the divorce Leo had kidnapped and raped a 7-year-old girl in 1962. In 1966 he got a life sentence for that. In 1969 he died of the consequences of a suicide attempt.

Aileen was married to a considerably older man for a while, and had several unhappy relationships with men. In 1978 she tried to kill herself, shooting herself in the belly. She was imprisoned for armed robbery in 1982. In 1986 she met Tyria Moore and lived a life on the road with her. Even after she had been caught, she did everything to protect her girlfriend. So Tyria was not put on trial.

During her trial Aileen Wuornos, who made an extremely battle-weary impression, became converted to the faith of Arlene Pralle, a "reborn Christian" and was adopted by her. Though in the trial her life was shown as one of constant abuse and repression by men she only wanted to defend herself against, and the sympathy of the jury was on her side, she was nevertheless sentenced to death by the electric chair on January 30, 1992. Locked up in Death Row since then, Aileen Wuornos has been fighting for a retrial and a milder sentence.

AILEEN WUORNOS – THE SELLING OF A SERIAL KILLER / GB 1992

Written and directed by Nick Broomfield. Camera: Barry Ackroyd. Music: David Bergeaud.

With this subtle and captivating documentary Nick Broomfield tries to find the real human being behind all the media hysteria around the "first female serial killer". At the same time the film, most of the time shot from the talented director's subjective position, tells us about his initial failure to get in touch with the 35-year-old prostitute, as well as the difficulties in getting the desired interview. His odyssey to get in touch with Lee shows mercilessly and ironically how different people have tried to enrich themselves by her popularity – like her allegedly self-sacrificing adoptive mother and friend in confession Arlene Pralle, and the lawyer Steve Glazer, a rather whimsical and unprofessional figure. Both want money for every scrap of information, although they basically cannot help Broomfield at all. They are more interested in film or book contracts, or lucrative interviews. Moreover, in the course of his talks with Aileen Wuornos, Nick Broomfield uncovers a police conspiracy. One month before arresting Aileen Wuornos, some police officials had already negotiated Hollywood deals. They had also sold the copyright on the story of Tyria More, who had herself been a main suspect at the time.

Broomfield confronts the audience with a hunted, hurt and cornered woman who sees herself caught in a web of intrigue, false friends and deceived hopes, and who indefatigably claims her rights. Aileen Wuornos is neither the feminist angel vengeance portrayed by certain magazines, nor a repressed girl, but an exploited criminal. The director and the cameraman know that they are part of the whole voyeuristic game, hence they never act pushily or indulge in cheap sensationalism. Aileen Wuornos is delinquent and victim at the same time, which is expressed quite impressively in this documentary.

"What I found interesting in Aileen Wuornos in the first place was the unique example of a prostitute who kills men instead of being killed by them." This is what Nick Broomfield said about the film that was awarded the British Grierson-Award.

OVERKILL: THE AILEEN WUORNOS STORY / USA 1993

Directed by Peter Levin. Written by Fred Mills. Soundtrack: Dennis McCarthy. Camera: Thomas Burstyn. With Jean Smart, Park Overall, Tim Grimm, Ernie Lively , Geoffrey Rivas, Erich Anderson

She liked drinking beer, bawled to the country-songs from the jukebox, and was arrested in the "Last Resort", a wild biker-bar. She is the prototypical girl from the gutter living a life of humiliation, disappointments, and human catastrophes. And she only wanted to "save men from their misery". Viewed through the distorting mirror of the media Aileen Wuornos seems to be an ideal dramatic soap character, a kind of aggressive super-Roseanne, whose life, adequately staged, numerous American women simply must identify with.

This TV production aims at such an image, including all the clichés of the medium. We get to know about the wounds, the booze, and the deplorable white trash milieu of the Highway Killer. Time and again flashbacks of her grandfather's beating hand interrupt the plot. Others show the traumatic birth of her child. Then again abusive, violent men, this time brutal lovers. Like the cops in his film Peter Levin does not believe in the idea of a female serial killer. "When women kill, they kill people they know. they kill their husbands, their lovers, or the mistresses of their husbands, but they never kill strangers. This is what serial killers do, they kill for killing's sake" (from the film's script).

For Peter Levin Aileen Wuornos is clearly a victim who becomes an angel of vengeance. He shows her deeds in the tradition of films like MS.45 or LIPSTICK (1976). But the film does not, ultimately, arouse too much compassion. It is much too lengthy and conventional for that. A vehicle for biased opinions, nothing more.

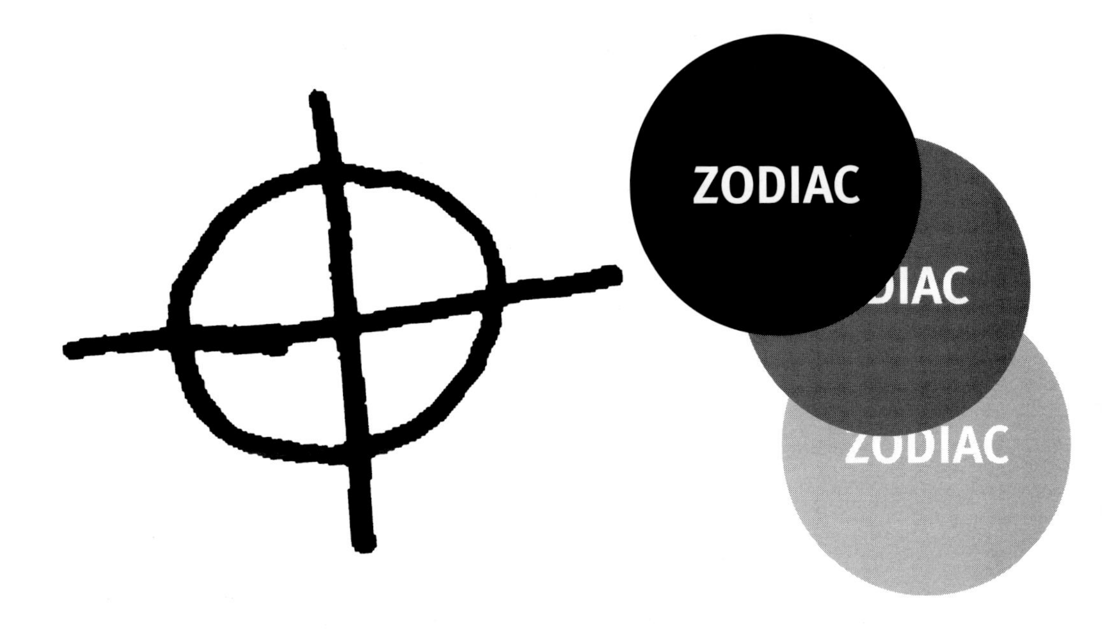

"I like killing people because it is so much fun it is more fun than killing wild game in the forrest because man is the most dangeroue anamal of all to kill."
–From an original letter of the "Zodiac" (original spelling)

The Case

Within nine months an unknown killer slew five people and seriously injured two in California. Most of the victims were young couples, shot or knifed at remote places. After his first murder in December 1968 the unknown terrorist sent three letters to newspapers, all signed with the symbol of the Zodiac. A coded message revealed Zodiac's motives to the public: man is the most dangerous animal of all. He liked killing people; yes, it was even better than sex. Once murdered his victims were supposed to become the Zodiac's slaves in the "afterworld".

Surviving victims described him as a rather stocky 30-year-old man with reddish hair and thick horn-rimmed spectacles. Once, he also wore some sort of hangman's costume with a hood and the Zodiac symbol emblazoned across its bib.

On October 21, 1969 he told the police he would surrender, if he got a famous counsel for the defence. Then he demanded an interview in a morning talk show. A few days later the mysterious killer made himself heard in the that show via telephone, and talked to a lawyer present. But his voice sounded different, and experts did not really believe in the authenticity of the caller. Moreover, he failed to show up at an arranged meeting. Despite repeated threats, he stopped killing.

In 1974 the San Francisco police received a final letter in which he claimed to have already killed 37 people. It was the last sign of the mysterious killer. Maybe he died; in any case, he has never been detected.

```
H E R > 9 ⅃ Λ V P ꓘ I ● L T G ● ᗡ
N 9 + B φ ■ O ◩ D W Y · < ◩ K ꟻ ⊖
B Y I Ɔ M + U Z G W φ ⊖ L ■ ✦ H J
S 9 9 △ Λ ⅃ ▲ ◩ V ● 9 O + + R K ●
□ △ M + ✦ ⊥ Ƭ ᗡ I ● F P + P ● ꓘ /
9 ▲ R Λ F ⅃ O – ◩ ᗡ C ■ F > ● D φ
■ ● + K ⊘ ◩ I ● U Ɔ X 6 V · ✦ L I
φ G ● J ꟻ Ƭ ■ O + □ N Y ✦ + ⊡ L △
ᗡ < M + 8 + Z R ● F B Ɔ Y A ⊙ ● K
– ✦ ⅃ U V + Λ J + O 9 △ < F B Y –
U + R / ● ⊥ E I D Y B 9 8 T M K O
● < Ɔ ⅃ R J I ◩ ● T ● M · + P B F
✦ ⊙ △ S Y ■ + N I ● F B Ɔ φ I ▲ R
⅃ G F N Λ ꟻ ● ● ● 8 · Ɔ V ● ⊥ + +
Y B X ● ◩ I ● △ C E > V U Z ● – +
I Ɔ · ● ✦ B K φ O 9 Λ · ꟻ M ⊘ 6 ●
R Ɔ T + L ● ● C < + F ⅃ W B I ⊖ L
+ + ⊖ W C ✦ W Ɔ P O S H T / φ ⊖ 9
I F ꓘ ᗡ W < △ ⊥ B □ Y O B ■ – C Ɔ
> M D H N 9 ꓘ · S ✦ Z O ▲ A I K I +
```

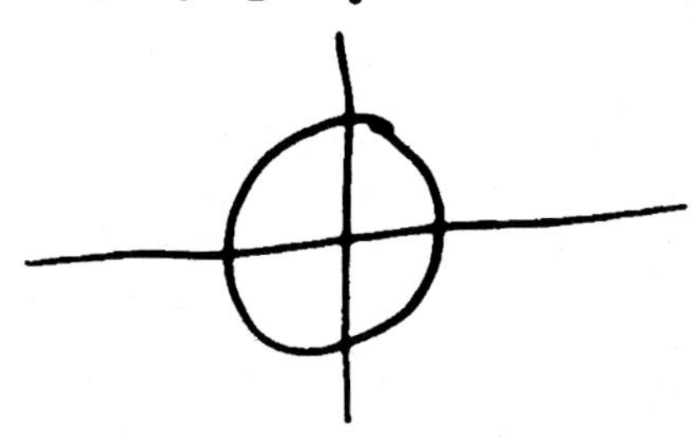

Coded message from Zodiac

DIRTY HARRY

DIRTY HARRY / USA 1971

Directed by Don Siegel. Written by Harry Julian Fink & Dean Riesner. Camera: Bruce Surtees. Music: Lalo Schifrin. With Clint Eastwood, Reni Santoni, Harry Guardino, Andrew Robinson

A killer named Scorpio, who kills people seemingly randomly to blackmail the municipal corporation of San Francisco is hunted by Detective Harry Callahan, who is notorious for his "unconventional" methods. After many innocent people have been killed, Callahan manages to track down the publicity-greedy angel of death. But liberal laws hamper "Dirty Harry", who has only tortured the villain a little bit, and Scorpio is released. When he hits again and kidnaps an entire school bus, the cop (first symbolically) throws away his hampering dog tag to finish the case "his way". In the final showdown Scorpio gets another chance, but when he reaches for his gun, he dies in Callahan's hail of bullets.

Basically Don Siegel's controversial thriller is a classical cop/criminal melodrama about two unequal characters who both halt at nothing to further their individual purposes. Clint Eastwood in his show-piece role of "Dirty Harry" Callahan, a lone wolf in a world of corrupt cops and liberal politicians who takes the law into his own hands, represents the forces of order. Yet Callahan is far away from the classical film noir cop, who is himself a wrecked melancholic and often as crazy as the bad guys. He acts soberly, rationally, and icy-coldly, delivering a quasi-fascist blueprint for a whole generation of vigilante-style exterminators.

His direct opponent is Andy Robinson (Edward G. Robinson's son) as the killer Scorpio. The psychotic criminal playing cat-and-mouse with the police is obviously inspired by the Zodiac killer, a case still raging in America's collective subconscious in 1971. Like Zodiac, Scorpio is addicted to publicity and enjoys the thrill of hunting and being hunted. But unlike the real Zodiac, this serial killer is tracked down and punished in DIRTY HARRY, whose right-wing subtext enraged some critics of the time.

THE ZODIAC KILLER / USA 1971

Written and directed by Tom Hanson. Camera: Robert Birchall & Wilson S. Hong. With Hal Reed, Bob Jones, Ray Lynch, Tom Pittman

"This film does not aim at commercial awards, but wants to point out a present danger". This is what the audience is told about the real intention of the film in the pre-titles sequence. But Tom Hanson wouldn't have won an Oscar anyway, with his minimal budget and a few amateur actors. Moreover, the noble message of the film cannot be taken too seriously. On the contrary, it is prototypical exploitation cinema somehow reminiscent of Herschell Gordon Lewis, yet without the latter's splatter-extremism. A lost piece of cheap dingy entertainment that says much about gender roles in America in its accumulation of petty bourgeois and misogynist characters.

Hanson uses many sources; the Zodiac letters are quoted word by word, original testimonies are employed, the details of the murders are authentic, but on the other hand he "solves" the killer's mystery in a rather ridiculous way. The Zodiac is a frustrated misanthropic postman, who is above all terribly afraid of women. He only loves the pet zoo full of rabbits in his basement. At night the serial killer prays in front of his zodiac altar and dreams of slaves for life after death, during the day he helps children climb trees on playgrounds, or satisfies lonely housewives *à la* postman. After the end of the obvious official series of murders, the hooded killer begins to simulate accidents (in an unintentionally funny way). So he helps lonely women when they have engine trouble or a puncture, then buries them under their cars. He even kills when he visits his father, who is locked up in a special cell in a hospital for the mentally ill. Daddy has not talked to his son for years, which drives him mad. Raging with anger he rushes out of the hospital, cuts the life suport of one patient and pushes another one in a wheelchair from behind. From off-screen he scorns, "Now you know that I exist. What do you want to do about it? I tell you, nothing. Your aspect makes me sick. You should lock me up, I am dangerous. But you haven't caught me yet. I'm still running around in freedom. Me and a lot of guys like me. Do you think I am going to give myself up to the police? You're kidding. [...]"

This is followed by scenes showing the Zodiac as a pretty normal citizen walking through the crowded streets of San Francisco, and even helping elderly ladies across the street. "You call us schizophrenic, psychopathic, but guys like me don't give a shit for this nonsense. Under 'crazy' you find 'absolutely senseless' in the dictionary. But how do I manage to live in my own ordinary daily routine, how can I work, or put on my clothes?" A guffaw of laughter from the soundtrack, the last shot freezes, and a final title threatens that "this is not the end".

What is remarkable in this context is a further gag of the producers. Every viewer of the film had to jot down in 25 words why the Zodiac commits his murders. He had to write it on a card to be placed into a box in the foyer. Invisible, someone was sitting there who read every card immediately. They were sure that the Zodiac was going to watch the film and betray himself by his comments.

PART TWO
SCREEN PSYCHOS

CHAPTER ONE
MAN AS A HUNTING OBJECT: THE SERIAL KILLER BETWEEN FILM AND REALITY

"Have you ever killed someone? It's always the same and it's always different."
–HENRY, PORTRAIT OF A SERIAL KILLER

"There's a killer on the road..."
–The Doors

"We love you, Mickey and Mallory!" The crowd in front of the court room falls into a hysterical chorus when the two media stars finally appear. The people begin to scream, ask for autographs, and greedily try to touch them. No rock stars or new Hollywood starlets are being enthusiastically cheered on by a yelling pack, but two celebrities of crime. Mickey and Mallory Knox are two serial killers, having killed dozens of times on the way to their trial. Nevertheless they are celebrated as glittering stars of pop culture.

One scene from Oliver Stone's mass murder staccato NATURAL BORN KILLERS, being much less a vision of the near future than a slightly exaggerated depiction of the present. Serial killers *are* hip. In youth sub-culture and beyond they enjoy almost idol-like adoration. Multiple killers grin broadly from the screen as bloody permanent fixtures, liven up books, videos, Reality TV, and the Yellow Press with their hideous presence, and have become a standard topic of journalistic as well as sociological analyses. Where does the enormous power come from that serial killers perpetrate on their victims? What drives a man to such deeds? Where is the germ of the mass murderer phenomenon? These are some of the questions already a whole industry is investigating.

The serial killer seems to impersonate something like the perfect ultimate villain in a profit-oriented as well as performance-oriented society, and this inspired the American novelist Bret Easton Ellis to create the character of the murderous killer-yuppie in *American Psycho*. Unlike the runner-amok, who almost always annihilates himself too, the serial killer seemingly wants to survive, triumph, and go on killing. Furthermore, the monster serial killer offers a manifestation of the absolute evil which is highly necessary for society and its values in a world of ethic twilight zones, corrupted ideologies and shattered values.

The motives of the real killers (no matter if they are so-called motiveless killers) disappeared long ago behind the reproduction of clichés in the flood of the media's permanent myth production. Only very few films attempt to illuminate seriously the poles round which the natures of the murderers circle: power, innocence, trance, sex, transcendence.

Born To Lose: The Revenge Of The Losers

"Exiled from the street. Isolated from other children. Unknown, unwanted, unloved."
–From a poem by the mass murderer Joe Kallinger

The world of cinema likes toying with the idea of stylising the serial killer to a monster larger than life, or a kind of artificial super-killer. This goes from the superior cool sociopath working on his memoirs together with a writer (WHERE SLEEPING DOGS LIE/1992, WHITE ANGEL/1993) to Satan incarnate like Dr. Lecter in SILENCE OF THE LAMBS (1990) or HANNIBAL (2001); the title character of MR. FROST (1990), or the mass murderer representing all killer clichés in the cop comedy THE HARD WAY (1990), just to mention some examples.

But reality is different. Even if you close in upon the multitude of personality profiles and analyses vacillating between an effort towards seriousness and a cheap spectacular approach rather critically, one thing becomes clear: real serial killers have very little to do with philosophical "gourmets" *à la* Hannibal Lecter, who consumes his victims with precious silver cutlery. Instead they are haunted by their existence and a mixture of fear, frustration, and feverish hate seethes inside them.

The untouchable superman created by cinema and TV is contrasted with failures like the British murderer of homosexuals Dennis Nilsen, accurately portrayed as a human wreck in THE COLD LIGHT OF DAY (1990). Or are they figures like skin-sewing "Buffalo Bill", the other nightmarish character in THE SILENCE OF THE LAMBS, who does not accept his transsexual disposition and compensates his physical and mental suffering with bloody deeds committed on young girls. If you scratch on Bill's facade, or on that of real killers like Jeffrey Dahmer, you find everything *but* superiority and strength.

Joel Norris says that "they are no mad geniuses" but helpless human zeros, repressed and obsessed by sex differences. Their enormous frustration is partly based on the fact that they are often highly intelligent people with a great potential, yet in the position of the loser who cannot profit from this potential. Instead they channel their intelligence into the act of killing. The psychologist and author Norris, who almost maniacally investigates the subject, has filtered several common features from the studies of more than 300 serial killers. They almost always show evidence of neurological or central-nervous-system impairment, ranging from dyslexia to epilepsy; they walk in their sleep or experience *déjà vu*; they have memory lapses, and their violence is almost always presaged by killing fantasies or hallucinations. They are fascinated with fire and at some point usually mutilate animals. According to Norris, most serial killers also abuse alcohol or drugs and it is a central point for him that almost all "have been abused, emotionally, physically and quite often sexually."

Henry Lee Lucas, one of the most gruesome mass murderers of criminal history, fits almost cliché-like into the picture of the victim of rape. He grew up in a whorehouse and was forced to go to school in girls' clothes. His mother abused him sexually and his stepfather used to beat him up.

If you study further cases, it seems as if many serial killers had from birth onwards a "born to lose" stigma tattooed on their fronts. Spat out into a planet full of hate and violence as unwanted children, beaten from early childhood on, and handed over to abuse; thus the biographies of many notorious delinquents, from Joseph Vacher to Carl Panzram, begin in reformatories and juvenile prisons. Someday, it seems, the anger at their predicament has eaten up the last traces of humanity. Traces of an existence wrecked from the beginning can be seen more than clearly in the faces of Lucas and his murder accomplice Ottis Toole. If you look at their aspect on file-card photographs, as the violence deeply carved in their gloomy faces stares at you, you are tempted to believe the dull theories of the Italian "criminal anthropologist" Cesare Lambroso, who in all seriousness suggested that a certain frame or physiognomy predetermines that certain people become criminals.

Your Neighbour, The Killer

But cases like the one of raped and abused Henry Lee Lucas, who mutated into a beast, only partly reveal the truth about the serial killer phenomenon.

In comparison with this, Joel Rifkin, who a few years ago was accused of having killed at least 13 prostitutes in New York, has a much more alarming character profile. From the outside he appears to be perfectly normal. Friends and neighbours said nothing had ever hinted at a murderous personality. The gardener who was given the nickname "The Turtle" in Junior High School never dated a girl. But this was the only odd thing in his banal facade. Nobody thought of suspecting people like him to have a second identity as a sex killer. On the surface he is nothing but the boy next door.

Further examples from the more recent history of crime: Donald Leroy Evans, from the outside a typical white male American in his mid-life crisis, with an intelligence above the average. Secret profession: mass murderer. Or the German Joachim Kroll. None of his neighbours suspected the washing-room guard to be "The Children-Slaughterer of Duisburg", until atrocious things were found in his fridge and cooking pot. Not to forget Ted Bundy, the All-American Boy, who was impersonated by homely Mark Harmon in THE DELIBERATE STRANGER, the TV-adaptation of his case. Bundy's middle-class existence made it clear that multiple murderers not always spent their childhood in girls' clothes, or must have been raped by one of their parents. Who suspected a brutish woman killer behind his charming smile? People like Rifkin, Evans, or Bundy are the flaws in the fundament of psychological profiles and statistics, for they (apparently) lived a banal life like millions of other people.

Some committed films have tried to look behind their facades of normality. Richard Attenborough as John Christie in TEN RILLINGTON PLACE (1971), or the loneliness-stricken hero of the German serial killer movie SCHRAMM (1993) are such average citizens with a power deficiency. The German director Jörg Buttgereit, who has been haunting German censors since NEKROMANTIK (1987), works with unvarnished raw images. His anti-hero Lothar Schramm has nothing in common with a diabolic beast. Basically, he is "an average German male" between masturbation, dull daily routine, and his secret "hobby".

The prototypical example for the horror rising in ordinariness and perhaps the most extreme killer in sheep's clothes, was Andrei Romanovic Chikatilo (portrayed in CITIZEN X, 1995). The 56-year-old former teacher from Russia confessed to have killed, raped, and dismembered over fifty young girls and boys, over a period of some ten years. Examples like Chikatilo, or Peter Sutcliffe, "The Yorkshire Ripper", make clear what is the link between many serial killers: the addiction to sex and power shrouded by an ordinary family life.

Married With Children

"Only retreat into the save harbour of the family remedies against the atrocity of the world. Only escape into the world helps against the terror of the family. Nobody can live without the world. Nobody can live without a family".

–Georg Seesslen

Neo-conservative advocates of restoration in politics and society supported by AIDS and social insecurity, do not want to hear it, but courageous cineasts know it better: the family is the origin of all the fright that mass murderers and serial killers give our society.

When in a scene of THE BOSTON STRANGLER (1968) Tony Curtis as Albert DeSalvo is sitting too peacefully together with his wife and his children, you can already guess the next shot: Curtis wraps gaffer tape around a woman's mouth before he rapes and finally kills her. Not only Catholics regard the family as the shelter of love and solidarity, the smallest cell of Humanism and charity. Depicting it like that, television daily confronts us with the "Mum-Dad-Kiddie-idyll" via sitcoms. Reality characterised by marriage crises, divorces and child abuse, and on the whole rather bathed in tears, gapes like an open wound beside this wishful thinking, a wound in which Oliver Stone sarcastically turns the knife with NATURAL BORN KILLERS. He shows the youth of his anti-hero Mallory Knox as a typical loud late-afternoon sitcom including the genre-specific laughter from the off. But you have to admit that Daddy (Rodney Dangerfield, the US-epitome of the TV-Daddy) does filthy things with his daughter in the bedroom.

This ingeniously nasty episode, after which the world of soap opera will never be the same says: we have always known it. Behind the kind facade of *Dear Uncle Bill* (alias Brian Keith in a series for children) hides a drooling pederast who is going to do unutterable things to his little foster-children. The kids from *The Brady Bunch*, too, celebrate night-time incest orgies. Under the one or other pink terry cloth pyjama-surface you may find stained blood, as well as sperm stains on cute little teddy bears.

Lost Innocence

"Not only in America the idyll is the icon of the consensus society. Everything the defenders of social compromise have always demanded is established in it: peace, joy, sanctity, and immobility."

–Andreas Ungerboeck

Very often serial killers have never overcome the break with innocence that is marked by growing up. For example, they want to see their parents pure and spotless. They do not accept that Daddy sticks his "stinking thing" into Mum's "dark, sticky opening". In PARENTS (1987) by Bob Ballaban a little boy watches his parents having sex. Because he has not the foggiest idea what they are doing, he mistakes the whole thing for a brutal cannibalistic game. Most of the children process such things sooner or later, but in some of them a fundamental shock continues to develop. They long for unspoilt fantasies. "Red Dragon", the crazy killer in Michael Mann's MANHUNTER, visits families in the night to annihilate them. Like the real "Night Stalker" Richard Ramirez, who set foot in other people's bedrooms in the night, the "Red Dragon" photographed his victims in bizarre death-tableaux. The family is the origin of all his nightmares, so he has to return there again and again. In the midst of children's corpses, fallen-down vases and destroyed living rooms the serial killer dreams of a happy family life.

In the shocking German television play DER HAMMERMOERDER (THE HAMMER-KILLER, 1990) that is based on a true case, an underpaid cop longs so intensely for the bourgeois idyll of home sweet home, a loving wife and happy children, a house and a car, that when he realises that his dreams won't come true he prefers to annihilate his family rather than accept his own capitulation. It is the gap between absolute innocence conjured up time and again (the perfect family sitting around the Christmas tree with radiant faces) and harsh reality that potential killers cannot digest. Even the "stepfather" in THE STEPFATHER (1987), who thanks to his charm again and again marries into new families, is a man looking for an intact world. But he is not able to bring his ideals into line with reality, and has to drown the idylls in blood.

MAN BITES DOG

The best films about serial killers thematize the family aspect without falling into cheap pseudo-psychology or the rigid schemes and checklists of the FBI statisticians. Mother Reece's gaze, distorted by pills in William Friedkin's RAMPAGE (1987) says everything about the breeding-ground of her vampiristic son. Nevertheless, Friedkin asks in his highly complex opus how many children have grown up under similarly desolate circumstances and yet have become ordinary workers, stock brokers, etc.

Finally, the shocking Belgian satire MAN BITES DOG realises that putting one's finger on the open sore of family might end up in movie clichés. So the serial killer is shown celebrating with his parents in unspoilt harmony.

"Father/mother/child, body/mind/soul; orders that break down time and again only to be reconstructed immediately afterwards. You have to go into the world to find family orders again", notes German film critic Georg Seesslen. If a killer was completely denied a family in his childhood, he must create an own family according to his own rules: the cannibal "family" in Tobe Hooper's THE TEXAS CHAINSAW MASSACRE, or the real Family around the Hippie guru Charles Manson are two random examples.

Death Orgasms

"What does physical erotism signify if not a violation of the very being of its practitioners? – a violation bordering on death, bordering on murder?"

–Georges Bataille

Innocence and perversion, the idyll and the anti-idyll: apparently opposites attract each other almost magically. Serial killers like Chikatilo conceal their feverishly

BLUE STEEL

distorted sexual fantasies behind the mask of the loving family father. The light in the eyes of the vicious stock-broker in BLUE STEEL (1990) when he strokes the burnished metallic penis/gun, the lingerie rites of Tony Curtis alias Albert deSalvo (THE BOSTON STRANGLER); the necrophiliac travesty games in MANIAC (1980), WHITE ANGEL, and THE SILENCE OF THE LAMBS, cinema again and again conjures up the bloody ejaculations and death orgasms of serial killers. The chain of motives behind many mass murders, no matter if in film or in reality, begins and ends with sex. The mass murderer either imagines himself as a sex-maniac (e.g. Albert deSalvo's sex drive was described as uncontrollable by doctors, Ted Bundy was always on the hunt for women), or he lives categorically in a self-inflicted celibacy, which reminds us of the chastity of Christian martyrs and the close relation between prohibition and excess.

No matter if you go as far as some feminist writers, who regard "masculine sexuality", or, more generally, "masculinity" as the fundamental basis of sexual murder, or if you differentiate between certain cases, it is an obvious fact that serial murder is almost a 100% domain of men. Aileen Wuornos, one of the very rare female serial killers who waylaid men on the highway, lacks the typical sadist serial killer characteristics, if you have a closer look at her case. Robert Ressler, ex-FBI agent and famous self-appointed expert in the subject of mass murder, confirms this assumption: according to him the sub-category of the sadistic, sexually oriented serial killer exclusively consists of usually intelligent white male loners. This type of killer, says Ressler, generally comes from a broken home, has had poor parenting and/or was abused early in his life, usually doesn't marry, is often an alcoholic or drug addict and can be suicidal. Most of these points seem to fit in the case of Jeffrey Dahmer, who, according to his father, was abused by a boy from the neighbourhood as an 8-year-old (although Dahmer himself denied this). Repressed homosexuality resulting in self-hate and a murderous homophobia are in the centre of Dahmer's case, as well as in that of his "colleague" John Wayne Gacy, who lead a double life as a respectable married businessman.

Repressed sexuality is an important element in the puzzle of serial murder. Gagged and enslaved forbidden forces lived out in public toilets, hidden basements, and lonely apartments mark the beginning of many murder series. John Christie in TEN RILLINGTON PLACE was not able to combine his shy insecurity towards women with his longing for dominance. In Buttgereit's SCHRAMM the title character fornicates a rubber doll (or, more precisely, a plastic torso with a hole) in his single-apartment while listening to the moaning of a prostitute in the adjoining apartment. Schramm dreams of the whore while masturbating into the plastic surrogate vagina. His isolation makes the room appear like a stalactite cavern. Only the death orgasm of murder liberates the serial killer from a circle of desire and repression.

The Myth Of Power

"I am a big man and I have a big gun, got me a big old dick and I like to have fun. Held against your forehead, I'll make you suck it, maybe I'll put a hole in your head. You know, just for the fuck of it. I can reduce you if I want. [...] I'm as hard as fucking steel and've got the POWER."

–Nine Inch Nails, "Big Man With A Gun"

In a simulated world of the present where nothing is real any more, the mass-dying, the daily abundance of atrocities in the storm-centres and war theatres of the world mediated via TV-news, makes the death of the individual a commonplace affair. A victim of one of the numerous wars seems irrelevant in the media overkill whereas the mass murderer even attributes singularity to his victims, and power to himself.

Such ultimate exercise of power, like that of the serial killer over his victim, fascinates, because it is better than sex, i.e. becomes the ultimate thrill in the combination of both: "Taking their lives, I knew them in their most exquisite moments of existence. Cutting them down young, ardent and healthy, I assimilated brashness and sex that would have gone timid had I not usurped it for my own use." (James Ellroy, *Silent Terror*.

Although entirely fictitious, *Silent Terror* is one of the most illuminating books about the phenomenon of the serial killer. This night-journey into the psyche of a serial killer was written by the US thriller-novelist James Ellroy, a specialist in such uncompromising subjects. The book tells about the life and murders of Marty Plunkett, a character constructed after real models as well as Ellroy's imagination unifying the characteristics of all known types of serial killers: the hedonistic killer who kills for thrill, the missionary one who liberates the world from "unnecessary" life, and especially the power-oriented type. A quote: "Part of it was to kill my nightmares and staunch my awful rage, and part of it was for the sheer thrill and high-voltage sense of power that murder gave me. (...) I have been to points of power and lucidity that cannot be measured by anything logical or mystical or human. Such was the sanctity of my madness."

When Ellroy's killer raves about his motives, you feel the cold blast of the real origins of the serial killer phenomenon.

Ecstasy And Ultimate Exceeding

"I need to get shaken, I need to feel something. I need that punch in the nose that wakes me up."

–Edward Norton about his character in FIGHT CLUB

The interaction of power and sex constitutes an important factor in the search for the motives of "motiveless" killers.

Moreover, here is the root of the magical attraction of cinematic adaptations of serial murder. In the cinema the brutal living out of sexual dominance until the bitter end is absorbed by an audience constantly on the hunt for stimulants, kicks, and extremes. Celluloid, video, and literature are surrogates where people want to live out forbidden fantasies. Hold your hand into the murderous flame for a few seconds, then quickly return to safe everyday life!

But the real killer wants much more. Just as, according to Georges Bataille the passionate lovers maybe be able to transcend the Self (as well as the eternal inextinguishable gap between human beings), and to dissolve the ego, people like Marty Plunkett feel that the act of murder can mean something mythical, ecstatic, and sacred for them. To deprive a fellow being of his/her life becomes an act of total exceeding that catapults the individual out of his senseless existence. Hence murder fulfils a function comparable to the animal sacrifice, or the human sacrifice of the Aztecs, or the ecstatic feast in earlier times.

It is a symptom of our time, that other forms of excessive transgression are not enough any more, that murder has remained as the endmost, perverted form of the ultimate state of ecstasy. After "God's death" (Nietzsche) and the deconstruction of all metaphysical castles in the air, after the end of all ideologies and values, even humanism is totally corrupted and has been sold to the technocrats, people are confronted with the structured transparent void of a world having lost its magic. A void that is mirrored *ad infinitum* in the media overkill. Images with nothing but a vacuum behind them. But the demand for other more bestial states of mind, for a delirious catapulting of oneself out of one's existence, is still there. Sexuality in its modern monogamous-couple-variety cannot fulfil this any more, the ecstatic feast has died out, and art can only contribute fragments (cinema, music). Apparently, death is the last remaining "real thing" in our simulation society. Hence the serial killers out there in the wilderness of the canyons and highways of megalopolis can to seen as performing murder as a ritual act.

Murder As A Ritual Act

"My whole existence is flawed, you get me closer to God"
–Nine Inch Nails, "Closer"

It may sound blasphemous to the majority of Christians, but in earlier times it was religion that offered something serial killers are addicted to. "Murders are exciting and lift people into a heart-beating awe as religion is supposed to do", E.L. Doctorow wrote in *Billy Bathgate*. William Friedkin's RAMPAGE, based on a novel by William P. Wood, who in his turn was inspired by the deeds of Richard Chase, "The Vampire", emphasises the ritualistic aspect of the moments of killing more than most of the other films. Moments of ecstasy felt by the murderer when he slaughters his victims comparable to moments in shamanism, certain sacrifices in Voodoo ceremonies, and especially pagan cults. It is the viewer who has to find the link in his/her mind when Friedkin edits long sequences of Communion and murder simultaneously, or when in the end the delinquent wants to taste the Body of Christ, murders the priest ritually, and fills his blood into a monstrance. In many of its scenes RAMPAGE symbolises the ecstasy of killing. While in reality he is butchering a whole family, the serial killer portrayed by Alex McArthur hallucinates squatting naked in front of a tiger's cage in a trance, covering himself ritually with blood. Finally, Friedkin seems to surrender to the ballast of socialisation theories and individuals directed by social structures that is discussed in other moments of the film. Obviously, the animal does not only stand for the brutish side of man, but rather for nature, cruelty as such.

Oliver Stone concluded similarly to William Friedkin. "I believe we are all born violent."

"I am a natural born killer", the serial killer Mickey Knox puts it in Stone's subject-relevant motion picture. James Ellroy, too, who relies on hundreds of pages of police records in the character description of Marty Plunkett, comes to a matching conclusion. In *Silent Terror* FBI agent Dusenberry puts it like this: "Checking out their school records, I found the all-American boy (...) but no mention of anything like pivotal, life-forming trauma (...) Evil exists, pre-packaged at birth, predestined in the womb."

"Oh poor heart, I was doomed from the start. Doomed to play the villain part", as the quasi-religious rock singer Nick Cave howls in the Old Testament fate ballad "Up Jumped The Devil".

The Killing Of America

The actor/director Sean Penn said in an interview that "hunting, the act of going out into the wilderness to shoot one's deer does not exist anymore. Everybody can go to a supermarket and buy a steak there". In THE INDIAN RUNNER (1990), a melodrama about two unequal brothers, Penn creates parallels between the hunting ceremonies of the Native Americans and the "ritual deer-slaying" in the end of the film when the aggressive protagonist slays a bar-keeper in bloodlust. The whole scene is accompanied by Indian hunting drums on the soundtrack. Penn supposes that "for many men violence is a valve. It has been invented and romanticised for them. At least when we are talking about the America society, this is true".

The serial killers prowling the vast American continent know or feel that they stand in a long tradition: "Killing has already been important in the times of the trappers. The shooting of the animal, the enemy, the mythical appropriation of the victim via the blood, the taking over Indian mythology, religion, and rituals, the evidence for a serious, unsolvable identity crisis [...] Bloodlust often got hold of the old trappers. We know that from many documents passed on to us" (Oliver Huzly in the German afterword of James Ellroy's *Silent Terro*r).

Having its origin in American history – for example the gunman John Wesley Hardin, who allegedly murdered over 40 victims – the serial murderer has become a prototypically American phenomenon. In the age of total mobility the almost infinite extentof the country grants a wide variety of hide-outs to the killers. The typically American infrastructure of transport and speed, anonymity, and decay of values are implied variables leading to top performance in the calculated production of death.

Moreover, no country in the world seems to be so obsessed by its serial killers as America: David Berkowitz alias The Son of Sam, Ed Gein, John Wayne Gacy, Henry Lee Lucas, Jeffrey Dahmer, Ted Bundy. American serial killers and rapist killers evoking images of blood, fear, and tears, are as popular in their country as the president or famous movie stars.

"They're young; they're bold; to an America egregiously entrenched in the mythology of good versus evil and inundated by slaughter flicks, hideous rock'n roll videos, and catastrophic bad news they're strangely groovy", writes James Ellroy. Nobody commercialises its murderers as well as the USA. Of course, England has its Jack the Ripper cult, but the Americans make superstars of their killers. Ed Gein's car was exhibited at fairs, the paintings of "Killer Clown" Gacy sell very well in the art business, the multiple woman killer Ted Bundy received love letters even in Death Row, not to mention the business with devotional articles around the sect-founder Charles Manson. Killing is big business.

The Serial Killer In The Age Of Simulation

"I've seen the future, baby, and it's murder"
–Leonard Cohen

We are nearing the beginning again. Welcome to the Present. In search of the "lost" individual in a faceless mass society the idea of the serial killer as a brutal drop-out from everyday life has become the ultimate subject of the media. Hannibal Lecter and John Doe (SEVEN, 1995) seem to be the last individualists.

If, according to Jean Baudrillard, the constant (mimetic) depiction of a thing sooner or later makes the thing itself disappear, and finally only the image remains (as the sex-boom has driven back real sex and infected all areas of everyday life with sex images instead), the deluge of reports about serial killers/merchandising/movies/videos, etc. has devaluated murder as the final act of exceeding. Killing itself has become a part of the capitalistic *mise-enscène* in an entirely simulated world. The "system" that had been afraid of the individual act of amok and violence for so long, because it had always come as an outcry of revolt, has integrated blood and death into commercialisation now. The modern killers do not kill for reasons of madness, lust, or sexual disturbance anymore, but for, with, and under the guidance of the media. In the past there had also been cases of mutual influence. TAXI DRIVER, a film that had been inspired by real assassin and in his turn "inspired" the real assassin John Hinckley would be a suitable example. But nowadays it goes much further. A new branch of industry has been born. Meanwhile, the murderer has become the partner of the media. True Crime books, comic strips, postcards, Reality-TV, and rock music (e.g. Death Metal) make use of serial killers. Vice versa, the delinquents are strongly media-oriented to achieve popularity, hence immortality. This is the approach of NATURAL BORN KILLERS, a film that does not aim at soberly illuminating reality, but makes that very myth-making the subject of a gloomy satire. The film states pessimistically: The outlaw, even in its ultimate form, the serial killer, is dead. Commercialised to death by a much viler demon that trivialises everything, even homicide.

Taking the massacre in the Heysel Stadium in Brussels where soccer fans trampled each other to death as an example, Baudrillard notes: "There is no atavistic resurgence of some archaic type of violence [...] The violence of old was both more enthusiastic and more sacrificial than ours. Today's violence, the violence produced by our hypermodernity, is terror. A simulacrum of violence emerging less from passion than from the screen."

Baudrillard defines this modern violence as "an aggravated form of indifference, no violence out of passion, but violence coming from the screen". That is why Mickey and Mallory, who represent archaic violence, shoot the head villain, the diabolic journalist Wayne Gale (Robert Downey Jr.) personifying the simulacrum-violence of the media. "Mickey and Mallory are, yes, irreverent and feel no guilt, drawn broadly in a Swiftian/Voltairian caricature of our worst nightmare", says Oliver Stone. "They do 'come' from violence. Violence is depicted as generationally handed down from father/mother to son/daughter and on and on, to the end of time. There will be no end of violence. But something particularly vicious about the 20th Century stands out in its faceless, genocidal quality".

Obviously, like Baudrillard, Oliver Stone plays the individual violence of Mickey and Mallory off against the violence of the media, the law, and the government. The murderous lovers are the last romantics in the totalitarian age of simulation. Stone notes: "The killers may be sick, but those characters representing the establishment are, on the contrary, completely perverted".

The most interesting and most cutting newer films on the subject mirror the

SEVEN

Reality-TV era. John Water's SERIAL MOM (1994), or the malicious Belgian film MAN BITES DOG were already produced in the time of the True Crime media overkill. The documentary AILEEN WUORNOS – THE SELLING OF A SERIAL KILLER (1992) has the commercialisation process in the rare case of a female delinquent as subject.

What is still left to serial killer cinema? Of course, it can ignore all developments and re-stage the old myths of the revolt commercialised to death in a post-modern way (THE CELL, 2000) as well as dark romantic way (as in SEVEN or IN DREAMS, 1999). Films about the community of serial killers and their media partners as a means to an end like WHITE ANGEL, WHERE SLEEPING DOGS LIE, or KALIFORNIA (1993) pretending to give insight into the abysmal inner lives of the killers, but only sticking to the perceptive faculty of their ignorant writing counterparts, are highly fashionable but shallow. The only thing you get to know in KALIFORNIA is what is going on in the minds of the dull young yuppie couple. Brad Pitt as the killer remains a grotesque cliché-figure. To be extremely vicious, as "pre-exorcised" by Hong Kong cinema with films like GAO YANG YI SHENG (DR. LAMB, 1992) or the infamous BA XIAN FAN DIAN ZHI REN ROU CHA SHAO BAO (BUN MAN: THE UNTOLD STORY, 1992), seems to be another dead-end street that can't be duplicated by the censorship-ridden Western cinema.

On the other hand, artistic "criminals of passion" like James Ellroy, the specialist for deranged psyches and murderous motives, neither want to criticise the media nor re-stage second-hand myths. That is why they have completely turned away from the subject of serial killers. James Ellroy said in a film interview: "I'm sick to death of serial killers. I think the public's fascination for serial killers is expressed as a means to avoid the real social ills that are consuming America right now. Self-contained serial killers that come out of nowhere [...] are easy, they're safe, they have nothing to do with anything important. I'm *dead* tired of serial killers".

SERIAL KILLER FILMS: A SELECTION

AMERICAN PSYCHO / USA 2000

Directed by Mary Harron. Written by Mary Harron and Guinevere Turner after the book of Brett Easton Ellis. Camera: Andrzej Sekula. Music: John Cale. With Christian Bale, Willem Dafoe, Chloe Sevigny, Jared Leto

Those who think that the New York feminist director Mary Harron links up with the era of ambitious serial killer movies with her screen version of AMERICAN PSYCHO get it wrong, at least partly. Though Harron's film is sparkling with wit and sarcasm, it rather deals with the excesses of capitalism and uncompromising consumerism than the subject "serial murder". What Brett Easton Ellis hasn't grown weary to emphasize is that his novel, far more explicit in its depiction of violence, aims at the same target. Super-yuppie Patrick Bateman is neither an outlaw, an Existentialist nor a Nietzschean/Sadean villain. He is rather a construct designed on the drawing board to personify the terror of sterile designer apartments, nouvelle cuisine and Phil Collins CDs. All these status objects don't thrill him anymore – that's why Bateman kills.

Harron, who unlike some of her feminist colleagues actually understood Ellis' message, distils the stockbroker's life into a piece of highly malignant social satire. Less shocking and disgusting than uncompromisingly funny. Best scene: honed axe in hand and grinning, Bale/Bateman approaches one of his victims and lectures about the benefits of the new Huey Lewis album. The banality of Evil.

BLUE STEEL / USA 1990

Directed by Kathryn Bigelow. Written by Eric Red. Camera: Amir Mokri. Music: Brad Fiedel. With Ron Silver, Jamie Lee Curtis, Clancy Brown, Louise Fletcher

A visually impressive but, in its contents not entirely convincing film by one of the great newcomers of the Eighties. Widely known through her gloomy vampire ballad NEAR DARK (1987), Kathryn Bigelow employs again her favourite themes: violence, action, and the plasticity of images. Again she puts obsessive love crossing all borders into the centre of the story and discusses the conflict between such passion and the law , i.e. moral values. Nevertheless, the love story of the yuppie serial killer (trite: Ron Silver) and a female cop (brilliant: Jamie Lee Curtis) lacks consequence and decisiveness. Not a spark of indecision or insecurity haunts the cop when she finally erases her evil ex-lover.

BODY BAGS / USA 1993

Directed by John Carpenter and Tobe Hooper. Written by Billy Brown and Dan Angel. Camera: Gray Kibbe. Music: John Carpenter and Jim Lang. With Deborah Harry, Stacy Keach, Mark Hamill, David Naughton, Sheena Easton, David Warner

A thrilling, but also amusing episodic film with two stories circling around serial killers ("Gas Station" and "The Eye"). The former quite thrilling story is about a gas station during the night-time, and its lonesome female attendant quotes John Carpenter and his HALLOWEEN movies. In the latter the ex-STAR WARS hero Mark Hamill plays a family father haunted by a serial killer. Average video stuff that has very little to do with the classic masterpieces of its makers.

BONE COLLECTOR, THE / USA 1999

Directed by Phillip Noyce. Written by Jeremy Iacone after the book of Jeffery Deaver. Camera: Dean Semmler. Music: Craig Armstrong. With Denzel Washington, Angelina Jolie, Queen Latifah, Michael Rooker, Leland Orser, Ed O'Neill

After an accident, a forensics expert (Denzel Washington) is left as a quadraplegic who is able only to move his head and one finger. Just with the help of a computer he can still manipulate his environment. When he is confronted with clues from a serial killer that are obviously pointed to forensics investigation, the case re-invokes his interest in life. Recognizing the talent of a sharp, young cop for forensics, he makes her (Angelina Jolie) his assistant. Via CB-radio she becomes his eyes and legs on the scene.

With the exception of shooting star Jolie's charismatic performance, this stereotyped thriller doesn't offer anything worth seeing. Elements of COPYCAT and BONE DADDY – Nothing new under the serial killer sun.

C'EST ARRIVÉ PRÈS DE CHEZ VOUS (MAN BITES DOG) / Belgium 1992

Written and directed by Remy Belvaux, André Bonzel, and Benoit Poelvoorde. Camera: André Bonzel. Music: Jean Marc Chenut. With Benoit Poelvoorde, Remy Belvaux, André Bonzel

Done by three fanatic Belgian film students with a minimal budget, this pitch-dark comedy very quickly achieved cult status. MAN BITES DOG dissects the every-day life of Reality TV with a satirical scalpel. The film shows cuts of the daily routine of a serial killer recorded by a young film crew that dogs his footsteps. Ben, a cold-blooded chauvinist/racist/misanthrope who likes reciting poems and kills for money from time to time, but most of the time for the fun of it, is shown "at work" in jumping realistic black-and-white images. Shots in the head, strangulation, rapes contrasted with cordial visits at Ben's grandparents' place and small talk in the bistro round the corner. The laughter coming up in the audience is constantly suffocated by a pulp of brain matter and blood.

THE CELL / USA 2000

Directed by Tarsem. Written by Mark Protosevich. Camera: Paul Laufer. Music: Howard Shore. With Jennifer Lopez, Vincent D'Onofrio, Vince Vaughn, Dylan Baker

"Enter the mind of a killer" – the tagline of THE CELL sounds promising at first. With the help of highly sophisticated technology the psychologist Deane (J. Lopez) has to enter the mind of the killer Stargher (D'Onofrio) to find out the whereabouts of Stargher's latest victim, who is still alive. Yet the world behind the eyes of the psychopathic pain-junkie is not at all as unsufferably bleak as one might imagine e.g. Jeffrey Dahmer's mindscape. Instead, it is as rather colourful and flashy and *goth-chic*, as a killer's mind imagined by an MTV-veteran like Tarsem Singh should be.

Hardly anything in this pretentious serial killer opus is original: the décor, though admittedly catchy, is sampled from the output of more innovative video artists like Floria Sigismondi or other postmodernist artists like Pierre et Gilles and Damian Hirst. The ideology behind this visual orgy too is all but new. For the killer, Jennifer Lopez may slip into every possible cliché between Mother, Whore, and Holy Virgin. The triumph of style over a reactionary content.

COPYCAT / USA 1995

Directed by Jon Amiel. Written by Ann Biderman & David Madsen. Camera: László Kovács. Music: Christopher Young. With Sigourney Weaver, Holly Hunter, Harry Connick Jr., Dermot Mulroney, William McNamara

Whether you want to admit it or not: we live in an age of total quotation terror, and the "new", according to postmodern everyday life, is only made up of random fragments that have always been there. Under such circumstances serial murder is no desperate final cry for individuality any more, but merely a quote. This is what the film COPYCAT quite correctly concludes. So this film shows a killer-fan/fan-killer who tries to copy to the last detail his great idols, Son of Sam David Berkovitz, the Boston Strangler, Jeffrey Dahmer, etc., in his own gory deeds. Yet this exciting premise, which

COPYCAT

might trigger off a cynical criticism of our time as well as media-philosophical considerations, merely serves Jon Amiel as a pretext for a highly predictable collection of cinematic quotes. He especially exploits the Thomas Harris-motives of *The Silence Of The Lambs* and *Red Dragon* and adds a little bit of political correctness and pseudo-feminism. But even stars like Holly Hunter and Sigourney Weaver cannot upgrade the slippery result.

THE EXORCIST III / USA 1990
Written and directed by William Peter Blatty. Camera: Gerry Fisher. Music: Barry De Vorzon. With Brad Dourif, George C. Scott, Jason Miller, Ed Flanders, Scott Wilson
What seems to be typical genre-cinema on the surface (although contemporary

horror fans actually find the subtle horror of this film rather boring) is in reality a highly intelligent reflection on violence, religion, philosophy, and serial murder. The best-selling author Blatty (he wrote the highly successful *Exorcist*) had already directed a similar box office flop (although it had been a fascinating dialogue film): THE NINTH CONFIGURATION (1980). In this theological discourse-shocker Blatty clashes metaphysics and rationality, humanism and individualistic anarchy.

IN DREAMS / USA 1999

Directed by Neil Jordan. Written by Bruce Robinson & Neil Jordan, based on a novel by Bari Wood. Camera: Darius Khondji. Music: Elliot Goldenthal. With Annette Bening, Aidan Quinn, Stephen Rea, Robert Downey Jr.

Apart from Hollywood Productions of rather debatable merits like INTERVIEW WITH A VAMPIRE (1994) Neil Jordan also stands for highly personal films like THE CRYING GAME (1992) and the fabulous THE BUTCHER BOY (1997). These are films where Jordan transforms outsider subjects into deliberately artificial larger than life images, whereas others end up in petty social realism. These images give all the freaks, transsexuals and mentally deranged in his films a beauty that outshines the "normal" by far. IN DREAMS can be placed in this context and deals with the subject of serial killers much more abysmally than many of the films flooding the movie theatres after the climactic SEVEN. The film carries us off into the dreams of the writer Claire (Annette Bening) which are reminiscent of the fairytales of the Grimm brothers and psychoanalytical puzzles. Only after her beloved little daughter disappears sdoes omething dawn on Claire: there is a mysterious man, a serial killer who taps the dreams of his favourite author and plays cat and mouse with her.

The story of Jordan's film is neither new nor without flaws, but *how* he tells it is unique in late Nineties mystery cinema. IN DREAMS hypnotizes and startles until the last frame – not least thanks to the breathtaking photography of SEVEN cameraman Darius Khondji.

KISS THE GIRLS / USA 1997

Directed by Gary Fleder. Written by David Klass after the novel of James Patterson. Camera: Aaron Schneider. Music: Mark Isham. With Morgan Freeman, Ashley Judd, Gary Elwes, Alex McArthur

Washington DC detective Dr. Alex Cross travels to North Carolina to investigate the kidnapping of his niece. Aided by an escaped kidnappee (Ashley Judd), Cross tries to hunt down the serial killer who operates under the pseudonym "Casanova". Until the final showdown all the usual scenarios and elements of successful genre contributions like SILENCE OF THE LAMBS or SEVEN are reeled off, but the film does not all reach the intensity of its models.

For insiders: Alex McArthur, who plays the minor part of an FBI agent here, played the threatening ritual killer in William Friedkin's far better film RAMPAGE.

KYUA (CURE) / Japan 1997

Directed and written by Kiyoshi Kurosawa. Camera: Tokusho Kikumura. Music: Gary Ashiya. With Koji Yakusho, Tsuyoshi Ujiki, Anna Nakagawa, Masato Hagiwara

A wave of gruesome murders is sweeping Tokyo. The only connection is a bloody X carved into the neck of the victims. In each case the murderer is found near the victim and remembers nothing of the crime. The investigating detective assumes that there must be someone who forces other people via hypnosis to commit such murderous deeds. Yet when the cop, himself a mentally unstable character, finally gets hold of the supposed malefactor, a former psychiatry student, the terror has only just begun.

At a time when Western serial killer cinema is becoming increasingly

MANHUNTER

paralysed in its formalism, Japanese cinema is electrifying us with new and startling contributions to the genre. The reason for this probably is that directors like Kurosawa don't contend themselves with cinematic quotes, but derive their inspiration from the fluid evolution of national traumata.

In the case of this very unique and trance-like opus the social phenomenon under examiniation is Japan's mind-control and mass psychosis paranoia, which has also been explored fascinatingly by Sogo Ishii in DASUTO (ANGEL DUST, 1994), as well as most of the films of Hisayasu Sato. Since the homicidal underground gas assault of the Aum sect this paranoia has become even stronger. KYUA is a gripping example of its legacy on the modern Japanese psyche.

MANHUNTER / USA 1986

Directed by Michael Mann. Written by Michael Mann after The Red Dragon by Thomas Harris. Camera: Dante Spinotti. Music: The Reds, Michael Rubini. With William Petersen, Kim Griest, Tom Noonan, Dennis Farina, Brian Cox

The quasi-forerunner of THE SILENCE OF THE LAMBS, where the character of the ultimate serial killer Hannibal Lecter (played by Brian Cox) appears for the first time. With the help of the locked up Dr. Lecter a cop tries to find a serial killer who brutally erases whole families. In order to detect him, the cop lets his mind slip deep into the killer's mind and risks his mental sanity. In the fashion of the Eighties Michael Mann, who invented *Miami Vice* and directed numerous aesthetic commercials, polishes the more than convincing plot with often much too stylish images. Nevertheless he also creates hypnotic scenes trenched in gleaming light, with Tom Noolan bewildering the viewer as "Red Dragon", a tattooed angel of death.

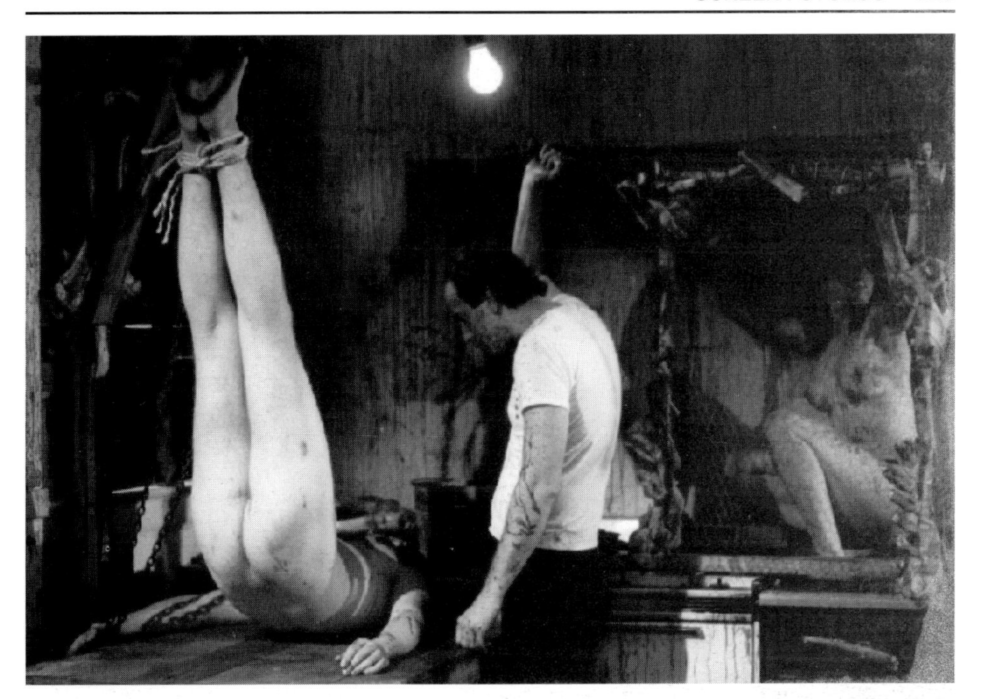

ROADKILL

MR. FROST / GB-France 1990

Directed by Philip Setbon. Written by Philip Setbon and Brad Lynch. Camera: Dominique Brenguier. Music: Steve Levine. With Jeff Goldblum, Alan Bates, Kathy Baker, Jean Pierre Cassel

Jeff Goldblum as an icy cold aristocratic slaughterer who only kills for the killing's sake and confronts a police detective with his anti-social philosophy. Mr. Frost could have become an even more radically formulated, more abysmal Hannibal Lecter, the whole film a subversive thriller about the Superman-fantasies of many serial killers, but Philip Setbon bungles it all, as his killer reveals himself as Satan. The escape into metaphysical nonsense saves the viewer from the confrontation with "the other side", the evil. Moreover, the film lacks any biting and intelligent fireworks of dialogue las featured in the already-mentioned theological serial killer spectacle, Blatty's EXORCIST III.

ROADKILL: THE LAST TEN DAYS OF JOHN MARTIN / USA 1987

Written and directed by Jim Van Bebber. Camera: Mike King. With Mark Gillespie, Marc Pitman, Maurine Alllisse

A short film by Jim Van Bebber, the insider bet for the American splatter-scene crown (DEADBEAT AT DAWN), who throws a 20 minute flashlight upon the everyday life of a serial killer with an ultra-cheap production that reveals much more of the truth about the horror behind the headlines than many "ambitious" films. Bloodstained dullness, an existence between drinking beer, killing rats, watching TV, and butchering people. Some gorehounds are awaiting the final product in a fever of anticipation, and with these ingredients the film might become THE TEXAS CHAINSAW MASSACRE of the Nineties. Yet Van Bebber still has to wait for the money necessary to finish ROADKILL or his major project, CHARLIE'S FAMILY.

SCHRAMM

SCHRAMM / Germany 1993

Directed by Jörg Buttgereit. Written by Franz Rodenkirchen and Jörg Buttgereit. Camera: Manfred Jelinski. Music: Max Mueller and Gundula Schmitz. With Florian Koerner von Gustorf, Monika M.

The German comment on the serial killer hype staged by Buttgereit, Rodenkirchen, and Jelinski, a team experienced in human extremes (sex with corpses in NEKROMANTIK; suicide and amok in DER TODESKING/THE DEATH KING, 1990). The portrait of a murderous petty bourgeois, desolate, bitter, and sometimes romantically melancholic loner. Whereas in McNaughton's HENRY the violence is born in a total emotional vacuum, and MAN BITES DOG stresses the media-critical gesture, Buttgereit cares a lot for the emotional state of his protagonist Lothar Schramm. A "man in his room" story in the sense of Paul Schrader with all related fears, desires, and deformations, where splatter effects serve as metaphors for psychic abysses. A highlight and safe bet in the only partly funny German film scene.

SERIAL MOM / USA 1994

Written and directed by John Waters. Camera: Robert Stevens. Music: Basil Poledouris. With Kathleen Turner, Sam Waterston, Ricki Lake, Susanne Somers

The most amusing contribution to the subject and its complete commercialisation is by a real serial killer expert. John Waters has attended a lot of trials over the years, exchanged letters with murderers, and collected macabre material. Kathleen Turner as a serial-killing housewife who collects Charles Manson autographs and has a lively correspondence with Ted Bundy. Cute, light entertainment with a serious subject.

SEVEN / USA 1995

Directed by David Fincher. Written by Andrew Kevin Walker. Camera: Darius Khondji. Music: Howard Shore, Nine Inch Nails, Gravity Kills etc. With Morgan Freeman, Brad Pitt, Gwyneth Paltrow, John C. McGinley, Kevin Spacey

At a time when mainstream cinema really does not seem to be able to add anything further to the thematic complex "serial killer", when everything has already been said and ticked off, a young director still manages to set new standards. David Fincher, previously responsible for a number of music video-clips and the totally underrated ALIEN^3 (1993), undermines Hollywood's conformism with an extra dose of bleakness and intensity. Morgan Freeman as the old detached cop and Brad Pitt as the young hot-headed cop, hunting a serial killer through a climate of decay in a nameless US metropolis.

The killer's morbid bible-fixation fits perfectly into this gloomy and melancholic world where it rains without surcease. As a self-appointed judge over the decadence of his fellows he murders according to the pattern of the seven Catholic mortal sins: gluttony, greed, lust, pride, sloth, envy, wrath. Fincher stages murder as a fine art: the corpses are discovered looking like the photographer Joel Peter Witkin's disturbing tableaux, while the breathtaking pre-titles sequence quotes the industrial-aesthetics of bands like Nine Inch Nails. Yet only in a very few moments does the perfect visual adaptation jar with the content, or distract from the story's tragic significance. A radically dark ending, not to be found elsewhere in the Hollywood-swamp of the Nineties, sweeps away any such second thoughts.

Undoubtedly, SEVEN is one of the most remarkable, and at the same time most successful, entries into the chapter of serial killer films. Its influence has been considerable, perhaps most notably in the giddy gore-splattered clone RESURRECTION (1999), in which a sick religious fuck amputates human body parts in order to construct his own personal Christ/Frankenstein on the cross.

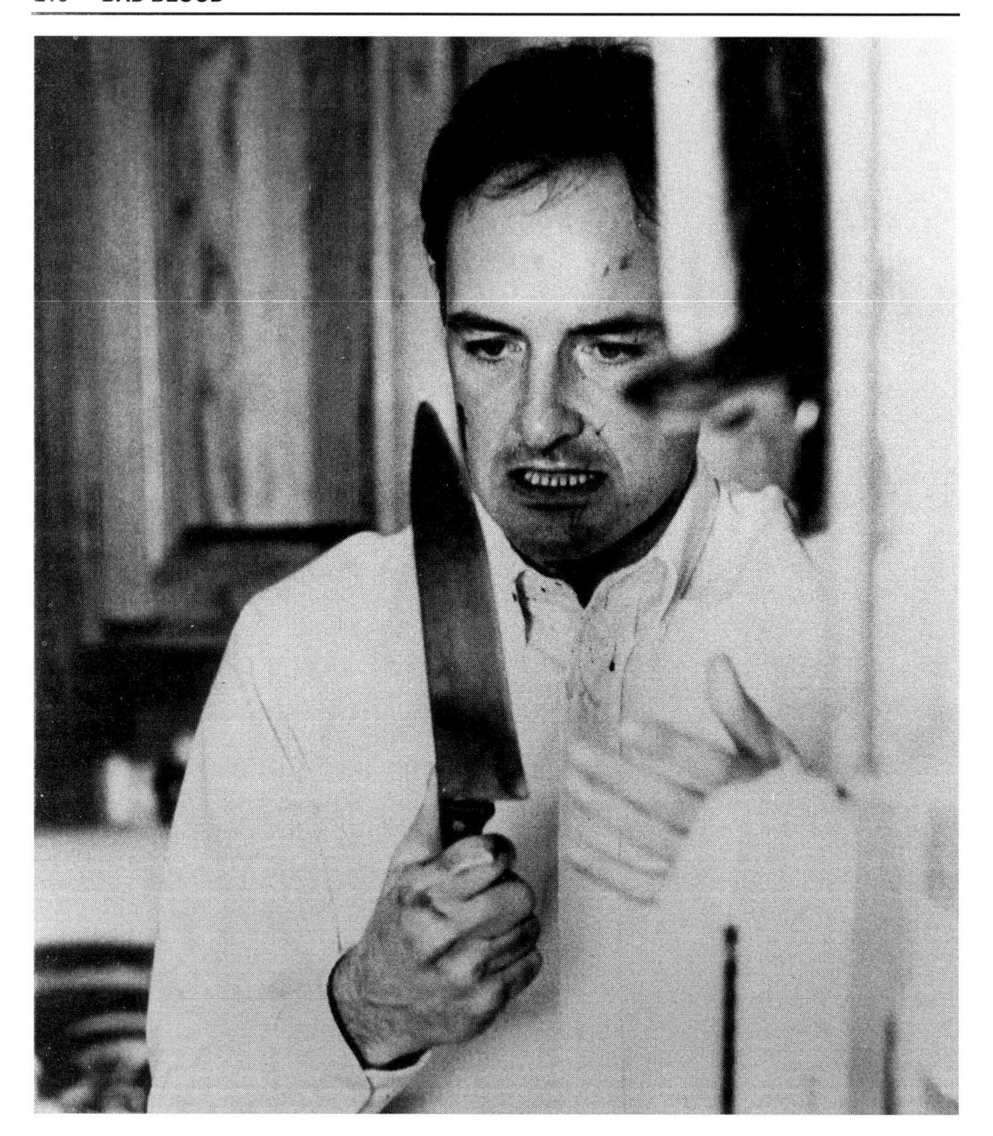

THE STEPFATHER

THE STEPFATHER / USA 1987

Directed by Joseph Ruben. Written by Donald E. Westlake. Camera: John Lindley. Music: Patrick Moraz. With Terry O´ Quinn, Jill Schoelen, Shelley Hack, Charles Lanyer

The starting-point sounds intriguing: a seemingly respectable gentleman in his middle ages approaches female singles with children and plays the nice-guy step-daddy, until he finally drowns the newly-found family idyll in carnage. What could have been a traumatic combination of family, sex, and violence, an autopsy of bourgeois desires and fears, is doomed to failure by Joseph Ruben's too conventional *mise-en-scène*. This variation of old Hitchcock motives lacks stringency from the beginning to the end, culminating in a classic happy ending and the restoration of the intact world *à la* Hollywood. Even worse, extremely dull sequels followed.

THE WATCHER / USA 2000

Directed by Joe Charbanic. Written by David Elliot & Clay Ayers after a story by Darcy Meyers & David Elliot. Camera: Michael Chapman. Music: Marco Beltrami. With James Spader, Keanu Reeves, Marisa Tomei

Another example of the repetitive formalism of serial killer cinema at the turn of the millennium. Most of the times the credit titles, since SEVEN a gloomy visual field of experimentation, are the best part of the film. In THE WATCHER this is the case too. The title sequence with its coarse-grained, intensely coloured images and electronic soundtrack promises much more than the film can deliver. For the story of the FBI agent (Spader) and his Nemesis, the sly women slasher (Reeves) is highly conventional in its staging. Highlight: James Spader, who manages to add some fascinating nuances to the good old cliché of the busted cop on the verge of a nervous breakdown. Anticlimax: teddy bear Keanu, who, deliberately cast against his MATRIX image, makes one of the most unimpressive killers of all times.

WHERE SLEEPING DOGS LIE / USA 1992

Directed by Charles Finch. Written by Charles Finch & Yolanda Turner. Camera: Miles Cooke. Music: Mike Figgis. With Dylan McDermott, Tom Sizemore, Sharon Stone

An interesting premise (a young unsuccessful script-writer lives together with a serial killer who dictates him his biography) is destroyed by a lack of purpose in its staging. A quickly and cheaply produced film for the video market.

WHITE ANGEL / GB 1993

Directed by Chris Jones. Written by Chris Jones and Genevieve Jolliffe. Camera: Jon Walker. Music: Harry Gregson-Williams. With Peter Firth, Harriet Robinson, Don Henderson

Another film where an author (female for a change) and a killer who wants his life recorded for posterity meet. Contents-wise a captivating film with ambitious actors (especially Peter Firth), but too conventional in plot matters and rather reminiscent of a TV movie rather than a picture made for the cinema.

Relevant films already discussed in Part One:

AILEEN WUORNOS – THE SELLING OF A SERIAL KILLER
THE BOSTON STRANGLER
COLD LIGHT OF DAY
CONFESSIONS OF A SERIAL KILLER
THE DELIBERATE STRANGER
HENRY – PORTRAIT OF A SERIAL KILLER
M
RAMPAGE
THE SECRET LIFE
SILENCE OF THE LAMBS
TEN RILLINGTON PLACE
TENDERNESS OF WOLVES
TO CATCH A KILLER
DER TOTMACHER

CHAPTER TWO
WEIRDOS, VOYEURS, SPLIT PERSONALITIES: PSYCHO KILLERS

"You think I'm psycho, don't you mama?"
–Eddie Noack, *Psycho*

" [...] and all that he could feel was an all-pervading sickness that seemed to flow through his body and into his arms and legs and fingers and bones and the sickness was almost visible within and its hideousness and grotesqueness fed itself and the sickness became more and more intolerable and all he could do was stay within himself and become more and more a part of his disease."
–Hubert Selby, *The Demon*

A young man, his name is Peter, hears voices in his head. There is whispering and screaming, sounds and fragments of words, uninterrupted and unbearable, like a radio perpetually searching for a station planted into his brain. Peter lives in a car with side windows covered with newsprint, wheels along the desolate roads of a Canadian island looking for his daughter. His gaze is hunted, his movements shaky. The police thinks he is a wanted serial killer.

Peter is the protagonist of the US movie CLEAN, SHAVEN and he is schizophrenic. In a long row of cinematic approaches to madness and crime this film is one of the most serious attempts to create realistic images of the shaken psyche. It is easy to put weird killers into the corset of stereotypes and portray them as repugnant monsters, like the random mad slashers of many horror movies representing nothing more than snarling, eye-rolling catalysts for various shock-sequences. Director Lodge Kerrigan confesses: "I felt that in recent cinema schizophrenia is portrayed in very unrealistic terms. It seems to be either that a schizophrenic character is portrayed as some kind of monster out of control or the other way – that it's kind of hip and cool to be crazy. The third way says it's not really an illness, all the character needs is just a little bit of love to help them feel better. Peter is definitely a psychotic character but I tried to portray him as a very normal person, in that his desires are very normal. He really is reaching out towards his family, he wants to be united with his daughter. I just tried to portray him as a human being. His violence is really a projection of the internal destruction of his mind".

Nevertheless, Kerrigan's psycho-study is, in its seriousness, much more shocking than most horror films: "I did a lot of research for this film. I tried to base a lot of it on medical facts. But the truth of the matter is, there's no real understanding of the causes of mental illness and schizophrenia. It's relatively unknown what causes the illness. I wanted to communicate the sense of anxiety that this character lives with on a day to day basis in his life, to an audience. In a very visceral way. How extreme that is and how disorientating".

The Lust Of Seeing: Voyeurmania

CLEAN, SHAVEN is a exceptional case in cinema. Only very few films are so authentic in their approach to minds spirited away from reality. Most of the movie psychos benefit from the exaggeration of their characters, from big spectacular performances. Madness in film must be extraordinary to leave an impression upon the audience. Yet genre films more than the average, too, though rather aiming at entertainment than Kerrigan's humane ideas, manage to subvert the fundament of "normality".

In its best moments cinema forces the viewer into the perspective of the psycho, forces a different point of view upon us, and simultaneously makes us reconsider our own safe view of "reality". In PEEPING TOM (1960) we see with the eyes of Mark Lewis, a young camera-man who has fixed a knife at the tripod. So he can film and kill his victims simultaneously.

The protagonist of Michael Powell's film lets himself deeper down into his obsessions than an average voyeuristic fetishist. He films people in the moment of their death. Moreover, the film clearly expresses that cinema makes us all voyeurs. We all want to participate in the doom of others if we watch Mark when he is watching. Author Robert Fischer states: "We are living in the age of scopophilia, in the age of the lust of seeing, the lust, the addiction of watching. Everybody stares at the telly in his living room every day, the children are literally bewitched by video and computer-games. Nobody escapes the deluge of images coming from poster walls, magazines, and monitors and penetrating all of us. It seems as if nobody *wants* to escape it".

Many killer films tell of the lust of seeing, the addiction of observation, which is closely related to the fundamental roots of cinema. Brian de Palma's BODY DOUBLE (1984) turns the situation around and brings together a psychotic killer who enacts being watched when murdering and a "harmless" voyeur (the protagonist), an ideal symbiosis.

If we see with the eyes of the psycho, this does not mean that we have to like the monstrous villains. But sometimes an insight into such seriously sick minds is like a flashlight illuminating the deep tunnel of our own emotional sewage.

Respectable Facades, And What Lurks Behind

An abundance of the most threatening, intelligent, and charismatic psycho killers of cinema belong to the category of the "perfectly disguised". Very often they are charming good-looking lady-killers like Albert Finney, the nice sub-tenant of NIGHT MUST FALL (1963). Finney paralyses all the women of the household with his gallant manners. Nobody ever suspects that he carries around a ripped-off head. Things like that can become dangerous for elderly widows.

Joseph Cotten too, polite Uncle Charlie ranks among the many welcome visitors hiding a corpse somewhere in a drawer. SHADOW OF A DOUBT (1943) is one of Alfred Hitchcock's most subversive films, because the vicious killer fleeing to his small-town relatives appears to be much sharper and much more mundane than his hillbilly hosts. Uncle Charlie, "Hitchcock's first complete psychopath" (Richard Schinkel), is a "murderer with an ideal" as "Hitch" put it, in a way a brutal anarchist who only occasionally steps across the thin border of real madness. In such moments the film lays bare Charlie's pathologic inner side, but in contrast to the suffocating petty bourgeoisie surrounding him, he is almost likeable.

Don't trust anybody! – This seems to be the message of many psycho films. Everybody might possibly be the insane killer, even the cool shrink you are telling your most intimate sexual secrets (DRESSED TO KILL, 1980), or the ship-wrecked beau with the sleepwalking Marlon Brando gaze (DEAD CALM, 1989). A shy well-groomed young man with genteel manners who manages Bates Motel for his mother sitting in a wheelchair became the prototype of many hidden killers. A long time before

PEEPING TOM

Norman Bates jumping from behind a shower curtain in 1960, other serial killers murdered under cover of a respectable facade. Peter Lorre made the character of Herr Beckert immortal, a man ambling through Berlin in 1931 whistling cute melodies and luring little kids with candy. What Beckert does with the kids is not shown in M – EINE STADT SUCHT EINEN MOERDER, but you get to know it if you read the biography of Peter Kuerten, which strongly influenced Lang's film. Like Norman Bates, Beckert is driven by his madness, kills in a kind of trance, and does not remember anything after returning to his "good side".

Christ And Antichrist, Love And Hate, Good And Evil

"Listen Ben! See this hand I'm holding up? See them letters tattooed on it? Love, Ben, Love! That' s what they spell! This hand – this right hand of mine – this hand is Love. But wait, Ben! Look! There's enough moonlight from the window to see. Look, boy! This left hand! Hate, Ben, hate! Now here's the moral, boy. These two hands are the soul of mortal man! Hate and Love, Ben – warring one against the other from the womb to the grave".

–Davis Grubb, *Night Of The Hunter*

"Harry Powell", NIGHT OF THE HUNTER

"Love" is tattooed on the knuckles of one hand, "Hate" on the other. The man wearing these tattoos looks like a preacher, one of the Lord's men, but the only messages he proclaims are lethal. Preacherman Harry Powell, too, is a well-disguised madman who elderly women like to invite for a cup of tea. In the Christian's garments dwells the greedy, hypocritical, and violent Anti-Christ marrying lonesome widows and killing them on their wedding night. In the multitude of psychopathic killers crowding the screen Robert Mitchum as the preacher in THE NIGHT OF THE HUNTER (1955) is an outstanding figure, a deluxe version of unpredictability, burning madness, and homicidal violence.

Charles Laughton shows Powell/Mitchum as a psychically defective monster throwing a sinister shadow over the scenery. In Davis Grubb's novel you also read about the religious mania, the repressed wantonness, the contradictions tearing apart the preacher. Love and hate not only fight each other via tattoos. The preacher himself is a split personality.

The US-painter Joe Coleman has been dealing with such Janus heads of cinema and their real counterparts in criminal history for a long time: "My interest in the tragic lives of infamous murderers such as Charles Manson, Carl Panzram, Albert Fish, can be traced to a fascination with the life of Jesus Christ which was like theirs filled with suffering, injustice and brutality. Like Jesus Christ these men had dual identities of ultimate masochist and sadist, hero and villain, Christ and Anti-Christ."

In David Lynch's opaque and enigmatic milestone BLUE VELVET (1986) Dennis Hopper recalls to life such a split interpretation of evil. Frank Booth, standing for the criminal dark side hidden in the intact small-town world of Lumberton, is one of the most impressive movie psychos of the Eighties and a deserving successor to the

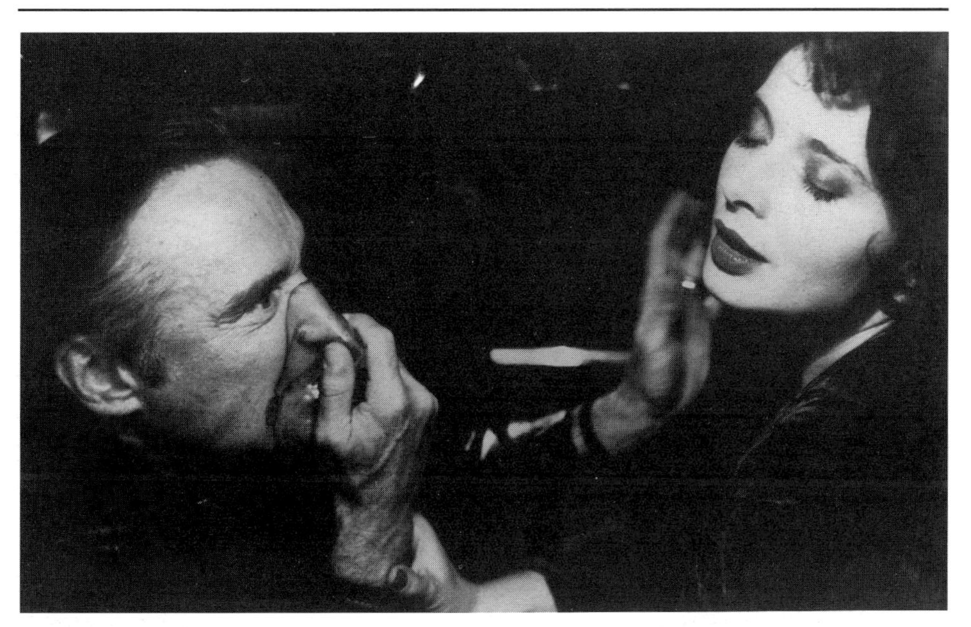

"Frank Booth", BLUE VELVET

preacher Powell. When he penetrates the apartment of Dorothy (Isabella Rossellini), a night-club singer whose husband he has kidnapped, attacks her sexually, hits her and calls her "cunt" while inhaling a strange non-identifiable gas, he seems to be the perfect personification of evil. But Frank also has a different, very sentimental side. He can hardly hold back tears when listening to the song "Blue Velvet", or when a fellow gangster with heavy make-up imitates Roy Orbison for him. "In dreams I walk with you...". Somewhere in the abyss of his lost soul Good and Evil might have fought each other bitterly.

Like Laughton in THE NIGHT OF THE HUNTER, Lynch juxtaposes psychopathic terror with pure innocence not broken through irony, which finally shoos away the demons. The preacher Powell is thwarted by the unspoilt world of the children, which he has been haunting like a living nightmare. Frank is killed by the upright hero Jeffrey. When THE NIGHT OF THE HUNTER is over and a new dawn breaks, you hear children singing like chimes. Robins chirp their song in the end of BLUE VELVET. But the birds are mechanically moved creatures, irritation intrudes into the final idyll.

Walking Time Bombs

There are film psychopaths who manage to live their split sides simultaneously. They murder in the night and re-transform to average citizens during daytime. This goes on until they are detected. Fritz Lang's Beckert belongs to this species as well as Powell, or the shrink in DRESSED TO KILL. Other are in such perfect control of their deviant sides that they never fully break out, or almost never. They accumulate suppressed aggression like a pressure cooker and only a minor occasion might ignite them. Human time bombs.

In the opening scene of MIAMI BLUES (1988) Frederic Frenger jr., a psychotic killer who tries to control his dangerous forces, arrives at Miami Airport and is approached by a Hare Krishna begging for money. Within a second he lets off steam and breaks the beggar's finger in a way that he dies of pain shock. In the end of Peter

"Killer Kane", THE NINTH CONFIGURATION

Blatty's THE NINTH CONFIGURATION you get to know that the peaceful, philosophical Vietnam veteran Colonel Kane has been treated legitimately in a mental institution. Endlessly provoked by a gang of bikers, something comes up in Kane that almost cannot be verbally expressed. None of the Hell's Angels survives "Killer Kane's" one-man assault. In THE INDIAN RUNNER by Sean Penn we get to know two brothers. The one, Joe, is a Highway Patrolman, the other an outlaw with suddenly erupting outbursts of psychotic violence sending him upstate time and again. Joe's philosophy is simple: try to love life, your wife, and your kid. But deep inside the cop, too, feels something of the fire of his angry brother Frank. Frank thinks he is an "Indian Runner", an Indian messenger, the personification of denial, negation, and disdain. He does not want to laugh like the others; as the poet Lautréamont put it: "Seeing these exhibitions I've longed to laugh, with the rest, but that strange imitation was impossible. Taking a penknife with a sharpened blade, I slit the flesh at the points joining the lips. For an instant I believed my aim was achieved. I saw in a mirror the mouth ruined at my own will! An error! Besides, the blood gushing freely from the two wounds prevented my distinguishing whether this really was the grin of others. But after some moments of comparison I saw quite clearly that my smile did not resemble that of humans: the fact is, I was not laughing".

According to William S. Burroughs, reality is a matter of definition, and normality all the more so. Usually something is normal if it fits into a framework of norms. Who "cannot or does not want to laugh like the others", soon ends up on the opposite side. Weirdos, freaks, and split personalities have their own logic working according to its own laws deviating from common-sense reason. This does not mean that there are no "sick" people, but cinema should at least try to break on through to the other side. The portrait of a psycho killer should not only content itself with evaluating the "healthy side" when stigmatising the dark opposite, as has been done in several horror films and action-films *à la* DIRTY HARRY. The journey into the universe of our soul with commanders like Mark Lewis, Frank Booth, Colonel Kane, or Uncle Charlie is much more informative and thrilling.

PSYCHO KILLER MOVIES: A SELECTION

BLUE VELVET / USA 1986

Written and directed by David Lynch. Camera: Frederick Elmes, Joe Dunton. Music: Angelo Badalamenti. With Kyle McLachlan, Isabella Rossellini, Dennis Hopper, Laura Dern, Brad Dourif, Dean Stockwell, Hope Lange

Only very few films can be interpreted in so many ways as David Lynch's visit to the "clean" small-town Lumberton: a film about structure and sound, about shining blue velvet stained with bloody brain tissue at the end. A Buñuelesque surrealist trip inside cut-off ears, sewage pipes, and ant swarms as well as a voyeuristic game about the breathtaking feeling of standing in a stranger's drawer and seeing what happens outside: violence, nudity, abyss. BLUE VELVET is a sado-masochistic melodrama where sex exclusively executed with a knife is followed by Roy Orbison-nostalgia. Above all David Lynch tells a story of man's Good/Evil duality, emphasising naïveté and juxtaposing a vision of innocence to the post-modern void of the Eighties.

CLEAN, SHAVEN / USA 1993

Written and directed by Lodge Kerrigan. Camera: Teodoro Maniaci. Music: Hahn Rowe. With Peter Greene, Robert Albert, Megan Owen, Molly Castelloe, Jennifer McDonald

An impressing low-budget study about the borderline between normality and madness. A cop chases Peter, the protagonist because he thinks he is a serial killer. The people in the audience have to draw their own conclusions as to whether Peter is really a killer, or not. "The few cases of schizophrenics actually tending to violence are blown up and exaggerated by the press. This is one of the reasons why I have not answered in the film if Peter is really a killer. The people in the audience have to draw their own conclusions and they shall think over their decision. It is not the aim of the film to find a solution or even to draw a moral conclusion." (Lodge Kerrigan)

CLEAN, SHAVEN confronts the physical as well as psychical violence of the everyday life of a schizophrenic with the repressive violence of society.

DEAD CALM / Australia 1989

Directed by Philip Noyce. Written by Terry Hayes after a novel by Charles Williams. Camera: Dean Semler. Music: Graeme Revell. With Sam Neill, Billy Zane, Nicole Kidman, Rod Mullinar, Joshua Tilden

Somehow he reminds us of the young Marlon Brando, this shipwrecked guy disturbing the sailing trip of a married couple in the open sea. After a lethal accident to their only child, they had retired into the midst of the ocean. But the new passenger seriously sabotages the peace on board and finally reveals himself as a highly dangerous maniac, who killed the crew of the last ship he was on. A war of nerves between the couple and the intruder flames up in the cramped space of the yacht. It is really fantastic how Noyce uses this space, thanks to an unbridled camera.

DRESSED TO KILL / USA 1980

Written and directed by Brian De Palma. Camera: Ralf Bode. Music: Pino Donnaggio. With Angie Dickinson, Nancy Allen, Michael Caine, Keith Gordon, Dennis Franz

Michael Caine as Dr. Robert Elliot, the mad slashing wolf in the sheep's clothing of a rational psychiatrist (a long time before Hannibal Lecter!) is one example of many psychopathic killers in the *oeuvre* of Brian De Palma. Besides the suspense-laden story the film also tells of repressed sexuality, rape, mental wounds, and death.

As all of De Palma's better films, DRESSED TO KILL is a modern tribute to Alfred Hitchcock which carries on the style of the past master of suspense

Shower scene, DRESSED TO KILL

uncompromisingly, and up-to-date with explicit nudity and violence. De Palma even includes a shower scene in this PSYCHO homage.

GANGSTER NO. 1 / GB 2000

Directed by Paul McGuigan. Written by Johnny Ferguson. Camera: Peter Sova. Music: John Dankworth. With Malcolm McDowell, David Thewlis, Paul Bettany, Saffron Burrows

Almost all new British gangster movies in the trail of Big Daddy Tarantino had one deficiency in common: they glorified their protagonists and their milieu in a too ironical and exaggerated way. Consequently, there are tough talkin' tough guys in sharp suits galore in this film, as well as a pulsating soundtrack and a cool retro décor. But at the same time GANGSTER NO. 1 and his fellows are some of the most disturbing psychopaths in British cinema since Alex and his droogs killed the defenceless and homeless in A CLOCKWORK ORANGE (1971). That Malcolm McDowell, who starred in this classic, acts at his nastiest again, fits perfectly. Yet the film's real discovery is youngster/gangster Paul Bettany, who writes psycho-killer history with some key scenes. This film disturbs you and makes you feel chill to the bone. The fun of LOCK, STOCK AND TWO SMOKING BARRELS (1998) is over.

HOMICIDAL / USA 1961

Directed by William Castle. Written by Robb White. Camera: Burnett Guffey. Music: Hugo Friedhofer. With Jean Arless, Glenn Corbett, Patricia Breslin, Eugenie Leontovich

After Hitchcock's triumph with PSYCHO the screens of drive-in cinemas were soon crowded with cheap imitations. The psycho-thriller genre was born. Not only because of his promotions and bizarre advertising gimmicks, William Castle was the most creative among the Hitchcock alumni. His films share a typical morbid style. In HOMICIDAL, his most outstanding opus, Castle packs transsexuality and the loss of identity in a perversely charming, spooky little black-and-white thriller which achieves the maximal degree of delirium.

THE INDIAN RUNNER / USA 1990

Directed by Sean Penn. Written by Sean Penn inspired by Bruce Springsteen's song "Highway Patrolman". Camera: Anthony B. Richmond. Music: Jack Nitzsche. With Viggo Mortensen, David Morse, Patricia Arquette, Dennis Hopper, Charles Bronson

Sean Penn's fascinating directing debut was inspired by a Bruce Springsteen song that had been haunting him for a long time: "Highway Patrolman", the story of two unequal brothers, a bloodcurdling country-ballad dealing with morals, responsibility, family, as well as with the dissolution of these values in a cloud of violence. Sean Penn delivered an emotional film about the severe, almost insoluble identity crisis of white male America represented by Viggo Mortensen oscillating between family life and psychotic outbursts of violence. His act of murder in bloodlust at the end of the film ranks among the most electrifying moments in the recent history of cinema.

THE KILLER INSIDE ME / USA 1976

Directed by Burt Kennedy. Written by Edward Mann after a novel by J.M. Thompson. Camera: William A. Fraker. Music: Tim McIntire. With Stacy Keach, Susan Tyrell, Tisha Sterling, Keenan Wynn, Charles McGraw

Hardly anyone has portrayed everyday madness as shockingly and as full of sardonic humour as James Myers Thompson, hard-boiled pulp novelist and analyst of the American nightmare. The characters in his detective novels live like undercover agents of paranoia, hiding their unpleasant propensities in perfect camouflage. Lou Ford, one of Thompson's darkest "heroes" (impersonated by the seriously underrated Stacy Keach) hides his murderous tendencies behind the mask of a small-town cop. Keach gives his best, but sadly this sub-average adaptation totally lacks the toughness and the intensity of the novel.

Psycho cops are the cracked mirror image that haunts us in such films as ORDER OF DEATH (1980), BUTCHER, BAKER, NIGHTMARE MAKER (1981), THE FANTASIST (1986) and MANIAC COP 1 and 2 (1988/1990).

MANIAC / USA 1980

Directed by William Lustig. Written by C.A. Rosenberg. Camera: Robert Lindsay. Music: Jay Chaltaway. With Joe Spinell, Caroline Munro, Gail Lawrence, Kelly Piper, Tom Savini

The story of a psychotic slasher lurking in the asphalt jungle of New York, modelled by director William Lustig on aspects of Ted Bundy and David Berkovitz, "The Son of Sam". The schizophrenic Frank Zito is brought to a horrible greasy existence by the now-deceased B-movie actor Joe Spinell. Zito suffers from an extreme mother complex, he vegetates in an apartment full of mannequins which he decorates in a bloody way. He skins and scalps his victims, hallucinates wildly. Myriads of "serious" critics have damned the film for its cynicism and the central role of the killer as (anti-)hero. But today MANIAC enjoys cult status in splatter-circles thanks to Tom Savini's ultra-gore effects.

MIAMI BLUES / USA 1988

Directed by George Armitage. Written by George Armitage after a novel by Charles Willeford. Camera: Tak Fuijimoto. Music: Gary Chang. With Alec Baldwin, Fred Ward, Jennifer Jason Leigh, Nora Dunn, Charles Napier

In the Seventies and Eighties Charles Willeford carried on the literary tradition of the best noir-authors and hard-boiled writers. His books are crammed with freaked-out

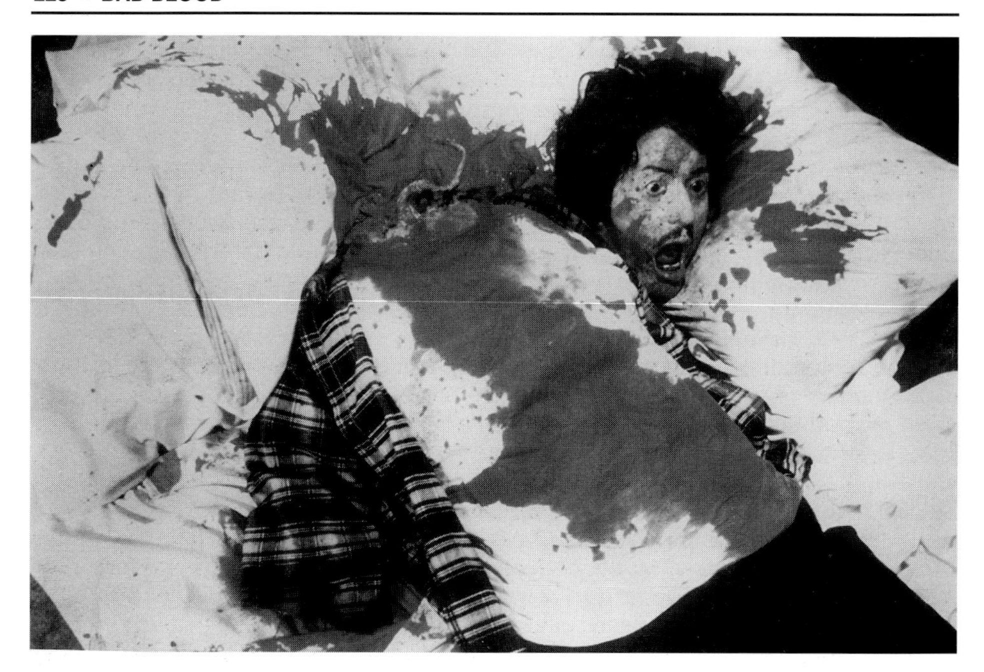

MANIAC

criminals at the gates of madness, and groggy cops who have looked down into the abyss more than once, getting away with deep scars. George Armitage's MIAMI BLUES is the rare case of a successful adaptation of these themes without the clichés of a designer thriller, but straight and unspectacular images. Especially the slippery mainstream-hero Alec Baldwin as a highly explosive schizophrenic killer, who shows how talented he actually is.

Perhaps one should not forget to mention another film daring to screen a contemporary hard-boiled writer, the James Ellroy adaptation THE COP (1987), which also deals with the confrontation of an intelligent psychopath and an obsessed police detective.

NIGHT MUST FALL / GB 1963

Directed by Karel Reisz. Written by Clive Exton based on a play by Emlyn Williams. Camera: Freddie Francis. Music: Ron Grainer. With Albert Finney, Mona Washbourne, Susan Hampshire, Sheila Hancock, Michael Medwin

Living in an English cottage the young sub-tenant Danny is idolised by the elderly Mrs. Bramson and her female personnel. But nobody knows that sometimes Danny has infernal fits of murder. He even carries the head of an earlier victim with him in a hatbox. The first cinema adaptation of the play *Night Must Fall* was done with Robert Montgomery in 1936. In the early Sixties Karel Reisz, an important representative of British Free Cinema, did this electrifying remake. Beside the atmospherically dense black-and-white photography, the film is dominated by Albert Finney, who masterfully evokes the nervously smiling serial killer Danny.

THE NIGHT OF THE HUNTER / USA 1955

Directed by Charles Laughton. Written by James Agree after the novel by Davis Grubb. Camera: Stanley Cortez. Music: Walter Schumann. With Robert Mitchum,

Shelley Winters, Lilian Gish, Peter Graves
When the actor Charles Laughton chose the successful detective novel *The Night Of The Hunter* for his debut behind the camera, he decided to transform the rather realistic book version into a gloomy Southern Gothic tale. His most brilliant idea was to cast Robert Mitchum. The murderous preacher Harry Powell was the key role in Robert Mitchum's career. Laughton turned the swamps of the South into an unreal fairy tale-landscape which became the setting for a mythical conflict between Good and Evil influenced by W.H. Griffith and German silent movies. What began as a conventional film project, became one of the great masterpieces of film history.

THE NINTH CONFIGURATION / USA 1980
Written and directed by Peter Blatty. Camera: Gerry Fisher. Music: Barry De Vorzon. With Stacy Keach, Scott Wilson, Jason Miller, Ed Flanders, Neville Brand, Joe Spinell
The US-government isolates some high members of the armed forces with serious Vietnam-traumata in a castle in the mountains, cut off from the outside world. Among the men with deep mental scars from the war is Colonel Kane, a highly decorated officer who transformed into an existentialist questioner after a nervous breakdown. Kane's mind meanders through spheres out of reach for his fellow veterans, and it seems as if he were secretly in charge of the strange sanatorium. Only when he rescues one of "his" patients from a gang of Hell's Angels down in the village, massacring the whole biker gang, does he again become the legendary "Killer Kane" who snuffed enemies with his bare hands back in Vietnam. Blatty reflects the small margin between philosophy and madness, normality and bloodlust. A fantastic film that has somehow disappeared, but urgently deserves to be rediscovered instead of turning to dust in forgotten archives.

PEEPING TOM / GB 1960
Directed by Michael Powell. Written by Leo Marks. Camera: Otto Heller. Music: Brian Easdale. With Carl Boehm, Anna Massey, Moira Shearer
Mark Lewis, an assistant camera-man in a London studio, kills people undercover of night and films them when they breathe their last. He stores hours of "real dying" in his attic room. The key to his perverse passion can be found in his childhood (as so often in the psycho killer genre). Mark served his father, a scientist as guinea pig for fear experiments put on celluloid. At the end, the death voyeur stages his own end in the harsh flashlight of the cameras.

The times are changing. When PEEPING TOM was shown for the first time, and the press shredded it to pieces, the film paralysed the careers of Powell and Boehm. Now, the film is regarded as a masterly analysis of an obsessed character, a psychoanalytical reflection about cinema and the lust of seeing in general.

SHADOW OF A DOUBT / USA 1943
Directed by Alfred Hitchcock. Written by Thornton Wilder, Alma Reville, and Sally Benson after a short-story by Gordon McDonnell. Camera: Joseph Valentine. Music: Dimitri Tiomkin. With Joseph Cotten, Theresa Wright, MacDonald Carey
Long before American directors dared to dissect petty bourgeois idylls, Alfred Hitchcock did it with diabolical precision. Santa Rosa can almost be seen as a forerunner of BLUE VELVET's Lumberton, a sleepy small town paralysed by boredom where all the people know each other. A perfect hideout for Charlie Oakley (Joseph Cotten), a cynical misanthrope and widow killer. Money was not his only motive. It rather was his hate of the "fat, wheezing animals", his urge to free the world of old women that drove him to murder. The killer lives in Santa Rosa with his relatives until his niece gets suspicious, and fate takes its run.

WHITE HEAT

WHITE HEAT / USA 1949

Directed by Raoul Walsh. Written by Ivan Goff & Ben Roberts after a novel by Virginia Kellog. Camera: Sid Hickox. Music: Max Steiner. With James Cagney, Virginia Mayo, Edmond O'Brien, Margaret Wycherly

Dominant mothers are stock figures of psycho killer-movies, from Norman Bates, the most famous of the wrongly brought up sons, to Dennis Hopper's Frank in BLUE VELVET screaming "Mummy!" during his brutal sex attacks. One of the most famous mother's boys in film noir is James Cagney in the role of the psychically labile gangster/killer Cody Jarret, who always thinks of his mother when robbing and killing. "Top of the world, Ma!", he screams in the apocalyptic climax, blasting a gas tank and himself to oblivion.

WHITE OF THE EYE / UK 1987

Directed by Donald Cammell. Written by Cammell & China Kong. Music by Rick Fenn, Nick Mason. Camera: Larry McConkey. With David Keith, Cathy Moriarty, Art Evans

Typically challenging psycho-killer film by Cammell, director of PERFORMANCE (1968), interspersed with violent set-pieces and driven by complex camera tropes and compositions. David Keith plays the husband who kills and mutilates housewives, keeping body parts in his bathroom. The film ends with a colossal explosion and conflagration, a veritable holocaust suggesting the latent power of the psychotic mind unleashed.

CHAPTER THREE
WHEN ALL FUSES BLOW: AMOK KILLERS

"When I was just a baby, my mama told me: 'Always be a good boy, never play with guns!' But I shot a man in Reno, just to watch him die."
–Johnny Cash, "Folsom Prison Blues"

"The simplest surrealist act consists of dashing down into the street, pistol in hand, and firing blindly, as fast as you can pull the trigger, into the crowd. Anyone who, at least once in his life, has not dreamed of thus putting an end to the petty system of debasement and cretinization in effect has a well-defined place in that crowd, with his belly at barrel level."
–André Breton

Runners amok are the rip in the social fabric, the unpredictable grain of sand in the system's rational machinery.

They come out of the blue, act beyond all traditional moral values, and hence represent the biggest threat to the established order. The authentic amok gunner is different from the "ordinary" criminal who kills to obtain wealth or power, as well as from the cool calculating assassin such as depicted by Fred Zinneman in THE DAY OF THE JACKAL (1973). The act of vengeance too is not 100% related to amok. The lynch-law and vigilante movies, a quasi-sub-genre of action cinema (from the DEATH WISH series to EXTERMINATOR, etc.) are dominated by strict morals, intentionality, and a strong will to survive. This has nothing to do with the runner amok surrendering himself to uncontrollable forces, mindless of his own safety.

The German author Bernd Mattheus writes: "Amok, like suicide culminates in the utmost transgression possible in the field of action. The runner amok does not only range beyond logic, society, and power in his own death, but sovereignty, an utter recklessness concerning the future, and the glory of life in the midst of death, precede the holocaust, make him capable of perpetrating it. Authentic sovereignty is in the here and now, even if its ephemeral character seems like an apology of failure. Amok, frenzy, ecstasy (of killing and being killed), the [...] waste of oneself is the death of thinking, the death of logos."

Though revenge is a term inherent in the mindscape of runners amok, it is most of the times not a vengeance for actually suffered physical or emotional harm, but rather an irrational revenge upon the whole of society, symbolically choosing some random victims. Motivated by a chain of random events, Travis Bickle/Robert De Niro chooses a gang of pimps in Martin Scorsese's TAXI DRIVER.

"You're Talking To Me?": The Runner Amok As Existentialist

"If anything, what I'm concerned about in films and in real life is redemption, because I do believe in purging and a kind of transcendence, either through contemplation or action."
–Paul Schrader

"Travis Bickle", TAXI DRIVER

"Loneliness has followed me all my life. The life of loneliness pursues me wherever I go: in bars, cars, coffee shops, theatres, stores, sidewalks. There is no escape. I am god's lonely man". This is what Travis Bickle writes into his diary, his imaginary addressee. Up to the present day TAXI DRIVER is perhaps best-known among the films documenting the development of an outsider from alienation to the outburst of violence. The epoch-making opus of the trio Scorsese (direction), Paul Schrader (script), and the protagonist Robert De Niro manage to unify and expose all symptoms generally connected with the image of the runner amok: the inability to communicate, isolation, and lingering madness.

The metaphors used by the scriptwriter to explain the protagonist's actions are not new, they have their origins in the symbol-laden world of film noir. Moreover, Paul Schrader combined them with motives from European existentialism, as he discussed in an interview with Richard Thompson: "Travis's problem is the same as the existential hero's, that is, should I exist? But Travis doesn't understand that this is his problem, so he focuses it elsewhere; and I think that is a mark of the immaturity and the youngness of our country. We don't properly understand the nature of the problem, so the self-destructive impulse, instead of being inner-directed, as it is in Japan, Europe or any of the older cultures, becomes outer-directed. The man who feels the time has come to die will go out and kill other people than kill himself [...]That's essentially how the existential hero changes when he becomes American. There is not enough intellectual tradition in this country, and not enough history; and Travis is just not smart enough to understand this problem".

American Nightmares

So Schrader has not only said something essential about the character he created, but also about the runner amok in his own country in general. It seems as if there is a typically American tradition of irrational, violent criminals. Just think of the authentic cases of Arthur Bremer, who tried to assassin Governor Wallace, or Charles Whitman, who shot aimlessly into the throng from the tower of a Texan university. The former is vaguely alluded to in TAXI DRIVER. It is a fact that the vast majority of amok-movies come from the USA. Only Japanese cinema deals similarly with suicide, or amok candidates (as in the classic films of Koji Wakamatsu such as VIOLATED ANGELS or GO, GO, SECOND TIME VIRGIN).

"What he [Travis] seeks is escape, to shake off the mortal chains and die a glorious death" (Schrader) and he would do this at any place and at any time, but the hell surrounding him, filthy Seventies New York, makes the situation much more plausible. It is the same stifling reality as described by David Lynch in his industrial horror opus ERASERHEAD (1977). But whereas there the anti-hero Henry Spencer sinks into a black hole of apathy and emptiness, Travis Bickle tries to shoot himself out of this state of mind. Schrader's trick to give the character of the taxi driver existentialist traits, even to stylise him as an ascetic martyr, prevents the film from exaggerating the social and environmental aspect. After all, millions of people live in awful circumstances in cities like New York, or have had a disfunctional childhood, etc. ... but still not every victim automatically becomes a delinquent. If you termed films exclusively explaining the motives of their protagonists by an alienated world "social reason movies", Scorsese's films would only partly belong to this genre.

Buddy Giovinazzo's COMBAT SHOCK (1985) is a depressive trash-version of TAXI DRIVER with elements of ERASERHEAD, and all Vietnam veteran dramas. The more suitable original title of this low-budget production distributed by the notorious Troma company, was AMERICAN NIGHTMARE. As a matter of fact, Giovinazzo compiles all American traumata in his protagonist, a completely down-and-out Vietnam vet living with his wife and a baby in the most run-down neighbourhood of New York. The quality as well as the weakness of the film lies in its excessively filthy surface. In its accumulation of social as well as private disasters, big city street detritus including junkies, hookers, and the unemployed, the hysterical wife, the permanently crying, deformed baby (resembling the ERASERHEAD baby), the bloody Vietnam-flashbacks, corrupt cops, organised crime etc, COMBAT SHOCK is a "social reason movie" *par excellence*. Finally the protagonist can't help shouting "Now I'm God!" and getting even with the criminals, the scum, his wife, the baby, and last but not least, himself. Compared to Giovinazzo's trashy New York of faeces and vomit, Travis Bickle's environment appears rather harmless. On the other hand, in favour of exploitation, COMBAT SHOCK foregoes a more profound depiction of mental decay.

Abel Ferrara's unsuccessful artist who becomes the DRILLER KILLER (1979) is another one of "God's lonely men". The isolation in which he is voluntarily living and painting is disturbed by a noisy punk band. This triggers off a bloody escalation of homicidal activity. Funnily enough, the runner amok uses a battery-powered drill instead of the usual gun. It remains unclear whether Ferrara associated it with simple phallic symbolism, or merely exploited the stylistic devices of the then highly *en vogue* splatter genre. The painter's character is similar to the taxi driver, and slightly similar to the hallucinating killer in BLOODY WEDNESDAY, another film about someone completely freaking out, based on the real case of James Huberty.

Sex As Threat

"Sex is a lie, boys. The truth, that's the chainsaw!"
–THE TEXAS CHAINSAW MASSACRE 2

Speechlessness. The inability to express oneself. An emotional void. The losers and fuck-ups of these films live drifting from one day to the next. Realising their inability to communicate, especially with women, they live in self-chosen exile. An ex-inmate of a lunatic asylum starts an affair with a social worker, but fails (BLOODY WEDNESDAY). Travis Bickle imagines his ideals, projects archetypal visions of womanhood, like the pure angel and the whore, into the teenage hooker Iris, as well as the pretty campaign worker Betsy. This was paralleled in reality by the famous case of the would-be Ronald Reagan-assassin John Hinckley who, influenced by TAXI DRIVER chose Jodie Foster/Iris as the object of his projection. He wanted to kill the President in her honour.

Sexuality is the area where these characters' inability to communicate becomes clearest. Constantly arguing the sense of sexually "sick" minds, which can also be called exploring minds, we are soon confronted with limitations. The celibate radical poet Antonin Artaud noted: "A real human being has no sex and ignores this ugly and narcotising sin. I despise all sexual relationships, of any kind, as debasing for humanity, and I find it deeply offensive that it should be believed my body could have been submitted to them at any moment of its life". And he talks of "the parasitical proliferation of the act known as orgasm, coitus, copulation, fornication". The protagonists of the films mentioned, too, react with wild bewilderment when confronted with the opposite sex. They are torn between gloomy masturbation fantasies and a longing for purity. "He has the smell of sex about him: sick sex, repressed sex, lonely sex, but sex none the less" is a quote from the TAXI DRIVER script. Like Travis Bickle, the nameless Butcher in Gaspar Noé's SEUL CONTRE TOUS (I STAND ALONE/1999) spents a lot of his time in late-night porn cinemas. What he sees on the screen, he finds attractive and repulsive at the same time.

In Penelope Spheeris' THE BOYS NEXT DOOR (1985), one of the most malicious "buddy" movies ever to be seen on the screen, the friendship between two nice American boys is so strong that the angrier of the two reacts with murder when girls try to break into their initially rather innocent, then latently homosexual relationship. When Roy (Maxwell Caulfield) hears Bo (Charlie Sheen) gasp and moan when fornicating a girl in the adjacent room, he becomes so enraged that he slays the blonde. Sex and the implied intimacy, bliss, and lust are revolting for Roy (and many real runners amok). Later on he also kills a young couple and a gay man who wanted to seduce him.

Outside Is The Enemy

Many potential amok-candidates escape into their ascetic isolation for similar reasons. They lock themselves up in their apartments and celebrate rituals of solitude there. Paul Schrader once called this "a man in his room stories", and most of his films deal with it in one or other way. Travis talks to the TV filling his apartment with artificial life. Or he observes himself in the mirror, on the one hand for narcissistic reasons, on the other, because he has a sense of profound alienation from himself. There is Willem Dafoe in LIGHT SLEEPER (1991), scribbling his thoughts into notebooks only to throw them away afterwards. Richard Gere doing exercise in AMERICAN GIGOLO (1980) in order to stay handsome, belongs here too. Writing. Insomnia. Steeling oneself. Men alone in their apartments, locked in their bodies and their occupational therapy. The runners amok go a step further. Celibacy and a posture of denial are supposed to help them to prepare for the ultimate, liberating deed. They plan their exit from the grotesque stage of life like a play whose final act almost always ends with self-extinction (cf. SHUFFLE by Sogo Ishii, Japan 1981). Hence the ritual character of the suicidal staging is so important, because longing for significance its originator wants to transcend his anonymity and senselessness. Travis Bickle does hard exercise,

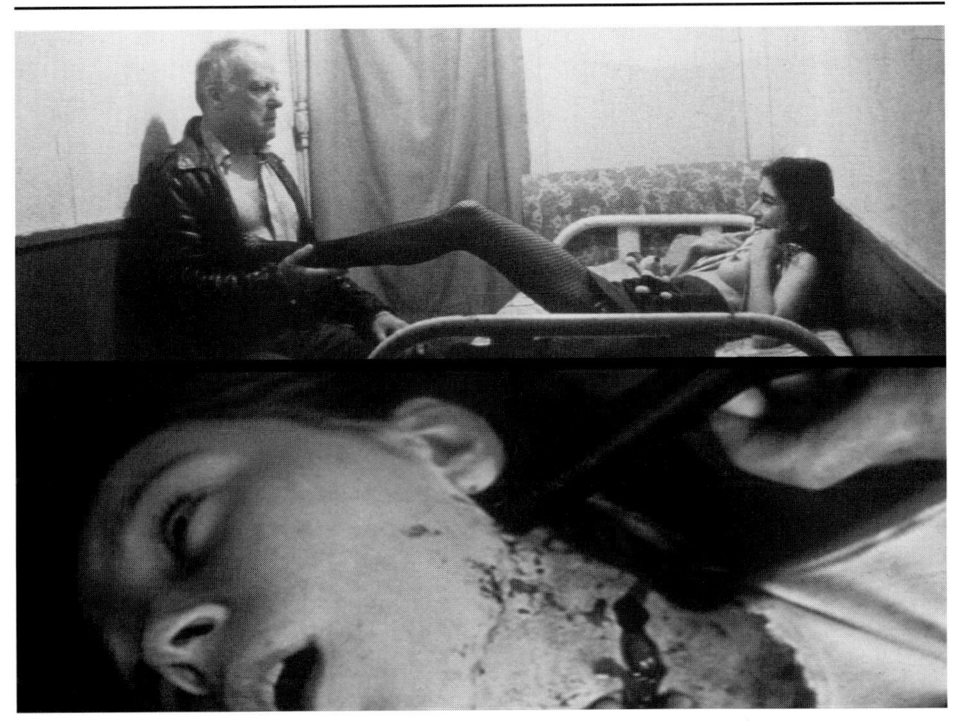

SEUL CONTRE TOUS

learns to handle guns, steels his body for weeks, and finally throws it away. The final triumph of wasting oneself. The ritual change of appearance is part of it: Bickle's Cherokee-look, the "driller killer"'s painted face, the paramilitary arming of the hallucinating madman in BLOODY WEDNESDAY, this all reminds us of the Samurai tradition masterly reconstructed by Paul Schrader in MISHIMA (1985). This film too is a kind of a "man in his room" story, telling of the writer Yukio Mishima and his transformation into a bodybuilder and warrior. With his public suicide the Japanese poet achieves something like the desired "unity of pen and sword", of artistic ideal and reality. This is, at least, what the film's glorifying final sequence suggests. TAXI DRIVER ends much more cynically. Travis Bickle fails in his purpose to erase himself in the final carnage, goes on cab-driving and even becomes a hero. Maybe on the outside his rage seems exorcised, his violence purged – but deep down he remains a human time bomb. Paul Schrader: "But, in time, the cycle will again come around and he'll succeed the next time."

Abel Ferrara ends DRILLER KILLER in complete darkness and derangement without telling us about the painter's fate. In BLOODY WEDNESDAY the protagonist storms a junk food restaurant and, like the real James Huberty, he massacres all the people who happen to be there. Finally the delinquent too burns in an inferno of blood, glass, and screams.

Urban Kamikaze-Rituals

God's lonely men – the protagonists of these films cannot be characterised better. "The man who moves through the city like a rat through the sewer", notes Paul Schrader, "the man who is constantly surrounded by people, yet has no friends. The absolute symbol of urban loneliness".

In his fascinating film DER TODESKING the German director Jörg Buttgereit adds a long-overdue female character to this lonely-men cliché. Approaching the mystery of suicide in seven completely different episodes, he finally also shows a female runner amok, her preparatory rituals and the final act, in the style of a fake documentary. Beside cartridge belts she also straps on a camera. So we see the murder scene happening in a cinema from her point of view. This not only hints at the menacing development of Reality TV, where the borderline between fiction and reality is slowly becoming semi-permeable, but at the same time the male point of view always connecting such "Samurai-acts" with masculine images, is subverted.

Buttgereit's amok-girl, the cab-driver, the frustrated artist, the all-American boys next door. They are all movie characters seemingly having nothing in common. Yet they are all single combatants, terrorists against law, order, and reason. Again Bernd Mattheus: "State and society fear the violence pointedly directed by the individual against himself, as well as the violence directed against society, its symbols and its representatives. Moreover, it is rather the uncompromising and irreversible breaking with the community of interests called society than the individual transgression, that is ostracised and persecuted. The rationalised, organised, collective protest is less outlawed than the arbitrary 'irrational' individual attempt on the norm."

"I'm Through!": Yuppies With Guns

The irreversible breaking with society does not take place any more in the amok-cinema of the late Eighties and the Nineties. Just as the serial killer has taken over the role of the Western outlaw, and hence has mutated from the absolute enemy to an admired anti-hero, the runner amok has replaced the angel of vengeance of the Charles Bronson era.

He kills blind with rage without transgressing social rules, and even becomes a partly sanctioned cleansing tool of bourgeois self-justice. Joel Schumacher's FALLING DOWN (1993) with Michael Douglas as petty bourgeois D-Fens venting his repressed aggression on a scorching L.A. summer morning is a prototypical example. It seems as if Douglas' character was designed on a sociological drawing board. He is so similar to the character-profiles developed by psychologists analysing real cases. These studies say that amok runners are ultra-conservative conformists, white males in love with the dominant ideology. Only their love is not reciprocated. And this drives them berserk. The journalist Graham Chester notes in his book *Berserk*: "By the time he is an adult, he will also have developed ambitions. expectations and a sense of personal sovereignty consistent with his gender, race and high self-regard; possibly even consistent, in an age of opportunity, with his realistic changes of success. Sooner or later, though, because of his modest social origins or his lack of talent, or both, he will discover that his dreams are beyond his means; in an era of recession, he will be particularly vulnerable" [...].

FALLING DOWN repeats these studies. The runner amok is no self-wasting irrational freak any more, but the classical Philistine representing the crisis of white male America. This could be an interesting plot, especially for the social satire which FALLING DOWN claims to be. Nevertheless, the film is highly problematic, because Schumacher & Co. try hard to give convincing social reasons for the frustrated yuppie's one-man campaign. "D-Fens" speaks for itself. Regarding the way the film portrays homeless people and Korean shop-owners he cannot but "defend" himself. The flaw: Schumacher does not show the individual view of a paranoid delinquent (like TAXI DRIVER, an otherwise rich source of inspiration for him), but pretends to deliver a reflection of the ill US society. That means that not only does D-Fens see things as stereotypically and black-and-white as depicted in the film, but FALLING DOWN alsor suggests that the world is actually like that. When D-Fens shoots a fanatical neo-Nazi (uttering "You sick asshole!"), he does so to assure us that Michael Douglas himself is neither sick, nor a Fascist.

Of course, Travis Bickle too constantly soliloquises about reasons (the same as D-Fens: big city decay, recession, etc.), but he only conjures up these outer reasons to justify his own disturbed personality. So Bickle is not like D-Fens, the simplistic cartoon of a Philistine gone berserk, but rather a typical tragic film noir character. On the other hand, D-Fens does not represent an outsider's point of view, but "healthy" America and its ideas about how to solve all social, ethnic, and economical problems: with a gun in one's hand.

AMOK KILLER FILMS: A SELECTION

71 FRAGMENTE EINER CHRONOLOGIE DES ZUFALLS (71 FRAGMENTS OF A CHRONOLOGY OF CHANCE) / Austria 1994

Written and directed by Michael Haneke. Camera: Christian Berger. With Gabriel Cosmin Urdes, Lukas Miko, Anne Bennent, Udo Samel, Otto Gruenmandl

The last sequel of Michael Haneke's trilogy about the "emotional freezing" of the Austrian soul is dedicated to a young man running amok. Seemingly without a motive he bursts into a subsidiary of a Viennese bank and opens fire there.

A series of episodes dealing with the emotional coldness and blankness of the modern urban bourgeois is constructed around this pivotal point. Haneke fascinates formally, letting the camera circle around the characters like an icy-cold observer. Yet considering the film's content Haneke is thwarted by his simplistic moral view of the world. Aa in the two other parts of the trilogy (DER 7. KONTINENT/THE SEVENTH CONTINENT, 1989, and BENNY'S VIDEO, 1992) which revolve around suicide and murder, Haneke only repeats commonplace culturally pessimistic clichés ("bad" TV, "selfish and loveless" parents, "debilitating consumer society"), and hence barely scratches the surface of the topics he is dealing with.

THE BOYS NEXT DOOR / USA 1985

Directed by Penelope Spheeris. Written by Mel Pearl & Don Levin. Camera: Arthur Albert. Music: George S. Clinton. With Maxwell Caulfield, Charlie Sheen, Christopher McDonald, Hank Garrett, Patti D'Arbanville

One of the most under-rated amok-films of the Eighties. In order to escape suburban *tristesse* and the prospect of working at an assembly line, two typical High School kids embark on a weekend trip to L.A. that turns into an orgy of violence. Though Penelope Spheeris' film is clearly against the two teenagers blindly bulldozing everything, you can also understand the overdose of frustration, anger, and hopelessness that makes their cute middle-class hell explode. Fortunately, the film does without hypocritical moral comments and warnings directed at parents, school, or society. Spheeris wants to provoke, to shock, and does not assume educational intentions.

COMBAT SHOCK aka AMERICAN NIGHTMARE / USA 1986

Written and directed by Buddy Giovinazzo. Camera: Stella Varveris. Music: Ricky Giovinazzo. With Ricky Giovinazzo, Veronica Stork, Mitch Maglio, Asaph Livni

A study in depression, poverty, and violence, produced by means of ultra-low budget cinema. One of the rare examples of a convincing synthesis of film aesthetics (filthy, primitively illuminated 16mm images) and content (the horror of an urban loser-existence). Though Giovinazzo constantly quotes (a fact that makes many amok-films of the Eighties and the early Nineties rather bloodless and shallow) and shamelessly exploits David Lynch and Martin Scorsese, COMBAT SHOCK works, as a filthy gutter-variation of TAXI DRIVER.

THE DRILLER KILLER / USA 1979

Directed by Abel Ferrara. Written by Nicholas St. John. Camera: Ken Kelsch. Music: Joe Delia. With Jimmy Laine (alias Abel Ferrara), Baybi Day, Bob de Frank, Peter Yellen

Mental conflicts, drugs, the perpetual rehearsal-din of a dilettante New Wave band, all this drives an eccentric painter to the brink of a nervous breakdown. His isolation in the megalopolis of New York functions as a catalyst for his urban running amok with a power-drill. The raw, gloomy debut of Abel Ferrara (BAD LIEUTENANT/1992, THE KING OF NEW YORK/1989) resembles a hard-core version of the then highly up-

COMBAT SHOCK

to-date New York New Wave cinema (Susan Seidelman, Amos Poe, etc). A film achieving cult status for its trashy splatter-sequences, and of course thoroughly denounced by the British censors as a "video nasty" *par excellence*.

FALLING DOWN / USA 1993

Directed by Joel Schumacher. Written by Ebbe Roe Smith. Camera: Andrzej Bartkowiak. Music: James Newton Howard. With Michael Douglas, Robert Duvall, Barbara Herschey, Frederic Forrest, Tuesday Weld

The one-man campaign of a frustrated businessman against the dark sides of the modern urban jungle. A solid, perfectly produced "discussion movie", yet as informative (and phoney) as the film version of an article in a *zeitgeist*-magazine. It is neither a shocking psychodrama, nor an existentialist tragedy, like other films relevant to the topic. But perhaps it is already a step in the right direction when a major production company depicts the urban apocalypse instead of the eternally intact Hollywood-world. Yet still the film follows the cheap "I'm through!" logic of the frustrated taxpayers that catapulted FALLING DOWN to the top of the US cinema charts.

SEUL CONTRE TOUS (I STAND ALONE) / Belgium 1998

Directed and written by Gaspar Noé. Camera: Dominique Colin. With Philippe Nahon, Blandine Lenoir, Franckie Pain, Martine Audrain

Somewhere in this book I talk about "movies that bite", films that really hurt and leave scars on the retina. SEUL CONTRE TOUS is one of the rare examples of this cinematic species.

In the opening scenes the *auteur* movie-maker Gaspar Noé seamlessly picks

DER TODESKING

up the threads of his excellent short film CARNE (1991). His protagonist is again the anonymous French butcher. After his release from custody – he had beaten up a lad who was going to abuse his mentally handicapped daughter – Noé's anti-hero is face to face with ruin. His shop has to be closed and his mistress is a notorious liar and walks out on him.

His attempt to start a new life fails too. First the old butcher contends himself with a verbal amok, then action follows his eruptive loathing for the world.

An off-screen voice that makes Travis Bickle's monologue in TAXI DRIVER sound like a manifesto of humanism, a face radiating sheer incandescent hatred, incest, pornography, blood, violence, alienation – SEUL CONTRE TOUS is probably the most radical cinematic commentary on the tragedy of human existence in the late Nineties. Yet it's a pity that the character of the butcher, who'd have the potential to become one of most intriguing incarnations of a sociopath throughout the entire history of cinema, has to be seen in a rather simplistic, xenophobic light in the second half of the film. The existentialist misanthrope shrinks somewhat to the cliché of a right-wing radical. But the formal aspects of Noé's film are consistently breathtaking: uncompromisingly unvarnished bleakness collides with strict stylisation and moments of aesthetic ecstasy.

TAXI DRIVER / USA 1975

Directed by Martin Scorsese. Written by Paul Schrader. Camera: Michael Chapman. Music: Bernhard Hermann. With Robert De Niro, Jodie Foster, Harvey Keitel, Cybill Shepherd, Peter Boyle

The amok-classic *par excellence* is based on autobiographical moments in the life of Paul Schrader, who wrote the script. After a wrecked marriage he fell into depression, drifted through the streets and bars at night, and ended his boozy odysseys in dim blue-movie theatres. Only a gastric ulcer and a long stay in hospital finished his solitary excursions. Scorsese too was fascinated the cab-driver as the absolute metaphor for urban solitude. So a film was created where religious and philosophical connotations flare up under the surface of a plain working-class character. Schrader: "Travis' is not a societally imposed loneliness or rage, it's an existential kind of rage. The book I re-read just before sitting down to write the script was Satre 's *Nausea*, and if anything is the model for TAXI DRIVER, that would be it".

DER TODESKING (THE DEATH KING) / Germany 1989

Directed by Jörg Buttgereit. Written by Jörg Buttgereit & Franz Rodenkirchen. Camera: Manfred Jelinski. Music: Daktari Lorenz, John Boy Walton, Hermann Kopp. With Hermann Kopp, Angelika Hoch, Michael Krause, Heinrich Ebber, Nicholas Petche, Eva M. Kurz

"The Todesking [King of Death] makes people want to kill themselves", says a little girl in the film. He is a mythical figure personifying the human urge to end his existence with his own hands. With this film Jörg Buttgereit, an underground director from Berlin mutated from the splatter-darling of German sub-culture to one of the most important German directors of *film d'auteur*. Seven stories, seven suicides. Amok, too, is a form of suicide. Buttgereit shows a female example. The episode around the woman staging her exit theatrically and preserving it for posterity with a video camera is introduced by a spoken treatise (*Greetings From Godard*) praising amok as the most liberating form of suicide. The last purification before finally snuffing oneself out.

Relevant films already discussed in Part One:

BLOODY WEDNESDAY
THE DEADLY TOWER
THE SNIPER
TARGETS
VIOLATED ANGELS

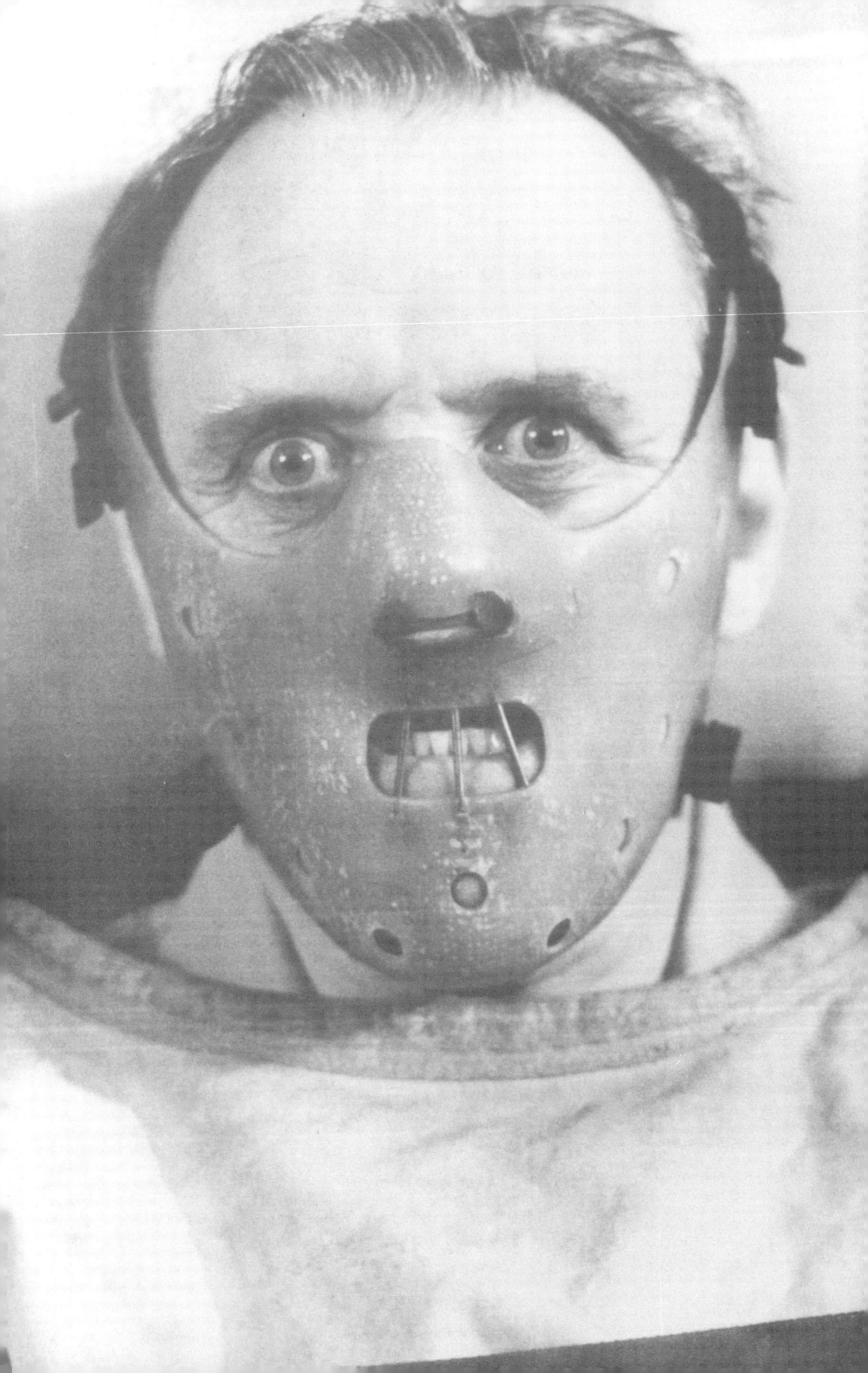

CHAPTER FOUR
THE KILLER AS MYTH, OUTLAW, OR ÜBERMENSCH: SADEAN MONSTERS

"He is a character so loaded with sexuality, and he knows this. He enjoys the role he plays, the manipulation of men. And he loves to shock people, to pull people's legs, to horrify people like the typical joker, like the Joker in 'Batman'. He is the ultimate joker."

–Anthony Hopkins in a interview about Dr. Hannibal Lecter

Hannibal "The Cannibal" Lecter, invented by the hard-boiled writer Thomas Harris and made immortal in the box-office-hits THE SILENCE OF THE LAMBS and HANNIBAL is an extreme, rare breed of screen villain. However, with all his gloomy erotic aura, his cutting humour, and the infinite terror behind psychotic eyes he is not really a brand-new figure, but rather a refined modern version of a species of cinema killer that has always been there in the history of film. They are murderers that have become mythical figures far beyond realistic depiction: mad scientists, super-gangsters, diabolical misanthropes like Fritz Lang's Dr. Mabuse, Edward G. Robinson as Captain Wolf Larsen in THE SEA WOLF (1941), or Charles Laughton's monstrous Dr. Moreau in ISLAND OF LOST SOULS (1933), to mention just a few examples. Whereas murderers in real life are most of the time just deplorable losers, the "masterfiends", as John McCarthy calls them, stand for strength, intelligence, and power. They are the great manipulators, the cruel killers always good for a sarcastic one-liner amid the bloody carnage.

If you want to explore the fascination and the origins of this type, you have to follow several tracks. One leads to Friedrich Nietzsche and the Marquis de Sade, two misinterpreted thinkers *par excellence*, others to outlaw-legends of US history and European fairy-tale figures. When Jodie Foster as Clarice Starling climbs down into the dark grotto (the high-security unit) where the wicked wolf is already waiting for her, one imagines the fairy-tales of the Grimm brothers rather than visiting Henry Lee Lucas in prison. Once upon a time there was..... an evil, evil man.

The Outlaw Factor

"Outside of society – that's the way I wanna be."

–Patti Smith

Before we analyse the cinema beasts who are larger than life, it should be clear that the film industry has simple reasons for transforming murderers into myths: super-human killers are much more interesting than the mediocre pervert next door. To elevate a miscreant to a hyper-villain, a criminal genius and puppet-master, helps to make the plot more spectacular. After all, exaggeration has always been a basic element of the medium.

Contemporary killer-"stars" like Freddy Krueger, the child-slaughterer of the horror film of the Eighties have so many fans because they are more bizarre, more filmogenic, and hence better film characters than their "good" counterparts. So fanatic subversive forces of film like the German Jörg Buttgereit or John Waters, the *agent provocateur* of US cinema, have preferred from their childhood the diabolical "bad guys" to the boring heroes. It was a key experience for John Waters to see THE WIZARD OF OZ (1939) as a toddler and to fall in love with the gloomy dangerous witch instead of Dorothy, like most of the kids of his age. "The bad ones are mostly more interesting than the good ones, who are always so morally correct," Buttgereit asserts. "They have fun and simply more to offer than the good ones".

But there is still more to the audience enthusiasm for the "masterfiends" of film. The supernatural demons into which Hollywood transforms serial killers and mass murderers today (replacing the Sea Wolf and Dr. Mabuse) also fascinate because they aim directly at the secret fantasies of many viewers. Many people subconsciously dream of transgressing the law like the killers on the screen, of exceeding all moral conventions and bans. A desire to unleash the uninhibited violence everyone of us feels at a given moment, e.g. when stuck in a throng in the tube, in a car during rush hour, among sweating fellow citizens in a queue, rudely accosted by an asshole still talking to you while you visualize his immediate annihilation in your daydreams. The super-human cinema killers realise these thoughts without batting an eyelash. They represent the anti-authoritarian figure *par excellence*, something like a modern, hyper-distorted variation of the classical outlaw acting far beyond all moral and social values or constraint.

Strangers Without Names

"[...] if the fate of twentieth century man is to live with death from adolescence to premature senescence, why then the only life-giving answer is to accept the terms of death, to live with death as immediate danger, to divorce oneself from society, to exist without roots, to set out on that uncharted journey into the rebellious imperatives of the self."

–Norman Mailer

Especially in American society, the lone wolf accountable to nobody, the man without a name, has been a traditional figure since the days of the Western Frontier. Traces of the outlaw-ideal can be found in all hipster and rebel-myths of US popular culture. But the romantic outcast acting according to a self-chosen, yet strict code of honour is an image of the past. Sam Peckinpah in his masterpiece THE WILD BUNCH, gave us the ultimate portrayal of this back in 1969.

Since then it has become impossible for cinema to show unbroken, heroic outlaw figures when out there in reality brutal murderers already regard themselves as the last word in anti-authoritarian rebels. "It also was a demonstration against the authorities," commented Edmund Kemper, a serial killer having murdered and chopped up dozens of people, and the mass murderer Carl Panzram declared shortly before his execution: "I expect to be a rebel right up to my last moment on earth. With my last breath I intend to curse the world and all mankind. I intend to spit in the warden's eye or whoever places the rope around my neck when I am standing on the scaffold. That will be all the thanks they'll get from me".

Nowadays the mass murderer-rebel has replaced the Wild West gunman. He is the outlaw of our time, an idea already anticipated by Norman Mailer in his famous essay "The White Negro" as early as 1957. Mailer defines the psychopathic outsider-hero as a necessary deviation from his conformist environment, for he develops out of a state of inner certainty that his rebellion is just a radical view of the world separating him from general ignorance, reactionary prejudices, and the self-doubts of the conventional psychopath.

A mixture of Mailer's hipster-view of the outlaw-psychopath and the old frontier images can be found in the contemporary myths of cinema. For example, Rutger Hauer as THE HITCHER (1986) is one such stranger without a name, a perverted version of the outsider-hero taking the law into his own hands. It is no coincidence that Hitcher, in his long fluttering coat reminds us of Clint Eastwood prowling lonely dusted roads in Italo-Westerns.

The completely exaggerated character of Dr. Hannibal Lecter transcends even the most twisted outlaw-ideals (to which Panzram and Kemper felt so closely related) in fascination, because essentially the murderous rebel still accepts the existence of an authority in all his vehement denial. But Dr. Lecter acts absolutely beyond mortal politics, ideologies, and ethical values. Outside of society. The killer stands above these things. Of course, he stands above all other criminals too, as the books of Thomas Harris and their respective cinema adaptations never get tired of emphasising. Whether it is the sex maniacs sharing his cell-block or the transsexual born loser Buffalo Bill (SILENCE OF THE LAMBS), or the paedophiliac lecher Mason Verger (HANNIBAL) – for Lecter they are all mere zombies driven by their instincts, who deserve contempt and punishment just like the bad guys who are in it for the money and act under cover of the FBI and psychiatry. Harris wants to tell us that his protagonist smiles at the traditional categories of Evil, just as he smiles at Good. The Doctor lives in his own world.

You could easily shrug this character off as a totalitarian fantasy of power, as some critics did. As a matter of fact, it is no wonder that "Hannibal the Cannibal" was so tremendously successful in the beginning of the Nineties, after a decade when yuppie-mania and numerous dreams of social rise had been smashed in a recession. The people were socially and economically shaken. The "No Future" vision of a regimented world full of people wearing bar-codes slowly became reality. Being such deplorable creatures we at least wanted the cinematic promise that somewhere out there, in the midst of impenetrable power conglomerates and political networks, deep in the fairy-tale-grottoes of high-security units, there was an untouchable renaissance man standing outside the existing status quo.

To Make Time Stand Still

"Daily life is dysentery. Escape this earthly Alcatraz. Get out of this penitentiary, crawl out of this century. Crack this cavity. I need release."

–Foetus Inc., "A Prayer For My Death"

Following THE SILENCE OF THE LAMBS many figures closely or more distantly related to Dr. Lecter appeared on the screen. Robert De Niro plays Max Cady, a violent, sexually insatiable, almost indestructible criminal in Martin Scorsese's remake of CAPE FEAR (1991). Films like BEYOND BEDLAM (1994), or JUST CAUSE (1995), where Ed Harris performs marvellously as a killer, are directly and bluntly in the mold of Hannibal the Cannibal.

The über-killers in these films are modern sorcerers, shamans of death moving almost magically, beaming their power through prison walls, and disappearing in the void whenever they feel like it. Society stigmatises them as madmen: yet an individuality we believe to have lost long ago sparkles in these self-appointed judges over life and death. Murder does not bring a man nearer to captivity, but on the contrary it is "the point at which, irremediably, man opts for his

"Max Cady", CAPE FEAR (1991)

own freedom" (André Gide).

"Murder is the absolute dividing line between material and transcendental, profane and sacred. Once crossed, the past no longer has any relevant existence, time ceases; the future is an open choice, and the necessity for choice has itself been freely chosen," wrote Jean Genet. The transgression of the dividing line drives the serial killer in SPOORLOOS (THE VANISHING, 1988) by the Dutch filmmaker George Sluizer to kidnap chosen persons, narcotising them, and burying them alive. Each murder should stop and influence the course of things. Like Dostoevsky's Raskolnikov in *Crime And Punishment*, who kills an old woman and justifies the deed with the following words: "I wanted to murder, Sonia, to murder without casuistry, to murder for my own satisfaction, for myself alone [...] I had to find out then, and as quickly as possible, whether I was a louse like the rest, or a man. Whether I can step over or not. Whether I am some trembling vermin, or whether I have the right".

Whoever makes time stand still and catapults himself out of existence, gets closer to God, wants to be God himself. There is no divine authority, hence no higher punishment for your deeds on earth. "Who could guess whenever he hugged a rosy-cheeked young child, that he was longing to hack off those cheeks with a razor and would have done so often had not the idea of justice and her long cartège of punishments restrained him on every occasion" (Lautréamont, *Maldoror*).

"Do what thou wilt shall be the whole of the Law" postulated the legendary occultist Aleister Crowley around the turn of the century. The misanthropic barkeeper impersonated by Dennis Hopper in Sean Penn's THE INDIAN RUNNER could be a disciple of this philosophy. In one of the key monologues of the film he explains to the indecisive anti-hero: "Did you ever want to kill someone, just out of rage? And you didn't do it, 'cause you 're afraid [...] and it's all about fear. Fear of the law coming down, sure, but mostly fear like in sin. Sin with God. Yeah, almighty God. What if He ain't almighty, what if He ain't sacred? You might just as well have done it, all right? Goodness, maybe it ain't nothing but fear, you know?"

Übermenschen And Little Students

"Tanz die Stimulanz. Was mich nicht umbringt, macht mich staerker. Friedrich N. Punkt!" [transl.: Dance the stimulance. What does not kill me, makes me stronger. Friedrich N. Full stop!]

–Einstürzende Neubauten, "Tanz das ZNS"

When you see the body-tattooed slaughterer Max Cady in his cell at the beginning of Martin Scorsese's CAPE FEAR, the picture of a certain German Philosopher hangs there on the wall beside Stalin. The "incarnation of Evil" (quote Robert De Niro), who has been steeling his body and mind to a hard battle-machine, looks for the super-structure for his war against the world (and his ex-lawyer) in Friedrich Nietzsche. Cady is not the first murderer who wants to be God (i.e. wants to kill God), and arms himself with quotes by the philosopher. For decades Nietzsche has provided the stuff "superhuman" killers are made of.

No doubt the unholy road-breed of THE HITCHER carries selected works of the controversial thinker with him, and likewise the family father in SPOORLOOS, who kills because he is superior according to his private philosophy, might have underscored the following sentence: "Let us stop brooding about the moral values of our actions". Nietzsche was concerned with erasing the dogmas of the world of ideas in his time when he wrote these lines. He deplored that "Since Plato, philosophy has been dominated by morality [...] Ulterior moral motives have hitherto most obstructed the course of philosophy." Language, words, were the battlefield of the fragile and always sickly philosopher, but Max Cady and co. do not want to know anything about philosophical discourse. The word must become flesh for them.

So some want to be physical representatives of Nietzsche's writings, whilst others are interested in a purely intellectual act. The Professor of Philosophy Rupert

Cadell makes a horrible discovery at the end of Alfred Hitchcock's ROPE. Cadell unveils two of his favourite students as murderers who cold-bloodedly killed a fellow student together. Yet the really bad thing about it is that the juvenile killers committed the deed to corroborate the ideas of their teacher, who has been lecturing about the superiority of elite people who can kill their inferior fellow citizens without moral remorse. According to their theory they have committed the "perfect crime" if they are not caught thanks to their intelligence; hence they are are on their way to becoming "supermen", Nietzsche's so often wilfully misinterpreted term, as a perverted blueprint for bored US College boys. Wracked by disgust, Cadell explains to the murderous couple that his lectures have only been mind games, theoretical provocation, and not manuals for such heinous acts.

Just as Hitchcock's College killers misunderstand their teacher (plus Nietzsche) and take him literally, so their real-life counterparts Nathan Leopold and Richard Loeb in the Chicago of the Twenties took the "superman" idea literally and killed little Bobby Franks. This attempt at "perfect murder" became a startling case that was also adapted in two other films, COMPULSION (1959) and SWOON (1992). It seems like a sick ploy of history that the two Nietzsche-fans were of Jewish origin, and triggered off a wave of anti-Semitism in Chicago. For just a few years later the Nazi regime in Germany adopted the explosive thinker, twisting his writings and thereby stigmatised his oeuvre for many years. What Hitchcock filmed with James Stewart in 1948, was already Nietzsche in a version distorted by the Nazis.

Philosophy can provide knowledge and awareness. It can help us to overcome abysses, or to look down into abysses; but for some of us it is poisonous.

Man Versus Nature: "Sadean Monsters"

"Thus it is that these murders our laws punish so sternly, these murders we suppose the greatest outrage that can be inflicted upon Nature, not only [...] do her no hurt and can do her none, but are in some sort instrumental to her, since she is a great murderess herself [...] The most wicked individual on earth, the most indefatigable murderer is therefore but the spokesman of her desires, the vehicle of her will, and the surest agent of her caprices."

–D.A.F. de Sade

"Let this be clear: nothing would be more fruitless than to take Sade literally, seriously."

–Georges Bataille

Another rebel of literary history, whose notoriety by far exceeds Nietzsche's, is also a main source of inspiration for cinema when inventing new monsters in human shape. The gloomy Marquis de Sade is present in various forms (and perversions), a little spark of him is hidden in most of the most diabolical film characters.

In Japan, where bondage films have been a popular commercial genre for decades, he has been the godfather of an avalanche of cineastic excess (see *Eros In Hell* by Jack Hunter, Creation Books). As a main inspiration of exploitation workaholics like Jess Franco, de Sade draws his trace of blood through European low-budget concoctions of the Sixties and Seventies (MARQUIS DE SADE: JUSTINE/1968; DE SADE 70). THE MOST DANGEROUS GAME (1932) shows how the early Hollywood imagined a Sadean criminal to look. Here, a sophisticated aristocrat hunts human quarry on his island. Count Zaroff (the protagonist) says in the film: "Only after the kill does man know the true ecstasy of love". The film deservedly enjoys an immoral cult status, and Leslie Banks deserves a special place in the gallery of "masterfiends" for his acting. But on the whole, the film only hints vaguely at de Sade's monstrous

SALO

imagination and the sexual ramifications of murder which he postulates.

Radical language almost always evades its adaptation in different media as well as "adaptation" in real life. Nietzsche's example proves this. Donatien Alphonse François Marquis de Sade too, left a gap between his radical writing and its staging in reality, a pit many interpreters, film-makers (see recent screen biographies SADE and QUILLS, both 2000), practising sado-masochists, and murderers alike have fallen into. De Sade, after all, provided the philosophical foundation and justification for the killing and prolonged sexual torture of two children for the British "Moors Murderers" Ian Brady and Myra Hindley. When a journalist asked them for their idols, Brady mentioned the "Divine Marquis", whose works were to be found beside Hitler's *Mein Kampf* in his library. An arrangement fully in tune with Pier Paolo Pasolini, the Italian godfather of art cinema, who transformed de Sade's fictional monsters into a shocking, scatological parable of fascism in his last opus SALO (SALO OR THE 120 Days OF SODOM, 1975).

Here, the fascist bosses meeting in an Italian castle to live out their violent sexual tastes without inhibition, fit well to Ian Brady's Hitler/de Sade fixation. Yet the philosopher Roland Barthes contradicts the tendency of SALO. For him, as for other representatives of the French de Sade front (like Pierre Klossowski or Maurice Blanchot, who also freed Nietzsche from the stigma of fascism) the terror spread by the "Divine Marquis" evades precise political classification. "Remaining faithful to the original words of de Sade's scenes, Pasolini finally deforms the object Sade and the object fascism," writes Barthes. "Sade cannot be depicted at all. Due to the imperious decision of the writer Sade this universe is exclusively left to the power of writing. [...] Seen from the political perspective Pasolini has erred too. Fascism is a too great and sneaking danger to be dealt with a simple analogy providing the fascist tyrants with the libertine's place. [...] Who won't state relieved in the face of the libertines in SALO, I, I am not like them, I am no fascist, because I don't like shit!"

The Heart Of Darkness

"Everything I saw told me that Kurtz had gone insane. The place was full of bodies. It smelled like slow death in there. Malaria, nightmares. This was the end of the river."
–Willard (Martin Sheen) in APOCALYPSE NOW

Of course, many diabolical killer-psychopaths have undeniable "member of the master race" tendencies (especially the "Doctors" Moreau, Mabuse and co.), whereas others like Max Cady stand for an exaggerated individual anarchism. Hyper-villains they are all, superhuman creations of scriptwriters without counterparts in the annals of the history of crime.

If you want to get to know one of the most dubious, unclassifiable characters representing the compendium and simultaneous fraction of all mythical villains of cinema, you have to embark on an apocalyptic voyage up river. At the end of the voyage, in a foggy zone where human heads are impaled on spears and chaos is reigning supreme, Marlon Brando is waiting as "superhuman" Colonel Kurtz in APOCALYPSE NOW (1979), Francis F. Coppola's ultimate Vietnam horror-trip.

"There must be a temptation to play God", someone says about the "fallen angel" Kurtz, but in the man who wants to be God all previousy discussed types are united. Undoubtedly, he has Nietzschean traits and traces of de Sade, and he is a "psychopathic outsider" (in Norman Mailer's sense) formed by an extreme situation (the war). This mass murderer, beyond Zaroff decadence and metaphysical figures like The Hitcher, presiding over the life and death of his followers as a mythical potentate, personifies a category of Evil that reminds one of Georges Bataille's idea of sovereignty.

Bataille, a theorist of transgression, differentiates between two completely different kinds of crime, "Evil viewed in the light of disinterested death fascination" which is opposed to "Evil motivated by selfish interests". Or in other words: the latter useful and rational murder (features: without emotions and self-preserving) absolutely detested by Bataille and attributed to the death-bureaucrats of political systems, as opposed to the self-destroying, excessive, and above all irrational crime ascribed with sovereignty by Bataille. Hereby the breaking with reason, the conversion to obsessive craze, is the most important point for a writer strongly influenced by Nietzsche and de Sade. Hating the war and acting in the *résistance*, he did not regard the terror of the NS-era as the excess of collective madness, as it has often been depicted, but as a cold mechanistic industry of annihilation. "The unchained passion raging in Buchenwald and Auschwitz was totally directed by reason", notes Bataille.

This Bataillean differentiation is elaborated in APOCALYPSE NOW, where Coppola puts the evil Colonel Kurtz in the middle of the evil of a war meticulously planned by a militaristic cartel of technocrats. Before meeting Kurtz we get to know a second slaughterer through the eyes of the protagonist Willard (Martin Sheen): Lt. Kilgore (Robert Duvall), who makes his GI's go surfing near the villages they have just annihilated with napalm. Kilgore, who loves "the smell of fresh napalm in the morning", is a symbol for the icy logistic murder-machinery that kills without batting an eyelash, seeing each victim as an abstract number. He is the opposite to Kurtz. Kurtz kills cruelly too, but he feels the pain, grasps the horror. APOCALYPSE NOW shows as if through a burning glass that Marlon Brando's Nietzschean killer-Colonel seems rather "humane, too humane" compared to the politicians and coolly calculating military men pushing the war ahead. Nietzsche had realised that many of the great massacres in history have been executed in the name of "degenerate reason" (its symbol here: Lt. Kilgore): "Ah, reason, seriousness, mastery over the affects, the whole sombre thing called reflection, all these prerogatives and

"Colonel Kurtz", APOCALYPSE NOW

showpieces of man: how dearly they have been bought! How much blood and cruelty lie at the bottom of all 'good things'!"

Maybe one should differentiate between two kinds of madness: the madness of being symbolised by the war that has driven Kurtz crazy, and lucid madness, a reaction against the omnipresent apocalypse impressively personified by the hulking genius of Marlon Brando.

The Lust For Apocalypse

"This is the end, my only friend, the end."
–The Doors

It has always been like that: the organisation of the rational mass murderers cannot accept an irrational rebel in its rows. So these people are locked in cages and stuck into leather face-masks so that they cannot bite. That's why the death-bureaucrats send the one-man-squad Willard upstream to annihilate Kurtz. The "clean" killers cannot bear the aspect of the "pathological". For the same reasons the NS regime so vehemently chased the mentally ill mass murderer Bruno Luedke. Whoever kills in the frenzy of madness, outside the fascist process, must be annihilated.

But the "superman" Kurtz has been anticipating for a long time that an executioner will come up the river. He constantly acts in full awarenesss of his own impending death. The sovereign Evil does not intend to preserve his power, but heads unerringly for his own self-chosen decline. Just as Zaroff, and The Hitcher, and the mysterious Colquhoun (RAVENOUS, 1999) choose their executioners, so Kurtz knows full well when he lets his murderer into his house. Willard says, "I felt like he was up there waiting for me to take the pain away. He just wanted to go out like a soldier, standing up, not like some poor wasted rag-assed renegade."

The sovereign Evil, as Phillipe Reliquet exemplifies with the mythical figure of the mass murderer Gilles de Rais, is not concerned with winning. Above all he wastes himself, excites himself at his own fall and ruin. "It's that the essence of his works is destruction: not only of the objects and victims brought into play [...] but of the author and the work itself." (Georges Bataille about de Sade).

SADEAN KILLER FILMS: A SELECTION

APOCALYPSE NOW / USA 1979

Directed by Francis F. Coppola. Written by John Milius & Francis F. Coppola after motifs from "The Heart Of Darkness" by Joseph Conrad. Camera: Vittorio Storaro. Music: Carmine & Francis F. Coppola. With Martin Sheen, Robert Duvall, Marlon Brando, Frederic Forrest, Dennis Hopper, Lawrence Fishburne, Harrison Ford

At the end of the Seventies Francis F. Coppola finally completed his vision of Joseph Conrad's novel *The Heart Of Darknes,* after a gigantic expenditure of material and human effort. In the mass of Hollywood movies attempting to evoke the American Vietnam trauma, Coppola's opus is farthest away from naked realism. It wants to be much more than an anti-war film, you are rather reminded of *Dante's Inferno* in a psychedelic horror-trip version. Yet APOCALYPSE NOW enters much more profoundly and universally into the shadow-world of human emotions than all the phoney PLATOON-type concoctions. Whereas conventional Vietnam movies stick to reactionary patriotism and talk of "good "and "bad" soldiers, Coppola shows total chaos, the negation of all values. The war as an absolute zone lays bare an atavistic bestiality that is otherwise veiled by civilisation. The archaic monster Kurtz thrones in the heart of the apocalypse, but the real monsters, the film says, are the technocrats pulling the strings of the war.

CAPE FEAR / USA 1962

Directed by J. Lee Thompson. Written by James R. Webb. Camera: Sam Leavitt. Music: Bernhard Hermann. With Robert Mitchum, Gregory Peck, Polly Bergen, Martin Balsam, Telly Savalas

In this suspenseful noir classic Robert Mitchum plays the ex-jailbird Max Cady, who wants to take vengeance upon his lawyer for putting him behind bars with false evidence. Cady starts a war of nerves against the lawyer (Peck) and his family. Finally the attacks become violent, and the peaceful lawyer is forced to counteract forcefully to get rid of his Nemesis. Mitchum's best psycho role since Preacher Powell in NIGHT OF THE HUNTER, laying the groundwork for de Niro's Nietzschean version of Cady 30 years later.

CAPE FEAR / USA 1991

Directed by Martin Scorsese. Written by Wesley Strick after a novel by John D. MacDonald and a screenplay by James R. Webb. Camera: Freddie Francis. Music: Elmer Bernstein after the original score by Bernhard Hermann. With Robert De Niro, Nick Nolte, Jessica Lange, Juliette Lewis, Joe Don Baker, Martin Balsam, Gregory Peck, Robert Mitchum

Maybe Martin Scorsese's grotesquely exaggerated remake lacks the subtly terrifying atmosphere of the original version, but it compensates for this by foregrounding those aspects nobody dared to show in the Sixties: the sexual seduction of a minor, the bloody harshness of Cady's acts of vengeance, the complete destruction of the bourgeois world. Yet it is already rotten anyway. The lawyer (Nolte) attacked by Cady reveals himself to be not at all innocent. His family life has been shaky for a long time, and he deliberately withheld the evidence which could have saved Cady from jail. Cady is primed to destroy the phoney middle-class idyll once and for all. You could criticise Robert De Niro's performance for its exaggeration, but you'd be missing the point; his character is basically a conglomerate of quotes from various sources (Nietzsche, de Sade, Jack Henry Abbott and True Crime myths, hardcore tattooed posturing *à la* Henry Rollins, and religious fanaticism), almost an ultra-rock star, whose depiction has been long overdue.

HANNIBAL

HANNIBAL / USA 2000

Directed by Ridley Scott. Written by David Mamet and Steven Zaillan after the novel by Thomas Harris. Camera: John Mathieson. Music: Hans Zimmer. With Anthony Hopkins, Julianne Moore, Gary Oldman, Giancarlo Giannini

Thomas Harris' sequel to his mega -success THE SILENCE OF THE LAMBS is hardly the most sophisticated thriller of the late Nineties. But just what makes the book most despicable in the eyes of many critics – its luxuriously celebrated sadism, its quite often exaggerated shock effects, the author's seemingly completely destructive view of the world – all this makes *Hannibal* almost subversive. How often does a malignant pulp novel make it to the top of the charts, a book that might throw more than one reader of best-selling novels into a deep moral crisis? How many mainstream books release the heroine into the heaven of love together with her most wicked, sociopathic antagonist?

Ridley Scott, who directed the film version after long discussions, wasn't able – and didn't want to – bring this immoral core of the novel to the screen. Instead, the film-maker indulged in opulent show effects and glossy surfaces, as he had often done before: Milan in summer, autumnal New England, stiflingly illuminated FBI archives and picturesque palaces, shoot-outs and splatter, and, of course, the mimic art of Anthony Hopkins. Jonathan Demme still oscillated between grim realism and the Grimm brothers' fairy tales in SILENCE OF THE LAMBS, but HANNIBAL is purely a modern version of Gothic horror. It has a sense of style, yes, it's gory and funny, but it's no wonder that Hannibal the Cannibal goes to the dogs somehow as he transmutes into a purely mythical, superhuman figure in this film.

THE HITCHER

THE HITCHER / USA 1986

Directed by Robert Harmon. Written by Eric Red. Camera: John Seale. Music: Mark Isham. Camera: John Seale. With Rutger Hauer, C. Thomas Howell, Jennifer Jason Leigh, Jeffrey DeMunn, Henry Darrow

You don't know his motives, his past, or even his name. The blond, powerful man standing lonely on the highway comes out of the blue and kills with superhuman vehemence. A young traveller can initially free himself from the claws of the killer, but the killer has smelled blood. The young man cannot get rid of him for long. The

Hitcher, invented by the ingenious script-writer Eric Red (BLUE STEEL, NEAR DARK), is a perfect cinema hybrid. He is an almost indestructible serial killer looking like an outlaw – hence far removed from real highway killers and their distorted ruinous personalities – but still more convincing than faceless modern movie slashers.

LOS SIN NOMBRE aka THE NAMELESS / Spain 1999

Directed by Jaume Balagueró. Written by Jaume Balagueró after the novel of Ramsey Campbell. Camera: Albert Carreras. M: Carles Casas. With Emma Vilarasau, Karra Elejalde, Tristan Ulloa, Jordi Dauder, Jessica Del Pozo

A few years after her daughter was killed by unknown kidnappers and her marriage broke down as a result, a woman tries to get a grip on her life again. But when one morning the phone rings and an all too familiar kid's voice whispers "Mama, I'm alive", the terror recommences. Together with an ex-cop, the woman follows the tracks of a dreadful mystery.

"Trying to reach the limits of evil... But evil *has* no limits" is the tagline of this Spanish film, a film that made fans of the genre once again true believers in perfect horror cinema. But it isn't only the film's Fincheresque atmosphere or the brilliantly timed shock sequences which create the horror. It is the story of the sect of The Nameless, a cult that began to create its world-wide web in the beginning of the 20th century, that gets most deeply under the skin. The cult's aim was to corrupt the innocent and create pure Evil. The exceptional talent Balagueró mixes influences of Aleister Crowley and Nazi-occultism with the Sadean belief in man at the mercy of an insatiable nature in order to evoke this picture of lightlessness.

A mixture that produces a highly fatalistic, hopeless conclusion. Instead of the foul compromise of a happy ending, there is only pitch-black darkness at the end of the tunnel.

THE MOST DANGEROUS GAME / USA 1932

Directed by Ernest B. Schoedsack & Irving Pichel. Written by James A. Creelman after a story by Richard Connell. Camera: Henry Gerrard. Music: Max Steiner. With Leslie Banks, Joel McCrea, Fay Wray, Robert Armstrong, Noble Johnson

The Russian Count Zaroff plays "the most dangerous game" on his private island, completely cut off from the outer world. He lets ships run aground with false signals and hunts and kills the survivors like animals. In a sequence only recently restored, we see his trophy room with its walls lined with human heads.

During a break in the filming of KING KONG (1932) Schoedsack and Cooper decided to use its scenery for a second project. The result is regarded as a bizarre late-expressionist jewel of horror. Though for some critics a precursor of Hitler, who obtained the power in the year the film was released, the worldly, highly sophisticated Count with a foible for sensual dishes and romantic music is still a Sadean hero *par excellence* (though, of course, *à la* Hollywood), a sado-masochist enjoying the fear of death, because this is the only thing that really stimulates his sexual appetite.

RAVENOUS / USA-GB 1999

Directed by Antonia Bird. Written by Ted Griffin. Camera: Anthony B. Richmond Music: Michel Nyman and Damon Albarn. With Guy Pearce, Robert Carlyle, David Arquette, Jeremy Davies, Jeffrey Jones

It is a sad fact that quality and resolution don't count for much at the box office. This sardonic deconstruction of the Western genre only reached a small audience. Probably, the young British director Antonia Bird heaped a little bit too much blood, guts and gore upon the sacrosanct myths of the American Frontier.

"Count Zaroff", THE MOST DANGEROUS GAME

It is the time of the Mexican-American War. Slightly similarly to THE HITCHER, this film discusses the basic ideas of Nietzsche, De Sade et al with two contrary protagonists: Captain John Boyd (Pearce), hyper-sensitive and a man of integrity, meets the mysterious Scotsman Colquhoun (amazing: Carlyle), the only survivor of a sojourn in a half-deserted fort. The stranger soon turns out to be a superhuman killer, feeding on his victims to gain animal strength.

When it comes to the showdown, the final confrontation of the opponents after a series of nerve-shattering and tragi-comic massacres, Boyd has already become similar to his antagonist. Colquhoun, a personification of the Windigo (a ravenous cannibalistic creature according to Indian myths), has shown him an abyss from which there is no possible return to humanity.

SALO (SALO OR THE 120 DAYS OF SODOM) / Italy 1975

Directed by Pier Paolo Pasolini. Written by Pier Paolo Pasolini & Sergio Citti after motives of de Sade's novel "The 120 Days Of Sodom". Camera: Tonino Delli Colli. Music: Ennio Morricone. With Sonia Saviange, Caterina Borrato, Aldo Vanelli, Giorgio Cataldi

Undoubtedly, Pasolini's last film ranks among the most insistent moral outcries in the history of film and, despairing of mankind, it is a deeply pessimistic valediction to his former utopias. Yet Pasolini entangles himself in inextricable contradictions when equating de Sade with fascism. The admixture of fascist radicalism, libertine sexuality, art, literature (Klossowski and again Nietzsche are quoted) and Nazi-atrocities seems at times highly dubious. Pasolini is conjuring a milieu in which all human values and aspirations are completely negated; the captives of the castle are less than animals, they are just lumps of meat to be raped, buggered, shat upon, tortured, mutilated or shot dead on a whim of the four übermenschen. Roland Barthes wrote: "Though the *mise-en-scène* is a failure Pasolini's film's value lies in dark recognition. [...] What touches so, shows an effect in SALO is its literalness. Pasolini has filmed the scenes totally literally, as described (I do not say: written) by de Sade. So these scenes have the sad icy-cold exact beauty of an encyclopaedic illustration." SALO remains one of the most extraordinary films ever committed to celluloid.

SPOORLOOS (THE VANISHING) / Netherlands-France 1988

Directed by George Sluizer. Written by Tim Krabbe & George Sluizer. Camera: Toni Kuhn. Music: Henry Vrienten. With Gene Bervoets, Johanna Ter Steege, Bernard-Pierre Donnadieu, Gwen Eckhaus, Bernadette LeSaché

Terror has a bourgeois face in SPOORLOOS. A 40-year-old chemistry teacher and family father reveals himself as a sociopath kidnapper and killer. He kidnaps Saskia, a girl on vacation with her boyfriend, and starts playing cat-and-mouse with him.

This brilliant thriller inexorably heading towards a shockingly pitch-black end, fascinates with its character descriptions. Sluizer lets the killer act highly intelligently, and consciously immorally. Almost like a Sadean figure he has replaced Good with pure Evil. Psychological explanations are replaced by ominous metaphors. Finally, Evil is not decoded.

In 1993 George Sluizer directed a US remake of the film (with Jeff Bridges and Kiefer Sutherland) that completely lacks the atmosphere, intensity and, above all, the bleak climax of the original version.

STRANGERS ON A TRAIN / USA 1951

Directed by Alfred Hitchcock. Written by Raymond Chandler and Czenzi Ormonde after a novel by Patricia Highsmith. Camera: Robert Burks. Music: Dimitri Tiomkin. With Robert Walker, Farley Granger, Ruth Roman, Laura Ellliot

Two men meet in a train from Washington to New York. The one, Bruno, proposes a devilish pact to the other, Guy. He shall dispose of Bruno's father. In return Bruno offers to kill Guy's unloved wife, who refuses to divorce him.

Again Hitchcock enters the Nietzsche-influenced realm of amorality, the question of "good" and "bad" in the shape of a perfect crime film. In a way Bruno, the psychopath believing in murder as an *acte gratuite* in the sense of André Gide as well as the "perfect murder" like the two "Thrill Killers" in ROPE, represents "good" Guy's repressed desire for murder too. In order to defeat the unpleasant side of his own nature, Guy must exterminate the gloomy stranger.

Relevant films already discussed in Part One:

COMPULSION
KILLER – A JOURNAL OF MURDER
ROPE
THE SILENCE OF THE LAMBS
SWOON

CHAPTER FIVE
ANGELS OF DEATH: MURDEROUS WOMEN

"My every waking moment was spent trying to control the beasts inside me. Nothing seemed to satisfy this unquenchable monster..."
–Lydia Lunch

Murderous women are not as exhaustively represented in cinema as male murderers. Moreover, their depiction lacks the dazzling variety dedicated to the staging of male perversion. If cinema deals with murderous women, they are mostly reduced to stereotypes. The poisoner putting arsenic into a cup of tea, the murderess of greed or jealousy swearing vengeance upon her unfaithful husband or lover, or, in rare cases, pure murderesses of passion. The era of American Film Noir was a chapter in the history of film where strong and dangerous women crowded the screen for a while. "She was calculating, manipulative, cruel and she used her sexual attractions blatantly and without regard for the polite conventions of the past. She [the Noir-woman] knew what she wanted and she didn't care what she did to get it." (Bruce Crowther, *Film Noir*). These women were usually punished at the end of the film – as is still the case with (sexually) aggressive women in Hollywood productions.

"Murder stands as a metaphor, the murderess symbolizing the breaking with the traditions of peacefulness and submission" states the preface of the catalogue of a Viennese festival on murderesses in film. Murder as an intentional lethal act of violence is just the last exceeding expression of violence as resistance against a society which on the one hand provides a woman only with the role of the victim, yet on the other fearfully, but lasciviously fantasises about the "demonic aspects" of the Female as such.

Feminists Deborah Cameron and Elisabeth Frazer define rape-killing as a form of sexual terror directed by men against the autonomy of all women as potential victims, in their book *Lust For Killing*. Basically, they deny the female sex the disposition to commit "motiveless" murder, or the killing of another person to obtain transcendence (like most of runners amok, serial killers, and sex killers).

On the whole, sociological and empirical investigations corroborate their ideas: murder, especially sexual and serial murder, is a domain of men. The FBI estimate that less than 5% of all serial killers are female. That's why the capture of Aileen Wuornos stirred so much attention. As the first "real" female serial killer she seemed to be as motiveless, misanthropic, and cold-blooded as her male counterparts.

Evidently, women only murder among their own families or acquaintances, if at all. They kill their children, husbands, or parents out of jealousy, revenge, or mental or material emergency. And this often happens in the shape of extended suicide. These women only defend themselves or see no way out any more. According to society's point of view, women are basically peaceful. Only man possesses the perverse lust for killing.

Digression: Honest Housewives And Amazons

"The myth I always aspired to was that of Artemis or Diana, the goddess of the hunt. She was a warrior and a fighter who had nothing to do with procreation."
–Diamanda Galas

People believe in the image of the peaceful woman. After all, killing, seen from a historical perspective, has always been a male domain. Either in hunting (the woman is attributed the position of the collector) or in war, women are excluded or their role in it is neglected. The Christian tradition has decisively contributed to the image of the peaceful woman brought up to silence and patient suffering. The woman is stylised as the child-bearing mother donating and maintaining life, hence as a symbolic counterpart to man, who alone had the right to kill over the centuries, as a hunter, judge, executioner, warrior, sovereign, slave-master etc.

In the dualistic system of the sexes the woman is provided with the passive, peaceful, and giving role in society, while man is active. His aggression is not only lethal, but can also be regarded positively as his urge for power or a career in economy and politics. Yet the woman is entirely fixed in the roles of the caring mother, the honest housewife, the sacrificing nurse, or the unselfish assistant. Many women could not bear this burden in the long run, and escaped into blood and death (cf. the notorious case of the Viennese "killer-nurses" around Waltraud Wagner).

Aggressive women are not socially acceptable. Anger and fierce struggle for power are regarded as unwomanly, and the most extreme form of aggression, murder, evokes more consternation and disgust than a man's murder. A male killer can even be stylised as an (anti-)hero.

Female killers are approached with a wild mixture of clichés and calls for damnation, as in the case of Aileen Wuornos (OVERKILL: THE AILEEN WUORNOS STORY, 1992). Or one makes the contrary reaction and presents the killer as a super-feminist finally penetrating the last bastion of men. But as a matter of fact, female killing is almost always a desperate cry for help or a psychopathic reaction to extreme personal situations. The motives are as numerous as they are individually different.

Poisoners

"Rhoda has some strange affinity for the cruelties of the Old Testament. There's something as terrible and primitive about her, as there is about them."
–William March, *The Bad Seed*

Poisoning is perhaps the most "typically" female way of killing. It is bloodless, silent, and takes no physical strength (Locusta, a female poisoner living in Rome around 54AD, is in fact regarded as the first recorded serial killer). There have been various reasons to use arsenic. Sometimes a husband had to die because his wife was afraid of a divorce, an existential disaster for women in former times. Sometimes she wanted to escape a years-long matrimonial hell. Many poisoners wanted to obtain their matrimonial fortune. In aristocratic circles poisoning was a popular political instrument for a while. Here two women became particularly notorious: Lucrezia Borghia and Katharine of Medici, the latter to be seen in LA REINE MARGOT (Queen Margot, 1994). The court's function as a "model" as well as the difficulty to prove this crime may have played a role in facilitating such practices.

Frank Capra deals with this topic very amusingly in his timeless black comedy ARSENIC AND OLD LACE (1944). Two elderly sisters kill male singles on the wrong side of forty with their elderberry wine, hence seriously embarrassing their nephew Cary Grant. The two ladies pretend to act out of pity (and hence wittily satirize some woman clichés). They claim that for a man life is not worth living anyway without a

BASIC INSTINCT

woman. The certain horror-effect behind the rapid sequence of puns and the occasional flaring of psychosis under the sisters' benevolent granny-surface, makes the film most enjoyable.

Chabrol's VIOLETTE NOZIÈRE (1977) acts completely differently. Seriously interested in the motives of the beautiful poisoner, he presents a pale pretty creature full of contradictions and mysterious womanliness. Violette is childlike and voluptuous at the same time, full of devotion and cold as ice, in love and greedy, faithful and phoney, hungry for life and murderous, a depraved, passionate Snow White handing over the poisonous apple to her parents.

Sex Murder In The Realm Of The Senses

"Love is cruel, love is truly absurd"
–Anita Lane

The deadly sex angel is the second popular cliché attributed to murderous women in cinema. Contemporary cinema is full of lasciviously erotic, but a at the same time coolly calculating women degrading men to will-less creatures with their bodies and their concentrated sex-appeal, and using them as playthings for their intricate intrigues. This has already been demonstrated fascinatingly in the Film Noir classic THE POSTMAN ALWAYS RINGS TWICE (1946). Bob Rafaelsen showed it even more explicitly in his remake of 1980. A similar story can also be found in BODY HEAT (1981) where long-legged Kathleen Turner seducees ignorant William Hurt into killing her husband.

This type of woman became particularly popular in the early Eighties when the sub-genre of erotic thriller was in vogue. Sharon Stone shows us in BASIC INSTINCT (1991) you can make tough men sweat. Don't wear panties under your mini-dress, then slowly uncross and cross your legs. Rather banally, of course, this erotic thriller mirrors a primeval fear: during intercourse the lovers are in their partner's hands as well as naked and helpless in case of an attack. Moreover, man's fear (and fantasy) of a (sexually) hyper-dominant and incalculable woman plays an important role. Fear and danger as aphrodisiac as well as lethal threat in times of an omnipresent Aids-paranoia. But this only works until a certain limit. The sexually aggressive demanding woman has to be defeated by man, especially in Hollywood. Unlike the real ice-pick killer Sharon Stone survives, but is finally domesticated. Glenn Close has to pay a higher price for her FATAL ATTRACTION (1987).

The Japanese prostitute Sada Abe, who in 1936 killed her lover from a surfeit of sexual passion and carried his severed penis with her for several days, inspired a film which puts these Hollywood efforts to eternal shame: Nagisa Oshima's AI NO CORRIDA (IN THE REALM OF THE SENSES).

Jörg Buttgereit too tells of drastic and lethal love in NEKROMANTIK 2 (1991), though he even goes a step further. The necrophile heroine kills her lover, because she covets him more as a corpse than alive. Ultimate pleasure through death.

Women On The Verge Of A Nervous Breakdown: Female Psychos

Male psychopaths have figured in countless films. Many of them have become real cult-figures. Their female counterparts are much rarer. Women are much more frequently the victims of psychopathic killers

Some female cinema psychos have been played by Joan Crawford and Bette Davis, especially in Robert Aldrich's WHATEVER HAPPENED TO BABY JANE? (1962) as breathtakingly duelling, hateful but still mutually dependent sisters. In Aldrich's similarly disturbing HUSH, HUSH, SWEET CHARLOTTE (1965) Bette Davis lives in a dream world for decades believing that she has slain her fiancé, until she finds out that her cousin (Olivia de Havilland) is the real, mad axe-murderess. Quite often these women are driven by jealousy or envy, they lust after their rival's success, admiration, wealth, the seemingly better life. Or they try to slip into the role of another woman, e.g. Jennifer Jason Leigh in SINGLE WHITE FEMALE (1992). She becomes more and more like her flat-mate Bridget Fonda, and takes over her haircut, her habits, and even her boyfriend. When Fonda realizes that there is more to this behaviour than mere admiration, it is almost too late.

Other women cannot stand being rejected or learning that the object of their desire is not as they want them to be. Disappointed love or admiration turns into downright hatred. The "nice" nurse (Kathy Bates) in MISERY (1990) reveals herself as

a sadistic nightmare for a writer (James Caan) completely in her hands after an accident. As he wants to let her favourite character in a series of novels die, she tries to talk him out of this decision with the most painful methods possible – including shattering his legs with a sledge-hammer. Only a trifle can make a good-natured, stocky housewife into a psychopathic sadist.

Clint Eastwood experiences similar things in PLAY MISTY FOR ME (1971), a film he also directed. When a radio DJ cannot stand a female fan's burning affection any more, she must make him change his mind with full-fledged threats and cop-murders. Fan-love can be lethal.

REPULSION

Catherine Deneuve in Roman Polanski's masterpiece REPULSION (1965) is a special case among the female psychopaths. She is no avenger-character, but a neurotic young lady extremely disgusted by her own burgeoning sexuality. Shrouded in gloomy black-and-white, the fragile protagonist loses herself in nightmarish hallucinations and commits a brutal murder by razor.

The Bad Seeds

"I'm born bad."

–Mallory Knox (Juliette Lewis) in NATURAL BORN KILLERS

"Varla" (right), FASTER, PUSSYCAT! KILL! KILL!

The representatives of the cinematic category "demon in a woman's shape" go a step further. They do not need an incident or excuse for their outbursts and murders. They are evil through and through and immoral from the beginning. Comparable real cases that lack every criminological explanation, like the one of the sisters Christine and Léa Papin, who killed their employers in 1933, are rare.

In THE BAD SEED (1956) little blonde Rhoda reveals herself as a demon in a child's shape. She kills an old neighbour to inherit something, drowns a classmate, and burns the gardener that finds her out. Evil lurks behind an angelic face.

Attractive Sue Ann's character in PRETTY POISON (1968) seems like a grown-up Rhoda, behind her harmless surface too lurks the bad seed.

ILSA, a platinum-blonde men-torturing sex-pot unscrupulously living out her sadistic and murderous desires in different ideological systems (Nazis, Stalin, Arabian harem) in a trilogy, is a trash-version of the demonic woman. But it is never the system that makes her evil, she is born bad and uses the political circumstances for her mean intentions, just like psycho real-life role model Ilse Koch.

Tura Satana in Russ Meyer's cult-movie FASTER, PUSSYCAT! KILL! KILL! (1965) offers a further, almost comic-like exaggeration of the female Devil. Her Meyeresque curves pressed into a skin-tight sexy outfit, she turns out to be more than a match for men. Laughing scornfully, Satana's "superwoman" Varla (desribed in the script as "a voluptuous beauty, tremendously physical, violent, dominating, evil") recklessly defeats every man, scorns him, abuses him, and sometimes even kills him. As in most of his films Russ Meyer comically turns the tables. The woman is superior to man, strong, and to be feared. Man is a weak coward, a poltroon helplessly surrendering to female attractions.

BLACK WIDOW

Amok Women

"I don't care if a rapist is white or black, if he is middle-class or poor – I only want to kill him."

–Diamanda Galas

"When I get mad and I get pissed I grab my pen and I run a list of all the people that won't be missed, you make my shitlist!

–L7

Amok women are the rarest cinema murderesses. Only in Film Noir, e.g. in GUN CRAZY (1949), in the B-movie GIRLS ON THE LOOSE (1958), or in THE BONNIE PARKER STORY (1958) did they appear as rare exceptions of their time. These women demand absolute freedom and uncompromising love. This is what they fight for, even with guns in their hands.

Only in the Eighties were women shooting again. Superficially examined, Abel Ferrara's MS.45 is a female counterpart to DEATH WISH (1974), but it also thematizes a woman striking back after being raped. The victim does not want to be a victim any more, does not want to be humiliated any more, but demands vengeance. Actress Zoe Tamerlis Lund stated: "In fact rape is not the issue. It is rather about the state of abuse in a general figurative sense". The more gratuitous I SPIT ON YOUR GRAVE (1977) is a similar case in point, but plays as a straight rape-revenge movie, rather than dealing with the rape-provoked, sociopathic amok of its protagonist.

In the Hong Kong action film DI YI LEI XING WEI XIAN (DON'T PLAY WITH FIRE, 1980) by the innovative director Tsui Hark it is a rebellious young woman who plays with fire. To escape the boredom and the confines of the city she manoeuvres herself and three male youths into a conflict with US soldiers of fortune – a conflict which ends up lethal for all concerned. In the French thriller MORTELLE RANDONNÉE (DEDALY CIRCUIT, 1982) an elderly private eye follows a chameleon-like young woman (Isabelle Adjani) who is marrying rich men and killing them afterwards like a black widow spider. The sleuth is fascinated by her ethereal beauty, which reminds him of his own late daughter, but also feels morally compelled to put a stop to her activities. Her real motive is her profound hate of all men. Nevertheless, she is also in search of pure love. In the similar Hollywood-produced BLACK WIDOW (1986), Therese Russell is the murdering serial wife whose victims include Dennis Hopper.

While male anti-heroes are allowed to survive in rare cases despite the blood dripping from their hands, female angels of vengeance and runners amok always die. Travis Bickle is still wheeling through N.Y.C. at the end of TAXI DRIVER, but Abel Ferrara's MS. 45 is stabbed in back by a friend, and Isabelle Adjani, the beautiful man-killer of MORTELLE RANDONNÉE has to rush into death in her car. Adjani meets a similar fate in POSSESSION (1980), where she portrays the ultimate female psychopath, although here she dies by shooting into her own back. The wild anarchic Chinese woman in Tsui Hark's DI YI LEI XING WEI XIAN is punished most severely. Without batting an eyelash the mercenaries shoot her down in cold blood. Unlike many male killers in cinema she does not experience a captivating, melodramatic death, but is executed rather randomly and incidentally, as if her rebellion as a woman had to be punished twice as harshly.

A woman's individual revolt in cinema has no chance against militarily drilled male violence. Female runners amok have to die for daring to break with a world dominated by the male sex.

MURDEROUS WOMEN FILMS: A SELECTION

ARSENIC & OLD LACE / USA 1941 (released 1944)

Directed by Frank Capra. Written by Julius J. & Philip G. Epstein after a play by Joseph Kesselring. Camera: Sol Polito. Music: Max Steiner. With Cary Grant, Priscilla Lane, Josephine Hull, Jean Adair, Raymond Massey, Peter Lorre

Thanks to its fantastic cast delivering fireworks of hilariously fast screwball-comedy dialogue, Frank Capra's film has become a black humour classic. The subtly comical Cary Grant as the seriously shaken nephew of the benevolent old ladies Josephine Hull and Jean Adair bringing elderly gentlemen eternal sleep; Raymond Massey as gloomy Boris Karloff-imitator mumming Frankenstein clichés *ad absurdum*; and the great Peter Lorre rolling his eyes in a brilliant and frighteningly ironical performance.

THE BAD SEED / USA 1956

Directed by Mervyn LeRoy. Written by John Lee Mahin after a play by Maxwell Anderson and a novel by William March. Camera: Hal Rosson. Music: Alex North. With Patty McCormack, Nancy Kelly, Henry Jones, Eileen Heckert, Evelyn Varden

When William March published his novel *The Bad Seed* in 1954, he whipped up controversy with his daring hypothesis that instead of environmental influences, only the genes were responsible for murderous instincts. March called the respective gene "the Bad Seed". In his novel, Evil manifests itself in nine-year-old Rhoda, a sweetly smiling girl with blonde tresses. Behind the cute facade lurks a cold-blooded murderess, portrayed by little Patty McCormack with a mixture of childlike innocence and anti-social depravity. McCormack's brilliantly diabolical performance makes Mervyn LeRoy's adaptation of the novel's stage-version a rare pearl for fans of dark, perverse and immoral B-movies, while the character of Rhoda foreshadows 11-year-old murderer Mary Bell, the schoolgirl who killed and mutilated two infants in 1968.

BASIC INSTINCT / USA 1991

Directed by Paul Verhoeven. Written by Joe Esterhasz. Camera: Jan De Bont. Music: Jerry Goldsmith. With Michael Douglas, Sharon Stone, Jeanne Trippleborn, George Dzunda

A mainstream collision of sex and murder. A cop investigating the sex murders of a brutal ice-pick killer becomes addicted to the aggressive eroticism of a writer involved in the case. Hated by critics, but celebrated by a world-wide audiences, BASIC INSTINCT seems like just another example of an ultimately lame "erotic thriller". But Paul Verhoeven, a veteran of European sex & crime cinema with films like FLESH AND BLOOD (1985) or THE FOURTH MAN (1983), adds a potent dash of cynicism and provocation to the mix of this Hollywood formula. Compared to other, mostly disastrous examples of the genre (BODY HEAT/1981, SLIVER/1993, BODY OF EVIDENCE/1993), Verhoeven's opus is actually much better than the average, and probably the best of the lot.

DI YI LEI XING WEI XIAN (DON'T PLAY WITH FIRE aka DANGEROUS ENCOUNTER – FIRST KIND) / Hongkong 1980

Directed by Tsui Hark. Written by Szeto Cheuk Hon. Camera: Chung Chi Man. Music: Alan Parsons Project, Jean Michel Jarre. With Bruce Baron, Nigel Falgate, Richard Da Silva, Pierre Tremblay, Lo Lieh

One of the most uncompromising statements of Hong Kong's "New Wave" in the early Eighties. An early opus by the celebrated director Tsui Hark that seems to be influenced by Peckinpah, Romero, and Godard, but also goes its own way beyond these models. A criminal teenage girl and three sheltered bourgeois boys get into a

THE BAD SEED

maelstrom of chaos and annihilation. The film condenses the scorching heat and suffocating atmosphere of Hong Kong with its 6 million people into hellishly claustrophobic images. In the midst of this anarchic story about the roots of aggression the female protagonist, an asexual, fragile little time bomb, finally explodes to devastating effect.

THE HAND THAT ROCKS THE CRADLE / USA 1992

Directed by Curtis Hanson. Written by Amanda Silver. Camera: Robert Elswitt. Music: Graeme Revell. With Annabella Sciorra, Rebecca De Mornay. Matt Mc Coy, Ernie Hudson, Julianne Moore

This thriller, conjuring up the image of the perfect US family idyll – which remains intact as long as no intruder disturbs the peace – was produced in one of the most conservative phases of the recent history of Hollywood (cf. FATAL ATTRACTION). Threat comes in the shape of the blonde nursemaid Rebecca De Mornay, a wicked witch who bears gloomy hatred against her employers, because of a tragic chain of fatal events. Curtis Hanson canonizes the successful, conformist upper-middle-class family, conjures up the wife's total devotion to her role as a mother, and degrades Afro-Americans to babbling retards in minor parts. All this for a few well-timed sequences of suspense.

MISERY / USA 1990
Directed by Rob Reiner. Written by William Goldman after a novel by Stephen King. Camera: Barry Sonnenfeld. Music: Marc Shaiman. With James Caan, Kathy Bates, Richard Farnsworth, Frances Sternhagen, Lauren Bacall
Instead of his usual ghost-train rides into pseudo-religious metaphysical worlds, Stephen King emphasizes realistic horror in *Misery*. His captivating novel about Sheldon, a successful writer getting into the claws of a highly dangerous fan, vacillates between suspense, breathtaking shocks, and the pungent smell of anaesthesia. Rob Reiner's celluloid version lacks much of that. The film backs old-fashioned actor's cinema and confronts James Caan as Sheldon with Kathy Bates, who has been awarded an Oscar for her psychotic, child-killing nurse Annie Wilkes.

MORTELLE RANDONNÉE (DEADLY CIRCUIT aka DEADLY RUN) / France 1982
Directed by Claude Miller. Written by Michel & Jacques Audiard. Gilbert Duhalde & Pierre Lhomme. Music: Carla Bley. With Isabelle Adjani, Michel Serrault, Guy Marchand, Stéphane Audran, Samy Frey
Isabelle Adjani's face alone can make a film sparkle. But if you have a look at her career, you do not find too many films where the directing, the script, and her acting perfectly fit together. Claude Miller's noir-homage to a man-murdering chameleon is one such film (as is Andrzej Zulawski's shattering POSSESSION).

Michel Serrault is her captivating partner in MORTELLE RANDONNÉE. Sometimes this story of voyeurism, desire, and death drifts into irrationality – which can either be seen as an achievement, or as a flaw due to ambiguity of content and

MS.45

lack of psychological insight.

Watch out too for the not as good, but still interesting remake the Australian director Stephan Elliot released in 1999, under the title EYE OF THE BEHOLDER starring Ewan McGregor and Ashley Judd.

Ms. 45 aka ANGEL OF VENGEANCE / USA 1981

Directed by Abel Ferrara. Written by Nicholas St. John. Camera: James Momel. Music: Joe Delia. With Zoe Tamerlis, Steve Singer, Jack Thibeau, Peter Yellen, Adida Sherman

Thana, a mute hyper-sensitive seamstress is raped by two different men in one afternoon. She manages to kill her second tormentor, dismembers his corpse, and throws the pieces into dustbins all over Manhattan. Afterwards Thana is not the same any more, something must have burnt through inside her. Wearing sexy outfits she starts a campaign of vengeance against pimps, crooks, and street gangs. But this film is some light-years away from petty-bourgeois & fascist vigilante movies like DEATH WISH. Thana is rather a sister of the torn Catherine Deneuve in REPULSION, and remotely related to Robert De Niro in TAXI DRIVER.

ODISHON (AUDITION) / Japan 1999

Directed by Takashi Miike. Written by Daisuke Tengan after the book of Ryu Murakami. Camera: Hideo Yamamoto. Music: Koji Endo. With Ryo Ishibashi, Eihi Shiina, Miyuki Matsuda, Renji Ishibashi

Since RINGU (RING, 1998), a supernatural thriller that broke many box office records

Isabelle Adjani, POSSESSION

in Japan, horror has reasserted an unequivocal face for the Japanese audience: a female phantom with long black hair covering her face, in the tradition of such classics as KWAIDAN (1964) and KURENEKO (1968). ODISHON pulls this image of an innocent yet at the same time threatening Lolita from the surreal world of ghosts into icy reality. At first the film deceives its audience, lulls it for an hour in the disguise of a subtle thriller. But then it exposes the defective relationship between men and women in Japan with pointed needles and delicate bone saws

Miike of all people, a hyperactive guy in ultra sex'n'violence futurism (e.g. FUDOH – THE NEW GENERATION/1996, DEAD OR ALIVE/1999), avenges generations of suppressed Japanese femininity. ODISHON is abysmally evil, though nonetheless melancholic. Love will tear us apart.

PLAY MISTY FOR ME / USA 1971

Directed by Clint Eastwood. Written by Jo Heims. Camera: Bruce Surtees. Music: Dee Barton. With Clint Eastwood, Jessica Walter, Donna Mills, John Larch, Irene Harway

There are many films about spurned women seeking brutal revenge (e.g. FATAL ATTRACTION), or maniacal fans wanting to devour their star's root and branch (e.g. MISERY). But none of those films is as thrilling as Clint Eastwood's early contribution.

A woman who adores a radio DJ manages to intrude into his life and to seduce him. When the (for him) rather casual affair ends, the real horror begins – because the lady does not want to give up "her" star. Omitting most of the usual clichés in her acting, Jessica Walter excels as the lethal groupie from Hell.

POSSESSION

Directed by Andrzej Zulawski. Music by Andrzej Korzynski. Camera: Bruno Nuytten. With Isabelle Adjani, Sam Neill, Heinz Bennent

Adjani's portrayal of Anna, a woman who suffers a complete psychopathic collapse in POSSESSION, is amongst the most harrowing ever filmed. The scene in a subway where she goes completely insane, screaming and injuring herself and finally suffering a miscarriage, is without equal. After this, Anna becomes a bloody knife-murderer and hallucinates(?) a sexual affair with a bizarre, inhuman creature which lurks in the gloomy, haunted-dungeon ambience of her apartment – an abode just once removed from Deneuve's in REPULSION. The film climaxes in bloody murder and suicide.

POSSESSION is an extraordinary movie whose complexities cannot be detailed here; suffice to say that Adjani's performance as a woman possessed remains the movie's central focus, and a key moment in the register of psychotic screen females.

REPULSION / GB 1965

Directed by Roman Polanski. Written by Roman Polanski & Gérard Brach. Camera: Gilbert Taylor. Music: Chico Hamilton. With Catherine Deneuve, Yvonne Furneaux, John Fraser, Ian Hendry, Patrick Wymark

Since Roman Polanski made this surreal, black-and-white nightmare in 1965, sexual hysteria has a face: Catherine Deneuve, who is at the centre of this study of creeping madness leading to hallucinations and murder. Her character, Carole, the manicurist, is based on a girl Polanski and Brach had known in St. Germain-des-Près in Paris: "What at first sight impressed me most besides her beauty was the image of sweet innocence and dry relaxation she offered. Only when she began to live together with one of our friends did another side of her personality appear. He told us strange stories about her, how she was at the same time attracted and repelled by sex, and had sudden outbursts of violence."

The way REPULSION exaggerated this true case and distilled it into a murderous film has become a stifling milestone in cinema history.

SINGLE WHITE FEMALE / USA 1992

Directed by Barbet Schroeder. Written by Don Roos. Camera: Luciano Tovoli. Music: Howard Shore. With Jennifer Jason Leigh, Bridget Fonda, Steven Weber, Peter Friedman, René Estevez

It is a rare case that cinema sides with the shy, mousy faces in the crowd. Those losers are usually contrasted to self-confident beautiful heroes and made to burn with envy and, finally, convert to Evil. Barbet Schroeder's psycho-thriller is no exception, and confronts Bridget Fonda as a tasty, attractive young woman with the "mousy" Jennifer Jason Leigh, who moves into her apartment as a sub-tenant. Dreaming of being like Bridget, Jennifer plots and schemes, changes her looks, and eventually kills. Of course, she is doomed to lose in Hollywood's clear-cut Good/Evil-universe, and peace is re-established after her deserved death.

STRAIGHT-JACKET / USA 1964

Directed by William Castle. Written by Robert Bloch. Camera: Arthur Arling. Music: Van Alexander. With Joan Crawford, Diane Baker, Leif Erickson, Howard St. John, John Anthony Hayes

One of the most beautiful psycho-slasher-films from the King of B's, William Castle, who had already produced the awesome HOMICIDAL, and here exploited many ideas from the then already released Aldrich masterpieces WHATEVER HAPPENED TO BABY JANE? and HUSH, HUSH, SWEET CHARLOTTE. Of course, Castle's film is black-and-white too. The newly-wed farmer's wife catching her husband red-handed with his mistress, then slaying both with an axe in front of her little daughter and thus ending up in a mental institution is a showpiece for Joan Crawford and her unmistakable half-diva, half-witch flair. You have to love her exaggerated, mannered acting derived from the large resource of Freudian clichés. When Joan Crawford plays on the piano of psychology, it always gives you the creeps.

Relevant films already discussed in Part One:

LES ABYSSES
AI NO CORRIDA
BIG BAD MAMA
BLOODY MAMA
CRAZY MAMA
THE GRISSOM GANG
ILSA, SHE-WOLF OF THE SS
JITSUROKU ABE SADA
THE MAIDS
VIOLETTE NOZIERE

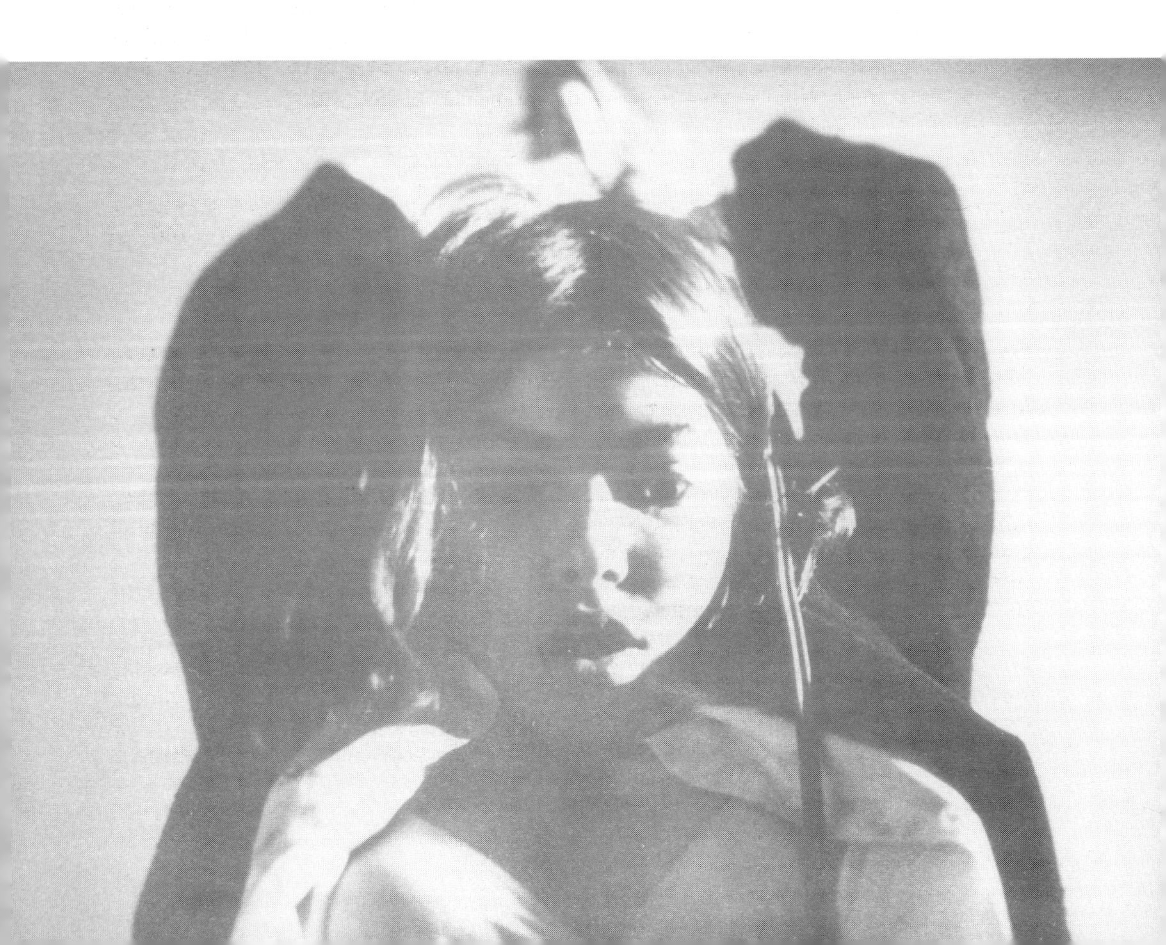

CHAPTER SIX
LOVE AND A BULLET: KILLER COUPLES

"Love me fierce in danger"
–James Ellroy, *White Jazz*

Films about amok killers and mass murderers are mostly situated in a masculine world of thoughts and feelings, filled with psychotic rituals of manliness and testosterone-fuelled sexual fantasies. Here women are restricted to a cathartic function, as in TAXI DRIVER, or are cast as hapless victims.

The few films about murderous amok-women, as we have seen, oscillate between *femme fatale* images and really strong women fighting their bloody way through a man-dominated world. Yet they all tell in a very radical, pessimistic way about the struggle of the sexes (e.g. Abel Ferrara's MS. 45) and emphasize the solitude and incompatibility of man and woman.

But in the road movie genre there are a lot of films which can be described in terms like obsession, passion, or death-lust, focusing on extraordinary men and women unified by their murderous instincts. Bonnie and Clyde, Kit and Holly, Clarence and Alabama, etc. Melodramas about young lovers crossing moral as well as geographical boundaries as they flee law and order. Love rises above itself in the face of death, many theorists of eroticism say, as it develops into an obsession unknown to normal relationships.

Digression: On The Road To Nowhere

"In the day we sweat it out in the streets of a runaway American dream. At night we ride through mansions of glory in suicide machines. Sprung from cages out on Highway 9, chrome wheeled, fuel injected. And steppin' out over the line"
–Bruce Springsteen, "Born To Run"

Keep moving. Constant movement is the quintessence of rushing, vertiginous epics of flight. The journey is an end in itself, the protagonists live on the road. Arrival, staying in one place signals stagnation, conformity, standstill – and when finally the cops arrive, even death. As long as you keep driving, the road promises freedom and adventure.

Those who seek perpetual motion, need wide, endless roads, landscapes where you can completely lose yourself. This makes road movies about criminal couples a prototypically American genre. The vastness of the American continent offers enough hideouts for asphalt-outlaws and gun-crazy drifters. Nowhere else is the cult of the car celebrated more extremely.

Sometime in the middle of the Sixties the road movie replaced the Western in "the land of infinite possibilities". The outlaw bartered his horse for a Harley Davidson, the cowboy became a trucker, and the sheriffs became highway patrolmen. Film critic Joe Hembus once wrote that "the freedom of the west was a crucial quality for the Westerner. When the west became the frontier between the wild free territory and civilisation, it was delivered to the dialectic of freedom and order." Road movie characters rebel against this order with their bikes and souped-up cars. The universe of lonesome highways and dusty roads has its own laws. The official guardians of law and order are nothing but enemies. Speed limits are breached with obscene gestures before you rush away with a howling engine. It is an apolitical, hedonistic revolt into the eternal street-myth of "freedom".

Whereas typical Seventies road movies (personified by cheesy actors like Burt Reynolds) only celebrate the cheap thrill of breakng speed limits and the beauty of polished Chevrolets or Corvettes, and basically stand for the true "upright" America where you are allowed to defend yourself against narrow-minded state troopers, other films are rather on the dark side of the road. BONNIE & CLYDE is one of the central classics where the vision of stepping out of society and living on the road ends in calamity. Or consider Martin Sheen and Sissy Spacek as juvenile killers in BADLANDS, fleeing in a Chevy through dreamlike, hallucinatory landscapes leaving behind piles of corpses. Finally there is Oliver Stone's hyper-real media-spectacle NATURAL BORN KILLERS, where Juliette Lewis and Woody Harrelson are sent on a horror-trip down Highway 666.

Rebellion with a gun inthe hand against parents, society, and the law, often begins with ardent romanticism, but ends in traumatic, blood-splattered one-way streets.

Thrill Crazy... Kill Crazy...Gun Crazy: Crimes Of Passion

"We discuss murder and the murder act. Murder takes the wheel of the Cadillac. And death climbs in the back. O Deanna. This is a car. O Deanna. This is a gun. O Deanna. And this is day number one. You are my friend now and my partner. And I ain't down here for your money. I ain't down here for your love. I'm down here for your soul."

–Nick Cave, "Deanna"

The two young gangsters' death in BONNIE & CLYDE is shockingly staged. Yet because they have lived their time before this moment in liberated anarchy, they seem to be satisfied. When two lovers knowing well they are going to die turn into the street of no return, this also means that their common passion will become eternal before it is washed away in mundane married life and domestic crises. Only a Magnum .45 makes love eternal. This "conservation" of passion, which is never eternal in everyday life, makes killer road movies perhaps the most romantic of killer films. The bloodstained hands of a man and woman clasping each other before they become weak in so many film endings, symbolically say that it is better to die together in the furnace of love than to get old together. Better to burn out than to fade away.

Many real killers were fascinated by this idea (we know the poems of Bonnie Parker and the notes of Charlie Starkweather), yet the best films about such gun-dominated romances reverberate with ambiguity. Though their makers are fascinated with the "live fast, die young" myths, they break with them at the same time. In BONNIE & CLYDE something like obsession shimmers through in short moments, but finally their dream turns out to be an affair of the more conventional kind. Even the rebellious mysticism running through the film seems rather a comment on 1967 and its youth revolts than the expression of *amour fou* going berserk. The seemingly rather detached gangsters Doc McCoy and Carol in THE GETAWAY (1972), Sam Peckinpah's study of violence, don't fall prey to an (anti-)heroic death. Peckinpah, who had been raving in death-embracing catharsis 1969 in THE WILD BUNCH (some gunmen sacrifice themselves for a friend) turns a blind eye this time, and grants the killer couple a happy ending without remorse behind the Mexican border. So he is milder than Jim Thompson, the author of *Getaway*, who lets the couple roast in a

GUN CRAZY (1949)

Kafkaesque city of Hell.

While the murders of Doc McCoy and Carol or Bonnie and Clyde are still partly *crimes de logique*, partly *crimes de passion* (money and love motivate them in equal parts), the late film noir opus GUN CRAZY (1949) is fully devoted to abysmal passion. A common love of weapons mixes with sexual desire to chain the lovers until the end. At the beginning we see a little boy staring with shining eyes into the shop-window of a gun store. Glass rattles, he steals a revolver. The boy is arrested and set straight by the judge, but his *penchant* for guns remains. As he grows up he does not become a friendly average citizen, but a perfect marksman. One day he meets a girl who more than matches him in an amusement park. She is a trick shooter who does not only aim better but, with her aggressive sexuality, totally captivates the passive man. Under her command the two begin to rob banks and to kill. Peggy Cummins as the gun-crazy lady, enjoys the thrill of killing and the lust of fleeing more than most women in the history of cinema before or after her. Director Joseph H. Lewis emphasizes the relationship between crime, depravity, and sex even more than Sam Peckinpah and Arthur Penn, who were operating in more liberal times. When she shoots someone, the woman's eyes shine like in the moment of orgasm. The film's promotional tagline is perfectly pitched: "Thrill Crazy...Kill Crazy...Gun Crazy". Of course, the end of GUN CRAZY is inextricably connected with death. John Dall kills his girlfriend in an argument with the friends of his youth. On the surface this seems to be Hollywood's victory of reason over wild devouring passion, but Dall is so fucked-up and broken that he won't be able to join "the right side" anyway. Neither a long farewell, nor a shared grave in the foggy swamp is granted the lovers. Basically, GUN CRAZY seems to distrust death romanticism too.

BADLANDS is the climax of the love-on-the-run-genre and a mystery at the same time. A disturbing, all-time milestone about the distorted dream of freedom. "The critics talked about influences and in most cases referred to films I had never seen,″ said director Terence Malick in one of his rare interviews. "My influences were books like *The Hardy Boys, Swiss Family Robinson, Tom Sawyer, Huck Finn* – all involving an innocent in a drama over his or her head. I wanted to make the film like a fairy-tale, out of time, like *Treasure Island*. I hoped this would take away a little bit from the radicalism of the film's violence and also keep the film's dream-like essence. Books for children are full of violence; Long John Silver cuts the throats of his faithful companions. Kit and Holly even believe that they live in a fairy-tale:"

Dangerous Friendships

One of the two alone would have never become a killer, but together they mutually trigger off acts of violence. Together their positive and negative poles melt to something potentially violent. This is what is often stated about killer-couples.

Not all killer couples function on the road, not all are male/female. The mutual destruction trope also works with partners of the same sex. The court claimed that neither Nathan Leopold, nor Richard Loeb would have ever killed a child, if they had not known each other. In Truman Capote's novel *In Cold Blood* Perry Smith and Dick Hickock only become capable of annihilating an entire family for a ridiculous sum because they are so dependent on each other. Richard Brooks' cinematic adaptation also follows this theory.

Juliet Hulme and Pauline Parker, the matricides from New Zealand sensitively portrayed by Peter Jackson in HEAVENLY CREATURES (1994), got into a highly explosive maelstrom of emotions. Jackson seems to be convinced that neither Juliet nor Pauline had murderous feelings. Only together did they become a dangerous "third person". Almost always in such relationships one half is more dominant, the other more passive. Quite often these roles reverse later on (Parker/Hulme, Smith/Hickock). Yet HEAVENLY CREATURES distrusts the Yellow Press fantasies of the lesbian killer couple. It need not always be openly mutual sexual dependence like in the case of Leopold and Loeb that triggers off murderous impulses. Games of dominance and submission can also be played in an asexual context.

It seems appropriate that one of the emotionally most radical films dealing with such an "innocent" but bloody friendship between two men is no product of occidental cinema. In the Western world the psychological relationship between male muscles and ammunition, sexuality and weapons is regarded as exhaustively investigated (by theorists like Germany's Klaus Theweleit), and it is already taken for granted, or has even become a cliché. An Asian director like John Woo is free of such interpretations. The myths of "honour, courage, and loyalty" are unbroken for him and devoid of any sexual connotation. A deep friendship between two killer-characters does not automatically mean latent homosexuality in the modern action cinema from Hong Kong. Here a wounded mercenary can be nursed by a fellow killer

WILD AT HEART

and one does not assume a perverted sub-text.

In Woo's modern action classic THE KILLER (1989), a contract killer meets a cop. Finally they fight side by side. Corpses pave their way. As if in a Greek tragedy, everybody dies around them. John Woo casually combines scenes which tremendously glorify violence with scenes of genuine, profound grief. Again and again he smashes the happy moments of his protagonists, and finally lets everything drown in a slow motion inferno of bullet-holes with fountains of blood spurting out. The viewer who not only enjoys the oceans of blood as a splatter-fan, but also gives the story a chance and entirely loses himself in the film, is captivated by narcotic catharsis.

A film about another masculine duo standing for violence and terror seems completely contrary and highly cynical. The male killer duo Cohen and Tate in the American film COHEN AND TATE (1988) by Eric Red, are only held together by money and a strange love-hate relationship. In the course of an admittedly thrilling story Eric Red dissects male rites and crime film clichés. And as you might have already guessed, death is waiting at the end; but unlike John Woo, it comes as completely unaffecting and without a trace of redemption.

"Wild Hearts" And "True Romances": The Nineties

"This whole world's wild at heart and weird on top!"
–Lula (Laura Dern) in WILD AT HEART

Life must be like rockabilly, wild and hard. "It's a matter of rockin' and rollin', livin' fast, dyin' young and leavin' a good-looking corpse." This is the philosophy of Clarence, a young cinema-freak identifying with Robert De Niro in TAXI DRIVER, living in a dreamworld of kung fu films and superhero comics. Moreover, he is even haunted by the ghost of Elvis Presley! Clarence loves Alabama , a platinum blonde white trash-callgirl with a golden heart and a foible for leopard-skin and shrill pop fashion. The two get into a brutal maelstrom of gloomy Mafiosi, icy-cold drug-smugglers, and outbursts of slow motion violence. But Clarence and Alabama dive through all this because they are passionately in love, no ordinary relationship but TRUE ROMANCE (1993). It´s the old story of "love me till death, kiss me in a hail of bullets!"

When you hear the sentimental title melody at the beginning of Tony Scott's film and Alabama's off-screen voice talking of true love, this could be a beautiful moment of cinema. Unfortunately, the emphasis is on *could be* because everything in this scene is second-hand, has been shamelessly stolen from Terence Malick's BADLANDS. There it was Sissy Spacek, who spoke from the off in a innocent young girl's voice. Even the same musical theme, only slightly altered, is used in TRUE ROMANCE. Recycling of ideas *à* la Hollywood.

There are many *déjà-vu* moments like that in TRUE ROMANCE. Allegedly, all the original stories have already been told. So what remains is the re-ordering of elements, courtesy of shooting star Quentin Tarantino. His films are prototypically examples that it is not reality anymore that provides the models, but film itself. TRUE ROMANCE is no new movie about an old subject, namely "Murderous Couples on the Run", no new BONNIE & CLYDE, or GETAWAY, but a film *about* those films, a metafictional statement entirely feeding on cinematic myths and clichés. In the brave new world of quotation-cinema of the Nineties, the term "true romance" is ironical in itself.

NATURAL BORN KILLERS, another film about a killer couple, could have been an ideal example for such a post-modernist disaster, but thematizing this danger itself the film does not fail at all, even though Oliver Stone's *tour de force* – through an incessant flood of stimuli – exceeds the films mentioned above by far. Of course (and this seems to be the doom of current cinema) this film too is only a reflection, a meta-film unthinkable without its forerunners from BADLANDS to GUN CRAZY. The road-movie romanticism conjured up in NATURAL BORN KILLERS in several scenes is an illusion; the film's surface is too perfectionist, too cold and calculated to purvey genuine passion.

In 1995, a film really trying to avoid the irony-traps of comparable films and following the great tradition of the Seventies was released in America. LOVE & A .45 (1994), the debut of the young director C.M. Talkington, sends Watty and Starlene, two proletarian heroes from the ghettos of American trailer parks on a killer tour together. The premise sounds good: the trigger-happy lovers enjoy the ecstasy of an aimless escape as did the protagonists of GETAWAY, BADLANDS and many others before them. Screeching tyres, whipping bullets, country songs from the radio, the myth of freedom on the road is investigated again in all its ambiguity. But soon you realize that Talkington's film is no exception from typical post-modern movie-making, and that the young director goes as far as including quotes from both Tarantino and Stone, besides numerous more classical film references. It´s the Hell of quotation-cinema again – but at least in LOVE & A .45 it's a very entertaining Hell.

KILLER COUPLE FILMS: A SELECTION

BAISE-MOI (FUCK ME aka RAPE ME) / France 2000

Directed by Virginie Despentes and Coralie Trinh Thi. Written by Coralie Trinh Thi after the book of Virginie Despentes. Camera: Benoit Chamaillard. Music: Varou Jan. With Raffaela Anderson, Karen Lancaume, Delphine MacCarty, Lisa Marshall, Estelle Isaac, Herve P. Gustave

Flash-frames from the dirty underbelly of Paris. Nadine kills her fellow-lodger in an argument. Manu shoots her brother after he has raped her. The two young murderesses meet by chance and go on an amok joyride across France. Cops, passers-by, lovers insisting on safer sex, the clientèle of a swinger club – they all die in the muzzle-flash of the carefree killer couple.

Fucked-up ghetto-chic and explicit genital shots, heavy guns and jerking penises. Though the film is obviously about women's self-determination in a concrete macho world, it seems above all greedy for the tough guys' respect. Every frame of this low budget digital video production screams "provocation". Every frame wants to be hardcore. Yet the young Parisian author and ex-stripper Virginie Despentes hasn't realised that the borders of pure exploitation aren't that far away. Instead of the story of an immoral life of transgression, she has created an unwitting exploitation film. No emotion, explicitness galore.

COHEN AND TATE / USA 1989

Written and directed by Eric Red. Camera: Victor J. Kemper. Music: Bill Conti. With Roy Scheider, Adam Baldwin, Harley Cross

Talented Eric Red, who wrote the script for HITCHER and NEAR DARK, created a masterpiece of the late Eighties with this three-character thriller. Unfortunately, it flopped terribly in the cinema as well as on video, and remains in obscurity. An unequal and lethal duo is in its centre: Cohen, an ageing killer with greyish hair and a hearing aid, and his adjutant Tate, who looks like the member of a hardcore punk band in his leather jacket and Doc Martens boots, and simply loves the sight of blood. They kidnap the nine-year-old boy Travis, who has witnessed a Mafia execution, and try to bring him to their clientele right across America. The only setting: the road, the endless Texan landscape. A road movie loaded with enmity and explosion-like outbursts of violence from the beginning until the end of the trip, culminating in a finale executed by Eric Red with an unflinching urgency rarely to be seen nowadays.

FREEWAY II: CONFESSIONS OF A TRICKBABY / USA 1999

Directed and written by Matthew Bright. Music: J.J. Holiday. With Natasha Lyonne, María Celedonio, Vincent Gallo, April Telek, Bob Dawson, Jennifer Griffin, Max Perlich

Though the film's title implies a sequel of the 1996 serial killer-comedy FREEWAY, Matthew Bright, who directed both underground flicks, follows a completely different path here. CONFESSIONS OF A TRICKBABY lifts the immoral tendencies of the first production into unheard-of dimensions and offers a long-awaited girls-on-the-run variant of the sub-genre "Murderous Couples". Compared to the skinny 15-year-old Crystal and her psychotic lesbian friend Cyclona, THELMA AND LOUISE (whose single killing was merely self-defence) seem like old-fashioned housewives. For these two young refugees don't spare anybody or anything on their amok trip, which leads them across America to Mexico. It is a mind-fucking, over-the-top-journey into the soft white trash underbelly, full of necrophilia, paedophilia, bingeing and purging, paint-sniffing and killing. In the end there is chaos and mayhem and Vincent Gallo (in drag) as sadistic Sister Gomez, who reveals himself as the witch from the "Jack and Jill" fairy-tale of the brothers Grimm. Sounds weird? It is. Where BAISE-

MOI, for example, the French version of the theme, tries desperately to provoke the audience, Bright tells his wicked and crooked fairy-tale unbelievably light-footedly and full of pitch-black humour. Sick, sexy and subversive fun.

FUNNY GAMES / Austria 1997

Directed and written by Michael Haneke. Camera: Jürgen Jürges. Music: John Zorn and others. With Susanne Lothar, Ulrich Mühe, Arno Frisch, Frank Giering, Doris Kunstmann

Two young men of seemingly good manners who call themselves Paul and Peter, enter a family's holiday domicile under the pretence that they need eggs. What is only a little intrusion at first, soon becomes a trip to Hell for the residents. The husband, his wife and their teenage son are locked up and slowly tormented to death by the strangers. The camera always tries to push the viewer into the perspective of an accomplice, who watches the disturbing FUNNY GAMES until the bitter end.

This is definitely the most controversial film by the Austrian director Michael Haneke, whose icily unemotional cinema feeds on deep moral perplexity. As in BENNY'S VIDEO, he takes the brutalization of the youth by media imagery and social violence as a starting point. On the one hand Haneke wants to hold up the mirror to an entire generation with the irrational sadism of his male couple, on the other the extreme violence of FUNNY GAMES should act as a deterrent. Potential voyeurs shall be healed forever by watching such films.

Two bold aims that can only have their origin in the mind of an ivory-towered intellectual. Yet grotesquely, and in spite of its built-in alienation effects, Haneke's anti-violence epic is very popular in the hardcore and splatter community.

THE GETAWAY / USA 1972

Directed by Sam Peckinpah. Written by Walter Hill after Jim Thompson's novel. Camera: Lucien Ballard. Music: Quincy Jones. With Steve McQueen, Ali McGraw, Ben Johnson, Sally Struthers, Al Lettieri, Slim Pickens, Richard Bright.

Like many other directors the great Sam Peckinpah was also shipwrecked in his attempt to screen a novel by the hard-boiled genius Jim Thompson. Whereas the novel never allows us to believe in a real togetherness of man (Doc McCoy) and woman (Carol) and ends in an existentialist Hell, Peckinpah grants a happy ending to the killer couple. Besides this flaw, the lack of the novel's uncompromising mercilessness, the film fits perfectly into Peckinpah's oeuvre, situated somewhere between his absolute masterpieces (THE WILD BUNCH) and straight craftsmanship (THE KILLER ELITE, 1975). Moreover, the plot's gloomy sub-plot, with the film's second kill-crazy couple, Al Lettieri and Sally Struthers, outshines Steve McQueen's and Ali McGraw's cool and ultimately anodyne presence.

THE GETAWAY / USA 1994

Directed by Roger Donaldson. Written by Walter Hill after Jim Thompson's novel. Camera: Peter Menzies Jr. Music: Mark Isham. With Alec Baldwin, Kim Basinger, Michael Madsen, Jennifer Tilly, James Woods

Roger Donaldson did not try to adapt Jim Thompson's novel adequately for the screen. He failed to take this opportunity, and merely made an exact remake of the Seventies version. Walter Hill recycled his old Peckinpah script and repeated the same mistakes. THE GETAWAY, 1994 again has a happy ending in sunny Mexico, and hence lacks Jim Thompson's gloomy and existentialist finale. Moreover, an unmotivated and dully acting Alec Baldwin (who showed his undisputed talent in MIAMI BLUES) and the over-taxed anti-talent Kim Basinger as protagonists, make the film rather worse than the original. Nevertheless, the minor parts make it worth seeing: Michael

KALIFORNIA

"RESERVOIR DOGS" Madsen as a cool psychopath, Jennifer Tilly as a sex-crazy witch beneath her housewife's apron who stops at nothing to sate her desire, and James Woods as an insidious gangster boss.

GUN CRAZY aka DEADLY IS THE FEMALE / USA 1949

Directed by Joseph H. Lewis. Written by Mac Kinlay Kantor & Millard Kaufman. Camera: Russel Harlan. Music: Victor Young. With Peggy Cummings, John Dall, Berry Kroeger, Morris Carnovsky, Russ Tamblyn

An icy-cold trick shooter (incisive as a noir *femme fatale*: Peggy Cummings) and a labile young man (helplessly lost in the web of passion: John Dall) are chained together by their love for guns. But ecstatic bliss only lasts for a few moments. As the noir-expert Foster Hirsch states: "Great pop psychology, GUN CRAZY makes passing stabs at a variety of meaty subjects: the place of violence in American life, the link between violence and sex; the emasculating obsession with masculinity."

Hardly a film before or afterwards so openly combined gun fetishism and erotic desire. Even Kathryn Bigelow screwed it up midway through BLUE STEEL. "Their love for each other was more fatal than their love for their guns", the director Joseph H. Lewis notes.

GUNCRAZY / USA 1993

Directed by Tamra Davis. Written by Matthew Bright. Camera: Lisa Rinzler. Music: Ed Tomney. With Drew Barrymore, James LeGros, Billy Drago, Joe Dallesandro

To begin with: this is no remake of Joseph H. Lewis' B-movie classic. The nice protagonists (Barrymore, LeGros) and the legendary minor actors (Dallesandro), the trendy hard soundtrack by Helmet and Sonic Youth, the beautiful American scenery, and, last but not least, Tamra Davis' credibility-bonus (she had made a name for herself with numerous rap/underground rock videos) – all these bonus factors bestow an attracting and interesting aura on this grunge-version of the killer couple on the road. Yet the film cannot live up to its great promise. Though, or rather because, all the glowingly hip ingredients perfectly fit together, GUNCRAZY does not work as a whole, but gives more the impression of a patchwork MTV confection.

KALIFORNIA / USA 1993

Directed by Dominic Sena. Written by Tim Metcalf. Camera: Bojan Bazelli. Music: Carter Burwell. With Brad Pitt, Juliette Lewis, David Duchovny, Michelle Forbes

A young Yuppie writer (future *X-Files* star Duchovny) is working on a book about the American media's favourite topic, serial killers and mass murderers. Hence he is going to embark on an all-across-America tour in order to visit the scenes of the most notorious cases and do research. He takes his stylish Yuppie girlfriend with him. On the road they meet a couple of hitchhikers, the filthy redneck Brad Pitt and his very young and naïve girlfriend Juliette Lewis (reprising their white trash killer double act from TOO YOUNG TO DIE/1994). They give the dubious duo a lift without having the faintest idea that they have picked up a wanted serial killer. What follows is a confrontation of Good (designer clothes, college education, uninspired sex, flirtation with the forces of the dark) and Evil (filthy second-hand clothes, proletarian origin, rough macho-sex, spiritaul corruption, eruptive violence). Brad Pitt and Juliette Lewis are experienced and entertaining in their performance of white trash criminality; the problem is that KALIFORNIA is cliché-infested cinema for exactly the clientele represented by the Yuppie couple. Their motto: a little bit of the bloodthirsty, filthy, horny road for a change, then back into the safety of our designer loft.

THE KILLER / Hongkong 1989

Written and directed by John Woo. Camera: Wong Wing-Hang. Music: Lowell Lowe. With Chow Yun Fat, Danny Lee, Sally Yeh, Kenneth Tsang

A contract killer, a cop, and a night-club singer, a handful of friends and a superior force of bad guys. A fatal plot and 100,000 bullets. John Woo further developed the gangland-style begun with A BETTER TOMORROW (1986), in this ballistic epic starring Chow Yun Fat (a modern Asian version of Delon/Belmondo/Eastwood). Wading knee-deep in human emotions, ordeals and guts, this roller-coaster ride through weird though nevertheless precisely choreographed action sequences, represents the climax of Woo's art and craftsmanship. *Film Comment* magazine notes that "every scene shows more tears than LOVE STORY and more explicit violence than THE WILD BUNCH".

LOVE AND A .45 / USA 1994

Written and directed by C. M. Talkington. Camera: Tom Richmond. Music: Tom Verlaine, Butthole Surfers, F.S.K. , Johnny Cash, Mazzy Star, Roger Miller. With Gil Bellows, Renee Zellweger, Rory Cochrane, Peter Fonda

Just at the time of collapses of the stock market, an enormous gap between the rich and the poor, and a daily increasing number of homeless people in the streets, the USA was experiencing the comeback of white trash romanticism. Suddenly it was cool to be dull, poor, and proletarian. Although this movie rides on the peak of the dubious wave of "white scum", it is at least an escape film full of breathtaking speed, action, violence and sex. Some US critics praise C.M. Talkington's debut as the ultimate

NATURAL BORN KILLERS

"Bonnie and Clyde"-style movie of the Nineties, though Gregg Araki's similar THE DOOM GENERATION, released the following year, pushes it in terms of slick sex, violence and twisted humour.

NATURAL BORN KILLERS / USA 1994

Directed by Oliver Stone. Written by David Veloz, Richard Rutkowski & Oliver Stone after an exposé by Quentin Tarantino. Camera: Robert Richardson. Soundtrack: Budd Car. With Juliette Lewis, Woody Harrelson, Tommy Lee Jones, Robert Downey Jr

The conspiracy theorist and self-appointed preacher of US cinema has landed a surprisingly big success. Though most of Oliver Stone's previous films turned out to be artistic disasters, NATURAL BORN KILLERS clinically exaggerates the American serial killer circus for its own ends. Machine-gun editing cuts deep wounds into the spectator's eyes, and the excellent soundtrack pulverizes the ears. Stone perfectly manufactures quotes of all kinds: white trash culture, pulp novels, noise music, industrial culture, classic road movies, etc. Beside its stupendous formal adaptation, its contextual position makes the film interesting. Stone, the old would-be Nietzschean, openly takes sides: against television, the Yellow Press, the police, and the rest of the world, in favour of true love in bloodlust on the old deserted highway.

PERDITA DURANGO aka DANCE WITH THE DEVIL / USA-Mexico 1998

Directed by Alex De La Iglesia. Written by Barry Gifford after his own novel. Camera: Flavio Martínez Labiano. Music: Simon Boswell. With Rosie Perez, Javier Bardem, Harley Cross, James Gandolfini, Screamin' Jay Hawkins

Those who have seen David Lynch's post-modernist road movie/fairy tale WILD AT HEART might remember the Mexican moll Perdita (played by Isabella Rosselini). Barry Gifford, the author of the book staged another novella in the same neo-Noir cosmos and put this minor character into the centre: *Perdita Durango*. And Alex de la Iglesia, Spain's most radical genre innovator (EL DIA DE LA BESTIA, 1995), made a film of it. This time it's Rosie Perez who plays the tough Latina and prowls the Texan highways together with her sadistic, homicidal, voodoo-priest lover Romeo (unbelievably monstrous: Javier Bardem).

Runaway couple romanticism, trash culture, blues, religious fanaticism, voodoo, sexual craving and an overdose of violence far beyond the borders of what censorship might be able to digest. Fully conscious of following the icon David Lynch, de la Iglesia has stuffed so much into this illegitimate WILD AT HEART sequel that one might expect the final result to burst in its profusion. Yet the opulent, sampled mix works fine, and this has to do with one simple fact: de la Iglesia seems to be a very obsessed person. A one-hundred-percent-passionate aficionado of the delirious dark aspects of pop culture. You can feel his intelligent fandom, a fandom that doesn't only copy pulp and hard-boiled myths but distils something new out of them at every angle. Oliver Stone in NATURAL BORN KILLERS finally demands some distance from his killer creations, but de la Iglesia would definitely share his apartment with Perdita and Romeo.

THEY LIVE BY NIGHT / USA 1948

Directed by Nicholas Ray. Written by Charles Schnee & Nicholas Ray after the novel "Thieves Like Us" by Edward Anderson. Camera: George E. Diskant. Music: Leigh Harline. With Cathy O'Donnel, Farley Granger, Howard da Silva, Jay C. Flippen, Helen Craig

One of the most highly romantic approaches to the theme of the criminal couple. Nicholas Ray's lovers on the run are less neurotic than related couples in other films. They lack the latently psychotic, trigger-happy element of GUN CRAZY. If Bowie (Farley Granger) had not been born into a criminal existence without escape, he and his girlfriend Keechie (Cathy O'Donnel) would have become a perfectly ordinary couple. They are two innocent protagonists, helplessly locked into a merciless film noir-world and much too weak to break out. A low score on the psycho-killer scale.

TRUE ROMANCE / USA 1993

Directed by Tony Scott. Written by Quentin Tarantino. Camera: Jeffrey Kimball. Music: Hans Zimmer. With Christian Slater, Patricia Arquette, Dennis Hopper, Christopher Walken, Gary Oldman, Brad Pitt

A film with a smooth, commercial-compatible surface and a wild exciting core. Quentin Tarantino knows a lot about the obsessions related to trash culture his heroes fall prey to. But Tony Scott, a rather plain and conventional Hollywood aesthete (TOP GUN, 1986) films the script in exactly the wrong way. He drowns the road movie romanticism in neon-blue images similar to TV commercials and emphasizes the ironic aspects instead of the gloomy and deadly. Nevertheless, when Dennis Hopper and Christopher Walken engage in a lethally funny conversation, when Patricia Arquette slays a Mafioso in an unleashed orgasm of murder, or kisses her injured lover in a hail of bullets, the form becomes unimportant and TRUE ROMANCE generates bloody and beautiful soap-bubbles of Pop.

WILD AT HEART / USA 1990

Directed by David Lynch. Written by David Lynch after a story by Barry Gifford. Camera: Fred Elmes. Music: Angelo Badalamenti. With Nicolas Cage, Laura Dern, Willem Dafoe, Harry Dean Stanton, Diane Ladd, Isabella Rossellini, Crispin Glover

Sailor wears a skin-tight snake leather jacket, his blonde playmate Lula skin-tight leopard-print dresses. Both like Elvis and speed metal and are on the run in their fancy sports car. They are hunted by the police, because Sailor has slain a guy who had harassed his girl, by Lula's nightmarish family, and, last but not least, they run away from themselves and their torn feelings. As a matter of fact, David Lynch was the first to revive the old myths of the road, love on the run, and the mythical relation of sex and violence in 1990. Moreover, his film became prototypical for the ironical post-modern road movie of the Nineties. Everything in WILD AT HEART is merely illusion, a series of sparkling quotes (BADLANDS, BONNIE & CLYDE, THE WIZARD OF OZ, Elvis Presley, Sam Peckinpah, etc.), but no real life pulsates beyond the surface. As David Lynch has already rewritten the history of film with two of his most intense contributions (ERASERHEAD and BLUE VELVET), this was really a pity. But in 1997 the master of moody, surreal cinema was back to nearly his best form with the bizarre noir trauma LOST HIGHWAY.

Relevant films already discussed in Part One:

BADLANDS
BONNIE AND CLYDE
HEAVENLY CREATURES
THE HONEYMOON KILLERS
IN COLD BLOOD
THE SADIST

CHAPTER SEVEN
MISOGYNY, SLAUGHTER AND GORE: HORROR FILM SLASHERS

In no other genre do mass murderers and serial killers belong more to the standard repertoire than they do in the horror film. Whether it is Norman Bates, the original psycho, Freddie Krueger, the child-slayer resurrected from the fire, Michael Myers, the masked Halloween phantom, or the many razor-blade slashers in Dario Argento's *giallo*-shockers; compared to the scores of serial killers lurking in the vaults of horror cinema, the number of fact-based True Crime films is relatively small.

The fact is that the majority of viewers do not want well-researched background information, nor depressing details of the everyday life of a killer, nor sociological/psychological/philosophical comments on the theme of murder. What they want is thrills, suspense, gore and an escape from their daily routine, not an analytical gaze into the mirror just to find the own monsters inside themselves. This is why cinema has transformed psycho-killers into the modern successors of Frankenstein, Dracula, or the werewolves. For what is part of the metaphysical world, pertaining to the Devil or the living dead, cannot truly seem dangerous for any sensible viewer. Freddy Krueger is forgotten immediately after consumption. But can you claim equal indifference to the protagonist of HENRY, PORTRAIT OF A SERIAL KILLER? He does not bite, but just in his everyday "normality" lurks a plausible nightmare you won't get out of your head so easily.

Yet one should not completely underestimate the horror genre. As a matter of fact, no other popular commercial film genre so explicitly devotes itself to the shadow-zones of the human condition: deformity, rotting flesh, visceral trauma, murder, terror, perverse sexuality, disgust, repulsion, violence, absurdity, madness. In no other celluloid genre are the protagonists annihilated in such brutal, bizarre, and unthinkable ways. Even in the most trivial horror film the viewer is confronted with bloody death, has to consider his/her own mortality. Only too often, via subjective camera, you are forced to be witness, victim, and perpetrator at one and the same time.

The Aesthetics Of Raw Flesh – About Splatter Cinema And Its Roots

It is not unequivocally clear where the origins of modern horror and splatter cinema lie. Yet it is a fact that the voyeuristic impulse to watch perverse atrocities is thousands of years old. Probably, the Roman gladiator fights and other forms of homicidal public entertainment from antiquity can be cited as origins. In the 18th century, essays with titles like "About The Pleasure In Subjects Of Terror", or "An Enquiry Into The Forms Of Misery Evoking Agreeable Feelings" were published in Europe. Besides such reflections, the German *Schauerroman*, and the Gothic horror of Shelley or Byron, the Parisian *Théatre Du Grand Guignol* of 1899 is considered as a forerunner of modern staging of horror. When cinema was introduced into our cultural history, some horror

LAST HOUSE ON THE LEFT

films were among the first epoch-making oeuvres, and the civilizing transition from the spectacle of public executions to screen simulations of death was well and truly underway.

In the course of its development, the horror genre seemed to become more and more some sort of magnifying-glass, making more visible the fears and neuroses of a film's time of production. The classic Universal monsters of the Thirties and the Forties reflect the political and economical insecurity of those decades. And the mirroring of social and cultural atmosphere can be seen most drastically in the films of the Fifties, when the fear of the nuclear bomb and the Cold War bred monsters, freaks, mutations, and mad scientists as never seen on the screen before.

The Real Horror

"I was just making a horor film, and I think the anger and the attitude and all that's there is just there because it was 1968."

–George A. Romero on NIGHT OF THE LIVING DEAD

At the end of the Sixties the horror became downright real. Some keywords: Vietnam, the decline of the hippie ideals, student and race riots, Altamont, the chaos of 1969 (see under *Charles Manson*). The old scenarios of remote castles, spooky cemeteries, or bubbling laboratories were finally replaced by the explosion of violence in reality. Artistic films like Sam Peckinpah's THE WILD BUNCH or Arthur Penn's BONNIE AND CLYDE reacted to that epoch with unbridled and stifling scenarios of realistic violence. As a side effect they tore down the barriers of censorship and helped pave the way for the splatter boom. In 1972 Wes Craven, as a reaction to the violence of Vietnam,

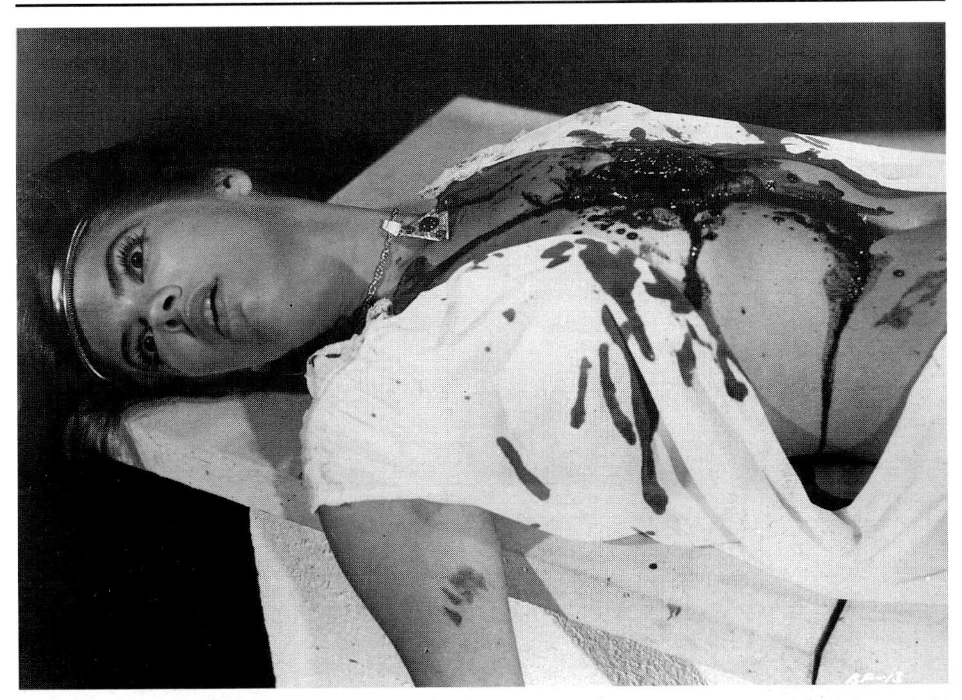

BLOOD FEAST

made one of the most gruelling, stomach-turning and realistic examples of psycho cinema ever, THE LAST HOUSE ON THE LEFT.

The horror genre had lost its innocence, it no longer focused on the old conflict of man vs. monster, but introduced the new struggle of man vs. man. Frankenstein's monster had been dethroned by the serial killer. He was replaced by axe- and chainsaw-swinging weirdoes and slashers in the direct line of succession succession of PSYCHO and the Ed Gein-influenced Norman Bates – usually acknowledged as the prototypical movie slasher.

But the trend for extreme blood-letting, and in particular the genre's predeliction for violence against women, had already been established. Back in the early Sixties, a clever exploitation film-maker previously successfully flooding the drive-in cinemas with "nudie" movies was looking for new lucrative topics. This man, named Herschell Gordon Lewis, finally had the flash of genius of his life: dismembered limbs, torrents of blood, guts, cut-out eyeballs – and all this in "blood-drenched colour", as a cannibal killer harvested body parts from his nubile victims. No major studio would dare to show something like that. And so BLOOD FEAST (1963), Lewis' guts'n'gore debut, may well claim to be the first splatter movie. From then until the middle of the Eighties, there was an era of artistic liberalism in horror, almost everything seemed to be allowed by progressive degree. George Romero (DAWN OF THE DEAD/1980), David Cronenberg (SHIVERS/1977), and Wes Craven (THE HILLS HAVE EYES/1977) produced milestones of the visceral genre. And numerous other independent directors, talented maniacs and lone wolves made films with minimal budgets that revelled in the spilling of blood. That was the golden era of splatter cinema.

BLOOD AND BLACK LACE

The Beautiful Murders Of Dario Argento

" I am in love with the colour red. I dream in red. My nightmares are dominated by red. Red is the colour of happiness and passion, the colour of the journeys into our subconscious. But above all red is the colour of fear and violence."

–Dario Argento

If 1963/4 was a key epoch for American slasher cinema with the release of BLOOD FEAST and its follow-up TWO THOUSAND MANIACS, it was no less important in the annals of Italian horror; for 1964 saw the release of Mario Bava's dazzling, violent killer-thriller SEI DONNE PER L'ASSASSINO (BLOOD AND BLACK LACE), a film often regarded as the first in the Italian genre of the *giallo*. Giallo fims were a type of visually slick murder thriller, usually featuring a plethora of inventive, misogynistic murders. Hundreds were produced over the next two decades, but among the most notable were Giulio Questi's DEATH LAYS AN EGG (1968), Ducio Tessari's THE BLOOD-STAINED BUTTERFLY (1971), and Paolo Cavara's BLACK BELLY OF THE TARANTULA (1971). Some *gialli* reached new heights of screen gore and violence against women, for example Riccardo Freda's IGUANA WITH A TONGUE OF FIRE (1971), Fernando Di Leo's SLAUGHTER HOTEL (1972), Renato Polselli's DELIRIUM (1972), Mario Landi's

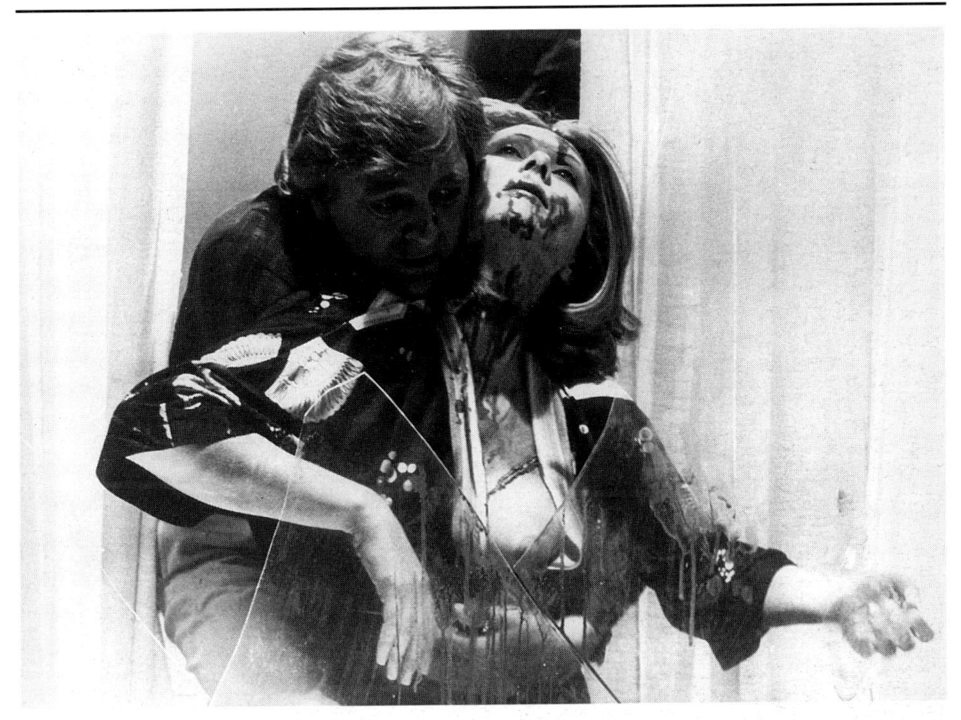

DEEP RED

GORE IN VENICE (1979), Ruggero Deodato's HOUSE ON THE EDGE OF THE PARK (1980), and Lucio Fulci's NEW YORK RIPPER (1982).

But no *giallo* film-maker has ever created such sparkling, sophisticated, blood-red aesthetic monuments to the serial killer as Dario Argento.

Logic and dramaturgy have only minimal importance in the world of Argento: the irrational laws of dream reign there. The maestro has so far worked up his dark violent dreams in a dozen films, psycho-thrillers sharp as razor-blades (CAT O'NINE TAILS/1970, FOUR FLIES ON GREY VELVET/1971) and surrealistic, stylized splatter-shockers (SUSPIRIA/1977, INFERNO/1979). Films where gory terror meets decorative elegance, where ultra-modern film technology serves a mind indulging in occultism, mysticism, and morbid visions.

If David Cronenberg personifies the cool intellectual among the dark stars in the cosmos of horror cinema and George Romero the critic of society, then Dario Argento is the last black romanticist, a visionary who still firmly believes in the unity of art and the artist and is, like his idol Edgar Allan Poe, obsessed by the macabre. When Argento himself wears the black gloves holding the unknown murderer's knife, this fits perfectly into his image. "I love my killers", Argento answered when asked about his spleen, "and I'm really good in such scenes. Probably, I'd also be a good killer."

Argento's THE BIRD WITH THE CRYSTAL PLUMAGE (1970) was a new milestone in the *giallo* genre. Many directors from Cinecittá had begun to make weird thrillers in imitation of Edgar Wallace, or Alfred Hitchcock, but hardly anyone generated the claustrophobic intensity of a "genuine" Argento. Unlike other psycho-thrillers his later classic *gialli* like TENEBRE (TENEBRAE aka UNSANE, 1982), or the awesome, unbeatable PROFONDO ROSSO (DEEP RED, 1975) completely lack moral

HALLOWEEN

distance. The murder scenes perversely, though highly elegantly, invite their viewers to take the killer's perspective, to share his gaze. Dario Argento neither wants to tell stories, nor deliver messages, nor celebrate box-office triumphs. He rather wants to exorcise his darkest visions with the camera as a weapon. His best films seem like modern cinematic descendants of the immoral writings of Huysmans, Poe, de Sade, or Baudelaire, created by a philosopher of death cinema.

"In such an intense physical act as murder a very sensitive, somehow deeply erotic relationship is established somewhere between the killer and his victim," says Mr. Argento. "There is something unifying between these acts, an erotic act and a bloodthirsty act. The knife, for instance, is a phallic symbol we all know, hence the link between the two orgasms: the orgasm of death and the sexual orgasm [...] I make films, but I am also a viewer who sides the killer. I cannot leave him alone. My killers are always around me."

Michael, Jason, Freddie: The Serial Killer As Bogeyman And Teenage Hero

Whereas Dario Argento has a genuine relationship to his killers, American splatter directors use the serial killer as a simple means to an end, a vehicle for a plot predominantly consisting of effectively timed moments of shock. In 1978 John Carpenter made a film that not only reserved him a permanent place in the Hall of Fame of horror, but also established an entire sub-genre. HALLOWEEN became the model for a series of subsequent slasher movies in which groups of teenagers (mostly girls) are stalked and butchered by a largely unseen assailant. Any girl discovered having sex by Myers is brutally killed, thereby establishing a cruel refinement to the already misogynist lore of the slasher genre. Only the virginal heroine Jamie Lee Curtis survives.

Michael Myers, the villain with the Halloween mask, is a hybrid like many related slashers. He isn't the rather realistic psycho-killer and maniac of the Sixties and Seventies (cf. LAST HOUSE ON THE LEFT) , but even much less the traditional monster. Myers, as after him Jason Vorhees and Freddy Krueger, exists somewhere in between. He stands for the serial killer from True Crime magazines, but he has a hint of the supernatural about him.

Vorhees, the slaughterer of whole legions of teenagers (his distinguishing feature: an ice-hockey mask), mutates to a zombie-like mega-monster time and again, rising from the dead in the course of the FRIDAY THE 13TH series. (In the first episode his avenging mother is the guilty party, but in the film's weird coda we see the drowned boy rise from the lake in slow motion, thus establishing a quasi-supernatural/oneiric tone for future sequelss).

NIGHTMARE ON ELM STREET (1980) finally elevated the movie slasher from mere mortal to undying monster. In the course of this film and its increasingly jokey sequels, Freddy Krueger, in his typical outfit consisting of hat, striped pullover, and famous razor-clawed glove, beats all grandfathers of horror like Dracula in his accumulation of diabolic tricks and strange powers. Add to this his wise-cracks and sadistic pranks, and you have the perfect modern-day screen slasher. Such serial killer hybrids, transformed into comic-book villains due to their magic faculties, soon won the hearts of the teenage splatter audience. A merchandising market featuring claw-gloves, hockey masks, and killer dolls has flourished since Freddie and co. started out. By the mid-Eighties, the serial killer had become the idol of millions of kids.

Epilogue: Bye, Bye Horror

Splatter films should strain any recipient to his/her breaking-point. They should shake us up, disturb us, and come down like sledgehammers on our nerve fibres. Besides entertainment, they should tell us something about our primal fears and open the door to the most taboo regions of our subconscious. Yet this stench of the slaughterhouse and torture-chamber is lamentably missing in the horror cinema of the last few years. The serial killer above all has degenerated into a random genre cypher. So films like SHOCKER (1989), THE GHOST IN THE MACHINE (1994) or BEYOND BEDLAM (1993), the ten thousandths mutations of Freddy Krueger do not even show the slightest promise of disturbing or scaring us. Instead of using the technical

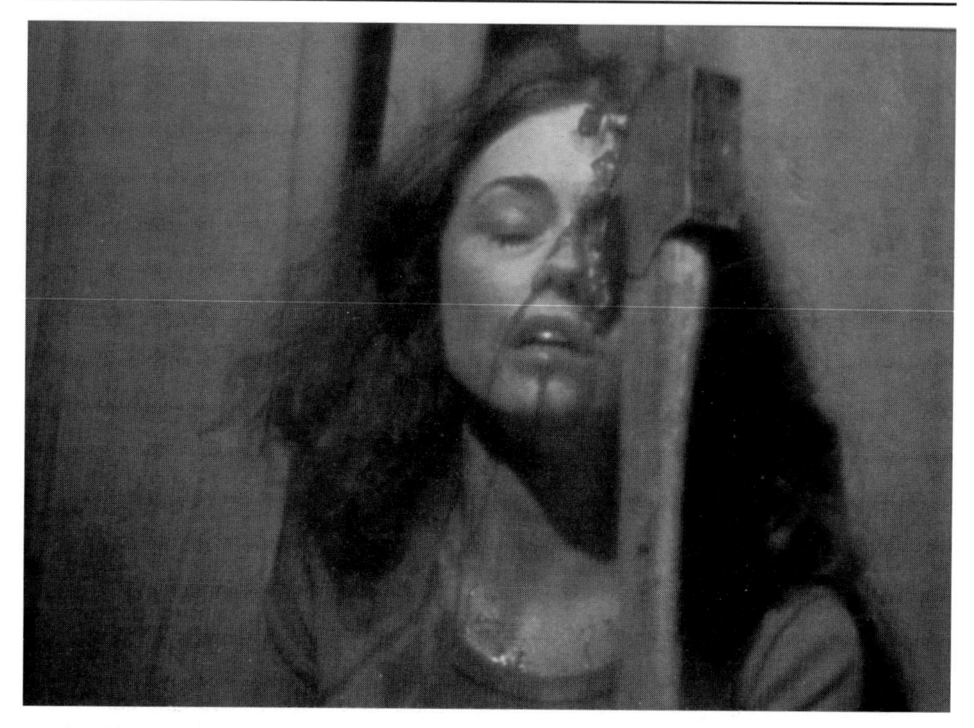

FRIDAY THE 13th

possibilities of the FX specialists to create images of terror never seen before, the industry favours well-tried, but used-up patterns, as horror films deteriorate to mere vehicles of a blunt make-up machinery. In addition to this, censorship is becoming stricter again, which is due to the fact that politicians are overtaxed and blame the increase of real violence exclusively on the media, without ever considering its social motives. Stricter censorship means a restricted market. So many films are now straight-to-video releases. In fact the video stores are flooded with such productions, waiting for their final grave in the audio-visual garbage-dumps of the future.

In addition to this, the fatal carousel of post-modernism began to turn wildly. The High School horror boom around the SCREAM series is more an infinite recycling of ideas than a genuine genre-comeback. A sad flaring up of old slasher-conventions under the guise of "irony". On the one hand too would-be clever, and too anaemic on the other, this wave is running on and reducing the slasher film to utter banality. The directors play up to their younger and younger audience and try to make the confrontation with death as bearable and funny as possible. But exploitation cinema and, above all, splatter movies need obsession and dark visions to fuel them. Genre productions from Europe, the current Spanish horror scene, for example, with talents like Jaume Balaguero, Alex de la Iglesia or Mateo Gil, seem to understand this – just like the dark masters of the new Japanese atrocity cinema such as Hisayasu Sato (NAKED BLOOD/1996). There the old hardcore spirit is still alive, and comes up in gloomy variations of the slasher movie and Sadean screen monstrosities. There they still know that without paranoia and sick sex, the genre becomes empty and boring. As Goethe once wrote to his friend Eckermann: "Only the abnormal imagination can save us."

HORROR SLASHER FILMS: A SELECTION

BLOOD AND BLACK LACE (SEI DONNE PER L'ASSASSINO) / Italy 1964

Directed by Mario Bava. Written by Marcello Fondato. Music by Carlo Rustichelli. Camera: Ubaldo Terzano. With Cameron Mitchell, Eva Bartok, Dante Di Paolo

The film which really established the tone, visual look and plot requirements of the classic *giallo* thriller. Six highly inventive yet gratuitous murders of women, performed with sadistic gusto by a masked, black-gloved stranger, and filmed in the most glorious, psychedelic saturated colours. The plot of the film is merely a peg on which to hang these dazzling set-pieces. A seminal movie from a seminal director.

BLOOD FEAST / USA 1963

Directed by Herschell Gordon Lewis. Written by Allison Louise Downe. Music by H.G. Lewis. Camera: H.G. Lewis. With Bill Kerwin, Mal Arnold, Toni Calvert, Ashlyn Martin, Sandra Sinclair, Astrid Olsen

Another seminal film moment, as Herschell Gordon Lewis invents the splatter movie. Mad priest Fuad Ramses is on a murder spree to collect pieces of female bodies for a cannibal offering. Lewis shows his butchery in gloating detail as limbs are hacked off, tongues pulled out by the root, brains hacked out and entrails strewn across the screen. Classic.

DEEP RED (PROFUNDO ROSSO) / Italy 1975

Directed by Dario Argento. Written by Argento, Bernadino Zapponi. Music by Goblin. Camera: Luigi Kuveiller. With David Hemmings, Daria Nicolodi, Carla Calamai

Argento's crowning *giallo* masterpiece, and the one in which he introduced more savage killings and gore effects into the proceedings. Teeth smashed out on a table edge, a man's head crushed by a truck, hatchet murders and drownings, all filmed in fantastic colours amidst a nightmare mood of psychosis and terror.

FRIDAY THE 13TH / USA 1980

Directed by Sean Cunningham. Written by Victor Miller. Camera: Barry Abrams. Music: Harry Manfredini. With Adrianne King, Betsy Palmer, Jeaninne Taylor, Robbi Morgan, Kevin Bacon, Harry Crosby, Mark Nelson

Like HALLOWEEN, FRIDAY THE 13TH begins with a ominous murder in the past and returns to the scene of the crime some years later. This time it is the vacation-camp Crystal Lake, a recreation centre that was closed in the time of those mysterious murders and is now re-opened. But once again the enigmatic killer begins to decimate the teenagers present, using machetes, wire slings, and other nasty accessories. It is finally the vengeful mother of little Jason, who drowned, while the supervising staff were celebrating an orgy.

FRIDAY THE 13TH has become famous for the fact that the shrill campaign for the film had started long before the film itself was available. Director and producer Sean Cunningham (an ex-porno director) showed great exploitation acumen, because the film became a tremendous commercial success. In the summer of 1980 it was only beaten by George Lucas' THE EMPIRE STRIKES BACK. Of course, this immense success demanded a number of sequels (about eight so far), all sharing the same pattern: one splatter-scene after the other, as the body count among the kids becomes stupendous. Yet Jason himself is the star of those films. In part one he rises from the dead after his Mum's death, and from this very moment he fights for leadership in the movie serial killer business. Unfortunately, no sequel ever reaches Cunningham's original version, which comes up with perfect shocks plus Tom Savini's make-up effects.

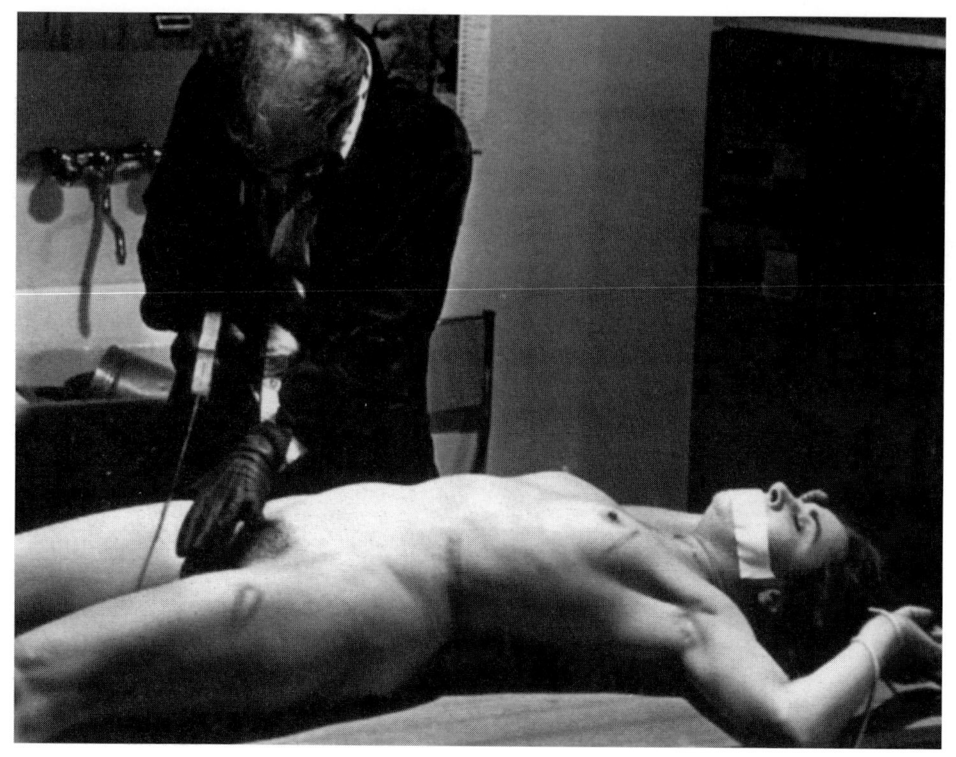

GORE IN VENICE

GIALLO A VENEZIA (GORE IN VENICE) / Italy 1979

Directed by Mario Landi.Written by Aldo Serio. Music by Berto Pisano. Camera: Franco Villa. With Leonora Fani, Gianni Dei, Jeff Blynn

Landi's ultra-gory, low-budget horrorshow is one of the most squalid examples of a *giallo*. Without the flair of Bava or Argento, he focuses on a series of brutal sadistic killings: a prostitute stabbed in the vagina, a man burned alive, and a woman tied nude to a kitchen table then slowly dismembered with a saw. Sleazy scenes of perverted sex complete the film's remarkably sordid ambience.

HALLOWEEN / USA 1978

Directed by John Carpenter. Written by Debra Hill & John Carpenter. Camera: Dean Cundey. Music: John Carpenter. With Jamie Lee Curtis, Donald Pleasance, P. J. Soles, Nancy Loomis

The archetypal mad slasher film: a numb, almost invincible phantom-killer whose mind and motives remain completely unimportant, a shy virgin scream queen (Jamie Lee Curtis) rising above herself in the struggle with the beast, a fanatic counterpart to the absolute Evil (Donald Pleasance as the shrink Loomis, who becomes a hunter), and a considerable number of nubile victims slaughtered by the masked killer. In his greatest moments John Carpenter totally focused on generating suspense and left aside everything else (like characters, message, or moral). This makes HALLOWEEN a strangely empty film, a polished surface with nothing beyond, though admittedly a technically perfect exercise in suspense. As you might have suspected the obligatory sequels followed soon, but none is in the least on Carpenter's level.

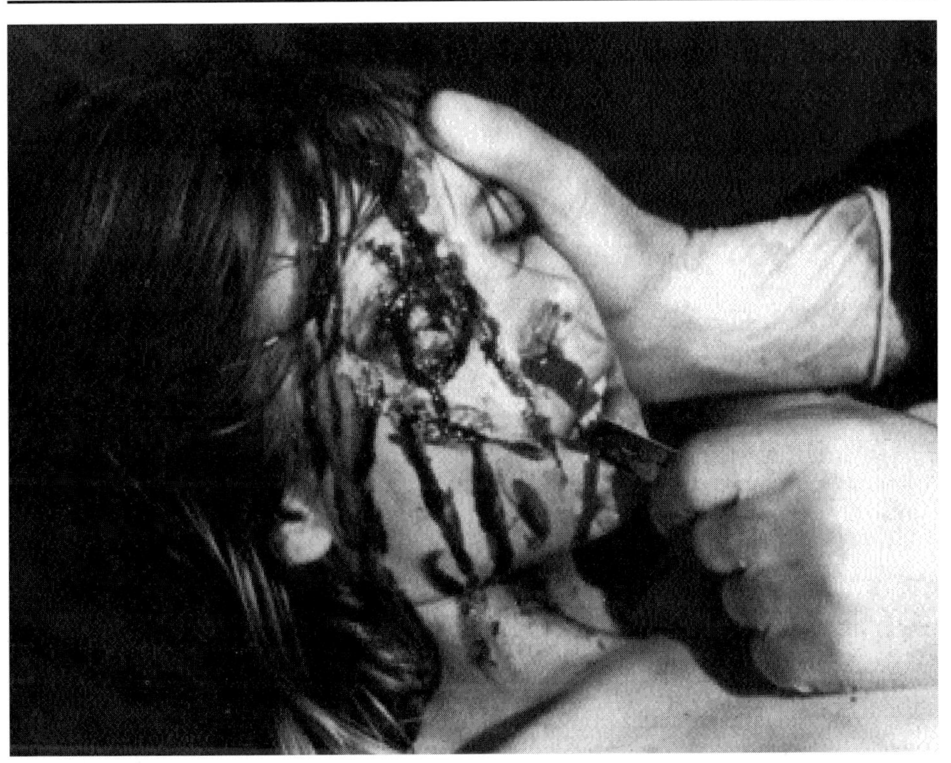

THE NEW YORK RIPPER

LAST HOUSE ON THE LEFT / USA 1972

Directed by Wes Craven. Written by Wes Craven. Camera: Victor Hurwitz. With David Hess, Lucy Grantheim, Sandra Cassell

Rape, murder and revenge by castration and other brutal methods, graphically portrayed with as much stomach-churning realism as possible. The result, a million miles away from the slow-motion death ballets of Sam Peckinpah, was the most harrowing display yet of naked hate and violence on screen. David Hess excels as the razor-slashing psychopath Krug, a type he would reprise in the later, ultra-violent *giallo* HOUSE ON THE EDGE OF THE PARK. An inspiration for grim future psycho movies such as LAST HOUSE ON DEAD END STREET (1978), as well as blood-soaked revenge tales like I SPIT ON YOUR GRAVE, Craven's first "horror" film success remains a classic of its kind.

THE NEW YORK RIPPER

Directed by Lucio Fulci. Written by Gianfranco Clerici, Vincenzo mannino, Fulci. Music by Francesco De Masi. Camera: Luigi Kuveiller

Look beyond its set-pieces of misogynistic ultra-violence and THE NEW YORK RIPPER is a visually striking, complex thriller with oneirc twists, a mutilated psycho and plenty of bizarre imagery. Yet the scenes depicting the ripper's violence against women – usually committed with a razor blade – are hard to ignore. A woman butchered to shreds in her car, another fatally gouged in the vulva with a broken bottle, a prostitute whose eyeball and nipple are sliced in two – Fulci presents us with his most graphic, sadistic slasher vison to date.

A NIGHTMARE ON ELM STREET / USA 1984

Written and directed by Wes Craven. Camera: Jacques Haitkin. Music: Charles Bernstein. With Robert Englund, Heather Langenkamp, Johnny Depp, John Saxon, Ronce Blakeley, Nick Corri, Amanda Weiss

The film which took the movie slasher out of reality and firmly into the realm of the supernatural, with the tale of a child-killer who comes back from the dead, resurrected in the dreams of the children of the vigilante mob who burned him to death.

The story of Freddy Krueger did not only generate a number of sequels (six films with varyingly bearable quality), but also infected the entire horror cinema of the Eighties with its images. The protagonists' seamless transitions from waking into dreaming soon belonged to the genre's standard repertory.

Freddie, who is destroyed in the basement by his victims' parents and reappears the kids' nightmares, mutated quickly into the ironic cult-icon of young Heavy Metal fans and comic-freaks everywhere. But NIGHTMARE ON ELM STREET is far removed from the involuntary farce of its sequels. Wes Craven's most convincing film to date – in form as well as in substance – is a surrealistic and bloody *tour de force* through the collective fears and repressed fantasies of American teenagers. Everything that makes adolescent American citizens sleepless – the lack of future perspectives, suburban dullness, sex and drugs, the generation conflict – flickers symbolically in the film's nightmarish landscapes. Of subsequent screen "monsters", only the Sadean übermensch Hannibal Lecter has managed to make a half-way comparable impact on audiences, and as we we have seen, with HANNIBAL even he has been thrust irrevocably into the same mythic terrain occupied by Freddie.

After this, there was no way for an average flesh-and-blood slasher to compete, and only a "post-modernist" comment like Craven's 1996 SCREAM could really say anything more (albeit trite) on a burnt-out subject. (Craven himself had tried to follow Krueger with the character of Horace Pinker in SHOCKER/1999, but to no commercial avail.)

SCREAM / USA 1996

Directed by Wes Craven. Written by Kevin Williamson. Camera: Mark Irwin. Music: Marco Beltrami. With Neve Campbell, David Arquette, Courteney Cox, Liev Schreiber, Skeet Ulrich

After – as they say – everything has been said (and massacred) in the splatter genre, SCREAM boasts to be the first meta-shocker: a horror film about fans of horror films who are killed by fans of horror films. Unfortunately, self-irony is the element that the genre needs least. So SCREAM and its two sequels (SCREAM 2, 1997 and SCREAM 3, 2000) certainly *don't* make us scream; at best they evoke a tired teenage smile. What horror cinema really needs are directors who treat their stories with deadly seriousness again. There *are* some, yet sadly you don't often find talents like Jaume Balagueró (LOS SIN NOMBRE) or Takashi Miike (ODISHON) on the beaten track(s) of slasher cinema. Which way forward now?

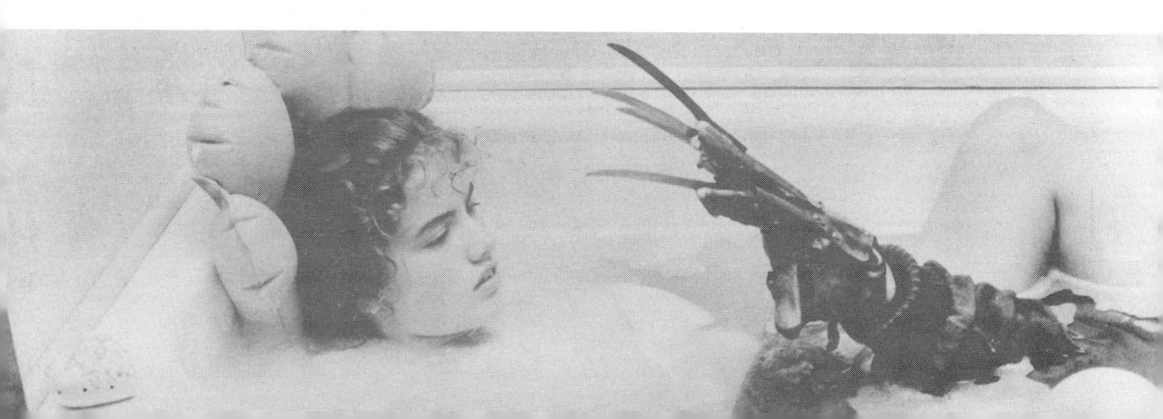

POSTSCRIPT
LIFE IMITATES ART: COPYCAT KILLERS

"I saw & think 'The Exorcist' was the best saterical comidy that I have ever seen."
–The Zodiac Killer, in a letter to the *San Francisco Chronicle*

When asked his name by police, a teenage murderer who had decapitated his mother in Maryland, in 1992, replied: "Hannibal Lecter". When reported in the media, this once more gave ammunition to those who have always insisted that cinema can influence young, impressionable or disturbed minds to perpetrate acts of violence or evil.

Columbine, Colorado, April 1999. Two black-trenchcoated students, Eric Harris and Dylan Klebold, stride through their school opening fire at will, massacring 13 other pupils, and eventually turn their guns upon themselves. This notorious incident leads to calls for a whole range of films and music artists to be censored, ranging from the shock-rock star Marilyn Manson for his lyrics containing "suicide messages", to the Leonardo DiCaprio movie THE BASKETBALL DIARIES. Ever-vigilant journalists spotted the striking similarity between events at Columbine and a dream sequence in the film, in which DiCaprio, armed and clad in a long black trenchcoat, strides through his school to the principal's office and blows him away with a shotgun. DiCaprio was subsequently obliged to respond, vowing he would not appear in any more films which glamourized the use of guns.

The accusations against Marilyn Manson were not new either; the hard rock band Judas Priest were actually brought to trial in on similar charges, namely that secret "back-masked" messages in their LPs were urging teenagers to kill themselves. They were acquitted. "Satan Teen" Ricky Kasso found the Devil through the band AC/DC and – aided by huge doses of crack – went on the kill. AC/DC's track "Night Prowler" is also cited as the main inspiration for "Satanic" killer Richard Ramirez. And it remains well-documented that Charles Manson found inspiration from the Beatles' "White Album" for much of his apocalyptic philosophy, in particular Helter Skelter – an attempted genocidal race war between blacks and whites which would leave America wide open for Charlie to take control.

Yet the moral watchdogs have been calling for film censorship of this kind for decades; in Los Angeles in 1927, the sadistic attacks perpetrated by William Hickman led to a move to ban violent movies. Probably the first well-documented case of a powerful film affecting the behaviour of the susceptible was in 1974, with the release of THE EXORCIST. This then-groundbreaking horror film led to all manner of disturbances, including: in Germany, a 19-year-old named Rainer Hertrampf shot himself through the head after viewing the film; in England, murderer Nicholas Bell blamed the film for his actions; a teenager also blamed the film for his murder of a 9-year-old girl; 31-year-old Michael Taylor, after viewing the film, underwent an exorcism after which he tore his wife to pieces with his bare hands; and dozens of other mentally frail people reported severe relapses after seeing the film, many with intense paranoia and fears of being possessed. THE EXORCIST reportedly had an

The "Gemini Killer", EXORCIST III

equally disturbing effect on pubescent girls.

Of course, THE EXORCIST and, in particular, its belated second sequel EXORCIST III, were reputed favourites of mass murderer/cannibal Jeffrey Dahmer. Dahmer no doubt saw a role model in the latter's "Gemini Killer" played by Brad Dourif, who indulged in the kind of mind control that Jeffrey tried to achieve by administering home-made lobotomies to his "slaves". When the police finally arrested Dahmer, EXORCIST III was playing on his TV.

The Mexican/US border, its satellite cities and surrounding miles of terrain have always been rife with homicidal cult activities of the type depicted in the film PERDITA DURANGO. It was here that acolytes of Ervil LeBaron's notorious Chuch Of

THE BELIEVERS

The Lamb Of God committed dozens of brutal slayings in the name of "blood-atonement" for sin; here that the "witch" Marti Enriqueta, executed in 1912, murdered children, cannibalized them and rendered down the remains to sell as love charms; and here that Adolfo de Jesus Constanzo founded his Matamoros cult, right in the heart of Mexico City, in 1984. This cult was essentially involved in drug trafficking, but Constanzo held its members together by the practise of *palo mayombe*, a form of *santeria* or voodoo-like witchcraft. This included the upkeep of a cauldron filled with human blood and body parts. At first the cult raided graveyards for these ingredients, but soon took to mutilation-murder in order to maintain the cauldron's potency.

When John Schlesinger's occult thriller THE BELIEVERS was released in 1987, both Constanzo and, in particular, his acolyte Sara Aldrete, became obsessed with the movie, even showing it to new recruits as a "training film" to be watched no less than 14 times. Although the Matamoros Cult was already well under way before THE BELIEVERS was released, there is little doubt that this movie both underlined Constanzo's existing beliefs and may even have encouraged him to push his murdering atrocities to new extremes.

Other films have fared little better. TAXI DRIVER – itself part-inspired by failed assassin Arthur Bremer – infamously encouraged John Hinckley Jr, who became obsessed with Jodie Foster in the role of teen hooker Iris, to take a pot-shot at then-President Ronald Reagan. Fortunately(?) Reagan survived, but the causal link was established, the damage done. And Oliver Stone's satrical NATURAL BORN KILLERS has been blamed for so many copycat slayings that when the uncensored "director's cut" was released, many leading chains in the US – including Blockbuster – refused to carry it.

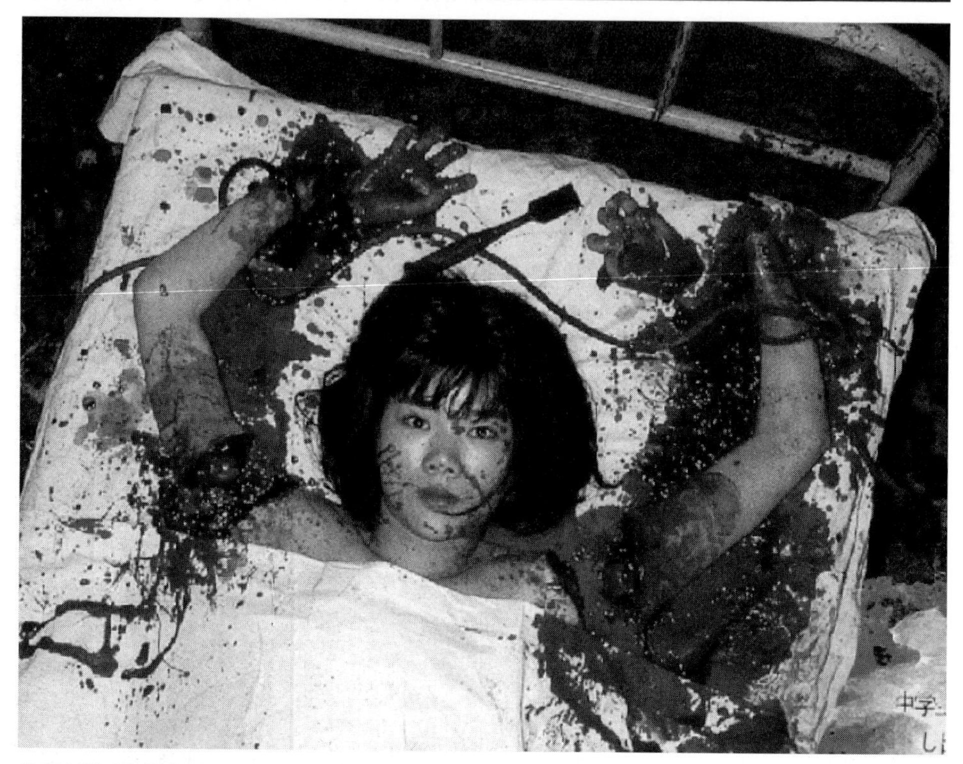

FLOWER OF BLOODY FLESH

In 1989 Japan, a country with an extremely low incidence of serial murder and – interestingly – a policy of almost zero censorship towards on-screen violence, was shaken by a murder case which caused them to question their liberal viewpoint. Tsutomi Miyazaki, an impotent paedophile vampire, was arrested for the grisly mutilation-murders of 4 little Tokyo schoolgirls. Police investigating the killer's apartment found a collection of over 5,000 videos, among them a short film of the underground *Guinea Pig* series, entitled FLOWER OF BLOODY FLESH. This film depicted with intensely graphic realism the drugging and dismemberment of a captive girl – so realistic is it, in fact, that as soon as actor Charlie Sheen saw a pirate copy he rushed out and reported it to the FBI as a genuine "snuff" movie. The butchery of the girl in this powerful film is very similar to the treatment meted out by Miyazaki to his pre-pubescent victims. As a result of the ensuing debate over issues of censorship, and whether this film could have inspired the killer to his hideous crimes, an age restriction was finally placed on the purchase of videos in Japan.

Nonetheless, Japan remains probably the only place in the world where a convicted murderer can achieve such celebrity that he gets to appear regularly on TV and act in movies. Issei Sagawa, the killer-cannibal who slew and then partially devoured his Dutch girlfriend in Paris, in 1981, plays a sex pervert in Hisayasu Sato's drug/murder concoction UNFAITHFUL WIFE: SHAMEFUL TORTURE aka THE BEDROOM (1992).

In England, the debate over film censorship rages continually. In several serious murder cases, films have been blamed for the dreadful crimes committed by killers. In August 1987 Michael Ryan, dressed in combat fatigues and armed with a

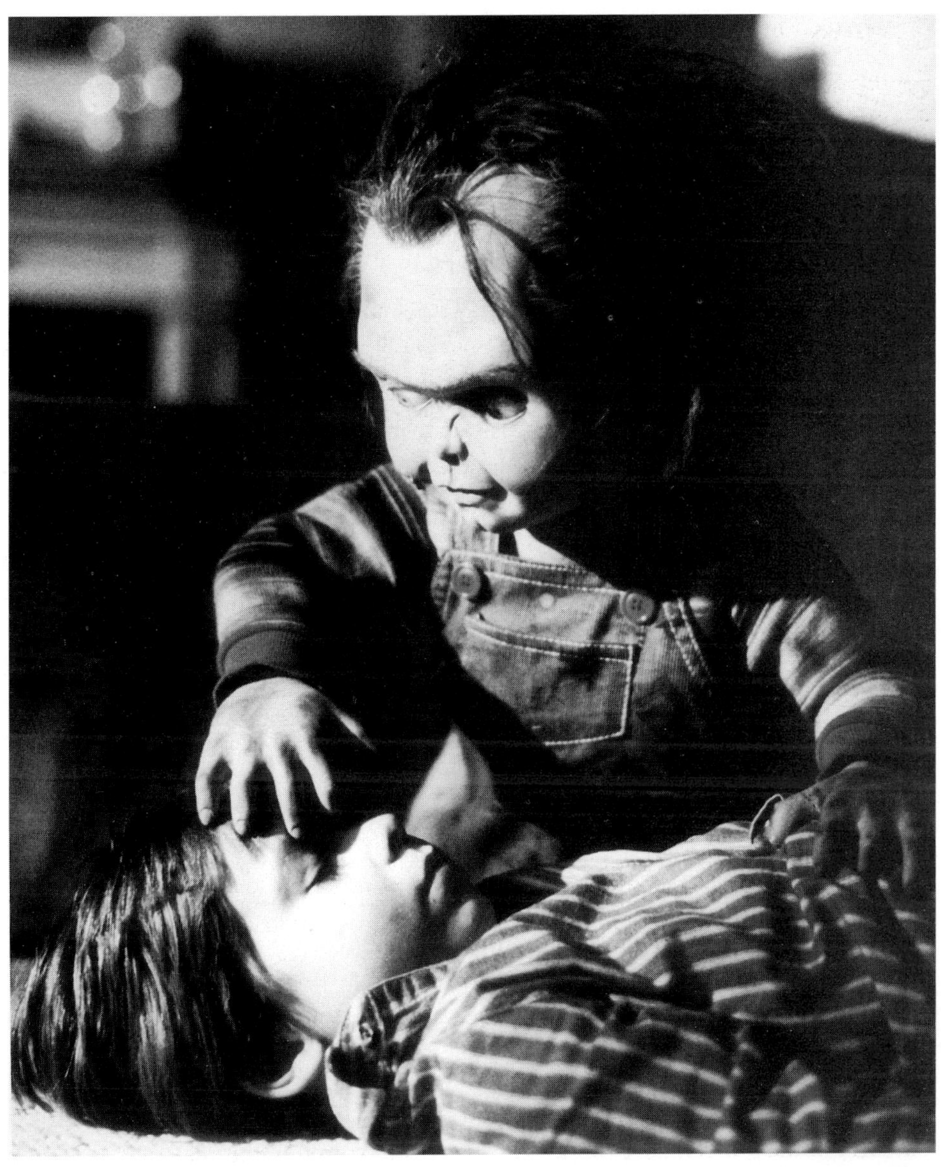

CHILD'S PLAY

Kalshnikov rife and Biretta pistol, stormed his home town of Hungerford shooting 16 people (including his mother) and finally blowing out his own brains. It turned out that Ryan was "obsessed" by the charcter of John Rambo in FIRST BLOOD, and had apparently modelled his killing spree on the rampage perpetrated by Rambo in the movie.

In 1989 one Robert Sartin, a mentally ill 23-year-old, gunned down 17 people in Whitley Bay. It came out at trial that his favourite movie was HALLOWEEN and – despite the fact that Sartin was obviously deranged anyway and in any case, the killer in HALLOWEEN uses a knife, not a gun – the movie was roundly blamed for the young man's homicidal eruption.

In February 1993 one of the most horrendous crimes in recent British history occurred, when two 10-year-old boys, Robert Thompson and Jon Venables, abducted and brutally beat to death the 2-year-old James Bulger. Bulger's stripped, battered and mutilated body was found across a railway track, where a train had sliced it in two. Unable to believe in the innate "evil" of the two boys, the British media and public clutched at straws to explain this aberration. When it came to light that the boys were avid fans of CHILD'S PLAY, the dopey horror flick about an animated killer doll, this fitted the profile. The young lads had clearly been turned into twisted killers by this evil movie.

Only one crime committed since the Bulger case has equalled it for atrocity value: the Dunblane Massacre. In March, 1996 paedophile ex-teacher Thomas Hamilton stormed into Dunblane Primary School in Scotland, shooting dead 16 young children and then himself. Another huge outcry over guns, and their depiction in cinema, ensued. Every film from PULP FICTION to NATURAL BORN KILLERS was blamed for Hamilton's lavish gesture.

And so the British media are ever vigilant, even trying in 1998 to ban David Cronenberg's amazing realization of J.G. Ballard's CRASH. They failed, but there were no subsequent reports of copycat motorists ramming other vehicles, or plowing their cars over the edge of motorway overpasses with half-naked women in the front seat.

It remains doubtful whether that many – if any at all – of the aforementioned delinquents were actually driven to murder by watching a movie. Movies can sometimes reassure us that we're "on the right track", but we have to be on it already. Nonetheless, the debate on this subject will run and run as long as there are movies, and as long as there are murderers – in other words, as long as society itself persists.

APPENDIX ONE
ADDITIONAL FILMOGRAPHY

Due to limited space, many instances of 20th Century true crime cases being made into films have had to be omitted. Below is an additional list of cases, plus in-brief details of related movies for those who wish to investigate this phenomenon further.

<u>BLACK DAHLIA MURDER</u>
BLACK DAHLIA, USA 1998
D: Lance Laspina & Eric Trow

TRUE CONFESSIONS, USA 1991
D: Ulu Grosbard

WHO IS THE BLACK DAHLIA, USA 1975
D: Joseph Pevney

<u>CHAMBERLAIN, LINDY</u>
CRY IN THE DARK, A, AUSTRALIA 1988
D: Fred Schepisi

<u>CHESSMAN, CARYL</u>
CELL 2455 DEATH ROW, USA 1955
D: Fred F. Sears

KILL ME IF YOU CAN, USA 1977
D: Buzz Kulik

<u>COOK, BILLY</u>
HITCHHIKER, THE, USA 1953
D: Ida Lupino

<u>CRIPPEN, HARVEY</u>
DR. CRIPPEN, GB 1968
D: Robert Lynn

DR. CRIPPEN AN BORD, GERMANY 1942
D: Erich Engels

DR. CRIPPEN LEBT, GERMANY 1957
D: Erich Engels

SUSPECT, USA 1944
D: Robert Siodmak

DOWNS, DIANE
SMALL SACRIFICES, USA 1989
D: David Greene

GOODBAR KILLER
LOOKING FOR MR. GOODBAR, USA 1977
D: Richard Brooks

TRACKDOWN: FINDING THE GOODBAR KILLER, USA 1983
D: Bill Persky

HEIRENS, WILLIAM ("THE CHICAGO LIPSTICK KILLER")
WHILE THE CITY SLEEPS, USA 1956
D: Fritz Lang

"JACK THE STRIPPER"
FRENZY, UK 1972
D: Alfred Hitchcock

KASSO, RICKY
WHERE EVIL DWELLS, USA 1985
D: Tommy Turner & David Wojnarowicz

RIVER'S EDGE, USA 1987
D: Tim Hunter

MY SWEET SATAN, USA 1994
D: Jim Van Bebber

KLEBOLD , Dylan and HARRIS, Eric
DUCK! THE CARBINE HIGH MASSACRE, USA 2000
D: William Hellfire

MacDONALD, JEFFREY
FATAL VISION, USA 1984
D: David Green

MAINLINE MURDERER
ECHOES IN THE DARKNESS, USA 1987
D: Glenn Jordan

MATIX, William Russel and BLUTH Michael
IN THE LINE OF DUTY: THE F.B.I, USA 1988
D: Dick Lowry

MOONLIGHT MURDERER OF TEXARKANA
BLACKOUT, USA 1985
D: Douglas Hickox

TOWN THAT DREADED SUNDOWN, THE, USA 1977
D: Charles Pierce

NEILSON, DONALD
BLACK PANTHER, THE, UK 1977
D: Ian Merrick

PETIOT, MAURICE
DR. PETIOT, FRANCE 1990
D: Christian De Chalonge

REID, MARK ("CHOPPER")
CHOPPER, AUSTRALIA 2000

SAGAWA, ISSEI
ADORATION, BELGIUM 1987
D: OLIVIER SMOLDERS

LOVE RITUAL, ITALY 1990
D: ALDO LADO

SARRET, GEORGES
TRIO INFERNAL, LE, FRANCE 1974
D: Francis Girod

SCHREUDER, FRANCES
AT MOTHER'S REQUEST, USA 1987
D: Michael Tuchner

NUTCRACKER: MONEY, MADNESS AND MURDER, USA 1987
D: Paul Bogart

SISTER GODFRIEDA
EL HUERTO DEL FRANCÉS, SPAIN 1977
D: Jacinto Molina

KILLER NUN, ITALY 1977
D: Giulio Berrute

WHERE LOVE HAS GONE, USA 1964
D: Edward Dmytryk

SUCCO, ROBERTO
ROBERTO SUCCO, FRANCE 2001
D: Cedric Kahn

WEINWURM, JOSEPH ("THE VIENNA OPERA MURDERER")
GEISSEL DES FLEISCHES, AUSTRIA 1965
D: Eddy Saller

YOUNG, GRAHAM
YOUNG POISONER'S HANDBOOK, THE, GB 1995
D: Benjamin Ross

Compiled by Harald Dolezal, Heimo Sver and Christian Fuchs

LOVE

APPENDIX TWO
INDEX OF FILMS

Page number in bold indicates an illustration

APPENDIX THREE
INDEX OF KILLERS

Page number in bold indicates an illustration

APPENDIX FOUR
SELECT BIBLIOGRAPHY

Abbott, Jack Henry: *In The Belly Of The Beast*, Random House. New York 1981.
Artaud, Antonin: *Selected Writings*, University Of California Press. Berkeley 1976.
Balun, Chas: *Horror Holocaust*, Fantaco. Albany 1986.
Barber, Stephen: *Artaud: The Screaming Body*, Creation Books. London 1998.
Bataille, Georges: *Eroticism*, Marion Boyars Publishers Ltd. London 1957/1987.
Bataille, Georges: *Visions Of Excess: Selected Writings, 1927-1939*, University Of Minnesota Press. Minneapolis 1985.
Baudrillard, Jean: *The Transparency Of Evil – Essays On Extreme Phenomena*, Verso Books 1993.
Black, Joel: *The Aesthetics Of Murder*, Johns Hopkins University Press. Baltimore/London 1991.
Bouzereau, Laurent: *Ultraviolent Movies*, Citadel Press. Toronto 1996.
Cameron, Deborah & Frazer, Elizabeth: *The Lust To Kill*, Polity Press/Basil Blackwell. 1987.
Capote, Truman: *In Cold Blood*, Random House. New York 1965.
Chester, Graham: *Berserk!*, Michael O'Mara Books Ltd. London 1993.
Ellroy, James: *Killer On The Road*, Avon Books. New York 1986.
Farin, Michael & Schmid, Hans: *Ed Gein – A Quiet Man*, Belleville. Munich 1996.
Gaddis & Long: *Panzram: A Journal Of Murder*, Amok Books. Los Angeles 2001.
Gilmore, John & Kenner, Ron: *The Garbage People*, Amok Books. Los Angeles 1995.
Gilmore, Mikal: *Shot In The Heart*, Doubleday. New York 1994.
Goad, Jim: *Answer Me!: The First Three*, AK Press. San Francisco 1994.
Gollmar, Robert H: *Edward Gein*, Pinnacle Books. New York 1981.
Hardy, Phil: *The Overlook Film Encyclopedia – Horror*. Woodstock/New York, 1993.
Hunter, Jack: *Eros In Hell*, Creation Books. London 1998.
Jackson, Kevin (ed.): *Schrader On Schrader*, Faber and Faber. London/Boston 1990.
Kerekes, David & Slater, David: *Killing For Culture*, Creation Books. London 1993.
Kerekes, David: *Sex. Murder. Art. The Films of Jörg Buttgereit*, Critical Vision. Stockport 1994.
Kilduff, Marshall & Javers, Ron: *The Suicide Cult*, Bantam Books Inc. New York 1978.
King, Brian (ed.): *Lustmord*, Bloat Books. Burbank 1996.
Kitses, Jim: *Gun Crazy*, BFI Publishing. London 1996.
Kristeva, Julia: *Powers Of Horror*, Columbia University Press. New York 1982.
Leyton, Elliott: *Hunting Humans*, Penguin Books. London 1986.
Mattheus, Bernd. Matthes, Axel (ed.): *Ich Gestatte Mir Die Revolte*, Matthes & Seitz, Munich 1985.
McCarthy, John: *Movie Psychos And Madmen*, Citadel Press. New York, 1993.
McDonnagh, Maitland: *Broken Mirrors, Broken Minds*, Sun Tavern Fields. London 1991.
Nietzsche, Friedrich: *Hammer Of The Gods*, Creation Books. London 1995.
Norris, Joel: *Serial Killers*, Arrow Books Ltd. London 1988.
Praz, Mario: *Romantic Agony*, World Publishing. Cleveland and New York, 1965.
Sade, Marquis de: *Philosophy In The Boudoir*, Creation Books. London, 1995/2000.
Sanders, Ed: *The Family*, E.P. Dutton and Co. New York 1971.
Sargeant, Jack: *Born Bad*, Creation Books. London 1996.
Schreck, Nikolas: *The Manson File*, Amok Press. New York 1988.
Unterweger, Jack: *Fegefeuer Oder Die Reise Ins Zuchthaus*, Heine. München 1983.
Vogel, Amos: *Film As A Subversive Art*, George Weidenfeld & Nicholson Ltd. London 1974.

www.creationbooks.com